D0665134

Praise for
On That Day
by
William M. Arkin

"Beginning in the spring of 2001, the CIA repeatedly warned the White House that Osama Bin Laden was planning terror attacks inside the USA. The Bush administration did nothing. The disaster that unfolded on 9/11— from the first minute of the day through the last—has now been meticu- lously recorded in Bill Arkin's new book. If you want to understand what happened, this is the place to start."

—Thomas Powers, author of *Intelligence Wars: American Secret History from Hitler to Al-Qaeda*

ON THAT DAY

ON THAT DAY

THE DEFINITIVE TIMELINE OF 9/11

WILLIAM M. ARKIN

PUBLICAFFAIRS

New York

Copyright © 2021 by William M. Arkin
Cover design by Pete Garceau
Cover copyright © 2021 by Hachette Book Group, Inc.

Hachette Book Group supports the right to free expression and the value of copyright. The purpose of copyright is to encourage writers and artists to produce the creative works that enrich our culture.

The scanning, uploading, and distribution of this book without permission is a theft of the author's intellectual property. If you would like permission to use material from the book (other than for review purposes), please contact permissions@hbgusa.com. Thank you for your support of the author's rights.

PublicAffairs
Hachette Book Group
1290 Avenue of the Americas, New York, NY 10104
www.publicaffairsbooks.com
@Public_Affairs

Printed in the United States of America

First Edition: August 2021

Published by PublicAffairs, an imprint of Perseus Books, LLC, a subsidiary of Hachette Book Group, Inc. The PublicAffairs name and logo is a trademark of the Hachette Book Group.

The Hachette Speakers Bureau provides a wide range of authors for speaking events. To find out more, go to www.hachettespeakersbureau.com or call (866) 376-6591.

The publisher is not responsible for websites (or their content) that are not owned by the publisher.

Library of Congress Control Number: 2021938209

ISBNs: 978-1-5417-0106-9 (trade paperback original) 978-1-5417-0107-6 (e-book)

LSC-C

Printing 1, 2021

To Rikki and Hannah

"Today: Less humid. Sunshine. High 79."
    Tuesday, September 11, 2001

"When it comes to foreign policy, we have a tongue-tied administration. After almost eight months in office, neither President Bush nor Secretary of State Colin Powell has made any comprehensive statement on foreign policy. It is hard to think of another administration that has done so little to explain what it want [*sic*] to do in foreign policy."
    Morton Abramowitz, "So Quiet at the Top," op-ed appearing in the
    Washington Post the morning of September 11, 2001

3:05 p.m. (10 minutes): "Small Group Meeting with Leaders of the Muslim Community" in the Oval Office.
    Schedule of the President, Tuesday, September 11, 2001

CONTENTS

LIST OF ILLUSTRATIONS

ON THAT DAY

INTRODUCTION

I count myself blessed that I've never had to ask myself what I wanted to do for a living and that I have found work—and a particular approach to my work—that fits an extremely patient and detail-oriented psyche. I served in US Army intelligence from 1974 to 1978 in West Berlin, responsible for keeping tabs on Soviet and East German military forces. And though I like to quip that I was once one of the world's leading experts on two militaries that don't even exist anymore, it taught me how to understand large systems and gave me a methodology to tackle a world of unknowns. After leaving the Army, I continued that same kind of nuts-and-bolts approach in delving into the secrets of nuclear weapons, building up my expertise by minutely ferreting out the topography of over 700 locations where US warheads were stored, filling index cards and then notebooks and then computer disks with data, even visiting sites to take a look. The product was the best-selling *Nuclear Battlefields*, featured on the front page of almost every newspaper in the United States and around the world, subject of an ABC *20/20* segment, the dense and serious book even mentioned in a late-night Johnny Carson monologue. After that, I worked on and coauthored four volumes of the *Nuclear Weapons Databook* series, the essential Cold War reference sponsored by the Natural Resources Defense Council.

When it came to the superstructure of everything from warheads to bunkers, I was a go-to expert for the news media. Eventually I found myself as a consultant to numerous organizations and at NBC, where I developed stories and made news. I developed sources inside the military, read the documents no one else did, wrote lists and timelines, obsessed about the details. And then with the end of the Cold War, I shifted my attention to understanding conventional warfare and airpower, ending up as the first military expert allowed into Iraq by the government of Saddam Hussein after Desert Storm in 1991. There, I methodically catalogued what had been bombed and the impact, both militarily and on the civilian population. Based on that, I was invited to present my findings to various military and intelligence audiences and eventually became an adjunct professor at the US Air Force's School of Advanced Airpower Studies, consulting for the Air Force on the direct and reverberating effects of warfare on the civilian population. Human Rights Watch and then the United Nations hired me to conduct post-bombing assessments in Iraq, the former Yugoslavia, Lebanon, Afghanistan, and other places.

On the day of 9/11, NBC News sent a limousine to my home in Vermont to bring me to New York to provide expert analysis. I remember quipping at the time that what I knew about al Qaeda could probably fit into a thimble. But NBC said that was an ocean compared to what most knew. And I was the guy who uniquely understood the secret world, and that meant I could explain what was going on behind the scenes in Washington and then in Afghanistan (and eventually Iraq). I can vividly remember sitting with Tom Brokaw and various senior producers, schooling them on emergency procedures of government, on this weapon and that target, and then eventually coming full circle back to weapons of mass destruction when the Iraq debacle approached. Suffice it to say I knew the details, how the military thought, and how government and the secret agencies worked.

For the final four months of 2001, I worked 18-hour days and lived out of a suitcase in New York, reporting on the aftermath of the al Qaeda attacks and the broadening Afghanistan war. As the United States recovered from 9/11, it was clear that there was so much going on in obscure corners as the system transitioned to a permanent wartime posture. And because it was wartime and in that post-9/11 frenzy, the secrecy was intense, and information was hard to get to. Pentagon spokespeople urged us not to do this and that story, to not reveal Dick Cheney's "secure location," to not talk about some new weapon, to not even mention organizations that were struggling with their own quick study. As a simultaneous consultant to the Air Force, I also *felt* the change—a tightening of the reins on information, a closing of doors and of minds, a change in day-to-day routines as people and institutions responded to perceived vulnerabilities and were overwhelmed by the task ahead.

I've applied my usual rigor and obsessiveness to try to make sense of the sequence of events that unfolded after 9/11, specifically the world of emergency procedures. Before 9/11, I'd already become one of the world's leading experts on the obscure subject of continuity of government. After the attacks, there was an eruption of new activity. I detected small clues of changes afoot, clues that I compiled into spreadsheets and timelines, tracking not just the seminal day but its effects. In *Codenames*, based on a ridiculous database I created, I wrote about the explosion of government secrecy and revealed thousands of programs. In *Top Secret America*, I researched the growth of post-9/11 organizations and the private companies that had just as much come to fight this new kind of war. In *American Coup*, I wrote about the encroachment of homeland security into every aspect of American civilian life. In *Unmanned*, I wrote about the advances in drone technology and the changes precipitated by the creation of a worldwide warfare network. And in *The Generals Have No Clothes*, I wrote about the resilience of that physical infrastructure of perpetual war, how it sustained the invisible enterprise and the task ahead in closing the chapter on 9/11.

Through it all, aided by trips to the Middle East and South Asia, I've become obsessed with the 9/11 terrorists—who they were, what they thought, how they did it. I compiled a million-word timeline of their lives and their paths to that day. I read everything, talked to the experts, contacted their families, and finally was leaked thousands of pages of interrogations and debriefings from black sites and Guantanamo Bay. That fed my labor of love, the 700-page *History in One Act: A Novel of 9/11*. It is a richly reimagined prequel and alternate history from the point of view of the terrorists and from the bowels of the secret agencies.

But 9/11 itself remains the day the world turned. We've seen, with every anniversary, with every new study, with every autobiography and contemporary history, that the day continues to stand front and center. Even in this past year, during COVID-19 and amid nationwide protests, the anniversary interrupted everything else. That Tuesday in September is undoubtedly the most studied day of our lifetimes. Almost everyone who was old enough remembers the details—where they were, how they felt, what it meant to them.

Yet so many of the memories are brief, visual, and fragmentary. Astoundingly, there is still no definitive account of what happened within the US

government. The official 9/11 Commission report was constrained by sani-
tizing bipartisanship and hampered by crushing government secrecy. Most
of the principals and agencies have written their own stories, but they are
filled with all the glory and obfuscation of self-promotion. There are some
fine outside books—particularly Garrett Graff's *The Only Plane in the Sky*
and Mitchell Zuckoff's *Fall and Rise: The Story of 9/11*—but these and most
others focus on the individual stories of human tragedy. The true facts of
the federal government's response, particularly the nooks and crannies of
the secret agencies and procedures, remain mysterious and overlaid with
misinformation. And yet what happened to those agencies that day has
shaped much of the world we live in now.

What went wrong—and why so many people had to die—is, of course,
where almost every narrative and study goes. That approach is essential,
but unfortunately for both public and expert understanding, the goal in
such studies seems to be to seek out explanations for government failure in
order to justify reform and greater spending. Others who are obsessed with
this day seem intent on finding conspiracies and intentional wrongdoing.
Herein lies the circular conundrum of secrecy: because the "story" of 9/11
hasn't been fully and transparently told, many believe that something sin-
ister is being intentionally withheld. Thus, two decades after 9/11, public
opinion remains deeply divided. Polling consistently shows that more than
half of Americans believe that the government is hiding something, while
one-quarter to one-half think that the government even had some involvement in perpetrating the attacks.[1] When as presidential candidate, Donald
Trump floated 9/11 conspiracy theories, he was consistently applauded.[2]

---

1. American public opinion polls show:
   - more than half of the American public believes that the US government is
     concealing information;
   - half believe the Bush administration and the intelligence agencies knew more than
     they admit;
   - as many as three-quarters do not accept government explanations; and
   - a quarter to a third believe the US government helped plan the attacks or
     consciously failed to act to stop them.
   See additional discussion (and sourcing) of public opinion around 9/11 in *The Generals
   Have No Clothes*.
   2. See, for example, Tim Hains, "Donald Trump on 9/11: 'You Will Find Out Who Really
   Knocked Down the World Trade Center,'" *RealClear Politics*, February 17, 2016.

So much dissatisfaction and confusion points to a problem of public trust, one that has grown since 9/11 and has been exacerbated by the economic failures of 2008, the government response to the COVID pandemic in 2020, and plenty of smaller crises along the way. Goaded by the internet of rumors and alternative speculations, the public is as confused as ever in believing that the government knows what it is doing.

My personality leads me away from speculation and feeds instead on the verifiable details that, far from hiding in plain sight, often require a certain expertise to be found. To create *On That Day*, I've plumbed the documents and recollections, new sources, and newly declassified documents. I've tried not just to put down on paper all the contradictions and mistakes but also to explain the inconsistencies and what they mean. As complete as I think *On That Day* is, there is also so much that is being kept secret: about the decision-making that day, about false alarms and confused intelligence, about the government's preparations for leadership continuity, about the workings of the Secret Service and the White House Military Office, about military alerts, and even about the role nuclear weapons played.

What the timeline shows is an astounding lack of thought regarding two issues that still very much shape our world: continuity of government (COG) and relations with Russia. In the former, only one of 16 constitutional successors to the presidency did as the prepared plans specified they should. Put another way, billions of dollars had been spent to prepare for this very type of event. But when the condition presented itself for the government to take action to increase its chances for survival, leaders brushed the apparatus aside. Only House Speaker Dennis Hastert—third in line to the presidency and now a convicted felon—went where he was supposed to. Everyone else refused to evacuate Washington. One would think that the experience that day would have led to reforms to create a workable and modern system. But the reality is that although billions of dollars were spent to make the flawed system better, its contradictions and irrelevance were once again showcased in the early months of COVID-19.

Never really discussed by the 9/11 Commission or others who specialize in matters of strategic stability is the Pentagon decision to shift US military forces to DEFCON 3, the highest level of alert for the US military since the 1973 Arab-Israeli war. The meager justification for a DEFCON 3 declaration on 9/11 was that the attacks in the United States might be followed by others overseas or that the attacks themselves were the opening salvo of a war. The decision by Donald Rumsfeld (egged on by Dick Cheney) reveals an appalling absence of intelligence regarding what was happening in the world but also a recklessness regarding a monumental decision where those ordering the shift had no idea what it actually would mean.

There is no evidence, moreover, apart from some ships based in Norfolk, Virginia, leaving port to assist in air defense, that the declaration had any actual effect—that is, that anything tangible resulted from the military declaring a historic alert. That is what we know based on the public record. What was actually done regarding the readiness of hidden intelligence assets or even the nuclear arsenal remains a closely guarded secret. What we do know is that the DEFCON order was alarming enough to Russian leader Vladimir Putin that the Kremlin contacted the White House to inquire what US intentions were. The official histories gloss over the tensions—and the implications. And yet truly another disaster could have been precipitated.

Two decades after 9/11, the government bureaucracy is constantly practicing, writing, and revising multiple plans of what to do in a crisis moment, even what to do if nuclear weapons are 30 minutes away from destroying Washington. It seems that little of what goes on connects back to the events and trauma of that day and to its significant lessons. That connection is essential because much of what happened on 9/11 was so seat-of-the-pants—government officials ignoring plans and procedures in the name of personal preference or expediency, decisions being made without any basis in fact, constant confusion ruling regarding what to do and even why. What the timeline shows is how much leaders were preoccupied with the most mundane of activities—getting phone calls through, finding and protecting their loved ones, keeping up with the news, struggling with the rumor mill.

Much of this sounds a lot like COVID-19. Continuity and emergency actions again became important when questions of the president and vice president separating were raised or whether Congress could have a "virtual" quorum, and then, later, who was in charge during the January 6, 2021, attack at the Capitol. We are told that so many of the organizational and technological deficiencies of 9/11 have been corrected, but in an age where information overload is exponentially worse, and where cyber-threats raise questions about the reliability of communications and decision-making, there is no particular reason to believe that the very same issues won't repeat themselves in future crises.

From the minute detailing of 9/11, I come away with the stark conviction that hardly any of the most difficult issues of government—even including basic accountability—have been resolved. It is my hope, as a national security specialist, journalist, and citizen, that this timeline serves as a reminder not just of how unexpected and earth-shattering the attacks were but also of how much scar tissue remains. To me, the nature of the chaos unleashed that day, its enduring nature, where everyone is to blame and no one is to blame, is a better starting point for understanding the impact—how it influenced how the United States undertook the largest federal reorganization ever, how the country went to war and then never stopped, and how we continue to repeat so many of the same behaviors. It should all help to explain the frailty of our world, the very human weaknesses and peculiarities of our leaders, and the power of gigantic systems—systems that sometimes do exactly what they're set up to do, taking over when humans falter, but also systems that are unable to pivot to new conditions and actual emergencies.

Twenty years on, we struggle endlessly over what to do about the wages of perpetual war; what to do with the poorly focused Department of Homeland Security; why we have a director of National Intelligence (and what the now-bloated organization does); what as a nation we should do about Russia, China, Iran, or North Korea; even what we should do (still) about Afghanistan and Iraq. Those persistent questions are the enduring legacy of 9/11.

Almost 60 years ago, another event equally seized the United States—the 1962 Cuban Missile Crisis—and it has similarly been closely examined, becoming a seminal event in debating Cold War strategies and models of decision-making. Graham Allison's *Essence of Decision* has been a staple at graduate schools and war colleges for decades, and the crisis itself has been the subject of tabletop war games and mock debates. And yet only with the end of the Cold War, when the Soviet participants themselves could tell their stories from their perspective—and as the public policy community took serious moves to revisit the crisis—did the truth emerge: of the mis-communications and autonomous actions of the armed forces, of a mercurial Soviet leader isolated and without much information. The theory that the two sides were deliberate in their counsel was punctured. It was also later revealed that President Kennedy used his brother as a back channel to the Soviets, a fact unknown for years—and one that also demonstrates how precarious established systems can be, particularly when they assume they are the only systems that exist.

On That Day aims to show the untidy, unsystematic nature of government faced with a wholly unexpected crisis. It contains more than 1,000 separate entries from 4:45 a.m. (EST) to 11:50 p.m., but this is itself a limited selection. Because the book focuses on federal government action, the story of what happened in New York City is given only the most cursory treatment. And for the best-documented agencies—the Federal Aviation Administration (FAA)[3] and the New York City Fire Department (FDNY),[4] only the most abbreviated entries are included. News media reporting from that day is also kept at a minimum. The focus is as much as possible

---

3. Numerous FAA logs exist, from Washington headquarters, from the Herndon Command Center, from the various regions, and from their subordinate centers. They are collectively referred to as "FAA logs" in the notes unless otherwise specified. The entries reflect the time that entries are made into logs, not necessarily the precise time of the event itself. The exceptional FAA documents referred to are as follows:

- Chronology of September 11, 2001, compiled by the FAA (AAT-20) on September 18, 2001, with no sources (located in the National Archives and retrievable as document 7602265; hereafter FAA Chronology of September 11, 2001).
- FAA, Chronology of Events, September 11, 2001, n.d. (2001) (located in the National Archives and retrievable as document 7597160; hereafter FAA Chronology of Events).
- FAA, 3 DCC 1708 Chronology 911 Timeline 1228-0044Z REDACT-SEALED.pdf (located in the National Archives and retrievable as document 7597219; hereafter DCC Timeline).
- The National Archives Catalog, FAA, Chronology of Events, n.d. (2001) (located in the National Archives and retrievable as document 7596061; hereafter National Archives Chronology).

4. The report, "FDNY Fire Operations Response on September 11," is archived at http://www.nyc.gov/html/fdny/pdf/mck_report/fire_operations_response.pdf (and is hereafter referred to as FDNY Report).

on federal government action and the tangle of information that flooded in as decision makers grappled with the day.

The timeline is based as much as possible on original government documentation and firsthand accounts from the key federal government participants. Most of the principals—Bush, Cheney, Rice, and so on—have written memoirs, and they are referenced throughout. Most are muddled about timing, and some—Donald Rumsfeld's, for example—have specificity while also glossing over any mistakes or controversies. When it comes to the federal government's official response, there aren't a thousand versions of what happened, but there are hundreds. For the FAA, the North American Aerospace Defense Command (NORAD), and the Pentagon's ongoing teleconferences, logs and transcripts are available, sometimes with precise times and sometimes with verbatim conversations. But there are also multiple versions of the same, and many disagree and are contradictory. Throughout, I've endeavored to correct mistaken times and reconcile the multiple versions. And where the official documentation and transcripts clearly disagree with the iconic (and unblemished) stories that persist in conventional retellings, I've provided the actual course of events. I have included the many contemporaneous reports of erroneous information—of planes going this way and that, of other hijackings, and of bomb threats—in cursory form to highlight the barrage of bad information that stressed decision makers. And I have tried to untangle many of the lingering controversies—for instance, when (and how) President Bush gave the order allowing military pilots to shoot down a civilian airliner, providing comments where mysteries still persist.

Though I have mostly used chronologies of the federal government and the 9/11 Commission, I have also found the reporting and chronologies of the Associated Press (AP) and CNN most useful, particularly in understanding when events were publicly reported or known. Numerous privately compiled timelines and histories were consulted, and my thanks go out to all who have diligently tried over the years to reconstruct what happened. The Internet Archive television news compilation for "Understanding 9/11" (https://archive.org/details/911/day/20010911) was invaluable and is recommended for further research.

The 9/11 Commission (the National Commission on Terrorist Attacks upon the United States) is, of course, the definitive source. Its final report did a fine job of providing a comprehensive overview, but it was also hampered in its desire to be nonpartisan and "useful" for organizational and legislative recommendations. In other words, it wasn't just a history. The archives of the Commission—its notes and working aids and its many interviews and memoranda—were far more important sources. The National Archives maintains a fine library and fully searchable index of the records (https://www.archives.gov/research/9-11), though thousands of documents remain partially or completely classified. For this timeline, the most useful materials contained within those archives are the records of NORAD and the Secret Service, available nowhere else.[5]

The George W. Bush Presidential Library and Museum (https://georgewbushlibrary.smu.edu/) is a second invaluable archive, containing photographs, documents, and finding aids. The library maintains an archival research guide specifically for 9/11. Its new and partially declassified Bush presidential diary for that day, released in 2016, was a valuable document in clarifying times and actions.[6]

The FBI Working Draft Chronology of Events for Hijackers and Associates, n.d. (2001–2002), Secret (partially declassified, hereafter FBI Working Draft Chronology) was obtained originally from agents who prepared the material. There are many versions of this document, as well as FBI timelines from Florida, New York, Boston, and other locations. They are the definitive source for the actions of the terrorists.

The final reports of the National Institute of Standards and Technology (NIST) investigation of the World Trade Center (https://www.nist.gov/el/final-reports-nist-world-trade-center-disaster-investigation) provides information available nowhere else. The NIST NCSTAR (National Construction Safety Team Act Report) 108, Chronology of Emergency Responder Operations, World Trade Center Attack, September 11, 2001

---

5. The 9/11 Commission, "Memorandum for the Record, Event: North American Aerospace Defense Command (NORAD) Field Site Visit, Type of Event: Interview with CINC-NORAD (Commander in Chief NORAD) General 'Ed' Eberhart, March 1, 2004" (hereafter 9/11 Commission NORAD MFR), is the most useful single document.

6. See "The Daily Diary of President George W. Bush, September 11, 2001," partially declassified (hereafter Presidential Daily Diary, partially declassified).

(hereafter NIST Chronology), was key to precisely matching early-morning events to government reactions.

Alas, though, the "official" Defense Department histories—*Pentagon 9/11* and *The First 109 Minutes: 9/11 and the US Air Force*—are largely promotional and not reliable for historical research. The oral histories and stories therein are useful, but the times are muddled, and as unclassified histories written for public consumption, they ignore any complicated or controversial issues. However, the Naval History and Heritage Command (https://www.history.navy.mil/browse-by-topic/wars-conflicts-and-operations/sept-11-attack.html) has compiled pointers to some fine oral histories.

For additional original reporting that, in particular, captures the vast emotional shock and trauma that people experienced and had to fight their way through, I recommend some excellent books: Garett M. Graff, *The Only Plane in the Sky*; Mitchell Zuckoff, *Fall and Rise: The Story of 9/11*; Erik Ronningen, *From the Inside Out: Harrowing Escapes from the Twin Towers of the World Trade Center*; and Jim Dwyer and Kevin Flynn, *102 Minutes: The Untold Story of the Fight to Survive Inside the Twin Towers*.

In commenting about the quality of the information he received on 9/11, President Bush later wrote, "When we did receive information, it was often contradictory and sometimes downright wrong."[7] NORAD commander Gen. Ralph "Ed" Eberhart later told the 9/11 Commission that the logs compiled that day "were not exactly correct." He said that in "no way" were the timelines created as a "falsification of the truth" but that the contemporaneous records, because of the Niagara Falls of information and human error, do not always agree with reconstructions of actual events.[8] I agree with him, and that is the point of this book.

---

7. George W. Bush, *Decision Points* (New York: Crown, 2010), p. 131.

8. See 9/11 Commission Memorandum for the Record, Interview with CINC NORAD (Commander in Chief NORAD), General Edward "Ed" Eberhart, March 1, 2004.

THAT DAY

On September 11, 2001, two hijacked commercial airliners crashed into the north and south towers of the World Trade Center. Soon thereafter, the Pentagon was struck by a third hijacked plane. A fourth hijacked plane, suspected to be bound for the US Capitol building, crashed into a field in Somerset County in southern Pennsylvania when passengers managed to overpower the hijackers.

The attacks that day killed 3,030 US citizens and other nationals.[9] There were 2,735 persons who died in the attacks on the twin towers in New York: 2,184 occupying the two buildings, 129 aboard the two aircraft (119 passengers and crew, and 10 hijackers), 343 New York City firefighters, 71 law enforcement officers (including 60 New York City and Port Authority police), and 8 private emergency medical technicians and paramedics. A total of 189 were killed at the Pentagon: 125 uniformed military, civilian, and contractor personnel and 64 passengers, crew, and terrorists.[10] Forty-four died in Pennsylvania.

---

9. It is important to note that years after the attack, the remains of 1,161 people killed in New York were still unidentified. And countless others have died from exposures to deadly substances; furthermore, there are victims and first responders who are still suffering two decades later.

10. The Department of the Army, with 75 dead, including 22 soldiers, 47 civilian employees, and 6 contractors, suffered more casualties than any other Department of Defense organization. "Most of the Army's losses were soldiers and civilians located in offices on the first and second floors of the Pentagon, between the fourth and sixth corridors. Two Department of the Army offices were particularly hard hit by the attack. Thirty-two civilians working for the Resource Management Directorate of the Office of the Administrative Assistant to the Secretary of the Army were killed. Twenty-six personnel in the Office of the Deputy Chief of Staff for Personnel lost their lives, including the deputy chief of staff, Lt. Gen. Timothy J. Maude. He was the highest-ranking soldier to die in the attack." See "Department of the Army: Historical Summary Fiscal Year 2001," p. 55.

CHAPTER 1

A ROUTINE TUESDAY

The Bush administration's national security titans—Cheney, Powell, Rumsfeld, Condoleezza Rice, and more—all Cold War (and Iraq) veterans, came into office to shepherd the inexperienced George W. through crises, covering the Texas governor's backside and covering the globe. With no particular threat to US national security on the horizon, the titans made a return to foreign policy fundamentals of US interest and a respect for the United States their priority. There'd be no more swatting at flies, no more soldiers wasted as peacekeepers, no more nation building or humanitarian crusades. Rice wrote that a foreign policy was required that "separates the important from the trivial" and that the Clinton administration "assiduously avoided implementing such an agenda." Terrorism, Rice wrote, only needed attending to insofar as it was used by rogue states to advance their interests.

Whatever intelligence there might have been about al Qaeda and whatever warnings were or were not conveyed and heeded, what was clear in this week after summer vacations and the Labor Day weekend was that the world was calm enough that the Bush administration could move forward with confidence that national security wasn't of concern. Carrying out the First Lady's agenda, the president went to Sarasota, Florida, to promote early reading. Neither of his primary national security advisers (Rice or her deputy, Stephen Hadley) accompanied him, itself an unprecedented practice. Secretary of State Powell was in Peru. Treasury Secretary Paul H. O'Neill was in Japan. Attorney General John Ashcroft was flying to Milwaukee, also to promote reading. Joe Allbaugh, the director of FEMA, was in Montana at a conference of state emergency managers. Even the head of government-wide COG didn't go to Florida (as he normally would). And neither was he in the White House. He was instead in New York, scouting locations for Bush's upcoming visit to the United Nations.

In the military, the chairman of the Joint Chiefs of Staff Army Gen. Henry "Hugh" Shelton, in his last weeks before his retirement, was also flying across the Atlantic on his way to say goodbye to his counterparts in Europe. Army Gen. Tommy Franks, commander of US Central Command (CENTCOM) and responsible for the Middle East, was also not at his headquarters in Florida but rather in Greece, on his way to a general tour of his domain, with terrorism not even a part of his agenda.

4:45 a.m.: UA Flight 93 hijacker pilot Ziad Jarrah starts making telephone calls at the Days Inn Newark Airport Hotel.[11] For the next two hours, he makes calls to local numbers and long distance to numbers in Lebanon, France, and Germany using an AT&T prepaid calling card.[12]

Jarrah places five telephone calls to Lebanon (his home country), one call to France, and one call to his wife, Aysel Senguen, in Germany. In this brief call, he is said to have told Senguen that he loves her.[13]

Jarrah flew from Atlanta, Georgia, to Germany on October 7, 2000, and then traveled with Senguen to Paris for a belated honeymoon before returning to Florida on October 29. During the trip, the Navy destroyer USS *Cole* was attacked in Yemen, and Jarrah thought he might have difficulty reentering. He didn't. The Paris trip was the first of five foreign trips Jarrah would take during his time in the United States. His relationship with Senguen remained close throughout his time in the United States, and he "made hundreds of phone calls to her and communicated frequently by email."[14]

5:00 a.m.: NPR's *Morning Edition* airs a story about President Bush visiting a school in Sarasota, Florida.

5:01 a.m.: UA Flight 175 hijacker pilot Marwan al-Shehhi is at the Milner Hotel in Boston and receives a call on his cell phone from Ziad Jarrah. The call lasts for one minute.[15]

---

11. FBI Working Draft Chronology.

12. FBI Working Draft Chronology.

13. National Park Service Flight 93 National Memorial, Timeline, Flight 93, September 11, 2001.

14. 9/11 Commission Report, p. 224; 9/11 Commission Staff Statement 16, p. 6.

15. FBI Serial MM-4035; FBI Serial PH-349.

5:30 a.m.: Laura Wunderlin-VanArsdal, a teacher at Emma E. Booker Elementary School, says, "Many of us had gotten up at 5:30 or earlier that morning, to be sure we made it to school at 7:30 to be checked through the metal detectors and receive our 'Stage Party' pass to allow us to meet the president."

President Bush is scheduled to appear at the school at 9:00 a.m.

5:33 a.m.: AA Flight 11 hijacker pilot Mohammed Atta and Abdul Aziz al-Omari (a "muscleman" on that flight) check out of Room 233 at the Comfort Inn, 90 Maine Mall Road, in South Portland, Maine. They pay for their room with Atta's Visa debit card.[16]

On September 9, Atta had rented a blue Nissan Altima from Alamo Rent-a-Car and picked up al-Omari on their way to Portland.[17]

"Shortly after noon on the day before the attacks, Atta left the Milner Hotel [in Boston], picked up Abdul Aziz al-Omari at the Park Inn [in Newtown, MA], and drove to Portland, Maine in a rented Nissan Altima." They check into the Comfort Inn in South Portland at 5:43 p.m. on September 10. Atta and al-Omari "are seen together on several occasions in the Portland area later that evening," according to the FBI.[18]

"The two spent their last night pursuing ordinary activities: making ATM withdrawals, eating pizza, and shopping at a convenience store. Their three fellow hijackers for Flight 11 stayed together in a hotel in Newton, MA, just outside of Boston."[19]

The two are caught on security cameras visiting a gas station, two ATMs, and a Walmart in Scarborough, Maine.

The FBI believes that on the morning of September 10, Atta drove through New York City, visiting the World Trade Center to obtain coordinates for a GPS navigation device that he used on 9/11 as a backup to locate the building.[20]

---

16. FBI Serial 302-11098; Government Exhibit 0G00020.2 01-455A.

17. FBI Working Draft Chronology.

18. Statement for the Record, FBI Director Robert S. Mueller III, Joint Intelligence Committee Inquiry, September 26, 2002. See also FBI Government Exhibit 0G00020.2 01-455A.

19. 9/11 Commission Report, p. 253.

20. Senator Bob Graham, *Intelligence Matters: The CIA, the FBI, Saudi Arabia, and the Failure of America's War on Terror* (New York: Random House, 2004), p. 78.

5:40 a.m.: AA Flight 11. Mohammed Atta's blue Nissan Altima enters the Portland Jetport parking facility.[21]

Atta is photographed by airport security entering the Portland Jetport. He leaves his rental car in the parking facility rather than return the car to the rental agency.[22]

5:43 a.m.: AA Flight 11. Mohammed Atta and Abdul Aziz al-Omari check in at the US Airways ticket counter at the Portland Jetport.[23]

Atta checks two pieces of luggage, one owned by al-Omari.[24]

"The agent who checked in the two hijackers recalled that when he handed Atta his boarding pass, Atta asked why he was not given a boarding pass for his connecting flight on American Airlines from Boston to Los Angeles. The agent explained to Atta that he would have to check in with American Airlines in Boston to obtain the boarding pass for the second leg of his itinerary. The agent remembered that Atta clenched his jaw and looked as though he was about to get angry. Atta stated that he was assured he would have 'one-step check-in.' The agent told them that they had better get going if they were to make their flight. He said that Atta looked as if he were about to say something in anger but turned to leave. Both Atta and Omari departed for the security checkpoint."[25]

Atta is randomly selected for additional security scrutiny by the Computer Assisted Passenger Prescreening System (CAPPS). His checked bag is held off the plane until it is confirmed that he has boarded. It is then loaded and checked through to AA Flight 11 (though it is never transferred).[26]

Al-Omari makes a cash withdrawal from an ATM at the Portland airport.[27]

---

21. 9/11 Commission Staff Report, August 26, 2004; FBI Serial 302-11062; FBI Serial BS-15885.

22. FBI Government Exhibit 0G00020.2 01-455A. The car is often incorrectly referred to as a Mitsubishi.

23. At 5:43 a.m., Atta and al-Omari are observed by security cameras and a videotaping system at the US Airways Counter at the Jetport. FBI Serial 302-37792.

24. FBI Serial 302-19106.

25. 9/11 Commission Staff Report, August 26, 2004.

26. FBI Working Draft Chronology; FBI Serial 302-11114.

27. FBI Working Draft Chronology.

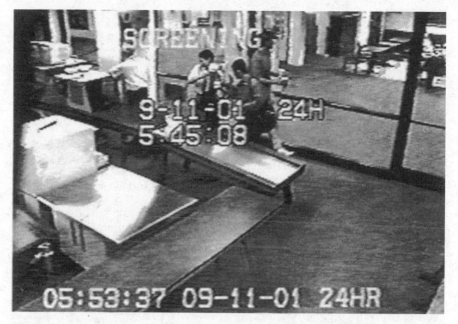

At the Portland, Maine, Jetport, Mohammed Atta and Aziz al-Omari go through security. (Source: FBI)

(Source: 9/11 Commission)

5:45 a.m.: AA Flight 11. Mohammed Atta goes through security at Portland Jetport. The security picture of him is taken around 5:45 a.m. as he passes through security before boarding a flight to Boston with Abdul Aziz al-Omari.[28]

"At 5:45 a.m., Atta and Omari arrived at the sole security checkpoint at the Portland International Jetport. This checkpoint was under the custodial responsibility of Delta Airlines, which contracted for security screening services with Globe Aviation Services. The checkpoint had two lanes, each outfitted with a walk-through metal detector and x-ray equipment to help detect weapons.

"The videotape showed that Atta and al-Omari entered the walk through metal detector at 5:45:03 a.m. A screener was stationed at the device to monitor the screening. Though not conclusive, the video suggests that neither of the subjects set off the metal detector. Both Atta and al-Omari proceeded from the magnetometer immediately to the x-ray belt. Atta picked up a black shoulder bag. Al-Omari claimed a similar bag, and also a smaller black case that he held in both hands. The item cannot be identified but resembled a camera or camcorder case. Neither of the bags was physically examined by a screener, a step that is required if the x-ray monitor displays a suspicious item. Both of the subjects passed out of view of the video camera at 5:45:15 a.m."[29]

5:52 a.m.: UA Flight 175. Hamza al-Ghamdi and Ahmed al-Ghamdi, musclemen, check out of Room 241, Days Hotel, 1234 Soldiers Field Road, Boston, Massachusetts.[30]

FBI investigators say that the desk clerk notes the heavy scent of cologne on Hamza al-Ghamdi. He requests that the clerk call for a taxicab.[31]

6:00 a.m.: AA Flight 11. Mohammed Atta and Abdul Aziz al-Omari board US Airways 5930 (operated by Colgan Air) leaving Portland, Maine, en

---

28. Government Exhibit 0G00020.2 01-455A.
29. 9/11 Commission Staff Report, August 26, 2004.
30. FBI Working Draft Chronology.
31. FBI Serial 2268.

route to Boston Logan. The Beechcraft 1900C model is carrying 8 passengers (19 are possible). Atta sits in seat 9, in the final row.[32]

"Seating aboard the Colgan flight was open rather than assigned. Eight passengers boarded the flight, including Atta and Omari. The flight crew included a pilot and a first officer who also served as the flight attendant. Atta and Omari were the last to board the aircraft and sat in the last row of the plane—row 9. . . . It departed from Gate 11 on time at 6:00 a.m., arriving at Gate B9 (A) at Boston Logan International Airport at approximately 6:45 a.m., one hour before the scheduled departure of [AA] Flight 11."[33]

Fellow passenger Roger Quirion will later say Atta and al-Omari kept quiet and did not draw attention to themselves. Quirion says, "They struck me as business travelers. They were sitting down, talking, seems like they were going over some paperwork."[34]

6:00 a.m.: In New York City, the polls open for primary elections for local offices, including for mayor.

6:00 a.m.: White House National Security Adviser (NSA) Condoleezza Rice arrives at her West Wing office. She reads various news clippings, cables, and intelligence reports. "There was nothing remarkable," she says.[35]

Usually Rice or her deputy, Stephen Hadley, goes along on presidential trips, but because President Bush's trip was short and did not have to do with national security, they sent Navy Capt. Deborah Loewer, director of the White House Situation Room (WHSR), in their stead.

6:00 a.m.: At command centers throughout the North American Aerospace Defense Command (NORAD), personnel prepare for day two of exercise Vigilant Guardian 01-2, a "homeland defense" exercise being held simultaneous with and as an adjunct to Global Guardian, the annual nuclear war game sponsored by US Strategic Command (STRATCOM).[36]

---

32. FBI Working Draft Chronology.

33. 9/11 Commission Staff Report, August 26, 2004.

34. "The Untold Story of Flight 11," CBS News, September 12, 2001.

35. Condoleezza Rice, *No Higher Honor: A Memoir of My Years in Washington* (New York: Crown, 2011), p. 71.

36. Hart Seely, "Amid Crisis Simulation, 'We Were Suddenly No-Kidding Under Attack,'" Newhouse News Service, January 25, 2002.

The interlocking series of domestic war games (still practiced today, mostly under different names) included not only Vigilant Guard and Global Guardian but also Apollo Guardian (a command-and-control exercise), Ellipse Alpha (a national-level emergency decision-making exercise), and Crown Vigilance (an air combat command exercise).[37]

Vigilant Guardian, planned for August 20–September 13, included "an exercise that would pose an imaginary crisis to North American Air Defense outposts nationwide" and "an air defense exercise simulating an attack on the United States." According to the 9/11 Commission, it "postulated a bomber attack from the former Soviet Union."[38] Though often referred to as a bilateral US-Canadian NORAD exercise, it was actually sponsored by US Space Command (SPACECOM), the US-only command responsible for Cold War homeland defense.

Global Guardian 01-2, scheduled for August 20–September 30, was the annual STRATCOM war game. Though the "live play" element of Vigilant Guardian was only in its second day, on the morning of 9/11, Global Guardian was in full swing. Three dozen real nuclear weapons had been loaded on board heavy bombers in North Dakota, Missouri, and Louisiana as part of the exercise. Land-based missile crews were on simulated alert, as were several Trident submarines. Three Nebraska-based E-4B National Airborne Operations Center (NAOC) aircraft were also participating, according to news media accounts.[39]

---

37. There were other military exercises going on or scheduled worldwide on September 11:

- Air Warrior II 01-10 and Joint Contingency Force Advanced Warfighting Experiment, September 1–20, at the Joint Readiness Training Center, Fort Polk, Louisiana;
- Cooperative Baltic Mix 01, September 9–12 in Europe;
- Cooperative Best Effort 01, September 10–12, a NATO-sponsored peacekeeping exercise, in Austria;
- Cooperative Key 01, September 10–21, a NATO-sponsored multinational task force exercise in Bulgaria;
- Dynamic Mix 01, September 1–October 31, in Europe;
- Sea Breeze 01, August 1–September 30, in Europe, a multinational naval exercise; and
- Ulchi Focus Lens 01, July 28–September 12, in South Korea.

38. 9/11 Commission Report, Notes to Chapter 1, p. 458.

39. Steve Liewer, "On 9/11, StratCom Leaders Were Practicing for a Fictional Threat When Real, Unprecedented Catastrophe Struck," *Omaha World Herald*, September 8, 2016.

Ellipse Alpha 01, September 1–14, is a periodic Joint Chiefs of Staff crisis decision-making exercise, conducted by US Joint Forces Command (JFCOM) Joint Warfighting Center. Nothing is known about this exercise.

`6:15 a.m.:` (Approximate time) AA Flight 77 hijacker pilot Hani Hanjour and Majed Moqed, one of the musclemen, check out of the Budget Host Valencia Motel in Laurel, Maryland.[40]

`6:15 a.m.:` (Approximate time) UA Flight 175. Hamza al-Ghamdi and Ahmed al-Ghamdi, musclemen, arrive at Boston Logan airport.[41] A Bay State cab driven by Jean Guerier picked the two up and took them to the airport. Guerier (incorrectly) reports that he arrives at the airport at 6:45 a.m. He specifically remembers the fare, he says, because the passenger only gave him a 15-cent tip.[42]

`6:20 a.m.:` UA Flight 175. Marwan al-Shehhi checks out of Room 308 at the Milner Hotel in Boston.[43] Fayez Banihammad and Mohand al-Shehri, musclemen, check out of Room 408 of the same hotel.[44] The three drive to Boston Logan in a Hyundai rental car.[45]

`6:20 a.m.:` UA Flight 175. Hamza al-Ghamdi and Ahmed al-Ghamdi check in at the United airlines ticket counter at Boston Logan. They approach a United Airlines customer service representative, who immediately refers them to another agent because one of the men presents an identification "certificate" that the first agent is unfamiliar with.

---

40. FBI Working Draft Chronology.

41. Statement for the Record, FBI Director Robert S. Mueller III, Joint Intelligence Committee Inquiry, September 26, 2002.

42. FBI Serial 302-24775.

43. FBI Working Draft Chronology.

44. FBI Working Draft Chronology.

45. FBI Working Draft Chronology. FBI Director Mueller will later incorrectly testify that at about 6:45 a.m., "Fayez Banihammad and Mohand al Shehri, also booked on UA Flight 175, checks [sic] out of the Milner Hotel in the Boston area and drove a rental car to the airport, where they returned the car to the rental company." See Statement for the Record, FBI Director Robert S. Mueller III, Joint Intelligence Committee Inquiry, September 26, 2002.

This second customer service representative says that one of the two men told her that he needed a ticket. She examines his documents and finds that he already has a UA envelope with an itinerary and ticket. She tells him that he does not need a ticket but should check in. The United agent recalls that the men checked two bags. She thought each had one carry-on bag resembling a briefcase. She recalled that each man had "problems" answering the standard security questions and that she had to repeat them "very slowly." After the questioning, the men depart the counter area for the security checkpoint.[46]

6:22 a.m.: AA Flight 77 muscleman Nawaf al-Hazmi and reportedly three other unidentified males check out of Room 122, Marriott Residence Inn, 315 Elden Street, Herndon, Virginia.[47]

6:28 a.m.: President Bush is picked up at the Colony Beach and Tennis Resort, Longboat Key, Florida, to go for a run.[48]

The president had arrived at the Colony Beach and Tennis Resort on Longboat Key at 6:30 p.m. on September 10 and spent the night. He was accompanied by, among others, White House Chief of Staff Andrew Card, Senior Adviser Karl Rove, White House senior staffers Dan Bartlett and Ari Fleischer, Capt. Deborah Loewer, and Secretary of Education Roderick R. Paige.

6:30 a.m.: AA Flight 77 muscleman Nawaf al-Hazmi and three unidentified males get a Dulles Airport taxi from the Marriot Residence Inn to Dulles International Airport (IAP).[49]

6:30 a.m.: UA Flight 175. Ahmed al-Ghamdi's two checked bags are loaded on the aircraft.[50]

---

46. 9/11 Commission Staff Report, August 26, 2004.
47. FBI Working Draft Chronology.
48. Presidential Daily Diary, partially declassified.
49. FBI Working Draft Chronology.
50. 9/11 Commission Staff Report, August 26, 2004.

6:31 a.m.: President Bush arrives at the golf course at the Colony Beach and Tennis Resort in Longboat Key to go for a run.[51]

6:40 a.m.: President Bush begins his morning run.[52]

6:45 a.m.: AA Flight 11. Mohammed Atta and Abdul Aziz al-Omari arrive at Boston Logan aboard US Airways Flight 5930 from Portland, Maine.[53]

"Atta and Omari arrived at Boston Logan, Terminal B, Gate B9A. Atta and Omari still had their carry-on shoulder bags. Atta's two checked bags were unloaded from the Colgan Air flight. The luggage tags indicated that they should be transferred to American Airlines Flight 11 from Boston to Los Angeles International Airport (LAX). Security rules did not require additional screening or special security handling of Atta's luggage. After exiting the aircraft, Atta and Omari crossed a parking lot that separated their arrival and departure terminals. They were observed asking for directions."[54]

6:45 a.m.: UA Flight 175. Marwan al-Shehhi and two of the musclemen arrive at Boston Logan in their Hyundai rental car. They park in the Central Parking Garage on the second deck in row W.[55]

6:45 a.m.: AA Flight 11. Wail al-Shehri, Waleed al-Shehri, and Satam al-Suqami, all musclemen, arrive at Boston Logan.[56]

Waleed spent the night at the Park Inn Hotel, Room 433, in Newton, Massachusetts. He rents a white Mitsubishi Mirage and drives to Boston Logan and parks. Witnesses later state that three males are in the car.[57]

"A witness, who parks in adjacent parking place, observes the arrival of the three hijackers and describes them as 'Palestinians.'"[58]

51. Presidential Daily Diary, partially declassified.
52. Presidential Daily Diary, partially declassified; *Decision Points*, p. 126.
53. 9/11 Commission Staff Report, August 26, 2004; FBI Serial 302-11114.
54. 9/11 Commission Staff Report, August 26, 2004.
55. FBI Working Draft Chronology; FBI Serial 302-6101.
56. 9/11 Commission Staff Report, August 26, 2004.
57. FBI Working Draft Chronology.
58. FBI Serial 302-5957.

6:50 a.m.: Vice President Cheney receives his President's Daily Brief (PDB) in the library of his residence, located on the grounds of the Naval Observatory in Washington, DC.

6:50 a.m.: UA Flight 175. Marwan al-Shehhi's checked bag is loaded.[59]

6:52 a.m.: AA Flight 11. Mohammed Atta receives a cell phone call from a pay phone located inside Terminal C at Boston Logan. This call is believed to have originated from one of the UA Flight 175 hijackers boarding in Terminal C.[60]

"Telephone records show that a phone call was placed from a pay phone in the gate area from which [UA] Flight 175 departed to Atta's cell phone at 6:52 a.m."[61]

The 9/11 Commission concluded that call suggested that the hijacking teams were in tactical communications and possible go or no-go determinations. Another consideration is that the hijackers were saying goodbye to each other, particularly Mohammed Atta and Marwan al-Shehhi, who had lived together and been inseparable for the previous three years.

6:53 a.m.: UA Flight 175. Fayez Banihammad (listed in the airline passenger record as Fayez Ahmed) and Mohand al-Shehri (listed as Mohald) check in. Banihammad checks two bags.[62]

6:54 a.m.: AA Flight 11. Mohammed Atta's cell phone receives a final phone call from a pay phone in Terminal C, Boston Logan, located between the screening checkpoint and the departure gate.[63]

---

59. 9/11 Commission Staff Report, August 26, 2004.

60. Statement for the Record, FBI Director Robert S. Mueller III, Joint Intelligence Committee Inquiry, September 26, 2002. See also Government Exhibit 0G00020.2 01-455A; 9/11 Commission Staff Report, August 26, 2004.

61. 9/11 Commission Staff Report, August 26, 2004.

62. 9/11 Commission Staff Report, August 26, 2004.

63. 9/11 Commission Staff Report, August 26, 2004. Banihammad's calling card number, 800-698-1174, and PIN, 29027646437, is used at a pay telephone. There are altogether three calls to Atta's cell phone, concluding with a call at 6:54 a.m. See FBI Serial 9756; FBI Serial Tel-1482.

6:57 a.m.: UA Flight 175. Fayez Banihammad's checked bags are loaded.[64]

7:00 a.m.: AA Flight 11. Satam al-Suqami, Wail al-Shehri, and Waleed al-Shehri check in at the American Airline ticket counter in Terminal B, Boston Logan.[65]

Al-Suqami, the only hijacker who does not have domestic US-issued identification, uses his Saudi passport to check in. He checks one suitcase and is assigned seat 10B.[66]

Waleed and Wail al-Shehri do not check any baggage and are assigned seats 2B and 2A, respectively.[67]

7:00 a.m.: UA Flight 93 pilot Capt. Jason Dahl enters a secure area of Terminal A at Newark IAP and begins preparations for his flight to San Francisco. He meets LeRoy Homer Jr., the first officer for the flight, in the operations center. The five flight attendants assigned also gather at the center for a briefing and to divide responsibilities.[68]

7:00 a.m.: In Shanksville, Pennsylvania, a small town of 245 residents, Rick King walks a block from his home to his business and opens Ida's Store for the day. He begins brewing coffee for his regular morning customers.[69]

7:01 a.m.: UA Flight 93 hijacker pilot Ziad Jarrah arrives at Newark IAP parking area.[70]

7:03 a.m.: UA Flight 93. Ahmed al-Nami and Saeed al-Ghamdi check in at Newark IAP. Al-Nami checks two bags. Saeed Al-Ghamdi checks no luggage.[71]

---

64. 9/11 Commission Staff Report, August 26, 2004.
65. FBI Working Draft Chronology.
66. FBI Serial 7134.
67. FBI Serial 302-19106.
68. National Park Service, Flight 93, September 11, 2001.
69. National Park Service, Flight 93, September 11, 2001.
70. FBI Working Draft Chronology.
71. FBI Working Draft Chronology; 9/11 Commission Staff Report, August 26, 2004.

`7:15 a.m.:` Gen. Henry "Hugh" Shelton, chairman of the Joint Chiefs of Staff, takes off from Andrews AFB, Maryland, in an Air Force passenger jet on his way to a meeting of the NATO Military Committee in Budapest, Hungary.

`7:15 a.m.:` AA Flight 77. Khalid al-Mihdhar and Majed Moqed, musclemen, check in with American Airlines at Dulles IAP.[72] Within the next 20 minutes, they are joined by Hani Hanjour and two other musclemen, Nawaf al-Hazmi and Salem al-Hazmi.[73]

`7:15 a.m.:` UA Flight 175. Hamza al-Ghamdi, muscleman, is reported to be observed at Terminal C, Boston Logan, by a United Airlines employee.[74]

`7:18 a.m.:` AA Flight 77. Khalid al-Mihdhar and Majed Moqed enter security screening at Dulles IAP. They place their carry-on bags on the x-ray machine belt and proceed through the first walk-through metal detector. Both set off the alarm and are directed to a second metal detector. Though al-Mihdhar does not trigger the second metal detector and is permitted through the checkpoint, Moqed fails once again. A security officer screens him with a handheld metal detection wand. He passes this cursory inspection.[75]

`7:20 a.m.:` UA Flight 93 is ready for boarding at Gate 17, Newark IAP. The plane is a Boeing 757–200, capable of seating 182 persons, but it is only 20 percent filled for the early-morning Tuesday trip to San Francisco. There are five flight attendants and 37 passengers.

The plane is loaded with 48,700 pounds of fuel for the nonstop cross-country trip. It is scheduled to depart the gate at 8:00 a.m. (the same time as UA Flight 175) and is expected to land in San Francisco at 11:14

72. 9/11 Commission Staff Report, August 26, 2004.
73. FBI Working Draft Chronology.
74. FBI Working Draft Chronology; FBI Serial 302-5493.
75. 9/11 Commission Staff Report, August 26, 2004.

a.m. Pacific time. Ten passengers (including the four hijackers) are seated in first class. The remaining 27 passengers have seats in the coach section.[76]

7:20:46 a.m.: AA Flight 77. Khalid al-Mihdhar and Majed Moqed arrive at the West Security Gate at Dulles IAP.[77]

7:23 a.m.: UA Flight 175. Fayez Banihammad and Mohand al-Shehri board, Banihammad sitting in 2A (first class) and al-Shehri seated next to him in 2B.

7:23 a.m.: President Bush's motorcade starts back to the Colony Beach Resort.[78]

7:24 a.m.: UA Flight 93. Ahmed al-Haznawi checks in with United Airlines at Newark IAP and checks a single bag.[79]

Of the four hijackers aboard UA Flight 93, only one, Haznawi, is selected for enhanced screening. As a precaution, his bag is held off the plane until he boards, but it is not opened.[80]

7:27 a.m.: UA Flight 175. Marwan al-Shehhi and Ahmed al-Ghamdi board, with al-Shehhi sitting in 6C (business class) and al-Ghamdi sitting in seat 9D (business class).[81]

7:28 a.m.: UA Flight 175. Hamza al-Ghamdi is the last hijacker to board for UA Flight 175, sitting in seat 9C (business class).[82]

7:29 a.m.: AA Flight 77. Nawaf al-Hazmi and Salem al-Hazmi check in at the American Airlines ticket counter at Dulles IAP.[83]

76. National Park Service Flight 93 National Memorial, Timeline, Flight 93, September 11, 2001.
77. FBI Working Draft Chronology.
78. Presidential Daily Diary, partially declassified.
79. FBI Working Draft Chronology; 9/11 Commission Staff Report, August 26, 2004.
80. National Park Service Flight 93 National Memorial, Timeline, Flight 93, September 11, 2001.
81. 9/11 Commission Staff Report, August 26, 2004.
82. 9/11 Commission Staff Report, August 26, 2004.
83. 9/11 Commission Staff Report, August 26, 2004.

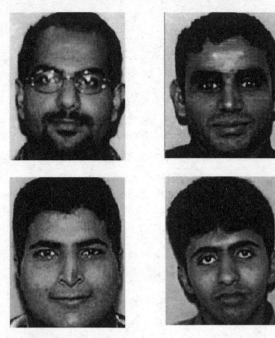

United Airlines Flight 175

Left to right, *Marwan al-Shehhi*, pilot; *Fayez Baniham-mad, Ahmed al-Ghamdi, Hamza al-Ghamdi, Mohand al-Shehri*, hijackers

(Source: 9/11 Commission)

"Nawaf al-Hazmi, along with three others [believed to have been three of the other Flight 77 hijackers], left the Marriott Residence Inn in Herndon, VA, and was later seen with Salem al-Hazmi approaching the American Airlines ticket counter at Dulles."[84]

7:29 a.m.: UA Flight 93. Ziad Jarrah checks in with United Airlines at Newark IAP. He does not check any luggage.[85]

7:30 a.m.: AA Flight 11. Waleed al-Shehri, Wail al-Shehri, and Satam al-Suqami board AA Flight 11 at Gate B32, Boston Logan.[86]

---

84. Statement for the Record, FBI Director Robert S. Mueller III, Joint Intelligence Committee Inquiry, September 26, 2002.

85. 9/11 Commission Staff Report, August 26, 2004. The FBI later reports that this Ziad Jarrah checks in for UAL Flight 93 at 7:39 a.m. FBI Working Draft Chronology.

86. FBI Serial 302-19160. 9/11 Commission Staff Report, August 26, 2004, says 7:31 a.m. The 9/11 Commission has al-Suqami boarding at 7:40 a.m. It is incorrect. 9/11 Commission Staff Report, August 26, 2004.

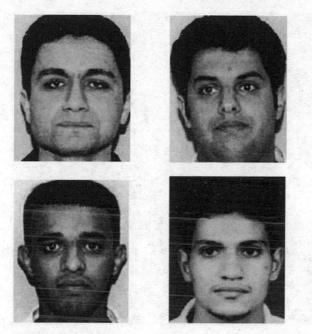

American Airlines Flight 11

Left to right,
Mohamed Atta, pilot;
Waleed al-Shehri,
Wail al-Shehri,
Satam al-Suqami,
Abdulaziz al-Omari,
hijackers

(Source: 9/11 Commission)

7:32 a.m.: A White House email from James R. Wilkenson, "Subject: President Action—Tuesday, September 11," lays out the president's schedule and the themes for the day.

"Attached are (1) today's Presidential Action, and (2) more detailed talking points on today's Presidential event on education in Florida."

7:35 a.m.: AA Flight 77. Hani Hanjour places two carry-on bags on the x-ray belt and passes through the metal detector at Dulles IAP. He picks up his bags and proceeds through the checkpoint.[87]

7:35 a.m.: President's schedule (written for September 11) states: "Phone call to the Prime Minister of Israel (Rice)."[88]

7:36 a.m.: AA Flight 77. Nawaf al-Hazmi and Salem al-Hazmi enter security at Dulles IAP. Salem, with one carry-on bag, successfully clears the

---

87. 9/11 Commission Staff Report, August 26, 2004.

88. Schedule of the President, Tuesday, September 11, 2001. Rice makes no mention of any such call in *No Higher Honor*, and there is no other reference to it.

Hijackers Salem al-Hazmi (right) and Nawaf al-Hazmi (left) clear security at Washington Dulles International Airport. (Source: FBI)

magnetometer and is permitted through the checkpoint. Nawaf sets off the alarms for both the first and second magnetometers. He is hand-wanded, and his shoulder bag is swiped by an explosive trace detector before he is allowed to proceed. The video footage shows that he was carrying an unidentified item clipped to the rim of his back pants pocket.[89]

7:39 a.m.: UA Flight 93. Ahmed al-Nami and Saeed al-Ghamdi arrive at Gate 17A, Newark IAP.[90]

7:40 a.m.: UA Flight 93. Ahmed al-Nami and Saeed al-Ghamdi and al-Nami board, sitting in seats 3D and 3C.[91]

---

89. 9/11 Commission Staff Report, August 26, 2004.
90. FBI Working Draft.
91. FBI Working Draft Chronology.

7:45 a.m.: Vice President Cheney leaves his residence at the Naval Observatory for the White House.[92]

7:45 a.m.: AA Flight 11. Mohammed Atta and Abdul Aziz al-Omari board at Boston Logan.

"They are apparently the last passengers to board the aircraft. Atta requests that the gate agent call the ramp personnel to check if his luggage has been transferred from US Airways Express Flight 5930 to American Airlines Flight 11."[93]

Atta's luggage is loaded on the US Airways flight but is never transferred to his Boston to Los Angeles flight.

7:45 a.m.: President Bush skims the morning papers after a shower and light breakfast. He writes, "The biggest story was that Michael Jordan was coming out of retirement to rejoin the NBA. Other headlines focused on the New York mayoral primary and a suspected case of mad cow disease in Japan."[94]

7:45 a.m.: At Secret Service headquarters in Washington, a routine staff meeting convenes.[95]

7:46 a.m.: (Approximate time) AA Flight 11 pushes back from the gate at Boston Logan. It is a nonstop flight from Boston to LAX, scheduled to lift off at 7:59 a.m. Capt. John Ogonowski and First Officer Thomas McGuinness pilot the Boeing 767-223. On board are 9 flight attendants and 81 passengers, including the 5 hijackers, led by Mohammed Atta.

---

92. Secret Service log; Secret Service Memorandum, White House Events on 9/11/01 (Special Agent James O. Scott), September 12, 2001, partially declassified.

93. FBI Serial 302-7431. 9/11 Commission Staff Report, August 26, 2004, incorrectly says they board at 7:39 a.m.

94. *Decision Points*, p. 126.

95. Paul L. Nenninger, "One Secret Service Agent's Experience," *Southeast Missourian*, August 29, 2011.

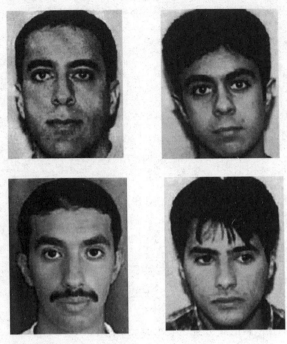

**United Airlines
Flight 93**

Left to right,
Ziad Jarrah, pilot;
*Saeed al-Ghamdi,
Ahmed al-Haznawi,
Ahmed al-Nami*,
hijackers

(Source: 9/11 Commission)

7:48 a.m.: UA Flight 93. Hijacker pilot Ziad Jarrah boards and sits in seat 1B, closest to the cockpit.[96]

7:50 a.m.: AA Flight 77. Majed Moqed and Khalid al-Mihdhar board, sitting in seats 12A and 12B in coach.[97]

7:50 a.m.: Condoleezza Rice receives her intelligence briefing.[98]

7:52 a.m.: AA Flight 77. Hijacker pilot Hani Hanjour boards, taking seat 1B, closest to the cockpit.[99]

7:55 a.m.: AA Flight 77. Nawaf al-Hazmi and Salem al-Hazmi board, occupying seats 5E and 5F in first class.[100]

---

96. FBI Working Draft Chronology; 9/11 Commission Staff Report, August 26, 2004.
97. FBI Working Draft Chronology; 9/11 Commission Staff Report, August 26, 2004.
98. Schedule of the President, Tuesday, September 11, 2001.
99. FBI Working Draft Chronology.
100. 9/11 Commission Staff Report, August 26, 2004.

American Airlines Flight 77

Left to right,
Hani Hanjour, pilot;
Nawaf al-Hazmi,
Khalid al-Mihdhar,
Majed Moqed, Salem
al-Hazmi, hijackers

(Source: 9/11 Commission)

7:56:27 a.m.: AA Flight 11. FAA Boston Airport Traffic Control Tower (Boston Tower) issues taxi instructions; this is the first of the four hijacked flights to depart.

7:57 a.m.: Vice President Cheney arrives at the White House.[101]

7:58 a.m.: UA Flight 175, scheduled to depart Boston Logan for LAX at 8:00 a.m., pushes back from its gate. It is then delayed 14 minutes on the runway before taking off.[102]

Capt. Victor Saracini and First Officer Michael Horrocks pilot the Boeing 767, which has seven flight attendants and 56 passengers on board.[103]

Hijacker pilot Marwan al-Shehhi is seated in 6C in business class. Mohand al-Shehri is in seat 2B, Fayez Banihammad is in seat 2A, Hamza al-Ghamdi is in seat 9C, and Ahmed al-Ghamdi is in seat 9D.[104]

---

101. Secret Service log; Secret Service Memorandum, White House Events on 9/11/01 (Special Agent James O. Scott), September 12, 2001, partially declassified.

102. 9/11 Commission Staff Report, August 26, 2004.

103. 9/11 Commission Report, p. 7.

104. FBI Working Draft Chronology.

7:59 a.m.: AA Flight 11, a Boeing 767, is cleared for takeoff from Boston Logan and departs for Los Angeles.[105]

It begins its takeoff roll on runway 4 Right and lifts off within one minute.[106] All communications with FAA Boston Tower and with Boston Departure Control are routine and normal.

8:00 a.m.: President Bush receives his daily intelligence briefing at his hotel. CIA briefer Michael Morell delivers the PDB, as he does most days. White House Chief of Staff Andy Card is present, as is Capt. Deborah Loewer, director of the WHSR. The briefing covered Russia, China, and the Palestinian uprising in the West Bank and Gaza Strip.[107]

According to Morell, that morning's briefing was "unremarkable, focusing on the most recent developments in the Palestinian uprising against Israel."[108]

Despite news media reports to the contrary, there was nothing regarding terrorist threats in that day's PDB. Morell says that in the first three months of the Bush administration, there was "little to no specific threat reporting on what al Qa'ida [sic] was plotting." That changed, he says, in the spring through early summer, when the volume of reporting increased and al Qaeda members spoke to each other of "very good news to come." By July, the reporting "suddenly dried up," Morell says, and it was during that period of "summer doldrums" that the famed August 6 PDB—"Bin Ladin [sic] Determined to Strike in US"—was written to summarize what the CIA knew of any direct threats to the United States.[109]

8:00 a.m.: At the Pentagon, Defense Secretary Rumsfeld hosts a congressional breakfast meeting in his private dining room. The meeting is to discuss the

---

105. Government Exhibit 0G00020.2 01-455A. FBI Serial BS-2909 says the aircraft then backs away from the gate and that Flight 11 took off from Logan Airport at 7:59 a.m.

106. FAA Chronology of the September 11 Attacks and Subsequent Events Through October 24, 2001 (eastern time is used throughout; hereafter "FAA Chronology"). AA Flight 11 takeoff time extrapolated from RADES radar data; NORAD 9/11 Timeline, n.d., prepared for the 9/11 Commission.

107. *Decision Points*, p. 126.

108. Michael Morell, *The Great War of Our Time: The CIA's Fight Against Terrorism— From al Qa'ida to ISIS* (New York: Twelve, 2015), p. 46.

109. *The Great War of Our Time*, pp. 39–43.

upcoming Quadrennial Defense Review (QDR), a congressionally mandated study.[110] Rumsfeld is scheduled to return to his office thereafter for his daily intelligence briefing—the same briefing given to Bush, Cheney, and Rice, supplemented by intelligence items relevant to the military. Others in attendance at the breakfast include Rumsfeld's senior military assistant, Navy Vice Admiral Edmund Giambastiani Jr.; Deputy Secretary of Defense Paul Wolfowitz; and Pete Geren, one of Rumsfeld's special assistants. The members of Congress include Rep. Doug Bereuter (R-NE), Rep. Christopher Cox (R-CA), Rep. Randy "Duke" Cunningham (R-CA), Rep. Kay Granger (R-TX), Rep. Robin Hayes (R-NC), Rep. John Hostettler (R-IN), Rep. Mark Steven Kirk (R-IL), Rep. John Mica (R-FL), Rep. John Shimkus (R-IL), Rep. Mac Thornberry (R-TX), and Rep. Roger Wicker (R-MS).

8:00 a.m.: Former president George H. W. Bush and former First Lady Barbara Bush depart Washington by private jet, bound for a speaking engagement in St. Paul, Minnesota. They had spent the night of September 10 at the White House.

8:00 a.m.: New York City public schools open for the fourth day of the new school year.

8:00 a.m.: In Shanksville, Pennsylvania, the post office opens for the day. Judi Baeckel, acting postmaster, opens and begins to sort the mail for the 165 boxholders.[111]

---

110. According to the Army, "By September, the review began to take shape. A new strategic framework formulated by Secretary Rumsfeld's office broke with the policies and guidance of the previous administration, which had based the previous QDR on the presumption that the United States should be able to wage two simultaneous major theater wars. The new concept became known as the '1-4-2-1' strategy, its name derived from the number of missions the US military had to be prepared to perform in order to meet different national security requirements. The 1-4-2-1 strategy articulated the following roles for the US military: homeland defense (1), forward deterrence in four critical regions (4), the ability to 'swiftly defeat the efforts' of enemy states in two near-simultaneous conflicts (2), and the ability to 'win decisively' in one of them, meaning the total defeat and overthrow of the enemy regime at the president's option in one of those conflicts." See Department of the Army Historical Summary: Fiscal Year 2001, p. 10.

111. National Park Service, Flight 93, September 11, 2001.

8:01 a.m.: UA Flight 93 pushes back from Gate 17A, Newark IAP, and taxies to its departure area. Because of typically heavy morning air traffic congestion, flight takeoff is delayed 42 minutes.[112]

8:04:55 a.m.: UA Flight 175 receives taxi instructions from Boston Tower.

8:05 a.m.: President Bush talks with Condoleezza Rice on the telephone.[113]

According to Bush's CIA briefer Michael Morell, who was in the room, the call was precipitated by an item in his PDB regarding the intercept of a conversation "between two (non-allied) world leaders." It is not related to terrorism.[114]

8:09 a.m.: AA Flight 77, a Boeing 757, pushes back from Gate D-26 at Dulles IAP.[115] It is scheduled to depart from Washington for LAX at 8:10 a.m. The aircraft is piloted by Capt. Charles F. Burlingame and First Officer David Charlebois. There are four flight attendants and 58 passengers aboard.[116]

8:09 a.m.: AA Flight 11, now in the air, establishes radio contact with FAA Boston Center. "Boston Center, good morning, American Eleven with you passing through one-nine-zero [19,000 feet] for two-three-zero [23,000 feet]."

Boston Center acknowledges. From this time until 8:13:31 a.m., all communications are routine and normal. The flight is instructed to climb to 28,000 feet and then subsequently to 29,000 feet.

8:09:18 a.m.: UA Flight 93 is issued taxi instructions from FAA Newark Airport Traffic Control Tower (Newark Tower).

8:10 a.m.: Condoleezza Rice receives her daily National Security Briefing.[117]

112. FBI Working Draft Chronology; 9/11 Commission Staff Report, August 26, 2004.
113. Presidential Daily Diary, partially declassified.
114. *The Great War of Our Time*, p. 46.
115. 9/11 Commission Staff Report, August 26, 2004.
116. 9/11 Commission Report, p. 8.
117. Schedule of the President, Tuesday, September 11, 2001.

`8:12:29 a.m.:` AA Flight 77 is issued taxi instruction from Dulles Traffic Control Tower (Dulles Tower).

`8:13 a.m.:` AA Flight 11. FAA Boston Center radios directional instructions: "American eleven turn twenty degrees right." AA Flight 11 replies: "Twenty right American eleven."[118]

"In its last routine communication, the cockpit crew acknowledged navigational instructions from . . . FAA's Boston Air Route Traffic Control Center, located in Nashua, New Hampshire. Sixteen seconds into the transmission, Zalewski instructed the pilots to climb to 35,000 feet. They did not acknowledge his direction."[119]

This is the last routine communication received with the flight.[120]

`8:14 a.m.:` Second Lady Lynne Cheney leaves the residence at the Naval Observatory for downtown.[121]

`8:14 a.m.:` UA Flight 175, a Boeing 767, begins takeoff roll on runway 9 and lifts off from Boston Logan, destination Los Angeles.[122] All communications with Boston Tower and with Boston Departure Control are routine and normal.

---

118. The FBI incorrectly says: "At 8:13 a.m. Flight 11 is directed by air traffic control to climb to 35,000 feet and maintain that altitude. The flight crew does not acknowledge this transmission from Air Traffic Control." This transmission did not happen until 8:14 a.m. See FBI Serial BS-11114.

119. Priscilla D. Jones, *The First 109 Minutes: 9/11 and the US Air Force* (Washington, DC: Air Force History and Museums Program, 2011).

120. FBI Working Draft Chronology.

121. Secret Service Memorandum, White House Events on 9/11/01 (Special Agent James O. Scott), September 12, 2001, partially declassified.

122. 9/11 Commission Report, p. 7; FAA Chronology. Takeoff from Boston extrapolated from RADES radar data; NORAD 9/11 Timeline, n.d., prepared for the 9/11 Commission.

CHAPTER 2

"WE HAVE SOME PLANES"

There were 19 of them: 15 Saudis, two citizens of the United Arab Emirates, one Egyptian, and one Lebanese national. Mohammed Atta, the sole Egyptian and the eldest at age 33, grew up in Cairo. The son of a lawyer and raised in a middle-class, educated family, he studied architecture before moving to Hamburg, Germany, to get his master's degree. He had been radicalized around 1995 and had written his last will and testament and offered his life as a martyr in response to the Israeli bombing campaign in Lebanon the next year. He joined an extremist mosque in Hamburg, started an Islamic student group at the university, made his pilgrimage to Mecca, and traveled to Afghanistan in early 1998, thought to be his first contact with al Qaeda central. Returning to Hamburg, he bonded with two of the other subsequent pilots—Lebanese student Ziad Jarrah and UAE student Marwan al-Shehhi—with all three receiving their assignments to be the pilots in Khalid Sheikh Mohammed's "planes operation" in November 1999.

All three entered the United States by June 2000, and for the next year and a half, they mostly lived in Florida, attending flight school, living normal lives, scouting targets, and studying airline operations and routines. Atta was always the leader, in charge of planning, finances, communications, target selection, and managing the overall group. The fourth pilot, Saudi citizen Hani Hanjour, wouldn't join until later, and the 15 "musclemen"— all Saudis except for one—would begin arriving in the United States in April 2001. The whole group was assembled by early August. Atta selected the final date and the synchronization of the attacks: two planes would strike the World Trade Center towers followed by simultaneous attacks in Washington, with one plane hitting the Pentagon and the other the US Capitol building.

8:14 a.m.: AA Flight 11, flying at about 27,000 feet, is taken over by hijackers.

"About this time the 'Fasten Seatbelt' sign would usually have been turned off, and the flight attendants would have begun preparing for cabin service."[123]

"At around 8:14 a.m. or shortly thereafter, the hijackers began their take-over of the aircraft. Information supplied by eyewitness accounts indicates that the hijackers initiated and sustained their command of the aircraft using knives (as reported by two flight attendants); violence, including stabbing and slashing (as reported by two flight attendants); the threat of violence (as indicated by a hijacker in radio transmissions received by air traffic control); Mace (reported by one flight attendant); the threat of a bomb, either fake or real (reported by one flight attendant); and deception about their intentions (as indicated by a hijacker in a radio transmission received by air traffic control)."[124]

Between 8:13:47 and 8:24:53 a.m., FAA Boston Center makes several radio transmissions attempting to contact AA Flight 11. None of them are acknowledged.[125] Investigators, including the 9/11 Commission, later conclude that Boston Center did not suspect for approximately 10 more minutes that AA Flight 11 had been hijacked.[126]

8:16 a.m.: In Shanksville, Pennsylvania, classes begin at Shanksville-Stonycreek School, with 490 students in pre-K through grade 12. It is the 10th day of the new school year.[127]

8:17:59 a.m.: AA Flight 11. A brief unknown sound (possibly a scream) from an unknown origin is heard over a radio at FAA Boston Center.[128]

8:18 a.m.: AA Flight 11 attendant Betty Ong calls American Airlines operations in Gary, North Carolina, to report a hijacking.

---

123. 9/11 Commission Report, p. 4.
124. 9/11 Commission Staff Report, August 26, 2004.
125. 9/11 Commission Staff Report, August 26, 2004.
126. *The First 109 Minutes: 9/11 and the US Air Force*, 2011.
127. National Park Service, Flight 93, September 11, 2001.
128. FAA Chronology of September 11, 2001.

FAA air traffic control regions as of September 11, 2001. (Source: 9/11 Commission)

According to the FBI: "At 8:18 a.m. a call is received by the American Airlines Southeastern Reservations Center in Gary, North Carolina. Flight attendant Betty Ong is calling from Flight 11 on the 'reservations telephone.' This telephone directly links American Airlines aircraft with the company's reservations centers. Ms. Ong identified herself to the reservations center employees answering the telephone as 'flight attendant number 3.' This designates an assignment in coach class, at the rear of the passenger cabin. She further stated that she was making the telephone call from 'jump seat 3R,' which is located at the rear of the coach class and the rear of the cabin.

"The emergency call from Betty Ong lasted approximately 25 minutes (8:19 [*sic*] a.m.–8:44 a.m.). Ong relayed vital information about events taking place aboard the airplane to authorities on the ground. Her call was received initially at the reservations office by an American Airlines employee. The call was transferred to another employee who, realizing the urgency of the situation, pushed an emergency button that simultaneously initiated a tape recording of the call and sent an alarm notifying Nydia Gonzalez, the reservations office supervisor, to pick up on the line. Gonzalez was paged to respond to the alarm and joined the call a short time later. Only the first four minutes of the phone call between Ong and the reservations center was tape-recorded because the recently installed recording system at that time contained a default time limit."[129]

8:19 a.m.: AA Flight 11. "At 8:19, Ong reported: 'The cockpit is not answering, somebody's stabbed in business class . . . and I think there's Mace . . . we can't breathe . . . I don't know, I think we're getting hijacked.'"[130]

"Ms. Ong stated that two other flight attendants had been stabbed and a passenger in first class had been killed. Ms. Ong said that the passengers had been forced to the rear of the cabin, because the hijackers had used some form of aerosol irritant, which she describes as 'Mace.' Ms. Ong identifies al-Suqami as the hijacker who killed the passenger. Al-Suqami is identified by his seat on the aircraft, 10B."[131]

"Passenger Daniel Lewin [seated in 9B], who was seated in the row just behind Atta and Omari, was stabbed by one of the hijackers—probably Satam al Suqami, who was seated directly behind Lewin. Lewin had served four years as an officer in the Israeli military. He may have made an attempt to stop the hijackers in front of him, not realizing that another was sitting behind him."[132]

"Ray Cornell Scott, manager on duty at the Information Center for American Airlines was advised of the Emergency phone call and listened to the call . . . Ong stated the individual who was seated in 9B appeared to be dead. Flight Attendant Number 1 was stabbed, in serious condition and had been placed on oxygen. Flight Attendant Number 5 had also been stabbed but was not described as being in serious condition. Ong relayed that a passenger who was seated in 10B was currently in the cockpit. The passenger's name was provided and phonetically reported as Samir Al Asaquami (Satam al-Suqami). Ong advised that passengers seated in seats 2A, 2B and 10B participated in the takeover of Flight 11. These individuals were identified by the manifest as Passenger 2A, Wail al-Shehri; Passenger 2B as Waleed al-Shehri and Passenger 10B as Satam al-Suqami. Ong

---

129. 9/11 Commission Staff Report, August 26, 2004.
130. 9/11 Commission Report, p. 5.
131. FBI Serial CE-1018; FBI Serial 302-30391.
132. 9/11 Commission Report, p. 5.

advised the First Class passengers had been moved to the coach section but did not specify if this was done by the flight crew or the hijackers."[133]

8:19 a.m.: AA Flight 77 is cleared for take-off at Dulles IAP.

> 8:19:20 a.m.: Dulles: "American seventy-seven, your departure frequency will be one two five point zero five, runway three zero cleared for takeoff."
>
> 8:19:27 a.m.: AA Flight 77: "Twenty-five point five cleared for takeoff, runway, ah, three zero American seventy-seven."[134]

8:20:48 a.m.: AA Flight 11's secondary radar return (from its transponder) is lost on FAA Boston Center displays. The aircraft is then observed as a primary radar target only.[135] Every commercial airliner is equipped with a radio transponder (sometimes called an "identification friend or foe" [IFF] transponder) that automatically broadcasts heading, speed, and altitude as well as a unique electronic code that identifies the airplane. The transponder data are converted into symbology on FAA scopes and maps. When a transponder is turned off, the aircraft "disappears" from scopes and maps.

The Air Force later explains that "because the transponder signal was lost, the [Boston] center would have to control the intercept until NEADS identification technicians could find the aircraft. Without the transponder signal and, therefore, without a radar point, NEADS personnel needed the plane's latitude and longitude coordinates."[136]

8:20 a.m.: AA Flight 77, a Boeing 757, begins takeoff roll on runway 30 and lifts off from Dulles IAP.[137] The departure is delayed 10 minutes. All

---

133. FBI, American Airlines Flight #11 Investigative Summary, FBI 02991.

134. NTSB, Flight Path Study.

135. 9/11 Commission Staff Report, August 26, 2004. There is a one-minute discrepancy in different timelines, with NORAD saying: "0820—AA 11 turns off transponder from RADES radar data"; NORAD 9/11 Timeline, n.d., prepared for the 9/11 Commission.

136. *The First 109 Minutes: 9/11 and the US Air Force*, 2011.

137. 9/11 Commission Staff Report, August 26, 2004; NORAD 9/11 Timeline, n.d., prepared for the 9/11 Commission. FAA Chronology says 8:21 a.m.

communications with Dulles Tower and Dulles Departure Control are routine and normal.

> 8:20:26 a.m.: Dulles: "American seventy-seven, turn left heading two seven zero, contact departure."
>
> 8:20:31 a.m.: AA Flight 77: "Two seventy heading departure American seventy-seven; thanks, sir, good day."
>
> 8:20:43 a.m.: Dulles: "American seventy-seven, Dulles departure radar contact; climb and maintain five thousand.
>
> 8:20:47 a.m.: AA Flight 77: "Five thousand American seventy-seven."[138]

8:20 a.m.: At NORAD NEADS, commander Col. Robert K. Marr says he was speaking with Maj. Gen. Larry K. Arnold, commanding general of the Continental NORAD Region (CONR), the higher headquarters of the Northeast Sector, located at Tyndall AFB, Florida, about the start of exercise Vigilant Guardian when he was informed that there was an FAA report of a real-world hijack.[139]

8:21 a.m.: AA Flight 11. At American Airlines in Gary, North Carolina, Nydia Gonzalez formally alerts central operations in Fort Worth, Texas, reaching Craig Marquis, the manager on duty.[140]

At about this time, an American Airlines dispatcher in Fort Worth receives a communication from a different American Airlines flight (traveling from Seattle to Boston) after FAA Boston Center asked other planes in the sky to try to contact AA Flight 11.[141]

8:22 a.m.: AA Flight 11. American Airlines manager Craig Marquis in Fort Worth "acknowledged the emergency and indicated to Gonzalez [in Gary,

---

138. NTSB, Flight Path Study.

139. Maj. Gen. Larry K. Arnold oversaw the Northeast, the Western, and the Southeast Air Defense Sectors. The locations of the departures, flight paths, and crash sites of the four aircraft were all in the Northeast Air Defense Sector, commanded by Col. Marr. See also 9/11 Commission Memorandum for the Record, Interview Colonel Robert Marr, January 23, 2004.

140. 9/11 Commission Report, p. 5.

141. 9/11 Commission Staff Report, August 26, 2004.

NC] that he would 'get ATC [air traffic control] on here.' At this same time, while Marquis was relating this information to Gonzalez, Ong reported to Gonzalez's colleague: 'I think the guys [hijackers] are up there. They might have gone there, jammed their way up there, or something. Nobody can call the cockpit. We can't even get inside.' Thirty seconds after contacting American Airlines' headquarters, Gonzalez rejoined the call from Ong."[142]

8:22 a.m.: AA Flight 11. A second flight attendant, Madeline "Amy" Sweeney, tries to contact the American Airlines flight services office at Boston Logan. The office managed the scheduling and operation of flight attendants, and its phone number was well known to the American flight attendants. Sweeney's initial attempt to get through on the Airfone failed.[143]

8:22 a.m.: AA Flight 77. FAA Dulles issues instructions:

> 8:22:08 a.m.: "American seventy-seven [AA Flight 77], climb and maintain one one thousand, eleven thousand."
> 8:22:08 a.m.: "AAL-seventy-seven up to one one thousand, American seventy-seven."[144]

8:23 a.m.: AA Flight 11. American Airlines flight dispatcher unsuccessfully tries to contact AA Flight 11 through the Aircraft Communications and Reporting System (ACARS) messaging system, a text-only email system that enables those in the cockpit of in-flight aircraft and company personnel on the ground to communicate: "Good morning . . . ATC looking for you on [radio frequency] 135.32." The dispatcher received no response to the message.[145]

"The tape recording of the call between Ong and the reservations center ceased because of the default time limit on the system. However, Gonzalez remained on the line with Ong for the next 21 minutes. Gonzalez continued to report the information she received from the flight attendant.

142. 9/11 Commission Staff Report, August 26, 2004.
143. 9/11 Commission Staff Report, August 26, 2004.
144. NTSB, Flight Path Study.
145. 9/11 Commission Staff Report, August 26, 2004.

. . . The call between American's reservations facility [in Gary, NC] and the SOC [American Airlines Service Operations Center] continued to be taped by the SOC until its conclusion."[146]

8:23:01 a.m.: UA Flight 175, now in the air, establishes radio contact with Boston Center. "Boston, morning, United one-seven-five out of one-nine [19,000 feet] for two-three-zero [23,000 feet]." FAA Boston Center acknowledges.

All communications between Boston Center and UA Flight 175 appear routine and normal. The flight is subsequently instructed to climb to flight level 310 (31,000 feet) and, after radar handoff, is issued a frequency change to contact FAA New York Center (New York Air Route Traffic Control Center).

FAA Boston Center is busy trying to contact AA Flight 11. The two flight attendants on board—Ong and Sweeney—have contacted American Airlines, not the FAA.

8:23 a.m.: AA Flight 77. FAA Dulles issues instructions and receives a response:

8:23:23: Dulles: "American seventy-seven cleared direct LINDEN contact Dulles one one eight point six seven."
8:23:28: AA Flight 77: "Direct LINDEN eighteen sixty-seven American ah seventy-seven."
8:23:43: AA Flight 77: "American, ah, seventy-seven with you passing nine decimal one for eleven one one thousand."
8:23:47: Dulles: "American seven seven, Dulles, approach climb maintain one seven thousand."
8:23:50: AA Flight 77: "One seven thousand, American seventy-seven."[147]

8:24 a.m.: AA Flight 11. Hijacker pilot Mohammed Atta keys the cockpit microphone in an attempt to communicate with the passengers. Instead,

---

146. 9/11 Commission Staff Report, August 26, 2004.
147. NTSB, Flight Path Study.

he transmits outside the aircraft, and those transmissions are heard on the ground.

FAA Boston Center controller Zalewski hears two clicks over the frequency assigned to the flight and radios in response, "Is that American eleven trying to call?"

> 8:24:38 a.m.: AA Flight 11 (Atta): "We have some planes. Just stay quiet and you'll be okay. We are returning to the airport."
>
> 8:24:38 a.m.: AA Flight 11 (Atta): "Nobody move. Everything will be okay. If you try to make any moves, you'll endanger yourself and the airplane. Just stay quiet."

According to flight attendant Ong's reporting, no announcement is heard in the cabin. Atta's transmission is at first garbled, and Boston Center cannot decipher the first sentence. It is understood only 30 minutes later, after a facility manager is able to locate and replay the tape and break it down.[148]

8:25 a.m.: President Bush finishes his 25-minute morning intelligence briefing.[149]

8:25 a.m.: AA Flight 11. FAA Boston Center begins notifications that a suspected hijacking is in progress, contacting Boston facility manager and the New England Regional Operations Center (ROC) in Burlington, Massachusetts, the regional center overseeing Boston. Additionally, controllers begin interfacility coordination with FAA New York Center, where the plane is headed.

An American Airlines specialist sends another ACARS message to AA Flight 11: "Plz contact Boston Center ASAP. . . . They have lost radio contact and your transponder signal." The aircraft does not respond to this or subsequent ACARS messages.[150]

---

148. *The First 109 Minutes: 9/11 and the US Air Force*, 2011.
149. *The Great War of Our Time*, p. 47.
150. 9/11 Commission Staff Report, August 26, 2004.

8:25 a.m.: AA Flight 11 flight attendant Sweeney makes another call to the American Airlines Flight Services Office at Boston and is briefly connected. Sweeney says that someone is hurt "aboard Flight 12," and then the phone call is cut off.[151]

Michael Woodward, the Boston flight service manager at Boston Logan, goes to American's gate area with a colleague. He sees that the morning flights have all departed, and the gate area is quiet. He further realizes that Flight 12 is a flight to Boston from the West Coast that has not even left yet, so he and his colleague return to the office to try to clarify the nature of the emergency call.[152]

8:25:49 a.m.: AA Flight 77, still flying normally, establishes radio contact with FAA Washington Center: "Center, American seventy-seven with you passing one-three decimal zero [13,000 feet] for one-seven-thousand [17,000 feet]." All communications between Washington Center and AA Flight 77 are routine and normal. AA Flight 77 is subsequently handed off to the Indianapolis Air Route Traffic Control Center (FAA Indy Center).

> 8:25:33 a.m.: Dulles: "American seventy-seven, contact Washington Center one two zero point six five, good flight."
> 8:25:37 a.m.: AA Flight 77: "Twenty [point] six five, American seventy-seven; thank you, ma'am, good day."
> 8:25:49 a.m.: AA Flight 77: "Ah, center, American seventy-seven with you, passing one three decimal zero for one seven thousand."
> 8:25:57 a.m.: Dulles: "American seventy-seven, Washington Center; roger, climb and maintain flight level two seven zero."[153]

8:26:30 a.m.: AA Flight 11, flying at 29,000 feet, begins a 100-degree southbound turn over Albany, New York, heading south toward New York City. "Near Albany, New York, the flight began a hard but level left turn to the south."[154]

---

151. 9/11 Commission Report, p. 6.

152. 9/11 Commission Staff Report, August 26, 2004.

153. NTSB, Flight Path Study.

154. *The First 109 Minutes: 9/11 and the US Air Force*, 2011. NORAD has a one-minute discrepancy: "0827—AA 11 Turns south from RADES radar data"; NORAD 9/11 Timeline,

Flight attendant Ong reports that the plane is "flying erratically."[155]

8:26 a.m.: AA Flight 77 radios to FAA Dulles: "Two seven zero, American seventy-seven."[156]

8:28 a.m.: FAA Boston Center calls FAA Air Traffic Control System Command Center (the national command center in Herndon, Virginia) to advise that it believes AA Flight 11, now flying south, has been hijacked and is heading toward New York airspace.

Herndon Command Center establishes a teleconference between Boston, New York, and Cleveland Centers to allow Boston Center to provide situational awareness to the centers adjoining Boston in the event the hijacked aircraft enters their airspace.[157]

Though the FAA now suspects a hijacking, no one imagines that the plane will be flown into a building. That is hardly the normal course of a hijacking, which previously had entailed demands for clearance to fly somewhere or a demand for ransom and the release of prisoners. The expectation was that the airplane would request permission to land in New York.

8:29 a.m.: AA Flight 11. American Airlines Operations Center in Fort Worth, Texas, contacts FAA Boston Center about the hijacking of AA Flight 11, nine minutes after the fight attendant reported the event to them. FAA Boston Center had just determined there was a hijacking.[158]

Flight attendant Sweeney again tries to get through to the American Flight Services Office in Boston and is connected.[159]

8:30 a.m.: At the Pentagon, Capt. Charles Leidig reports for duty as deputy director of operations (DDO) for Operations Team 2 (one of five) at the

---

n.d., prepared for the 9/11 Commission. The 9/11 Commission then incorrectly states that at 8:27 a.m., AA Flight 11 turned south toward New York City. 9/11 Commission Report, p. 6.

155. 9/11 Commission Report, p. 6.
156. NTSB, Flight Path Study.
157. 9/11 Commission Staff Report, August 26, 2004.
158. 9/11 Commission Report, p. 5.
159. 9/11 Commission Report, p. 6.

National Military Command Center (NMCC). He receives the intelligence and other turnover briefings on the status of US forces. The assistant DDO is Navy Commander Pat Gardner.[160]

Normally a "flag" officer (a general or admiral) would be the DDO, but Capt. Leidig is sitting in for Army Brig. Gen. Montague Winfield, the DDO for Operations Team 2, who is attending a meeting and does not return until about 10:45 a.m.

8:30 a.m.: AA Flight 77 again has normal communications.

> 8:30:38 a.m.: Dulles: "American seventy-seven, contact Washington Center, one three three point two seven."
> 8:30:42 a.m.: AA Flight 77: "Ah, thirty-three twenty-seven, American seventy-seven; thanks, sir, good day."[161]

8:30 a.m.: (Approximate time) Pakistan Intelligence (ISI) Director Lt. Gen. Mahmood Ahmed (Ahmad) is at a breakfast meeting in Washington with the chairmen of the House and Senate Intelligence Committees, Sen. Bob Graham (D-FL) and Rep. Porter Goss (R-FL), as well as with Sen. Jon Kyl (R-AZ).[162] Also present at the breakfast meeting is Pakistani ambassador to the United States Maleeha Lodhi.

According to Sen. Bob Graham, "We were talking about terrorism, specifically terrorism generated from Afghanistan" and Osama bin Laden.

During the next few days in Washington, Ahmed meets with US officials regarding Pakistani cooperation to facilitate the war in Afghanistan. He meets with CIA Director George Tenet, Secretary of State Powell, Deputy Secretary of State Armitage, Undersecretary of State for Political Affairs Marc Grossman, and Chairman of the Senate Foreign Relations Committee Sen. Joseph Biden (D-DE).

---

160. 9/11 Commission Memorandum for the Record, Interview, Captain Charles Joseph Leidig, USN, April 29, 2004.

161. NTSB, Flight Path Study.

162. George Tenet later writes that Sen. Lindsay Graham is also present, but that is probably a mistake. See George Tenet, *At the Center of the Storm: My Years at the CIA* (New York: HarperCollins, 2007), p. 162.

8:31 a.m.: AA Flight 77 still has normal communications.

> 8:31:05 a.m.: AA Flight 77: "American seventy-seven passing two five decimal one for two seven oh."
> 8:31:23 a.m.: Dulles: "American seventy-seven, ah, climb, climb maintain flight level two niner zero, sir."
> 8:31:30 a.m.: AA Flight 77: "Two nine zero, American seventy-seven."[163]

8:31 a.m.: AA Flight 11 flight attendant Sweeney reconnects to American Flight Services Office in Boston, her third call.[164]

8:32 a.m.: AA Flight 11. FAA Herndon Command Center notifies the FAA HQ Operations Center (WOC) of a possible hijacking. Herndon is told that FAA security personnel have just begun discussing the hijacking on a conference call with regional centers.[165]

8:32 a.m.: AA Flight 11. American Airlines flight service manager at Boston Logan, Michael Woodward, returns to his office to find that flight attendant Sweeney is on the phone. Woodward, who is a friend of Sweeney's, takes over the call. Sweeney says that she is sitting in the back of the plane next to Ong, who is still on the phone with Gonzalez.

The phone call between Sweeney and Woodward lasts approximately 12 minutes. It is not taped. According to Woodward, Sweeney is calm and collected. She provides the following information: the plane has been hijacked, a man in first class has had his throat slashed and is believed dead, and two flight attendants have been stabbed. The number-one flight attendant in first class has been stabbed seriously and is on oxygen, whereas the number-five flight attendant in business class's wounds are not life-threatening; a doctor has been paged. The flight attendants are unable to contact the cockpit, and there is a bomb on board.[166]

---

163. NTSB, Flight Path Study.
164. 9/11 Commission Report, p. 6.
165. 9/11 Commission Staff Report, August 26, 2004.
166. 9/11 Commission Staff Report, August 26, 2004; FBI American Airlines Flight #11 Investigative Summary, FBI 02991; FBI Serial 302-47851.

"Sweeney believed there were three hijackers in the business class section of the aircraft. All three hijackers were of Middle Eastern descent. At least one of the hijackers spoke English very well. Sweeney described the atmosphere in the aircraft as calm while the hijacking was carried out. At one point, the hijackers entered the cockpit, the plane changed direction and began to descend rapidly. During the descent phase, Sweeney attempted to contact the cockpit; she did not get a response."[167]

8:33:59 a.m.: AA Flight 11. FAA Boston Center hears a third partially unintelligible radio transmission, presumably by hijacker pilot Mohammed Atta: "Nobody move, please. We are going back to the airport. Don't try to make any stupid moves."[168]

8:33 a.m.: UA Flight 175 reaches its assigned cruising altitude of 31,000 feet.[169]

8:34 a.m.: AA Flight 11. FAA Boston Center contacts Cape Terminal Radar Approach Control (TRACON) (located at Otis Air National Guard Base [ANGB] in Falmouth, Massachusetts, on Cape Cod) and requests they notify the military of a hijacked flight.[170]

Flight attendant Ong tells American Airlines supervisor Gonzalez that there has been a fatality on board the flight. Gonzalez tells Marquis at 8:34 a.m.: "They think they might have a fatality on the flight. One of our passengers, possibly on 9B, Levin or Lewis, might have been fatally stabbed."[171]

At 8:34 a.m., there is the first possibility of any military organization being alerted, though the actual time when the Otis unit is contacted is

---

167. FBI American Airlines Flight #11 Investigative Summary, FBI 02991; FBI Serial 302-47851.

168. 9/11 Commission Staff Report, August 26, 2004, says 8:34 a.m. *The First 109 Minutes: 9/11 and the US Air Force* (2011) says 8:33 a.m.

169. 9/11 Commission Report, p. 7; 9/11 Commission Staff Report, August 26, 2004.

170. The Air National Guard installation was part of a Massachusetts military facility and former Otis air force base. TRACON refers to a terminal air traffic control (ATC) facility that uses radar and nonradar capabilities to provide approach control services to aircraft arriving, departing, or transiting airspace controlled by the facility.

171. 9/11 Commission Staff Report, August 26, 2004.

unknown. Boston Center decides not to wait for the request for assistance
to be passed up the chain of command and takes the initiative by calling
the Cape Cod facility directly. They ask if nearby Otis can get fighters airborne to "tail" the hijacked aircraft.[172]

8:34 a.m.: AA Flight 77 still has normal communications.

> 8:34:16 a.m.: Dulles: "American seventy-seven, turn twenty degrees
> right vector for your climb."
> 8:34:19 a.m.: AA Flight 77: "Turn twenty right, American
> seventy-seven."[173]

8:35 a.m.: AA Flight 11. American Airlines begins identifying hijackers,
as Ong and Sweeney pass on seat numbers. Supervisor Gonzalez confirms
the details regarding the identity of one of the hijackers: "He's the one that's
in the . . . he's in the cockpit?" she asks Ong. "Okay, you said Tom Sukani
[Satam al-Suqami]? Okay—okay, and he was in 10B. Okay, okay, so he's one
of the persons that are in the cockpit. And as far as weapons, all they have
are just knives."[174]

8:36 a.m.: AA Flight 11. FAA HQ Operations Center (WOC) notifies FAA
Office of Civil Aviation Security Intelligence of the hijacking and enters the
conference with New England Regional Operations Center in Burlington,
Massachusetts, and the Herndon Command Center.

The only external notification of any hijacking outside the FAA or American Airlines is Cape Terminal Radar Approach Control (and presumably,
through them, the Otis fighter interceptor unit).

In Fort Worth, Marquis initiates action to "lock out" AA Flight 11. This
procedure is standard for airlines in safety and security incidents. It isolates
information and prevents tampering or release without the input of top
leadership at the airlines. Lockout also protects the identities of passengers
and crew.[175]

---

172. 9/11 Commission Staff Report, August 26, 2004.
173. NTSB, Flight Path Study.
174. 9/11 Commission Report, p. 6; 9/11 Commission Staff Report, August 26, 2004.
175. 9/11 Commission Staff Report, August 26, 2004.

CHAPTER 3

"WE HAVE A HIJACKED AIRCRAFT"

On American Airlines Flight 11—the plane that would hit the North Tower— at 8:24 a.m., Mohammed Atta, in the pilot's seat, tried to use the aircraft intercom system to communicate with the passengers. His radio transmission was heard by FAA flight controllers, but it took them nearly 30 minutes to decipher what he said and finally confirm that a hijacking was underway.

By then, United Airlines Flight 175 from Boston to Los Angeles—the plane that would hit the South Tower—had already taken off, and American Airlines Flight 77—the plane that would hit the Pentagon—had also left Washington Dulles IAP bound for Los Angeles. AA 77 would fly a giant loop all the way to Ohio to stay on the operation's timeline of reaching Washington at the same time as United Airlines Flight 93, which was delayed on the runway at Newark International for 40 minutes. Evidently Mohammed Atta had taken into consideration that the New York–area airport regularly struggled with morning congestion, and the Newark plane would be the last to take off.

At 8:37 a.m., FAA Boston Center contacted the NORAD Northeast Air Defense Sector (NEADS) for the first time to inform them that AA Flight 11 had been hijacked, 23 minutes after the plane had already been taken over. The airplane was headed for New York, the FAA told them, but other than the fact that it had been hijacked, no one knew anything else. The military was merely asked if it could scramble a fighter jet to take a look. And the assumption at first was certainly that the single hijacked plane would land somewhere and that the hijackers would make demands.

Two minutes after the Boston Center call, President Bush left his Florida hotel to go to the Emma E. Booker Elementary School. Vice President Cheney was already at the White House, and an apparently normal day was starting. Neither the FAA nor NORAD had yet alerted anyone outside of their own channels of a hijacking. The first word in Washington (other than at the FAA) was literally when Mohammed Atta's plane crashed into the North Tower and was seen on television.

8:37:24 a.m.: FAA Boston Center contacts NORAD NEADS headquarters, located in Rome, New York, and tells them that AA Flight 11 has been hijacked.[176]

Joseph Cooper in the FAA Traffic Management Unit (TMU) reaches NEADS senior director, TSgt. Jeremy W. Powell of the New York Air National Guard on the operations floor:

> FAA Boston Center (Cooper): "Hi. Boston Center TMU. We have a problem here. We have a hijacked aircraft headed towards New York, and we need you guys to . . . we need someone to scramble some F-16s or something up there, help us out."
> NORAD NEADS (Powell): "Is this real world or exercise?"
> FAA Boston Center (Cooper): "No, this is not an exercise, not a test."[177]

Powell is taking part in exercise Vigilant Guardian when the call comes in. The DOD later writes: "It took some time for NEADS to realize 9/11 was a real-world scenario and not part of the exercise."[178] One news media report says, however, that "though at first some officers believe [sic] the call is part

---

176. *The First 109 Minutes: 9/11 and the US Air Force*, 2011. NORAD told the 9/11 Commission that the FAA contacted NORAD NEADS by phone with information on the possible hijack of American Airlines Flight 11 at 8:40 a.m.; 9/11 Commission, NORAD Questions for the Record, partially declassified; FAA Chronology. FAA reports possible hijack from NORAD/PA News Release on September 18, 2001, from "FAA Responds."

According to NORAD: "Note: Former FAA administrator, Jane Garvey, testified that the notification took place at 8:34. According to NEADS Commander, Colonel Robert Marr, 'This is the time [0840] captured in the primary operations log maintained by the Mission Crew Commander Tech (MCC/T). SSgt Powell answered the call from Mr. Joe Cooper of Boston Center at 08:37:24 and put a supervisor, Maj Deskins, on the line to get the information needed to take action. By the time this information was gathered the time was between 0839 and 0840, leading to the logged time of 0840L.'" See NORAD 9/11 Timeline, n.d., prepared for the 9/11 Commission.

177. *The First 109 Minutes: 9/11 and the US Air Force*, 2011.

178. Katie Lange, "8 Things You May Not Know About Our Air Defense on 9/11," DOD News, September 11, 2019.

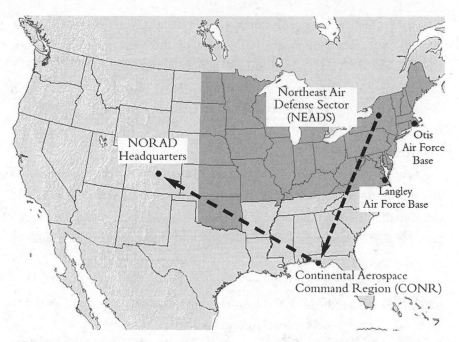

NORAD divided its area of responsibility into three regions (Continental, Canada, and Alaska) and subordinate sectors. Inside the United States, the NEADS in Rome, New York, and the Western Air Defense Sector (WADS) in Washington State were the relevant sectors, with both reporting to the Continental Aerospace Command Region (CONR) in Florida. (Source: 9/11 Commission)

of the ongoing Vigilant Guardian exercise, others knew right away it was 'real world.'"[179]

According to the Air Force: "[The FAA's] Cooper did not know that any military exercises were planned for September 11, 2001."[180]

NEADS commander Col. Marr seeks authorization for Otis fighters to go to "battle stations." Maj. Gen. Arnold directs Col. Marr "to go ahead and scramble the airplanes and we'd get permission later."[181]

---

179. Hart Seely, "Amid Crisis Simulation, 'We Were Suddenly No-Kidding Under Attack,'" Newhouse News Service, January 25, 2002.

180. *The First 109 Minutes: 9/11 and the US Air Force*, 2011.

181. 9/11 Commission Memorandum for the Record, Interview, Colonel Robert Marr, January 23, 2004.

Arnold then calls the senior operations officer at NORAD (in Colorado Springs), who tells him: "Yeah, we'll work with the National Military Command Center [NMCC]. Go ahead and scramble the aircraft."[182]

The Air Force later writes: "Both men [Marr and Arnold] were well aware . . . that hijacking was considered a law enforcement issue, and they realized that a number of notifications and clearances—from the FAA to the National Military Command Center and all the way up to the Office of the Secretary of Defense—were required under the federal government's anti-hijacking protocol before a scramble could be launched. But Arnold decided that the scramble should proceed." Arnold later recalls, "We didn't wait for that. We scrambled the aircraft, told them get airborne, and we would seek clearances later."[183]

8:37 a.m.: AA Flight 11. FAA Boston Center asks UA Flight 175 (soon to be hijacked itself) to look for AA Flight 11.[184]

8:37 a.m.: AA Flight 77 has normal communications.

> 8:37:31 a.m.: Dulles: "American seventy-seven, recleared direct CHARLESTON; climb, maintain correction, recleared direct HENDERSON, sir; climb, maintain flight level three niner zero."
>
> 8:37:39 a.m.: AA Flight 77: "Direct HENDERSON out of two nine for three nine oh requesting three five zero for a final American seventy-seven."
>
> 8:37:55 a.m.: AA Flight 77: "Center, American, ah, seventy-seven, you copy request for three five zero as a final?"
>
> 8:37:59 a.m.: Dulles: "American seventy-seven, ah, roger; maintain flight level three five zero. I'll show that as your final."[185]

8:38 a.m.: AA Flight 11 attendant Ong tells Gonzalez that the plane is flying erratically again and in a rapid descent. Manager Marquis asks a fellow

---

182. 9/11 Commission Staff Report, August 26, 2004.
183. *The First 109 Minutes: 9/11 and the US Air Force*, 2011.
184. 9/11 Commission Staff Report, August 26, 2004.
185. NTSB, Flight Path Study.

employee if AA Flight 11 is descending. The employee replies, "We don't know. The transponder is off, so we have no active read on him."[186]

American Airlines completes its lockout.

8:38:03 a.m.: AA Flight 77 routinely radios: "Ah, three five zero for a final, American seventy-seven; thank you, sir."[187]

8:39 a.m.: President Bush departs Colony Beach Resort for the Emma E. Booker Elementary School.[188]

Though the FAA and NORAD are now aware of a hijacking (and NEADS has alerted NORAD command centers in Florida and Colorado Springs), there is still no external notification (outside American Airlines, the FAA, or NORAD) of any hijacking. There is no evidence that the Pentagon or White House have been alerted. According to the 9/11 Commission, no one in the White House or anyone traveling with President Bush knows that a flight has been hijacked before 8:46 a.m. The 9/11 Commission finds no evidence that the hijacking was reported to any other agency in Washington before that time.[189]

8:40 a.m.: AA Flight 11. NORAD NEADS contacts Otis ANGB on Cape Cod, located about 153 miles away from New York City, where two F-15C Eagle fighter aircraft are on alert. NEADS tells the pilots to increase their "readiness posture."[190]

At FAA Boston Center, "as the situation escalated during what would be the missing aircraft's [AA 11] last six or seven minutes of flight, John Hartling . . . a former US Air Force air traffic controller, expands the center's search by contacting US Air Flight 583 and United Airlines Flight 175.

---

186. 9/11 Commission Report, p. 6; 9/11 Commission Staff Report, August 26, 2004.

187. NTSB, Flight Path Study.

188. Presidential Daily Diary, partially declassified. Schedule of the President, Tuesday, September 11, 2001, says Bush is scheduled to depart at 8:30 a.m.

189. 9/11 Commission Report, p. 35.

190. 9/11 Commission Staff Report, August 26, 2004. Without specifying the time, the 9/11 Commission (p. 20) suggests that this happened three minutes earlier: "NEADS orders two Air Force F-15 alert aircraft at Otis ANGB in Falmouth, Massachusetts to prepare to launch."

These flights have visual contact with the hijacked plane and identify its altitude as between 27,000 and 29,000 feet."[191]

8:40:32 a.m.: UA Flight 175 establishes radio contact with the FAA's New York Center at Ronkonkoma, New York, leaving FAA Boston Center territory.

> 8:40:31 a.m.: UA Flight 175: "United one-seventy-five at flight level three-one-zero."
> 8:40:37 a.m.: FAA New York Center: "United one-seventy-five, New York Center, roger."[192]

8:40 a.m.: AA Flight 77, after proceeding normally through FAA Washington Center airspace, is handed off to FAA Indianapolis (Indy) Center, with whom it makes routine radio contact.

> 8:40:03 a.m.: FAA Dulles: "American seventy-seven, contact Indy Center one two zero point two seven."
> 8:40:06 a.m.: AA Flight 77: "Twenty, twenty-seven, American seventy-seven, thanks, sir; good day."
> 8:40:13 a.m.: AA Flight 77: "Center, American seventy-seven with you, level three three zero."
> 8:40:15 a.m.: FAA Indy Center: "American seventy-seven, Indy Center, roger; squawk, three seven four three." [Note: *Squawk* is a control instruction to change the transponder setting within the aircraft.]
> 8:40:19 a.m.: AA Flight 77: "Three seven four three, American seventy-seven."[193]

When Indy Center acknowledges receiving AA Flight 77, the sector is responsible for 14 aircraft; additionally, 4 aircraft are in handoff status to this sector.

---

191. *The First 109 Minutes: 9/11 and the US Air Force*, 2011.
192. 9/11 Commission Staff Report, August 26, 2004.
193. 9/11 Commission Staff Report, August 26, 2004.

8:40 a.m.: Second Lady Lynne Cheney arrives at the Nantucket Salon, 15th and H Streets NW, to get her hair done.[194]

8:41 a.m.: AA Flight 11. Flight attendant Sweeney tells Michael Woodward in Boston that "passengers in coach were under the impression that there was a routine medical emergency in first class. Other flight attendants were busy at duties such as getting medical supplies while Ong and Sweeney were reporting the events."[195]

At 8:41:32 a.m., the pilot or first officer aboard UA Flight 175, which had entered New York Center airspace, radios: "Ah, we heard a suspicious transmission on our departure out of Boston, ah, with someone, ah, ah, sound like someone—sound like someone keyed the mike and said, ah, 'Everyone, ah, stay in your seats.'" FAA New York Center acknowledges and replies, "Okay, I'll pass that along."[196]

At American Airlines, Marquis is told that the air traffic controllers have declared AA Flight 11 a hijacking and "think he's [AA Flight 11 is] headed toward Kennedy [Airport]. They're moving everybody out of the way. They seem to have him on a primary radar."[197]

8:42 a.m.: UA Flight 175 is hijacked; less than two minutes after communicating with the FAA about a "suspicious transmission" overheard from AA Flight 11, the airliner has its last radio communication with the ground.[198]

Between 8:42 a.m. and 8:46 a.m., the hijackers begin their takeover of the flight over northern New Jersey. They use knives (as reported by two passengers and a flight attendant), Mace (reported by one passenger), and the threat of a bomb (reported by the same passenger). They stab flight crew members (as reported by a flight attendant and one passenger) and kill both pilots (as reported by a flight attendant).[199]

---

194. Secret Service, Interview with SA (Special Agent) Michael Seremetis, October 1, 2001.

195. 9/11 Commission Report, p. 6.

196. 9/11 Commission Staff Report, August 26, 2004.

197. 9/11 Commission Report, p. 6.

198. 9/11 Commission Report, p. 7. "It is believed, based on changes in course by Flight 175, that the hijackers gained control of the aircraft at approximately 8:42 a.m." FBI Serial 302-9269.

199. 9/11 Commission, p. 7; 9/11 Commission Staff Report, August 26, 2004.

8:42 a.m.: UA Flight 93 begins takeoff roll, runway 4 left, at Newark IAP.[200] After having waited in the holding area on the tarmac for 42 minutes, the flight departs for San Francisco, about 25 minutes later than its anticipated waiting time.[201] All communications with Newark Tower, with New York Departure Control, and with FAA New York Center are routine.

8:43 a.m.: AA Flight 11. Flight attendant Ong says that the plane continues to rapidly descend and that they are going down fast. Thereafter the phone call is disconnected.[202]

8:43 a.m.: UA Flight 175. FAA Herndon Command Center warns that UA Flight 175 is a "possible hijack" and will be headed toward Washington Center's airspace if it continues on a southbound track.[203]

FAA notifies NEADS concerning UA Flight 175 also being a suspected hijacking at 8:43 a.m., now in addition to AA Flight 11.[204]

---

200. According to NORAD: "UA 93 takeoff from Newark extrapolated from RADES radar data"; NORAD 9/11 Timeline, n.d., prepared for the 9/11 Commission.

201. FBI Working Draft Chronology; 9/11 Commission Staff Report, August 26, 2004; National Park Service Flight 93 National Memorial, Timeline, Flight 93, September 11, 2001.

202. FBI, American Airlines Flight #11 Investigative Summary, FBI 02991.

203. 9/11 Commission Staff Report, August 26, 2004; NORAD/PA News Release, September 18, 2001.

204. FAA Chronology. According to NORAD: "According to NEADS Commander, Colonel Marr, 'The time that the FAA notified NEADS of the hijacking of UAL 175 is listed as 0843L. None of the NEADS logs, transcripts, or audio recordings support this time. My recollection of the events was that the first indication we had of a second hijacking was the media transmission of the second tower being hit. The first transcript indication that the FAA had contacted NEADS was background voices at 0903L providing the call sign of UAL 175 . . . 0843L was labeled as the reporting time, but this time was attributed to an early effort by Operations people to build a timeline using a faulty computer time indication (numerous entries that used this method were later proven to be inaccurate by the transcript that used the Naval Observatory Time Hack on the tape). It is my speculation that this early, incorrect time was used to build the early NORAD timeline.'" See NORAD 9/11 Timeline, n.d., prepared for the 9/11 Commission.

At NORAD NEADS, technicians are trying to find AA Flight 11 in "the swarm of a Tuesday morning aerial rush hour" when they hear that a second plane, UA Flight 175, is also not responding.[205]

8:43 a.m.: AA Flight 77 has normal communications.

> 8:43:51 a.m.: FAA Indy Center: "American seventy-seven, climb and maintain flight level three five zero."
>
> 8:43:55 a.m.: AA Flight 77: "Thirty-three, three five oh, American seventy-seven."[206]

8:44 a.m.: AA Flight 11. Flight attendant Sweeney says over the phone: "Something is wrong. We are in a rapid descent . . . we are all over the place." Woodward asks her to "describe what she sees out the window." She responds, "I see the water. I see the buildings. I see buildings." After a short pause, she reports, "We are flying low. We are flying very, very low. We are flying way too low." Seconds later she says, "Oh my God, we are way too low." The call ends with a burst of very loud, sustained static.[207]

The American Airlines operations center also loses phone contact with flight attendant Ong.[208]

Another flight in the sky, US Air Flight 83, transmits to FAA New York Center: "I just picked up an ELT [emergency locator transmitter] on 121.5 [emergency VHF frequency]. It was brief, but it went off." New York Center acknowledges the call.

FAA reports: "AAL 11, B767, BOS [Boston Logan] . . . LAX [Los Angeles IAP] lost radar and communication by ZBW [FAA Boston Center]."[209]

8:45 a.m.: AA Flight 11. American Airlines director of security in Fort Worth, Texas, contacts the special agent in charge of the FBI Dallas Field Office.[210]

---

205. *The First 109 Minutes: 9/11 and the US Air Force*, 2011.

206. NTSB, Flight Path Study.

207. 9/11 Commission Report, pp. 6–7; FBI American Airlines Flight #11 Investigative Summary, FBI 02991; FBI Serial 302-47851.

208. 9/11 Commission Report, p. 6.

209. FAA logs; National Archives Chronology.

210. 9/11 Commission Staff Report, August 26, 2004.

8:45 a.m.: NORAD Commander Gen. Ralph "Ed" Eberhart at Peterson
Air Force Base (AFB) in Colorado Springs receives a call from the Cheyenne Mountain Operations Center (CMOC) command director (CD) to
inform him of a suspected hijacking on the East Coast. Eberhart is told that
this is not part of the ongoing Vigilant Guardian exercise.[211]

---

211. 9/11 Commission, Memorandum for the Record, Event: North American Aerospace Defense Command (NORAD) field site visit, Type of event: Interview with CINC-
NORAD (Commander in Chief NORAD) General "Ed" Eberhart, March 1, 2004 (hereafter
9/11 Commission NORAD MFR).

CHAPTER 4

THE NORTH TOWER IS STRUCK

It's still jarring, two decades later, to describe what happened when American Airlines Flight 11 struck the North Tower of the 110 story World Trade Center, impacting at close to 500 miles per hour. The Boeing 767-200ER aircraft plowed into and through the tower, destroying everything in its path, severing and damaging support columns and destroying the structural core running up the center of the building. The momentum of the airliner shot fragments of the building and the plane itself to the ground as far as five blocks away. Thousands of gallons of burning aviation fuel exploded, fireballs shooting down elevator shafts and bursting out onto lower floors, with the main fire erupting out of the opposite (south) face of the building.

It is estimated that between 16,400 and 18,800 people were in the World Trade Center complex, including about 14,100 in the two towers. About 300 people are thought to have died instantly; another 1,300 were trapped on the 11 upper floors. About two minutes before the attack, the last elevator carrying breakfast customers down from the Windows on the World restaurant on the 107th floor managed to leave. As more people below the severed stairwells started to evacuate, fuel was pouring down stairwells, elevator shafts, and the outside frame of the building.

When the airliner struck the North Tower, a mighty shock wave traveled down to the ground from the impact, reverberating back up again. The North Tower leaned from the impact, swaying back and forth several times, eventually managing to right itself. But more than half of its upper support columns had been destroyed. Exposed to the intense heat (as hot as 1,000 degrees Celsius, or 1,800 degrees Fahrenheit), floors, columns, and supporting steel trusses began to sag, collapse, and melt.

8:46:35 a.m.: AA Flight 11 strikes floors 94 to 98 of the north side of 1 World Trade Center (WTC 1), the North Tower.[212]

At the World Trade Center, the FDNY battalion chief assigned to Battalion 1 witnesses the impact of the plane from the corner of Church and Lispenard Streets in lower Manhattan. He immediately signals second alarm and proceeds to the World Trade Center. En route, he requests additional resources by transmitting a third alarm at 8:48 a.m. He informs the FDNY Communications Office (Dispatch) that the corner of West and Vesey Streets, one block north of WTC 1, will be the designated staging area for third alarm units.[213]

The Port Authority Police Department (PAPD) report reads: "A unit reports by radio to the Police Desk at the World Trade Center that there has been an explosion at the World Trade Center. A PAPD unit reports that there are major injuries at the Plaza."[214]

8:46 a.m.: Lt. Col. Thomas Gould, military aide to the president, is on a treadmill in Florida when his pager goes off; the White House provides him with a heads-up that an airplane has crashed into the World Trade Center. Gould recalls that as next up in the rotation of military aides (and scheduled to work on September 12), he also was the aide who had tactical control of presidential aircraft.[215]

8:46 a.m.: NORAD NEADS issues orders for a flight of two F-15C Eagle fighters ("PANTA" flight) to scramble from Otis ANGB six minutes after the FAA first contacted the New York sector command (but unrelated to the crash of AA Flight 11 into the North Tower).[216] The pilots' futile orders are to locate and tail the hijacked AA Flight 11.

---

212. The FAA in its official chronology, based on contemporaneous logs, later incorrectly states that the "1st impact World Trade Center" took place at 9:47 a.m. The 9/11 Commission Report states 8:46:40 a.m. (p. 7).

213. FDNY Report.

214. NIST Chronology.

215. Janene Scully, "Vandenberg Officer at Bush's Side During Attacks," *Santa Maria Times*, September 11, 2011.

216. See NORAD 9/11 Timeline, n.d., prepared for the 9/11 Commission; and FAA Logs. Note: Though many sources say that the F-15 fighters are scrambled at 8:46, they are

American Airlines Flight 11 (AA 11)
Boston to Los Angeles

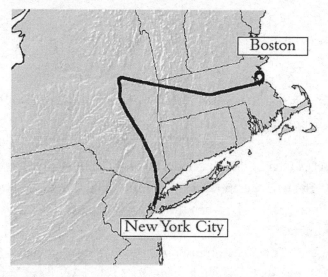

(Source: 9/11 Commission)

According to interviews with Lt. Col. Kevin J. Nasypany, NEADS mission crew commander (MCC) and the head of the ops floor: "Based on standard protocol, the military is tasked with establishing a fighter tail on hijacked aircraft. . . . Nasypany described his tactic in mind was to place the fighters over the New York Manhattan area as quickly as possible. He knew that the flight was headed south, and knew that the flight could most likely be intercepted somewhere over the New York area. . . . He commented that the latitude and longitude points that were passed to NEADS by the FAA indicated the flight was north of New York City."[217]

---

not airborne until 8:52–8:53 a.m. See also Hart Seely, "Amid Crisis Simulation, 'We Were Suddenly No-Kidding Under Attack,'" Newhouse News Service, January 25, 2002; FAA Chronology; 9/11 Commission Report, p. 20.

217. 9/11 Commission Memorandum for the Record, Interview with NEADS Alpha Flight Mission Crew Commander (MCC), Lt. Col. Kevin J. Nasypany, January 22, 2004, and January 23, 2004.

Though different rules of engagement (ROE) will yet come into play on 9/11, the standard intercept is a rear intercept, whereas the next, more aggressive intercept level—the so-called transitional ROE—calls for a "stern" (frontal) intercept.

8:46 a.m.: AA Flight 77 reaches its assigned cruising altitude of 35,000 feet.[218]

8:47 a.m.: The first 911 call is logged in New York City, with the caller reporting "a building explosion."

8:47 a.m.: UA Flight 175 transponder code changes twice in a one-minute period.[219] "The first operational evidence that something was abnormal on United 175 comes at 8:47, when the aircraft changed beacon codes twice within a minute."[220]

UA Flight 175's assigned transponder code of 1470 changes, first indicating 3020 and then changing again to 3321. FAA New York Center computers do not associate either of these codes with UA Flight 175. Consequently, UA Flight 175's secondary radar return (transponder), indicating aircraft speed, altitude, and flight information, is no longer associated with the primary radar return.

FAA New York Center controller David Bottiglia, responsible for UA Flight 175, is also handling AA Flight 11, which, he is told, has been hijacked. At this point he is trying to locate Flight 11 and does not notice the transponder code changes on UA Flight 175 until 8:51 a.m.[221]

218. 9/11 Commission Report, p. 8; 9/11 Commission Staff Report, August 26, 2004.

219. NORAD logs: "0846—UA 175 changes transponder code from 1470 to 3020, then to 3321 from RADES radar data." See NORAD 9/11 Timeline, n.d., prepared for the 9/11 Commission.

220. 9/11 Commission Report, p. 7.

221. 9/11 Commission Staff Report, August 26, 2004. Note: The controller communicating with UA Flight 175 was also monitoring the flight track of AA Flight 11. Based on coordination received from Boston Center indicating a possible hijack, most of the controller's attention had been focused on AA Flight 11.

8:47 a.m.: AA Flight 77. FAA Indianapolis Center (Indy Center) has routine communications with the flight:

> 8:47:16 a.m.: FAA Indy Center: "American seventy-seven, turn ten degrees to the right vectors for traffic."
> 8:47:20 a.m.: AA Flight 77: "Ten right, American seven-seven."[222]

8:47 a.m.: At the World Trade Center, the NYPD calls for Level 1 mobilization. Level 3 mobilization is called eight seconds later.

According to a PAPD report: "The top ten floors of the Trade Center are on fire, possible aircraft."[223]

8:48:08 a.m.: The first television report of an incident at the World Trade Center is broadcast locally in New York by Fox5 News (WNYW) less than two minutes after the plane crashes into the North Tower. WNYW breaks into a Paramount Pictures movie trailer for *Zoolander* with the first live TV pictures of black smoke coming from the Center, relayed by a WNYW cameraman at ground level. One of the station's camera crews is out on the street to cover New York's mayoral primary election.[224]

8:48 a.m.: At the World Trade Center, the first of at least 50 people jump to their deaths from the North Tower. The earliest jumpers are probably fleeing the intense heat of the impact zone, but later, people are seen jumping and falling from the stories above where AA Flight 11 impacted the building, desperately trying to escape growing fire and smoke.

8:48 a.m.: AA Flight 11. FAA New York Center manager provides an update report over the FAA teleconference.

None of the participants are yet aware that the airplane has already crashed into the World Trade Center.

---

222. NTSB, Flight Path Study.
223. NIST Chronology.
224. Television Archive, "Fox 5 News—September 11, 2001 Archive," https://archive.org /details/fox5news911.

8:49:34 a.m.: CNN breaks into a commercial and broadcasts the first national television report of an explosion or incident at the World Trade Center. The CNN chyron first reads, "WORLD TRADE CENTER DISASTER." Carol Lin, the first TV network anchor to break the news of the attacks, says:

> This just in. You are looking at obviously a very disturbing live shot there. That is the World Trade Center, and we have unconfirmed reports this morning that a plane has crashed into one of the towers of the World Trade Center. CNN Center right now is just beginning to work on this story, obviously calling our sources and trying to figure out exactly what happened, but clearly something relatively devastating happening this morning there on the south end of the island of Manhattan. That is, once again, a picture of one of the towers of the World Trade Center.

About a minute after CNN's initial broadcast, Sean Murtagh, CNN vice president, in an on-air phone call, says from his office in the CNN New York bureau that a large passenger commercial jet was seen to hit the World Trade Center. The first email bulletins of breaking news from CNN and MSNBC report "fire at tower of World Trade Center." Both CNN and MSNBC's websites receive such heavy traffic that many servers collapse.

"At the White House, the vice president had just sat down for a meeting in his office when an assistant told him to turn on his television because a plane had struck the North Tower of the World Trade Center. He said he wondered how a plane could hit the Trade Center, not thinking terrorism in any way."[225]

At the Pentagon, Secretary Rumsfeld is finishing his breakfast meeting with members of Congress when his senior military assistant, Vice Adm. Edmund "Ed" Giambastiani, passes him a note that an airplane has crashed into the World Trade Center. "It was, I assumed, a tragic accident," says Rumsfeld.[226]

---

225. "Twelfth Public Hearing," National Commission on Terrorist Attacks upon the United States, June 17, 2004, http://www.9-11commission.gov/archive/hearing12/9-11 Commission_Hearing_2004-06-17.htm.

226. Donald Rumsfeld, *Known and Unknown: A Memoir* (New York: Sentinel, 2011), p. 335.

In the NMCC, a call is made to the FAA HQ Operations Center (WOC), and they are told that the FAA has a report of a hijacking on a plane that had departed Boston.[227]

At NORAD NEADS command center in Rome, New York, a technician says: "I remember somebody running into the Ops Room. . . . They said they'd just seen on CNN that an aircraft hit the World Trade Center." A quiet tremor rolled through the room, replaced by the buzz of urgent questions into phones. What kind of aircraft hit the building? A small plane? A large plane? Could it be Flight 11? Boston Center was still tracking a blip believed to be Flight 11."[228]

8:49 a.m.: At the World Trade Center, the PAPD reports: "Start doing the evac, the upper levels. Have the units put on the Scot air-packs . . . [breathing] apparatus."[229]

8:49 a.m.: FAA DC logs: "ZNY [New York Center] asked if DC . . . has any direct lines to the military. DCC [Washington Center] responds that the supervisor is on his way back to CARF [Central Altitude Reservation Function]."[230]

FAA CARF is the Washington-based entity of the Herndon Command Center that supports special activities associated with government (e.g., presidential and foreign dignitaries), military, "national security" (e.g., FBI, CIA, Open Skies Treaty), and emergency flights, as well as FAA interactions with war plans. CARF was established in 1956 to enable the military services (primarily the Strategic Air Command) to conduct realistic bomber training missions at high altitude under simulated combat conditions while avoiding interference with civil aviation.

8:49 a.m.: (Approximate time) NORAD Commander Gen. Eberhart, in his office, watches the CNN broadcast of the World Trade Center attack.

---

227. 9/11 Commission Memorandum for the Record, Interview, Captain Charles Joseph Leidig, USN, April 29, 2004.

228. Hart Seely, "Amid Crisis Simulation, 'We Were Suddenly No-Kidding Under Attack,'" Newhouse News Service, January 25, 2002.

229. NIST Chronology.

230. DCC Timeline.

"He asked if the aircraft that was suspected of impacting the World Trade Center was the same aircraft that he had been told at 8:45 a.m. was a suspected hijack and he was told that they were not."[231]

8:50 a.m.: President Bush is told by Karl Rove that a plane has crashed into the World Trade Center.[232]

Bush later shares his memories with *National Geographic*. He explains that when he received news of the first plane crash at 8:50 a.m.—just before arriving at the school—he believed it was "a light aircraft," and his reaction was "Man, the weather was bad or something extraordinary happened to the pilot."[233]

8:50 a.m.: (Approximate time) CIA Director George Tenet is at breakfast with old friend and mentor former Sen. David Boren (D-OK) at the St. Regis Hotel, three blocks from the White House. He hears of the first attack (sometime after 8:46 a.m. but probably not before the CNN report) and says he rushes back to CIA headquarters in McLean, Virginia.[234]

Later reports claim that George Tenet tells Boren: "You know, this has bin Laden's fingerprints all over it," adding that he wonders "if it has anything to do with this guy taking pilot training," in a reference to Zacarias Moussaoui, arrested on August 16. Later it is reported that Moussaoui watched the attacks unfold from inside his jail cell, cheering.

8:50 a.m.: At the World Trade Center, FDNY First Battalion Chief Joe Pfeiffer establishes an incident command post (ICP) in the lobby of the North Tower in accordance with the fire department's high-rise firefighting procedures.

In approximately 10 minutes, from 8:50 a.m. to about 9:00 a.m., incident command is established and passed (according to protocol) from

---

231. 9/11 Commission Memorandum for the Record, Interview with CINC NORAD (Commander in Chief NORAD), General Edward "Ed" Eberhart, March 1, 2004.

232. Many timelines say that White House Chief of Staff Andrew Card first alerted President Bush. This is an error.

233. Elisabeth Bumiller, "Inside the Presidency: Few Outsiders Ever See the President's Private Enclave," *National Geographic Magazine*, January 2009; *Decision Points*, p. 126.

234. *At the Center of the Storm*, p. 161.

Pfeiffer to the first division chief (D1) to the citywide tour commander 4D (CWTC-4D) and finally to Chief of Department (COD) Peter James Ganci Jr.[235]

8:50 a.m.: (Approximate time) FAA HQ Operations Center (WOC) is processing the crash into the World Trade Center and activates a tactical net at the request of Civil Aviation Security Intelligence, teleconferencing in all centers and regions and used for tasking and implementation of directives within the FAA.

Delta Airlines Flight 1489, in the air, advises FAA New York Center that there is "a lot of smoke in lower Manhattan" and "the World Trade Center looked like it was on fire."[236]

Deputy FAA Administrator Monte Belger goes to WOC, describing the situation as "'chaotic but organized.' . . . He talked to FAA Administrator Jane Garvey on the phone. She was on her way to the WOC from Secretary Mineta's office."[237]

8:50 a.m.: AA Flight 77 transmits its last routine radio communication.[238]

8:50:47 a.m.: FAA Indy Center: "American seventy-seven, cleared direct, ah, FALMOUTH [Falmouth, KY]."

8:50:51 a.m.: AA Flight 77: "Ah, direct FALMOUTH, American seventy-seven, thanks."[239]

8:51 a.m.: AA Flight 77 hijacking commences, less than a minute after the message that all is normal. Between 8:51 and 8:54 a.m., over eastern Kentucky, the hijackers take over the plane.[240]

---

235. FDNY Report; NIST Chronology.

236. 9/11 Commission Staff Report, August 26, 2004.

237. 9/11 Commission Memorandum for the Record, Interview Monte Belger, former Deputy Administrator of the Federal Aviation Administration, November 24, 2003.

238. 9/11 Commission Staff Report, August 26, 2004.

239. NTSB, Flight Path Study.

240. According to NORAD: "0851—Transponder and radar returns lost from RADES radar data." NORAD 9/11 Timeline, n.d., prepared for the 9/11 Commission.

They initiate and sustain their control of the aircraft using knives and box cutters (reported by one passenger) and move all the passengers (and possibly crew) to the rear of the aircraft (reported by one flight attendant and one passenger). Neither of the firsthand accounts to come from Flight 77, from a flight attendant and from a passenger, mention any actual use of violence (e.g., stabbings) or the threat or use of either a bomb or Mace. Both of these witnesses began their flight in the first-class cabin. Unlike the earlier flights, hijackers are reported to have box cutters.[241]

8:51 a.m.: UA Flight 175 deviates from its assigned altitude over New Jersey, making a left turn and descending.[242] "New York air traffic controllers [could not see the plane but] began repeatedly and unsuccessfully trying to contact it."[243]

> 8:51:43 a.m.: FAA New York Center to UA Flight 175: "UAL 175, recycle transponder, squawk code one four seven zero."

No response is received. New York Center makes several attempts, repeatedly trying to contact UA Flight 175 via radio for the next four minutes.[244]

8:52 a.m.: CBS News broadcasts its first breaking news of the plane crash into the North Tower. Bryant Gumbel interviews a restaurant worker in Soho and then the doorman to the Marriott Hotel located between the two towers. He describes falling debris that set a man's clothes on fire. Gumbel is talking with another eyewitness when UA Flight 175 strikes the South Tower.

8:52 a.m.: Air Force F-15C Eagle fighters go airborne from Otis ANGB, six minutes after AA Flight 11 has already hit the World Trade Center.[245]

---

241. 9/11 Commission Report, p. 9; 9/11 Commission Staff Report, August 26, 2004.

242. 9/11 Commission Staff Report, August 26, 2004.

243. 9/11 Commission Report, p. 7.

244. 9/11 Commission Staff Report, August 26, 2004.

245. According to NEADS logs, in accordance with NORAD 9/11 Timeline, n.d., prepared for the 9/11 Commission. Some sources say the F-15Cs are airborne at 8:53 a.m. According to the Air Force: "The first two fighters launched from Otis Air National Guard

"The order to scramble the Otis fighters was passed from the NORAD NEADS Battle Commander (BC) to his Mission Crew Commander (MCC) [Lt. Col. Nasypany], who passed it to the Weapons Director (WD). Almost immediately, however, a problem arose. The Weapons Director asked: 'MCC. I don't know where I'm scrambling these guys to. I need a direction, a destination.' . . . The fighters were vectored to military air space near Long Island while NEADS personnel searched frantically for the missing flight."[246]

Lt. Col. Nasypany, NEADS MCC, later tells the 9/11 Commission: "Once the fighters were scrambled the FAA controlled their travel until they reached a military controlled airspace over the water. At that point the military controllers had the ability to redirect the flight to its correct point. Nasypany explained . . . that there are several airports and heavy GA (general aviation) and small aviation flights that are in the direct path between Otis ANGB and the New York area. He noted that not only other aircraft, but in most circumstance [sic] weather conditions as well effect [sic] the choice of the most appropriate scramble route."[247]

The F-15 fighter pilots are unaware that AA Flight 11 has already crashed. Though NEADS knows that UA Flight 175 is missing, it also has no knowledge that the second hijacked aircraft is heading toward the South Tower.[248]

8:52 a.m.: UA Flight 175. NORAD logs: "UA 175 alters course toward WTC from . . . [acquired] radar data."[249]

Base in response to an FAA request for assistance with Flight 11, but it had already crashed by the time the fighters took off." See *The First 109 Minutes: 9/11 and the US Air Force*, 2011.

246. 9/11 Commission Staff Report, August 26, 2004. National Guard Bureau, *A Chronological History of the Air National Guard and Its Antecedents, 1908–2007*, compiled by Dr. Charles J. Gross, NGB-PAH, April 2, 2007, is misleading in suggesting that Otis and Langley fighters were scrambled at the same time.

247. 9/11 Commission Memorandum for the Record, Interview with NEADS Alpha Flight Mission Crew Commander (MCC), Lt. Col. Kevin J. Nasypany, January 22, 2004, and January 23, 2004.

248. 9/11 Commission Staff Report, August 26, 2004.

249. NORAD 9/11 Timeline, n.d., prepared for the 9/11 Commission. The 9/11 Commission report (p. 8) strangely concludes that UA Flight 175 "took a heading toward New York City" at 8:58 a.m., but this is six minutes later and after others had already reported the deviation in course.

FAA New York Center controller Ed Bottiglia continues his attempts to contact Flight 175 and spends the next several minutes handing off the other flights on his scope to other controllers and moving aircraft out of the way of an unidentified aircraft as it moves southwest and then turns northeast after it makes its left turn toward New York City.[250]

Aboard UA Flight 175, a male flight attendant phones into United Airlines maintenance in San Francisco and speaks for two minutes, saying, "Oh my God, the crew has been killed, a flight attendant has been stabbed. We've been hijacked."[251]

In Easton, Connecticut, Lee Hanson receives a phone call from his son Peter, a passenger on UA Flight 175, who says, "I think they've taken over the cockpit. An attendant has been stabbed . . . and someone else up front may have been killed. The plane is making strange moves. Call United Airlines. . . . Tell them it's Flight 175, Boston to LA." Lee Hanson then calls the Easton Police Department, relaying the information from his son to a police captain and asking for his help.[252]

8:52:49 a.m.: At the World Trade Center, the PAPD report over the radio that "people are jumping out the windows" of the North Tower.[253]

There is a 10-60 alarm, the code that denotes a major emergency. NYPD responds; five teams deploy into the WTC buildings and plaza, and one additional team prepares for helicopter rescue (later canceled for safety reasons).

Thirty extra NYPD staff members are assigned to take 911 calls.[254]

---

250. 9/11 Commission Staff Report, August 26, 2004.

251. Marc Policastro, an employee at the United Airlines maintenance office in San Francisco, receives the phone call from a male flight attendant who reported that the airplane had been hijacked. The call lasted about two minutes. Policastro tried unsuccessfully to contact the flight via ACARS (text message). Another employee at the maintenance office also tried to contact Flight 175 with an ACARS message around the same time, with a message requesting the flight crew to confirm reports of an incident on board. None of these or any subsequent attempts to contact the flight were ever acknowledged from the aircraft. 9/11 Commission Report, pp. 7–8; 9/11 Commission Staff Report, August 26, 2004.

252. 9/11 Commission, p. 7; 9/11 Commission Staff Report, August 26, 2004.

253. NIST Chronology.

254. NIST Chronology.

8:53 a.m.: UA Flight 175. FAA New York Center controller asks other controllers whether they can see UA Flight 175 and whether they know who the unidentified radar target was on transponder code 3321. None of the other controllers reply in the affirmative.[255]

8:53 a.m.: At the World Trade Center, Conditions Car 042, the first responding EMS unit, establishes operations outside the North Tower near West Street.[256]

8:54 a.m.: President Bush arrives at Emma E. Booker Elementary School at 2350 Dr. Martin Luther King Way, Sarasota, Florida, and goes to a holding area.[257]

According to CIA briefer Michael Morell, who is in one of the White House vans with Ari Fleischer, "just as we were pulling up to the school," Fleischer's cell phone rings, and he listens for a few seconds. "He turned to me and asked, 'Michael, do you know anything about a plane hitting the World Trade Center?' I said, 'No,' but told him I would make some calls. As the motorcade came to a stop, I said, 'Ari, I sure hope this is an accident and not terrorism.'" Morell calls the CIA Operations Center and is told the plane in question was a large commercial airliner. "My hope that this was not terrorism started to fade."[258]

8:54 a.m.: UA Flight 175. United Airlines attempts to contact the pilot following a phone call from a flight attendant.

8:54:43 a.m.: AA Flight 77 deviates from its assigned course and makes a turn to the south. Shortly after the turn, the aircraft, at 35,000 feet, is observed descending.[259]

---

255. 9/11 Commission Staff Report, August 26, 2004.

256. FDNY Report; NIST Chronology.

257. Presidential Daily Diary, partially declassified. Schedule of the President, Tuesday, September 11, 2001, says he is scheduled to arrive at 8:50 a.m.

258. *The Great War of Our Time*, pp. 47–48.

259. 9/11 Commission Report, p. 9; 9/11 Commission Staff Report, August 26, 2004.

8:54 a.m.: At the World Trade Center, FDNY reports people trapped on the 106th floor of the North Tower. The PAPD orders the shutdown of all PATH tunnels and trains.[260]

8:55 a.m.: President Bush, inside the holding room at Emma E. Booker Elementary School, speaks to Condoleezza Rice for one minute.[261] When her executive assistant first told her that a plane had hit the World Trade Center, Rice says she remembers thinking, *That's odd.*

Rice tells President Bush that the plane was not a light aircraft, adding, "That's all we know right now, Mr. President." Bush responds, "That's a strange accident."[262] "I was stunned," he later writes. "That plane must have had the worst pilot in the world. . . . Maybe he'd had a heart attack."[263]

"Everyone was glued to the [television] coverage coming out of New York," Michael Morell recalls.[264]

8:55 a.m.: At the World Trade Center, announcements are made over the building-wide public address system by officials in the South Tower, saying that the building is "secure" and that "there is no need to evacuate." Some do not hear the announcement; others ignore it and evacuate anyway; others congregate in common areas like the 78th-floor sky lobby. Some return to their offices; others leave the building, depending on whom they speak to and even which police authorities they contact.

The first fire companies arrive, and some firefighters start up the stairs of the North Tower.[265]

8:55 a.m.: UA Flight 175. FAA New York Center declares UA Flight 175 a hijacking that may be heading "right towards the city."[266]

---

260. NIST Chronology.

261. 9/11 Commission Report, p. 35, says Rice was in the WHSR, but she says in her autobiography that she goes down to the Situation Room after speaking to the president. See *No Higher Honor*, p. 72.

262. *Decision Points*, p. 126; *No Higher Honor*, pp. 71–72.

263. *Decision Points*, pp. 126–127.

264. *The Great War of Our Time*, p. 48.

265. NIST Chronology; FDNY Report.

266. 9/11 Commission Staff Report, August 26, 2004.

FAA New York Center reports that a Delta Airlines flight was given instructions to avoid an unknown aircraft, and a US Airways flight was reporting having to take evasive action from an unknown aircraft.

8:55 a.m.: (Approximate time) Adm. Richard Mies, commander of STRAT-COM, is in Omaha, Nebraska. "Mies had stopped by Offutt's Officers' Club to have breakfast with some VIPs who were in town for Warren Buffett's charity golf tournament . . . he planned to escort them on a brief tour of StratCom's famous underground command center. During breakfast, Mies learned that a plane had struck at the World Trade Center."[267]

8:56 a.m.: AA Flight 77 transponder is turned off, and the plane is lost to FAA radar displays. Air traffic controllers can now only find the plane when it crosses the path of ground-based radar.[268]

At this point, FAA Indy Center still has no knowledge of the situation in New York or that other aircraft might have been hijacked. They believe that AA Flight 77 has experienced some sort of serious electrical or mechanical failure. Indy Center makes the first of 10 unsuccessful attempts over the next six and a half minutes to contact the aircraft via radio.[269]

Indy Center contacts American Airlines to advise the airline that contact has been lost. Airline dispatchers make the first of several unsuccessful attempts over three minutes to contact the flight using ACARS.[270]

8:56:32 a.m.: FAA Indy Center: "American seventy-seven, Indy."
8:56:46 a.m.: FAA Indy Center: "American seventy-seven, Indy."
8:56:53 a.m.: FAA Indy Center: "American seventy-seven, American, Indy."[271]

---

267. Steve Liewer, "On 9/11, StratCom Leaders Were Practicing for a Fictional Threat When Real, Unprecedented Catastrophe Struck," *Omaha World Herald*, September 8, 2016.
268. 9/11 Commission Report, p. 9; 9/11 Commission Staff Report, August 26, 2004.
269. 9/11 Commission Staff Report, August 26, 2004.
270. 9/11 Commission Staff Report, August 26, 2004; 9/11 Commission Report, p. 9.
271. NTSB, Flight Path Study.

Shortly after 8:56 a.m., Indy Center reaches out to controllers in adjacent sectors to advise them of the situation. They agree to "sterilize the air space" along AA Flight 77's projected westerly route.[272]

8:56 a.m.: At the World Trade Center, the NYPD says it is sending a team to meet helicopters for possible roof rescue. The PAPD report that trains are still coming into the World Trade Center station.[273]

8:57 a.m.: UA Flight 175 is now flying northeast, leveling off at 28,500 feet after turning around, and heading toward New York City.[274]

8:57 a.m.: AA Flight 77. FAA reports: "AAL 77 [AA Flight 77], B757, IAD [Dulles IAP] . . . LAX [Los Angeles IAP], ZID [Indy Center] lost radar vicinity York, KY."

FAA Indy Center continues to try to contact the plane:

> 8:57:12 a.m.: Indy Center: "American seventy-seven, American, Indy radio check; how do you read?"
> 8:57:27 a.m.: Indy Center: "American, ah, seventy-seven American, radio check; how do you read?"[275]

8:57 a.m.: At the World Trade Center, WTC complex security radios that no one should be let into the North Tower and that the plaza outside should be evacuated.[276]

8:58 a.m.: UA Flight 175. FAA New York Center controller Ed Bottiglia, searching for UA Flight 175, tells another New York controller that "we might have a hijack over here, two of them."[277]

8:58 a.m.: AA Flight 77. FAA Indy Center continues to make several attempts to contact AA Flight 77.

---

272. 9/11 Commission Staff Report, August 26, 2004.
273. NIST Chronology.
274. 9/11 Commission Staff Report, August 26, 2004.
275. NTSB, Flight Path Study.
276. NIST Chronology.
277. 9/11 Commission Staff Report, August 26, 2004.

8:58:16 a.m.: Indy Center: "American seventy-seven, Indy radio check; how do you read?"

8:58:20 a.m.: Indy Center: "American seventy-seven, center."

8:58:41 a.m.: Indy Center: "American, ah, seventy-seven, ah, Indy Center; how do you read?"

8:58:51 a.m.: Indy Center: "American seventy-seven, Indy radio check; how do you read?"[278]

8:58 a.m.: At the World Trade Center, EMS staging is established at Church and Fulton Streets. WTC complex security radios that "all security guards" should hold their posts. People are reported trapped on the 79th floor.[279]

8:59 a.m.: AA Flight 77. FAA Indy Center controllers begin coordinating with other controllers to protect the airspace and altitude of AA Flight 77's filed westward route of flight. Indy Center continues to try to contact the plane.

8:59:32 a.m.: FAA Indy Center: "American seventy-seven, Center."[280]

8:59 a.m.: UA Flight 175 passenger and former US Navy pilot Brian David Sweeney tries to call his wife, Julie. He leaves a voice mail on their home answering machine that the plane has been hijacked:

> Jules, this is Brian. Listen. I'm on an airplane that's been hijacked. If things don't go well, and it's not looking good, I just want you to know I absolutely love you. I want you to do good, go have good times. Same to my parents and everybody, and I just totally love you, and I'll see you when you get there. Bye, babe. I hope I call you.[281]

Sweeney then calls his mother, Louise Sweeney, tells her the flight has been hijacked, and he adds that the passengers are thinking about storming the cockpit to retake control.

---

278. NTSB, Flight Path Study.

279. NIST Chronology.

280. NTSB, Flight Path Study.

281. Drew Weisholtz, "Former Navy Pilot's Voicemail to Wife on 9/11 Is Still Heart-Wrenching, 19 Years Later," *Today* (NBC News), September 11, 2020. See also 9/11 Commission Report, p. 8.

United Airlines maintenance in San Francisco sends three ACARS messages to UA Flight 175. Each reads: "I heard of a reported incident aboard your acft [aircraft]. Plz verify all is normal."[282]

Shortly before 9:00 a.m., one of the San Francisco supervisors calls the United Airlines manager in Chicago to tell him of the reported hijacking of UA Flight 175. The operations center manager initially thinks the report refers to the American Airlines hijacking, but the supervisor in San Francisco reiterates that it is about Flight 175. The Chicago manager notifies his boss, United's operations center director, who in turn contacts United's chief operating officer, company CEO, and security chief. They all begin the process of activating the crisis center at United's headquarters, which takes about 30 minutes to complete.[283]

8:59 a.m.: At the World Trade Center, the NYPD says its first teams have entered the North Tower. By now, 18 fire apparatuses are parked outside the complex. The PAPD radios: "As soon as we're able, I want to start a building evacuation, building one and building two, till we find out what caused this." They then say that the entire complex is to be evacuated: "All buildings, copy?"[284]

9:00 a.m.: President Bush arrives at Room 301 at Emma E. Booker Elementary School, a second-grade classroom, for a demonstration of the school's early reading program.[285] He is accompanied by Secretary of Education Rod Paige; Florida Lt. Governor Frank Brogan; and two local congressmen, Rep. Dan Miller (R-FL) and Rep. Adam Putnam (R-FL).[286]

9:00 a.m.: "Speaker Dennis Hastert [Rep. Dennis Hastert (R-IL)] calls the House to order at 9 a.m. for morning-hour debate. By then, most House offices knew a plane had crashed into . . . [the] World Trade Center in lower Manhattan, but not much else."[287]

---

282. 9/11 Commission Staff Report, August 26, 2004.
283. 9/11 Commission Staff Report, August 26, 2004.
284. NIST Chronology.
285. Presidential Daily Diary, partially declassified.
286. Presidential Daily Diary, partially declassified.
287. "Whereas: Stories from the People's House: Unique Circumstances: A Look at the House Journal on September 11, 2001," House of Representatives Oral History on September

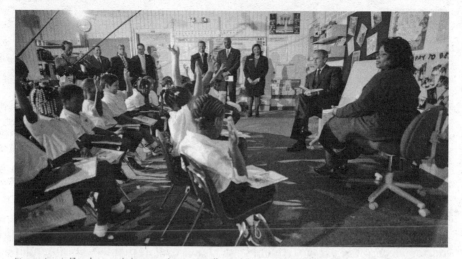

President Bush participates in a reading demonstration at Emma E. Booker Elementary School in Sarasota, Florida. (Source: George W. Bush Presidential Library and Museum / Eric Draper)

9:00 a.m.: UA Flight 175. FAA New York Center informs United Airlines that the flight is missing from radar.[288]

Lee Hanson receives a second call from his son Peter, a passenger aboard UA Flight 175. They talk for a little more than two minutes:

> It's getting bad, Dad. A stewardess was stabbed. They seem to have knives and Mace. They said they have a bomb. It's getting very bad on the plane. Passengers are throwing up and getting sick. The plane is making jerky movements. I don't think the pilot is flying the plane. I think we are going down. I think they intend to go to Chicago or someplace and fly into a building. Don't worry, Dad. If it happens, it'll be very fast. My God, my God.

The call ends abruptly as Lee Hanson hears a woman scream in the background. He turns on a television and sees the second aircraft hit the World Trade Center (at 9:03 a.m.).[289]

11, 2017, https://history.house.gov/Blog/2017/September/9-11-House-Journal2/ (hereafter Whereas: Stories from the People's House).

288. 9/11 Commission Staff Report, August 26, 2004.

289. 9/11 Commission Report, p. 8.

9:00 a.m.: AA Flight 77. American Airlines Executive Vice President Gerard Arpey learns that communications have been lost, and he orders all AA flights in the northeast that have not taken off to remain on the ground. The airline then extends the ground stop nationwide.[290]

FAA Indy Center continues to try to contact the flight:

> 9:00:25 a.m.: FAA: "American seventy-seven, Indy."
> 9:00:56 a.m.: FAA: "Indy Center calling American seventy-seven, American seventy-seven."[291]

9:00 a.m.: (Approximate time) At the World Trade Center, at about 9:00 a.m., FDNY Chief of Department Ganci takes over as incident commander. He moves the ICP from the lobby of the North Tower to across West Street (the eight-lane west-side highway) because of falling debris and other safety concerns. Officers on the scene consider a limited, localized collapse of the tower possible but do not think that a building could collapse entirely.

Operations Post 1 (OP-1) is established in the lobby of the North Tower so that rescuers have direct access to building systems, such as controls for alarms, elevators, and communication systems.

The FDNY, NYPD, and PAPD are placed at their highest mobilization levels.[292]

9:00 a.m.: (Approximate time) FAA Boston Center stops all departures from airports within its jurisdiction.[293]

9:00 a.m.: (Approximate time) Secretary Rumsfeld receives his daily intelligence briefing. "As we reviewed the threat reports from around the world, September 11 seemed to be no more different [*sic*] than any other day," Rumsfeld later writes. During the briefing, the second plane hits the South Tower.[294]

---

290. 9/11 Commission Report, p. 9; 9/11 Commission Staff Report, August 26, 2004.
291. NTSB, Flight Path Study.
292. FDNY Report.
293. FAA Chronology.
294. *Known and Unknown*, p. 335.

9:00 a.m.: (Approximate time) Gen. Richard Myers, vice chairman of the Joint Chiefs of Staff and chairman-designate, arrives on Capitol Hill for a meeting with Sen. Max Cleland (D-GA) to talk about his upcoming confirmation hearings.[295] He later writes what he thought after the initial attack on the World Trade Center: "Must have been a light aircraft, I thought. Maybe on a sightseeing flight."[296]

9:00 a.m.: (Approximate time) Gen. John Jumper is chairing his first staff meeting as the new Air Force chief of staff in the Air Force Council conference room on the mezzanine level of the Pentagon basement when he learns of an airplane hitting the World Trade Center.[297]

9:00 a.m.: (Approximate time) Federal Emergency Management Agency (FEMA) Director Joe Allbaugh is at a conference in Montana.

"Allbaugh, who didn't have a cellphone, knew nothing. . . . As the FEMA director walked through the lobby after breakfast, [Craig] Fugate stopped him to ask if he knew what was going on in New York. Allbaugh shrugged. Fugate then told his deputy at the other end of the phone, 'I'm handing you over to the director of FEMA—brief him.' He then pressed the receiver into Allbaugh's hand."[298]

Allbaugh would make it back to Washington for a 7:15 p.m. press briefing and to attend the evening Cabinet meeting. FEMA would play no other substantive role on 9/11, overshadowed by New York state and city organizations, the White House, and the military, which took charge of outside medevac and other rescue efforts.

9:00 a.m.: (Approximate time) Australian Prime Minister John Howard is in Washington to meet President Bush and address a session of Congress on September 12. He meets with Bush for the first time on September 10.

295. James Bamford, *A Pretext for War: 9/11, Iraq, and the Abuse of America's Intelligence Agencies* (New York: Doubleday, 2004), p. 39.

296. Richard Myers, *Eyes on the Horizon: Serving on the Front Lines of National Security* (New York: Threshold, 2009), p. 8.

297. Defense Studies Series, Pentagon 9/11.

298. Christopher Cooper, *Disaster: Hurricane Katrina and the Failure of Homeland Security* (New York: Times Books, 2006), p. 74.

"We didn't talk about terrorism. Nobody knew this terrible event was just around the corner," Howard later says.

Howard is in his hotel when the first attack occurs.[299]

9:01 a.m.: UA Flight 175. United Airlines flight dispatch manager tells Ed Ballinger, the dispatcher responsible for the airline's East Coast to West Coast flights, that San Francisco believes that UA Flight 175 has been hijacked.[300]

Though FAA Herndon Command Center is told about this "other aircraft" at 9:01 a.m., FAA New York Center still contacts New York TRACON and asks for assistance in locating UA Flight 175.[301]

9:01 a.m.: At the World Trade Center, the assistant chief of FDNY EMS Operations (Car 6A, the second-highest-ranking EMS officer) arrives and assumes the position of EMS Command, making him responsible for managing the overall emergency response. He assigns Conditions Car 042 to establish a division on Church Street and decides to move the EMS command post to the lobby of North Tower, next to the ICP that had been established by Fire Operations. FDNY protocols require that EMS Command report to the incident commander.[302]

NYPD says First and Fifth Precinct executive officers advise of new mobilization points at Vesey and West Streets. The PAPD is still ordering over the radio for "all buildings in the complex" to be evacuated.[303]

9:02 a.m.: UA Flight 175. FAA New York TRACON (radar) locates UA Flight 175 rapidly descending into lower Manhattan. A New York Center manager states: "All right. Heads up, man, it looks like another one coming in."[304]

---

299. James Grubel, "Australia's Howard a Surprise 9-11 Witness," Reuters, September 4, 2011.

300. 9/11 Commission Staff Report, August 26, 2004.

301. 9/11 Commission Staff Report, August 26, 2004.

302. FDNY Report.

303. NIST Chronology.

304. 9/11 Commission Staff Report, August 26, 2004.

9:02 a.m.: At the World Trade Center, evacuation is ordered. After initially instructing tenants of the South Tower to remain in the building, Port Authority officials now broadcast orders to evacuate both towers via the public address system.[305]

9:02 a.m.: UA Flight 93 reaches its cruising altitude of 35,000 feet.[306]

Several FAA dispatchers send ACARS messages to several United Airlines flights indicating that an aircraft has crashed into the World Trade Center. These messages provide no details or warnings, however.[307]

According to the 9/11 Commission, the UA Flight 93 flight crew is unaware of the hijacking of AA Flight 11. The Commission states: "No one at the FAA or the airlines that day had ever dealt with multiple hijackings. Such a plot had not been carried out anywhere in the world in more than 30 years, and never in the United States. As news of the hijackings filtered through the FAA and the airlines, it does not seem to have occurred to their leadership that they needed to alert other aircraft in the air that they too might be at risk."[308]

---

305. FDNY Report. The NIST Chronology records no such order at 9:02 a.m. Port Authority Police ordered evacuation of the complex earlier.

306. 9/11 Commission Staff Report, August 26, 2004.

307. 9/11 Commission Staff Report, August 26, 2004.

308. 9/11 Commission Report, p. 10.

CHAPTER 5

"AMERICA IS UNDER ATTACK"

When UA Flight 175 hit the south face of the South Tower at 9:03 a.m., it was clear to everyone who saw it, now on live television, that a massive terrorist attack was underway. The plane, flying at a higher speed than AA Flight 11, also careened into the South Tower at a greater angle, inflicting more damage, projecting fireballs and parts of the plane and fragments of the building itself much farther away. About 200 people were instantly killed, and another 600 were trapped on the upper floors. The plane also destroyed the 78th-floor sky lobby, the link to the upper floors, destroying elevator banks and all but one set of stairwells. The impact of the greater force and location of the attack resulted in the South Tower collapsing before the North Tower, though fewer people were thought to have died because many had already left the building of their own volition because of the adjacent attack, and, more importantly, so many more didn't get to work because of the earlier crash.

Mohammed Atta had planned the attacks so that the four flights would depart nearly simultaneously (AA Flight 11 at 7:45, UA Flight 175 and Flight 93 at 8:00, and AA Flight 77 at 8:10), thwarting any warning from the ground of hijacked planes. But the attacks in New York and Washington were to have taken place at different times, with the two flights hitting the World Trade Center at the same time around 8:45–9:00 a.m., while the two that were headed for Washington would hit an hour later. Three of the flights actually took off within 10 to 15 minutes of their planned departure times. The fourth plane, UA Flight 93, would ordinarily have taken off about 15 minutes after pulling away from the gate. When it left the ground at 8:42 a.m., more than 25 minutes late due to air traffic congestion in the New York area, the plot was disrupted, because by then, passengers aboard the last flight would know that other hijacked airliners had hit the World Trade Center.

Also, UA Flight 93 had only three "musclemen" on board (the other planes all had four), which might have contributed to the ability of the passengers to overpower the hijackers. The 9/11 Commission later speculated that the fifth muscleman might have been Mohamed al-Qahtani (the "20th hijacker"), who had been refused entry by a suspicious immigration inspector at Florida's Orlando International Airport in August.[309] That in itself is illuminating with regard to the impact one individual can have: if just one airline check-in person or one airport security person (or one intelligence analyst or FBI agent) had acted extraordinarily and had detected or stopped the hijackers, history might have been very different.

9:03:14 a.m.: UA Flight 175 strikes floors 78–84 of the south side of the South Tower (WTC 2).[310]

All 65 people on board the aircraft die instantly on impact. By this time, several news media organizations, including the three major networks (who have interrupted their morning shows) are covering the disaster. Parts of the plane, including the starboard engine, leave the building from its east and north sides, falling to the ground six blocks away.[311]

The FAA is still looking for the flight on radar even as it hits the South Tower. United Airlines dispatcher Ed Ballinger sends an ACARS message to the flight: "How is the ride. Anything dispatch can do for you." Another ACARS is sent at the same time by the United air traffic control coordinator: "NY approach lookin' for ya on [frequency] 127.4."[312]

An FAA Newark Center controller later states: "At approximately 9:00, I observed an unknown aircraft south of the Newark, New Jersey airport, northeast bound and descending out of twelve thousand nine hundred feet in a rapid rate of descent, the radar target terminated at the World Trade Center."[313]

---

309. 9/11 Commission Report, p. 11.

310. According to NORAD, "from RADES radar data and from 'FAA Responds'"; NORAD 9/11 Timeline, n.d., prepared for the 9/11 Commission. The 9/11 Commission Report (p. 8) strangely says 9:03:11.

311. NIST Chronology.

312. 9/11 Commission Staff Report, August 26, 2004.

313. 9/11 Commission Staff Report, August 26, 2004.

United Airlines Flight 175
(UA 175)
Boston to Los Angeles

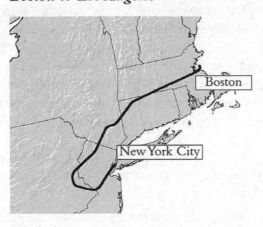

Boston

New York City

(Source: 9/11 Commission)

Fire chiefs immediately call in additional fire units and deploy units from the North Tower. "As the mobilization escalates, dispatchers instruct responding Fire units to report to staging areas that senior chiefs had designated near the World Trade Center. However, as these units approach the area, many fail to report to the staging areas and instead proceed directly to the tower lobbies or other parts of the incident area. As a result, senior chiefs could not accurately track the whereabouts of all units. In addition, the failure to stage prevents fire units from getting necessary information and orientation before going into the towers."[314]

Sixteen firehouses from lower Manhattan have units responding. Five of the 16 firehouses have multiple units responding.[315]

9:03 a.m.: In Sarasota, at the Emma E. Booker Elementary School, White House staffers in the holding room watch as a second plane hits the South Tower.[316]

---

314. FDNY Report.
315. NIST Chronology.
316. *The Great War of Our Time*, p. 48.

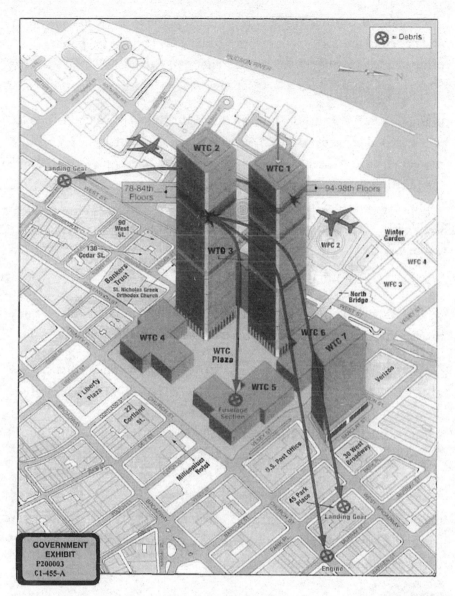

Map of the World Trade Center area depicting the paths of Flights 11 and 175.
(Source: FBI)

9:03 a.m.: At the White House, Vice President Cheney is watching television, still wondering "how the hell a plane could hit the World Trade
Center," when he sees the second plane strike the South Tower.[317]

---

317. "Twelfth Public Hearing," National Commission on Terrorist Attacks upon the United
States, June 17, 2004, http://www.9-11commission.gov/archive/hearing12/9-11Commis
sion_Hearing_2004-06-17.htm.

Condoleezza Rice is at a staff meeting in the WHSR conference room and goes into the adjacent operations center. She says she called the "NSA principals," including CIA Director Tenet and Secretary Powell in Peru. She is unable to reach Secretary Rumsfeld.[318]

9:03 a.m.: At the Pentagon, in the NMCC, duty officers watch the impact of the second plane live on TV. DDO Capt. Leidig later tells the 9/11 Commission that they "discussed who needed to be in on a conference call and the need for a Significant Event Conference (SIEC) so that a discussion could ensue on what they were going to do. Concerning the SECDEF and the VCJCS, the watch called their Executive Assistants (EA) and it was up to the EA's [sic] to notify the principals."[319]

A senior operations officer calls the FAA operations center and requests more information.[320]

The NMCC is evidently not yet aware of the scrambling of fighter jets by NORAD.

9:03 a.m.: NORAD NEADS receives their first official notice of a second hijacked aircraft when FAA New York Center tells a NEADS identification technician that UA Flight 175 is a "second possible hijack."[321]

The plane has just hit the World Trade Center, and the technicians in Rome, New York, are now watching on television. Cape Cod–based F-15s are still 71 miles away from Manhattan.

"The staff looked to Col. Robert Marr, who rallied the operation: Get to the phones. Call every Air National Guard unit in the land. Prepare to put jets in the air. The nation is under attack. They would rouse the homeland defense unit by unit, if necessary."[322]

9:03 a.m.: (Approximate time) NORAD commander Gen. Eberhart initially tries to call Chairman of the Joint Chiefs Gen. Shelton but is unable to

---

318. *No Higher Honor*, p. 72.

319. 9/11 Commission Memorandum for the Record, Interview, Captain Charles Joseph Leidig, USN, April 29, 2004.

320. 9/11 Commission Report, p. 38.

321. 9/11 Commission Staff Report, August 26, 2004.

322. Hart Seely, "Amid Crisis Simulation, 'We Were Suddenly No-Kidding Under Attack,'" Newhouse News Service, January 25, 2002.

connect.[323] He calls Vice Chairman Gen. Myers and talks to him "as he was coming out of the Senator Cleland's office. Myers believes he took the call from Senator Cleland's outer office, and that it was after the second tower had been hit (sometime between 0903 and 0930). It was a short conversation. Eberhart updated him on the situation (i.e., two towers hit, several hijack codes in the system), and informed Myers that NORAD would be scrambling fighters. The issue of ROE [rules of engagement] was not discussed. Myers mainly listened and responded that he needed to get back to the NMCC because he could not communicate from a cellphone."[324]

Gen. Eberhart says that after the attack on the South Tower, it is "obvious" that there is an ongoing and coordinated terrorist attack. Eberhart initially stays at the headquarters of NORAD in Building 1 at Peterson AFB in Colorado Springs, as he does not want to lose his tether to secure communications. Later in the morning, he is driven to the underground Cheyenne Mountain Operations Center (CMOC), an hour away.[325]

9:03 a.m.: AA Flight 77. FAA Indy Center, now unable to find AA Flight 77 for 10 minutes, begins notifying other agencies that the plane is missing and has possibly crashed.

9:03:06 a.m.: FAA: "American seventy-seven, Indy."[326] In Indianapolis, they are still unaware of the other hijackings, even what has been reported on television.

9:03 a.m.: AA Flight 11. FAA Boston Center reports to FAA New England Region (Burlington, Massachusetts) that they have deciphered what they heard in one of the first hijacker transmissions from AA Flight 11 at 8:24 a.m., that the hijacker (Mohammed Atta) said, "We have some planes."[327]

---

323. 9/11 Commission Memorandum for the Record, Interview with CINC NORAD (Commander in Chief NORAD), General Edward "Ed" Eberhart, March 1, 2004.

324. 9/11 Commission, Memorandum for the Record, Interview of General Richard Myers, February 17, 2004, partially declassified.

325. 9/11 Commission NORAD MFR.

326. NTSB, Flight Path Study.

327. 9/11 Commission Report, p. 10; 9/11 Commission Staff Report, August 26, 2004.

9:03 a.m.: FBI Special Agent Arthur R. Eberhart, in charge of the administrative and technical division of the 650-person Washington Field Office (WFO) and the senior officer present, activates the Rapid Response Team, established after the African embassy bombings in 1998. He then activates the WFO Command Center and then the National Capital Response Squad (NCRS).[328]

Because there is no intelligence warning, and because it is the week after Labor Day slowdowns, almost the entire office is away at trainings and meetings.[329]

9:03 a.m.: (Approximate time) At Secret Service headquarters, Special Agent Paul Nenninger remembers: "As we gathered up our personal effects [at the morning staff meeting] . . . [I explained] that the Training Center had been crashing planes into the White House since 1998 on a simulation program provided by the military. One of my previous assignments had been to run SIMLAB—Security Incident Modeling Lab. It was done to test the security responses of the various agencies that interact to provide security and support at the White House. . . . The agents knew without stating it that one plane could be an accident, two was an attack. We disbanded and went to various support roles defined by the day's events, known in government circles as The Continuity of Government Plan."[330]

9:03 a.m.: In the Air Force Command Center, Gen. Jumper and others present watch UA Flight 175 crash into the South Tower. After viewing

---

328. See 9/11 Commission, Memorandum for the Record, Arthur R. Eberhart, former SAC, FBI, December 15, 2003.

329. Special Agent Christopher Combs of the NCRS was teaching a class at the District of Columbia Fire Academy when he receives a page from the WFO Command Center. Special Agent Van Harp (the ADIC) is on vacation in South Carolina. Special Agent Timothy Bereznay, recently appointed to the position of National Security SAC, had not yet reported to the WFO, and his predecessor, Special Agent James "Tim" Caruso, had already left. Special Agent Ellen Knowlton, who headed the Criminal Investigative Division, had recently been reassigned to FBI headquarters. See 9/11 Commission, Memorandum for the Record, Arthur R. Eberhart, former SAC, FBI, December 15, 2003; Arlington County: After-Action Report on the Response to the September 11 Terrorist Attack on the Pentagon.

330. Paul L. Nenninger, "One Secret Service Agent's Experience," *Southeast Missourian*, August 29, 2011.

televised news for about eight minutes, Jumper resumes the meeting, concludes it quickly, and departs for his office.[331]

9:03 a.m.: (Approximate time) "[Army Chief of Staff] General [John] Shinseki was in Kuala Lumpur, Malaysia, attending a conference of the chiefs of staff of Pacific nation armies. He telephoned Assistant Deputy Chief of Staff for Operations and Plans Maj. Gen. Phillip R. Kensinger, and Brig. Gen. Peter W. Chiarelli, the director of operations, mobilization and readiness in the Office of the Deputy Chief of Staff for Operations and Plans. As General Shinseki was on the telephone, a second hijacked aircraft struck the South Tower of the World Trade Center. Following General Shinseki's instructions, Generals Kensinger and Chiarelli activated the Army Operations Center's Crisis Action Team."[332]

"Chiarelli gave Shinseki as much up-to-date information about the New York attacks as he could glean from CNN. . . . Chiarelli told Shinseki that in his additional capacity as [DOD executive agent] director of military [civil] support he had activated the Crisis Action Team to respond to the contingency in New York if requested by state and local officials. He anticipates that the World Trade Center disaster would require enormous rescue, firefighting, and recovery efforts. During the conversation with Shinseki an intelligence analyst interrupts to inform Chiarelli that other aircraft had been hijacked. One was thought to be headed toward Washington. Sensing the urgency of the situation, Shinseki ends the phone call, saying that he would call back later."[333]

9:04 a.m.: FAA Boston Center stops all departures from airports in its jurisdiction (New England and eastern New York State). Controller Terry Biggio advises FAA New England Region in Burlington, Massachusetts, that he is going to stop all departures at airports under their control and suggests that they "do the same elsewhere."[334]

---

331. Defense Studies Series, Pentagon 9/11.

332. Department of the Army, Historical Summary: Fiscal Year 2001, p. 55.

333. Defense Studies Series, Pentagon 9/11. See also Stephen J. Lofgren, ed., *Then Came the Fire: Personal Accounts from the Pentagon, 11 September 2001* (Military Studies Press, 2011).

334. 9/11 Commission Staff Report, August 26, 2004.

9:04 a.m.: At the World Trade Center, the PAPD report over the radio: "Be advised that a second plane has struck the building. . . . Not known if it was a second plane, possibly a missile."[335]

9:05 a.m.: President Bush is about to begin reading *The Pet Goat* to students at Emma E. Booker Elementary School when White House Chief of Staff Andrew Card whispers in his ear: "A second plane hit the second tower. America is under attack."

Bush says: "My first reaction was outrage. Someone had dared attack America. They were going to pay. . . . I saw reporters at the back of the room, learning the news on their cell phones and pagers. Instinct kicked in. I knew my reaction would be recorded and beamed throughout the world. The nation would be in shock; the president could not be."[336]

9:05 a.m.: AA Flight 77 reemerges on FAA Indy Center radar scopes, east of its last known position, rather than west, indicating that the plane has turned around. It remains on Indy Center scopes for another six minutes and then crosses into the western portion of FAA Washington Center's airspace at 9:10 a.m.

9:05 a.m.: (Approximate time) After the second plane hits, Speaker of the House Hastert attempts to contact Vice President Cheney on a secure telephone line but is unable to reach him.[337]

Hastert, as Speaker of the House of Representatives, is the third in line to the presidency, behind Vice President Cheney. Exactly when he tried to contact Cheney is unclear, but later he will be moved to Mount Weather in Bluemont, Virginia, to create maximum separation from Cheney.

9:05 a.m.: (Approximate time) At the CIA, in Alec Station (in charge of intelligence on Osama bin Laden): "When reports of the second plane's hitting the World Trade Center reached the Station, everyone instantly

---

335. NIST Chronology.

336. *Decision Points*, p. 127; Presidential Daily Diary, partially declassified.

337. Whereas: Stories from the People's House.

thought and said the same thing: 'So this is what al Qa'ida was planning. This is what we were waiting for.'"[338]

9:05 a.m.: (Approximate time) In Omaha, upon hearing of a second crash, Adm. Mies leaves the VIP tour he is conducting. The *Omaha World Herald* later reports:

> "I heard about the second plane," recalled Mies . . . "I realized it was a terrorist attack. . . ."
>
> "Early in the day, Mies considered the possibility that Bush might fly to Offutt. He asked the 55th Wing to prepare Quarters 13, a building for VIP guests on General's Row, for the presidential party just in case."
>
> Canceling the VIP tour, Mies returned to his command post at StratCom. He quickly pulled the plug on [exercise] Global Guardian so the military could focus on the terror crisis.[339]

The Global Guardian strategic nuclear war exercise is actually canceled at 9:50 a.m.

9:05 a.m.: AA Flight 77. American Airlines begins lockout procedures, restricting and preserving data on the flight.[340]

9:05 a.m.: FAA Boston Center contacts FAA New England Region in Burlington, Massachusetts, and confirms that the pilot on board AA Flight 11 said, "We have planes."[341]

9:05 a.m.: NORAD NEADS logs indicate the command is notified by the FAA of the events concerning UA Flight 175, after it has already watched the plane crash on television.[342]

---

338. *The Great War of Our Time*, p. 49.

339. Steve Liewer, "On 9/11, StratCom Leaders Were Practicing for a Fictional Threat When Real, Unprecedented Catastrophe Struck," *Omaha World Herald*, September 8, 2016.

340. 9/11 Commission Staff Report, August 26, 2004.

341. 9/11 Commission Staff Report, August 26, 2004.

342. According to NORAD: "0905–0907: Discussion about UA 175 between NEADS ID and FAA (Boston Military) from NEADS logs;" NORAD 9/11 Timeline, n.d., prepared for the 9/11 Commission.

9:05 a.m.: At the World Trade Center, the PAPD radios that it needs every ambulance the city can spare.[343] From the top of one of the buildings, security guards report that smoke is developing, and people can't breathe.[344]

9:06 a.m.: FAA New York Center declares "ATC zero," meaning that aircraft are not permitted to depart from, arrive at, or travel through New York Center's airspace until further notice.[345]

The FAA bans takeoffs of all flights bound to or through the airspace of New York Center from airports in that center and the three adjacent air route traffic control centers—Boston, Cleveland, and Washington. This is referred to as a first-tier ground stop and covers the Northeast from North Carolina north and as far west as eastern Michigan.

9:06 a.m.: At the World Trade Center, FDNY Chief of Department Ganci orders that no aerial rescue is to be attempted.

The PAPD report that a missile has launched from the Woolworth Building roof.[346]

9:07 a.m.: FAA Boston Center decides, on the advice of FAA New England Region in Burlington, Massachusetts, to contact Air Transport Association (ATA) representatives and ask that they formally request that airline companies warn their aircraft to heighten cockpit security. Not content to solely rely on the airlines, the Boston Center also decides to issue a Notice to Airmen (NOTAM) to heighten cockpit security in light of the attacks on New York.[347]

The 9/11 Commission will later say that Boston Center "requested at 9:07 that [FAA] Herndon Command Center 'get messages to airborne aircraft to increase security for the cockpit.' There is no evidence that Herndon took such action."[348]

---

343. NIST Chronology.
344. NIST Chronology.
345. FAA Chronology. 9/11 Commission Staff Report, August 26, 2004, says 9:05 a.m.
346. NIST Chronology.
347. 9/11 Commission Staff Report, August 26, 2004.
348. 9/11 Commission Report, p. 10.

`9:07 a.m.:` AA Flight 77, now flying east, levels off at 25,000 feet and makes a slight course change to the east-northeast.[349]

`9:07 a.m.:` At the World Trade Center, WTC security reports over the radio that it is evacuating other complex buildings—4 and 5 World Trade Center: "I have people going crazy."[350]

FDNY and NYPD chiefs receive a briefing from the FBI.

`9:08 a.m.:` FAA follows up on the 9:06 a.m. "ATC zero" order and issues a written advisory that "sterilizes" New York airspace, meaning that all aircraft are ordered to leave, and all takeoffs nationwide for flights going to or through New York Center airspace are also banned.[351]

United Airlines dispatcher Ed Ballinger begins to send out ACARS messages notifying United's transcontinental flights that have not yet taken off for the United States that a ground stop has been ordered in the New York area.[352]

`9:08 a.m.:` AA Flight 77. FAA Indy Center asks its military liaison to request that they be on the lookout for an accident involving AA Flight 77 because of the simultaneous loss of radio communications and all radar contact.[353]

`9:08 a.m.:` At the World Trade Center, the FDNY establishes a lobby command post inside the South Tower. WTC security reports over the radio that debris is coming down from the towers, endangering people leaving the other buildings, including 2, 4, and 5 World Trade Center.[354]

`9:09 a.m.:` NORAD orders additional interceptor aircraft, F-16 Fighting Falcon fighters at Langley AFB, just north of Norfolk, Virginia, to go to battle stations and prepare to launch.[355]

---

349. 9/11 Commission Staff Report, August 26, 2004.

350. NIST Chronology.

351. FAA Chronology.

352. 9/11 Commission Staff Report, August 26, 2004.

353. 9/11 Commission Staff Report, August 26, 2004.

354. NIST Chronology.

355. 9/11 Commission Staff Report, August 26, 2004. Three F-16 fighters from Langley AFB are launched to provide backup. Two are armed with air-to-air missiles and one, a

NEADS MCC Lt. Col. Nasypany says that "the strategy was to 'lean forward' in case of another event. He placed Langley on Battle Stations without a specific target, put with the intention of using them in response to another threat. He notes that the Langley Battle Stations order was generated by the events taking place in New York. Nasypany thought to put the Langley scramble over Baltimore, and place a 'barrier cap' between the hijack and Washington, DC."[356]

9:09 a.m.: Otis-based F-15Cs arrive in military-controlled airspace off Long Island, New York.

At about this time, the NEADS MCC Lt. Col. Nasypany decides that they need to move the fighters nearer to New York City. Anticipating additional attacks, he says:

> This is what I foresee that we probably need to do. We need to talk to FAA. We need to tell 'em if this stuff is gonna keep on going, we need to take those fighters, put 'em over Manhattan. That's best thing, that's the best play right now. So coordinate with the FAA. Tell 'em if there's more out there, which we don't know, let's get 'em over Manhattan. At least we got some kind of play.[357]

Though some 9/11 histories say the planes begin searching for AA Flight 11, the fighter pilots know that the plane had already crashed. Lacking a target to intercept, and to avoid New York area air traffic and uncertain about what to do, they are told to "hold as needed" in military airspace. From 9:09 to 9:13 a.m., the Otis fighters stay in this holding pattern.[358]

---

training plane, only with a Gatling gun. "More than thirty-five minutes later [after the Otis fighters were scrambled], the second three fighters launched from Langley Air Force Base in response to a faulty FAA report that Flight 11 was still aloft and was headed toward Washington, DC." See *The First 109 Minutes: 9/11 and the US Air Force*, 2011. See also NORAD 9/11 Timeline, n.d., prepared for the 9/11 Commission, with data from NEADS logs.

356. 9/11 Commission Memorandum for the Record, Interview with NEADS Alpha Flight Mission Crew Commander (MCC), Lt. Col. Kevin J. Nasypany, January 22, 2004, and January 23, 2004.

357. 9/11 Commission Staff Report, August 26, 2004.

358. 9/11 Commission Staff Report, August 26, 2004.

9:09 a.m.: AA Flight 77. FAA Indy Center reports loss of contact and a possible accident to the FAA Great Lakes Regional Office.[359]

9:09 a.m.: At the World Trade Center, the PAPD report over the radio that there are 75–100 people trapped in the Windows on the World restaurant on the 106th floor of the North Tower. People are "starting to panic."[360]

9:10 a.m.: FAA DC logs the situation: "[New York ATC] . . . asks for help from military. Coordinated . . . to stop ZNY [New York Center] and 1st tier traffic. . . . Coordinated with east and west to GS [ground stop] all traffic in the country. After that coordination to find out which way AAL 77 [AA Flight 77] was going, then coordination to assist in finding AAL 247, USA 41, DAL 1989, NWA 197, UAL 641, UAL 57, USA 633."[361]

Over the next nine hours, the FAA will struggle with reports of additional hijacked planes, including some of these same seven flights, as well as suspect aircraft arriving from overseas.

9:10 a.m.: At the World Trade Center, 100 percent of New York's rescue and high-rise units are deployed; most of the later-arriving units (from Brooklyn, Queens, and the Bronx) are directed to the South Tower (WTC 2) and the Marriott Hotel (WTC 3). Some of the rescuers, including fire and EMS units, are unable to communicate. The New York City Office of Emergency Management's Emergency Operations Center, located in 7 World Trade Center (WTC 7), is evacuated, with the staff moved to a police academy building on the Lower East Side.[362]

9:11 a.m.: AA Flight 77 flight attendant Renee May attempts to call her parents, but the call does not connect.[363]

359. 9/11 Commission Staff Report, August 26, 2004.
360. NIST Chronology.
361. DCC Timeline.
362. FDNY Report; NIST Chronology.
363. 9/11 Commission Staff Report, August 26, 2004.

9:11 a.m.: At the World Trade Center, the FDNY starts to ask responding units to stop short of the WTC complex due to the large number of vehicles on the scene as well as debris falling from the buildings. A backup transmitter is put into service in anticipation of potential problems with the primary transmitter located on top of the North Tower.[364]

The last PATH train leaves from the station under the World Trade Center. The station is vacant when the towers collapse.

9:12 a.m.: AA Flight 77 flight attendant Renee May makes a second call and talks to her mother, Nancy May, in Las Vegas. May tells her mother that her flight was being hijacked by six individuals who had moved them—the mother was not sure whether her daughter meant all the passengers or just the crew—to the rear of the plane. May asked her mother to call American Airlines and make sure they knew about the hijacking, giving her three phone numbers to call.[365]

9:12 a.m.: At the World Trade Center, FDNY Chief of Department Ganci issues a fifth alarm for the South Tower.[366]

9:13 a.m.: Otis-based F-15C fighters exit their holding pattern over Long Island and set a direct course for Manhattan.[367]

NORAD commander Gen. Eberhart has the authority to order scrambled air defense assets to shoot down hijacked planes under Joint Chiefs of Staff Standing Rules of Engagement[368] but "took positive action not to do so."[369]

364. FDNY Report; NIST Chronology.

365. 9/11 Commission Report, p. 9; 9/11 Commission Staff Report, August 26, 2004.

366. FDNY Report.

367. 9/11 Commission Staff Report, August 26, 2004. FAA logs state that Otis-based F-15 fighters reach their holding pattern above Manhattan at 9:09 a.m. This is likely in error.

368. Chairman of the Joint Chiefs of Staff Instruction 3121.01A, "Standing Rules of Engagement for US Forces [SROE]," January 15, 2000, was in effect on 9/11. The document is classified.

369. 9/11 Commission, Memorandum for the Record, n.d., 2012-042-doc24, partially declassified.

The fighters do not arrive over Manhattan until 9:25 a.m. According to NORAD, this is the first of three occasions where Gen. Eberhart was given an opportunity—in discussions with his command center—to order aircraft to shoot down civilian airliners but declined to issue any such order.

9:13 a.m.: At the World Trade Center, WTC security radio reports that the North Tower is flooding.[370]

---

370. NIST Chronology.

CHAPTER 6

GOODBYE, PET GOAT

Though much has been said about President Bush's reaction in the Sarasota classroom, what is most puzzling about the initial reaction to the attacks on the twin towers is that the Secret Service made no attempt to immediately evacuate the president, either from the classroom or from the school, a standard practice that follows even the most trivial incident. Yet from the first realization that an airliner had hit the North Tower (8:55 a.m.) until the president got into his limousine to go to the airport (at 9:32 a.m.), it took 37 minutes. That's 37 minutes of vulnerability at an unprotected elementary school—an eternity in the world of presidential protection.

When the second plane hit the South Tower at 9:03 a.m., everyone knew that a terrorist attack was underway. As the president's CIA briefer Michael Morell recounts, thinking of those minutes ticking by: "I was growing increasingly concerned about the president's safety as well as the safety of others at the school. The fact that the president would be at Booker Elementary at this hour, on this day, had been public knowledge for days."[371]

No one yet knew for sure what was going on. Standing on the sidelines, to the president's left, was Ari Fleischer, the White House press secretary. He says he immediately thought that President Bush shouldn't make a statement until he was briefed on the facts. "DON'T SAY ANYTHING YET," he wrote on the back of a yellow legal pad in big letters and held it up for the president to see.

President Bush later said that his instinct was to project calm, not to have the country see an excited reaction in a moment of crisis. The national press corps was standing behind the children in the classroom, and he says he saw them alerted when their phones and pagers start to ring. Thus he remained

---

371. *The Great War of Our Time*, p. 49.

in the classroom for another five to seven minutes, while the second graders continued reading. It would be nine minutes before President Bush left the classroom. Even back in the holding room, no particular extraordinary security measures were taken, and he returned to a classroom, schoolchildren surrounding him, to make a public statement. It was like the Secret Service itself was in a state of shock.

`9:14 a.m.:` President Bush returns to the holding area at the Emma E. Booker Elementary School.[372] Secretary of Education Rod Paige takes over his presentation.

Secretary Paige and his chief of staff are left at the school and have to make their way back to Washington themselves the next day, renting a car and driving.[373]

`9:14 a.m.:` At the World Trade Center, the PAPD continue to ask for help in rescuing people at Windows on the World. "They're losing . . . [garbled] . . . options at the location," the dispatcher says over the radio. But the upper elevators are not working any longer in the North Tower.[374]

`9:15 a.m.:` President Bush is briefed and watches television coverage of the World Trade Center now burning, with two planes having attacked. According to Bush, his first words are "I want to talk to my wife."[375]

At 9:15 a.m., he speaks on the telephone with Vice President Cheney.[376]

For the next 15 minutes, as the staff is busy arranging a return to Washington, President Bush consults other senior advisers about remarks he will give.

"Staff are in contact with the White House Situation Room, apparently no one with the President was in contact with the Pentagon. The focus was

---

372. Presidential Daily Diary, partially declassified.

373. Rick Martinez, "Former White House Official Talks About 9/11," KFSN (ABC Local, Fresno, CA), September 6, 2011.

374. NIST Chronology.

375. Laura Bush, *Spoken from the Heart* (New York: Scribner, 2010), pp. 202–203.

376. Presidential Daily Diary, partially declassified.

President Bush watches news coverage from Emma E. Booker Elementary School in Sarasota, Florida, replaying UA Flight 175 hitting the South Tower. Chief of Staff Andrew Card is at his left; Deputy Assistant Dan Bartlett and Karl Rove are at his right. (Source: George W. Bush Presidential Library and Museum / Eric Draper [P7058-21A])

on the President's statement to the nation. The only decision made during this time was to return to Washington."[377]

It takes almost until noon before a reliable line can be established with the First Lady, after numerous tries to connect President Bush with his wife.

9:15 a.m.: The CIA convenes a National Operational Intelligence Watch Officer's Network (NOIWON), an intelligence community-wide teleconference among senior officers in command centers throughout Washington, to discuss any signs of early warning of an external attack on the United States, such as missile launches from Russia or other signs of hostile intent on the part of US adversaries.[378] Included are CIA national

---

377. "Twelfth Public Hearing," National Commission on Terrorist Attacks upon the United States, June 17, 2004, http://www.9-11commission.gov/archive/hearing12/9-11Commission_Hearing_2004-06-17.htm.

378. 9/11 Commission, Memorandum for the Record, n.d., 2012-042-doc24, partially declassified.

intelligence officers, DOD intelligence components, the national agencies (e.g., NSA, NRO), and the WHSR.

9:15 a.m.: UA Flight 93 automatic pilot is engaged. The plane has reached its assigned altitude of 35,000 feet and is flying normally across northern Pennsylvania.[379]

9:15:15 a.m.: AA Flight 77. AA Flight 683 radios in from the air: "Called AAL 77 on guard [channel] at center request."[380]

9:15 a.m.: FAA New York Center advises NORAD NEADS that UA Flight 175 is the second aircraft that has crashed into the South Tower.[381]

FAA Indy Center requests that the FAA notify Air Force Search and Rescue of a possible missing and downed aircraft. The operations manager also contacts West Virginia State Police, advising them of a possible downed aircraft, and asks if they have any reports of a crash.[382]

9:15 a.m.: At the World Trade Center, emergency radio communication is increasingly poor, with static and multiple signals garbling communications.[383]

In New York City, officials begin closing bridges and tunnels to all but emergency vehicles and pedestrians.[384]

With the surge in cell phone use, networks start to clog not just in New York but also nationwide, and an increasing number of calls cannot be connected.

9:16 a.m.: AA Flight 77. Barbara Olson, a passenger on AA Flight 77, speaks to her husband, Ted Olson, for about one minute before the call is cut off (between 9:16 a.m. and 9:26 a.m.). Ted is the solicitor general of the United States and is in Washington. She reports that the flight has

379. National Park Service, Flight 93, September 11, 2001.
380. NTSB, Flight Path Study.
381. At the same time at 9:15 a.m., the FAA Logs record: "UAL 175, B767, lost radar, South of Kingston [sic]."
382. FAA logs.
383. NIST Chronology.
384. NIST Chronology.

been hijacked and that the hijackers are wielding knives and box cutters. She does not mention stabbing or slashing of the crew or passengers. The hijackers, she says, are not aware of her phone call. All the passengers are in the back of the plane. Barbara Olson had been seated in first class.

After this call, Ted Olson tries unsuccessfully to reach Attorney General John Ashcroft, who is traveling and not in Washington. He then contacts the Department of Justice Command Center. He tells them that his wife's flight has been hijacked and gives them the flight number.[385]

9:16 a.m.: At the World Trade Center, the NYPD begins to establish a perimeter two blocks around the complex. The FDNY radio dispatchers advise that there are people trapped in the North Tower at the 82nd floor, east side; 83rd floor, Room 8311; 103rd floor, Room 103 near the corner; 104th floor; and 106th floor. In the South Tower, people are trapped at the 82nd floor, west side; 88th floor; and 89th floor.[386]

9:17:02 a.m.: Jim Stewart of CBS News, reporting from Washington, says that Osama bin Laden is considered a probable suspect, according to the intelligence community.

This is the first known national news media mention of Osama bin Laden.

9:17 a.m.: NORAD: "0917–0918: Discussion between NEADS MCC [Lt. Col. Nasypany] and FAA (Boston) about fighter availability."[387]

9:17 a.m.: At the World Trade Center, the PAPD radios that people on the 106th floor of the North Tower are losing oxygen.[388]

9:18 a.m.: Secret Service Special Agent in Charge of the Presidential Protective Division Carl Truscott is in his office at the Eisenhower Executive

---

385. 9/11 Commission Report, p. 9; 9/11 Commission Staff Report, August 26, 2004.
386. NIST Chronology.
387. NORAD 9/11 Timeline, n.d., prepared for the 9/11 Commission.
388. NIST Chronology.

Office Building, adjacent to the White House, watching the CNN broadcast of the aircraft crashing into the World Trade Center.

He meets with special agents in charge of various White House protective details to discuss security enhancements. "SAIC Truscott said that issues addressed during the meeting included the following: placing counter sniper (CS) support on the White House; providing counter assault team (CAT) support to the First Lady detail . . . at the US Capitol; opening the Emergency Operations Center; increasing the number of Emergency Response Teams . . . ; placing counter surveillance units . . . near the White House; providing protection for . . . Condoleezza Rice; increasing [Technical Security Division] support; [deleted] . . . and alerting the Army Corps of Engineers/Structural Collapse Team."[389]

There is still no mention of anything other than routine protective actions in Washington, particularly of evacuating the White House or moving the president.

9:18 a.m.: At the World Trade Center, the FDNY, outside the burning buildings, starts to move because of falling debris.[390]

9:19 a.m.: UA Flight 93. United Airlines dispatcher Ed Ballinger, now aware that two hijacked airliners have crashed into the World Trade Center, begins sending ACARS messages to the 16 flights he is handling, including UA Flight 93: "Beware any cockpit intrusion—Two a/c [aircraft] hit World Trade Center."[391]

The messages are sent out in groups. UA Flight 93 receives its message at 9:23 a.m. This represents the first occasion when either American or United Airlines sends out warnings to airborne aircraft.[392]

9:19 a.m.: FAA New England Region in Burlington, Massachusetts, now worried about other transcontinental flights, calls FAA Herndon Command

---

389. Secret Service Memorandum, Interview with SAIC Carl Truscott, October 1, 2001, partially declassified.

390. NIST Chronology.

391. National Park Service Flight 93 National Memorial, Timeline, Flight 93, September 11, 2001.

392. 9/11 Commission Report, p. 11; 9/11 Commission Staff Report, August 26, 2004.

Center and asks that it advise incoming Delta Flight 1989 (another Boston Logan flight) to use extra cockpit security.[393]

9:20 a.m.: President Bush talks with Gov. George E. Pataki (R-NY).[394]

9:20 a.m.: Rep. Timothy Johnson (R-IL), who serves as speaker pro tempore of the House of Representatives, recesses the House. It does not reopen for business again on 9/11.[395]

9:20 a.m.: At the Pentagon, a Significant Event Conference (SIEC), a worldwide conference call, is initiated at the NMCC.[396]

DDO Capt. Leidig directs the SIEC with the commanders-in-chief (CINCs) of the unified commands and the military services.[397]

"This is Captain Leidig, DDO at the NMCC with the significant event conference. This conference is convened in response to the two aircraft that crashed into the World Trade Center. I will provide an update as to what I know at the National Military Command Center and then ask for updates from conferees."[398]

As Leidig later explains: "There was not a specific procedure for a terrorist attack, so they opted for an SIEC because there is flexibility to add in people as needed. They decided that the SIEC conference best fit their

---

393. 9/11 Commission Report, p. 10.

394. Presidential Daily Diary, partially declassified.

395. Whereas: Stories from the People's House.

396. It should be noted that there are also contradictory reports that the conference started at 9:29 a.m. "NMCC initiated a key teleconference that started at 9:29 as a 'Significant Event Conference' and then at 9:37 resumed as an Air Threat Conference call." See http://www.9-11commission.gov/archive/hearing12/9-11Commission_Hearing_2004-06-17.htm; and 9/11 Commission, Memorandum for the Record, n.d., 2012-042-doc24, partially declassified.

397. The SIEC provides "the means to characterize and assess events not identified as aerospace (non-NORAD), land, maritime, cyberspace or CS events, but have the potential to impact or threaten North America or US forces, interests or allies in other theaters of operation. This conference will be used when no other emergency conference is appropriate"; JCS EAP Conference Procedures, fact sheet, n.d., partially declassified.

398. Secretary of Defense Info Memo, Subject: 9/11 Air Threat Conference Call Transcription, Top Secret SCI, October 20, 2003; partially declassified (hereafter 9/11 Air Threat Conference Call Transcription, partially declassified).

needs that morning. He made the decision to initiate the conference; he had that authority. He convened it and he ran it. No one called him with any guidance at that point. He did not recall if there has been a call to the White House at this point."[399]

Bush, Cheney, Rumsfeld, Gen. Myers, and Deputy NSA Hadley all participate at various points in the day, as do military personnel from the White House underground shelter (the PEOC). The president's military aide, Lt. Col. Gould, traveling with President Bush, also participates.[400]

A separate National Operational Intelligence Watch Officer's Network (NOIWON) teleconference is initiated at the CIA at 9:15 a.m., connecting intelligence watch centers. An FAA internal teleconference is also set up at 9:20 a.m., linking at least the Herndon Command Center to DOD and the FBI. It is on a separate line from the SIEC. The WHSR conference begins at 9:25 a.m., separate from the SIEC. A Secret Service conference also opens with the FAA at 9:25 a.m., separate from the broader conference. The Secret Service, from its Joint Operations Center (JOC) in the Eisenhower Executive Office Building, also maintains conferences with President Bush's detail, with the Pentagon, with the DC National Guard, and with other Washington-based organizations. Different officials participate in each of these conferences, but there is little coordination between the different efforts, and the participants are physically separated. Ultimately, the Pentagon teleconference ends up being the most important and relevant.

9:20 a.m.: AA Flight 77. FAA Indy Center learns by 9:20 a.m. that there were other hijacked aircraft in the system and begins to doubt its initial assumption that AA Flight 77 has crashed.

At approximately 9:20, the Indy Center operations manager contacts Chicago Air Route Traffic Control Center (Chicago Center) and advises

---

399. 9/11 Commission Memorandum for the Record, Interview, Captain Charles Joseph Leidig, USN, April 29, 2004.

400. "Twelfth Public Hearing," National Commission on Terrorist Attacks upon the United States, June 17, 2004, http://www.9-11commission.gov/archive/hearing12/9-11Commis sion_Hearing_2004-06-17.htm. See 9/11 Commission, Memorandum for the Record, n.d., 2012-042-doc24, partially declassified.

them of concern that AA Flight 77 may have been hijacked and that Chicago Center should be on the lookout for a potential attack.[401]

Between 9:20 a.m. and 9:31 a.m., Barbara Olson again calls her husband. During their second conversation, she reports that the pilot had announced that the flight had been hijacked. Ted Olson asks for her location. She says that the aircraft is flying over houses. Another passenger tells her they are traveling northeast. Ted Olson informs his wife of the two previous hijackings and crashes. According to later reports, she does not display signs of panic or indicate any awareness of an impending crash. Then the call abruptly ends.[402]

9:20 a.m.: (Approximate time) At FBI headquarters, counterterrorism specialists begin examining passenger manifests of the known hijacked flights: first AA Flight 11, followed by UA Flight 175, and then AA Flight 77. By midmorning, they establish that two names of passengers on AA Flight 77—Khalid al-Mihdhar and Nawaf al-Hazmi—are in intelligence databases. The FBI also starts to investigate other Arabic names on the lists.

After the FBI Washington Field Office (WFO) Command Center is notified that AA Flight 77 was hijacked after takeoff from Dulles IAP, Special Agent Eberhart dispatches a team to investigate and provide additional airport security. He sends a second team to National Airport as a precautionary step.[403]

For the WFO, the "first eight hours was a whirlwind of activity. The hijacking of Flight 77 led to a full investigation. Identifying the hijackers, obtaining a passenger manifest, luggage, photographs, and ongoing surveillance. . . . Eberhart was juggling conference calls with FBI HQ and handling [calls] from US senators and other VIPs. Flight 93 was in bound to Washington, DC Attorney General Ashcroft was in the air and almost got shot down."[404]

---

401. 9/11 Commission Staff Report, August 26, 2004; DCC Timeline. FAA DC logs at 9:20 a.m.: "AAL 77 west of HVQ [?]. Lost comm. radar, no primary."

402. 9/11 Commission Staff Report, August 26, 2004.

403. Arlington County: After-Action Report on the Response to the September 11 Terrorist Attack on the Pentagon.

404. See 9/11 Commission, Memorandum for the Record, Arthur R. Eberhart, former SAC, FBI, December 15, 2003.

9:20 a.m.: At the World Trade Center, three fire companies make it to the 40th floor of the South Tower by work elevator.[405]

Thirty Manhattan firehouses now report that they have companies dispatched, and Brooklyn has seven firehouses dispatched.[406]

9:20 a.m.: "The FAA, following its protocol, set up a hijacking teleconference at approximately 9:20 with several agencies, including DOD and the FBI. However, FAA and Defense Department participants in this teleconference told us the call played no role in coordinating the military and FAA response to the attacks."[407]

9:20 a.m.: Deputy FAA Administrator Monte Belger says that though FAA Boston and New York Centers had taken the initiative to initiate ground stops in their sectors, the FAA HQ Operations Center (WOC) and Herndon Command Center were both discussing a national ground stop.[408]

9:21 a.m.: AA Flight 77. NORAD NEADS receives a report from FAA Boston Center "that AA Flight 77 was still airborne and 'heading towards Washington.' NEADS personnel begin an active radar search for the aircraft."

FAA Herndon Command Center advises a supervisor at the Dulles TRACON (radar) facility that FAA Indy Center has lost contact with AA Flight 77 and that others are trying to find the aircraft. They are instructed to look for "primary targets," radar returns of otherwise unidentified aircraft.[409]

9:21 a.m.: UA Flight 93, still flying normally, checks in with United Airlines. Capt. Jason Dahl is not yet in receipt of the ACARS warning. He sends a routine message to dispatcher Ed Ballinger:

---

405. NIST Chronology.

406. NIST Chronology.

407. "Twelfth Public Hearing," National Commission on Terrorist Attacks upon the United States, June 17, 2004, http://www.9-11commission.gov/archive/hearing12/9-11Commis sion_Hearing_2004-06-17.htm.

408. 9/11 Commission Memorandum for the Record, Interview Monte Belger, former Deputy Administrator of the Federal Aviation Administration, November 24, 2003.

409. 9/11 Commission Staff Report, August 26, 2004.

"Good mornin'. . . . Nice climb outta EWR [Newark IAP] After a nice
   tour of the APT Courts Y GRND CNTRL. . . . At 350 OCCL
   LT [occasional light] chop. Wind 290/50 ain't helping. J [Jason
   Dahl]."[410]

The pilot, Jason Dahl, is a friend of United dispatcher Ed Ballinger.[411]

9:21 a.m.: Port Authority orders all bridges and tunnels in the New York
area closed.

9:22 a.m.: UA Flight 175. United Airlines issues an advisory, under the
name of UAL Chief Operating Officer Andy Studdert, to all facilities,
including flight dispatchers, stating that UA Flight 175 has been involved in
an accident in New York City and that the crisis center had been activated.
Just prior to the Studdert advisory, United HQ begins lockout procedure to
restrict access to passenger and crew information about the flight.[412]
   United Airlines advisory: "There may be Addnl [additional] hijackings
in progress. You may want to advise your flts to stay on alert and shut down
all cockpit access Inflt [inflight] . . . per Mgmt."[413]

9:22 a.m.: UA Flight 93. First Officer LeRoy Homer receives an ACARS
message from United Airlines at the request of his wife, who is concerned about her husband after learning of the attacks on the World Trade
Center.[414]

9:22 a.m.: The NYPD requests mobilization of off-duty personnel.[415]

9:23 a.m.: President Bush talks over a secure phone with FBI Director
Mueller for one minute.[416]

---

410. National Park Service, Flight 93, September 11, 2001.
411. 9/11 Commission Staff Report, August 26, 2004.
412. 9/11 Commission Staff Report, August 26, 2004.
413. 9/11 Commission Staff Report, August 26, 2004.
414. 9/11 Commission Staff Report, August 26, 2004.
415. NIST Chronology.
416. Presidential Daily Diary, partially declassified.

Mueller is in his office at FBI headquarters on Pennsylvania Avenue. He has been on the job for less than a week.

Officers from CIA Counterterrorism Center are on their way to brief Mueller on the status of the USS *Cole* investigation—the attack on the Navy ship in Yemen in October 2000. The commander of the *Cole*, Navy Cdr. Kirk Lippold, is at the CIA, briefing the group on his experiences. The group was to have left for the FBI just as the planes hit the twin towers.[417]

9:23 a.m.: UA Flight 93. The United Airlines ACARS message warning transmitted at 9:19 a.m. is received (circa 9:23–9:24 a.m.): "Beware any cockpit intrusion—Two a/c [aircraft] hit World Trade Center."[418]

9:23 a.m.: At the World Trade Center, FDNY radio dispatcher advises that 100 people were dead or dying from fire, heat, and smoke on the northwest and southwest corners of the 103rd floor of the North Tower.[419]

9:23 a.m.: NPR's *Morning Edition* rebroadcast is interrupted, and Bob Edwards says that two planes have struck the World Trade Center; NPR begins its live coverage.

9:24 a.m.: AA Flight 77. FAA officially notifies NORAD NEADS concerning a suspected hijacking. FAA and NORAD establish an open line to discuss AA Flight 77 and other flights, separate from the multiagency conference call that the FAA is also participating in.[420]

NORAD later writes: "At 0924L it was reported to the operations floor from Boston Center that AA 11 had not impacted the WTC, but was still airborne enroute to Washington, DC (which later proved to be inaccurate). Simultaneously, there were indications of UAL 93 as a possible hijack in Ohio . . . and a reported 'third' hijacking. Numerous other uncorroborated reports were coming in that increased the likelihood that an attack would be

417. *The Great War of Our Time*, p. 49; *At the Center of the Storm*, p. 198.
418. 9/11 Commission Report, p. 11; 9/11 Commission Staff Report, August 26, 2004.
419. NIST Chronology.
420. FAA Chronology.

possible against Washington, so the 0924L [local time] report time is more accurately a general indication of a possible targeting of Washington."[421]

AA Flight 11 has, of course, already hit the North Tower and is probably confused with AA Flight 77, which the FAA had determined was a hijacking. There is no indication that UAL 93 had been hijacked by 9:24 a.m., so this NORAD summary prepared for the 9/11 Commission shows how confused the information was.

9:24 a.m.: NORAD orders three F-16 fighters to scramble from Langley AFB, Virginia (the planes are not airborne until 9:30 a.m.).[422] NORAD: "0924—Fargo alert fighters at Langley AFB scramble order."[423]

Fargo refers to the North Dakota Air National Guard Unit that was deployed at Langley AFB for rotational East Coast air defense duty.

Lt. Col. Nasypany, NEADS mission crew commander, issues an order to scramble alert F-16 fighters from Langley AFB. "The initial strategy of NEADS personnel was to use the alert fighters scrambled from Otis ANGB . . . [to] chase down Flight 11 [*sic*] if they could find the aircraft, and to vector the Langley fighters on a northerly heading to an area between the (reported) southbound Flight 11 and the nation's capital."[424]

AA Flight 11 has crashed into the World Trade Center 38 minutes earlier. Again NORAD confuses the two flights. The official DOD history states that "[Capt.] Leidig . . . [the DDO at the NMCC] rejected the erroneous FAA warning that [AA] Flight 11 was heading for Washington."[425]

"Now, NEADS was phoning Air Guard commanders across the Northeast, posing questions that hours earlier would have seemed ludicrous. Did the unit have available pilots? Mechanics? Crew chiefs? What could it get airborne in two hours? In 24 hours? In 48?"[426]

421. NORAD 9/11 Timeline, n.d., prepared for the 9/11 Commission.
422. Hart Seely, "Amid Crisis Simulation, 'We Were Suddenly No-Kidding Under Attack,'" Newhouse News Service, January 25, 2002.
423. NORAD 9/11 Timeline, n.d., prepared for the 9/11 Commission.
424. 9/11 Commission Staff Report, August 26, 2004.
425. Defense Studies Series, Pentagon 9/11.
426. Hart Seely, "Amid Crisis Simulation, 'We Were Suddenly No-Kidding Under Attack,'" Newhouse News Service, January 25, 2002.

9:24 a.m.: UA Flight 93, after reporting that it experiences some "light chop," is handed off from FAA New York to FAA Cleveland Center. "Good morning Cleveland, United ninety-three, three-five-oh [35,000 feet], intermittent light chop."[427]

The FAA later says that Cleveland Center did not respond to this initial transmission as the controller had 16 flights under his control and was issuing new routes to several aircraft based on the ground-stop decisions in New York and Boston.

9:24 a.m.: AA Flight 77. Though others now have reported a hijacking, FAA Great Lakes Regional Office passes information to FAA Washington Operations Center that AA Flight 77 has had a possible accident.[428]

9:24 a.m.: At the World Trade Center, FDNY radio communications reports that they have received a report from Morgan Stanley: "They've taken the brunt of the stuff. There are a lot of bodies." The Port Authority Police report that "other bodies are coming down and that people are on the street. There's a lot of debris."[429]

---

427. 9/11 Commission Staff Report, August 26, 2004; National Park Service, Flight 93, September 11, 2001.
428. 9/11 Commission Staff Report, August 26, 2004.
429. NIST Chronology.

CHAPTER 7

"AN APPARENT TERRORIST ATTACK ON OUR COUNTRY"

"I was sitting there thinking about it. It was a clear day, there was no weather problem—how in hell could a plane hit the World Trade Center?" That's what Vice President Cheney says was going through his mind as he sat at his desk, watching the television images of an airplane hitting the North Tower of the World Trade Center.

It was only after the second plane hit the South Tower, and when the first bits of information came in that another plane seemed to be heading toward Washington, DC, that it became clear to the experts—and then to the principals—that al Qaeda was behind the attack. The organization was barely known outside of specialist circles, and even there, many in Washington doubted Osama bin Laden's global reach and his conviction to attack the United States directly. But al Qaeda's signature had become the spectacular strike, not just in bombing two embassies in Africa (in August 1998) nearly simultaneously but also in attacking the Navy destroyer USS *Cole* (in October 2000).

Still unknown to the experts (and not known until well after 9/11) was Khalid Sheikh Mohammed (KSM), the mastermind of the 9/11 operation, a US-educated Pakistani national who conceived the idea of using airliners as missiles. His road to 9/11 was a long one. After the February 1993 garage-level bomb attack on the World Trade Center by Ramzi Yousef, KSM worked with the global fugitive in the Philippines to hone the plot. Their first iteration was sneaking a bomb onto a flight to test whether it could be remotely detonated. Then KSM conceived of a plot to blow up ten American-flagged airliners while they flew over the Pacific Ocean. That idea then shifted to hijacking and landing in the United States, with KSM himself announcing that the country was under attack. Osama bin Laden took on sponsorship of the plot, and he wanted the planes to attack a combination of financial, governmental, and military targets. Though four viable pilots were eventually found to carry out the attacks, KSM's ambitions were endless—had he been able to find more pilots and planes, there would have been attacks on the CIA, the Saudi embassy in Washington, and even a nuclear power plant.

Though US intelligence didn't yet know who KSM was—how important he was within al Qaeda—it would be wrong to say that they didn't "know" or that they could never have imagined such a plan, as many government and intelligence officials would later insist. For one, the World Trade Center had already been attacked. And from the Philippines plotting, one of KSM and Ramzi Yousef's accomplices who was apprehended told the FBI not only that he had completed flight school in the United States but also that he had been given the assignment of flying a plane into the CIA. Two "known" al Qaeda terrorists were in San Diego, and one of them even took a flight out of the United States and then returned in July 2001 at the very time when the intelligence community was looking for him. So despite all the later blame on legal or policy impediments to counterterrorism, this was not just a failure of imagination or to "connect the dots." It was a matter of not appreciating how far the enemy was willing to go.

One figure from that day who understood the threat is the Clinton administration's counterterrorism "tsar" Richard Clarke, a holdover from the previous White House. He insists that he tried to warn the Bush principals and, indeed, the evidence confirms that he and CIA Director George Tenet tried—until they had made themselves irritants and were told either to get with the new program or be ignored. Clarke's is the quintessential Washington story of success in failure: he became a kind of hero afterward because he was willing to apologize to the American people. In the end, though, whatever intuition or fear he possessed before 9/11, none of it was adequately conveyed to those who mattered. Perhaps Washington culture—the undifferentiated medley of warnings and other threats that DC subsists on—was the ultimate reason the Bush principals were so disbelieving and unprepared. But in the intelligence community at least, and among the counterterrorism specialists, there are no heroes.

9:25 a.m.: (Approximate time) Vice President Cheney is in his West Wing office, watching television, when Secret Service agents decide to evacuate him.

Cheney watches the attack on the North Tower. (Source: National Archives)

At 9:25 the Secret Service JOC broadcasts an alert about "unidentified aircraft coming toward the White House." Cheney's detail decides to move him to a safer location, the so-called ZP shelter tunnel, an underground area in the "ZP" basement level of the White House, a makeshift bomb shelter and the blast door entrance to the tunnel that goes farther onward to the underground Presidential Emergency Operations Center (PEOC) located beneath the East Wing.[430]

9:25 a.m.: Otis-based F-15 fighters arrive over Manhattan for the first time.[431]

Though the planes have arrived over New York City, the pilots have no orders of what to do except to find and escort errant planes, now many fewer in the skies due to ground stoppages and movements of planes out of the area.

---

430. Secret Service, "Actions of TSD Related to Terrorist Incident," partially declassified; Secret Service, Interview with ATSAIC Scott Johnson and SA James Scott, October 1, 2001, partially declassified.

431. 9/11 Commission Staff Report, August 26, 2004.

9:25 a.m.: FAA orders a "nationwide ground stop," an order that bans takeoffs of all civilian aircraft regardless of destination—a national ground stop. The order is actually transmitted at 9:30 a.m.

9:25 a.m.: AA Flight 77. Dulles Tower observes a primary radar target tracking eastbound at a high rate of speed (later confirmed to be AA Flight 77) between 9:25 and 9:30 a.m.[432]

9:25 a.m.: UA Flight 93 again routinely radios FAA Cleveland Center, checking in at 35,000.[433]

9:25 a.m.: At the World Trade Center, the FDNY advises that people are now trapped in World Trade Center Building 5 (WTC 5).[434]

9:25 a.m.: The Secret Service establishes an open line with FAA Presidential Operations.[435]

9:25 a.m.: The WHSR initiates an interagency teleconference of deputies. With the official title of Special Adviser for Cyberspace Security, Richard Clarke says he chaired the conference. He was at a conference in the Ronald Reagan Building three blocks from the White House when the North Tower was hit. He returns to the WHSR, where he joins Franklin Miller, another NSC senior staffer.[436]

Logs indicate that the video teleconference began at 9:25 a.m. and included the FBI; the Departments of State, Justice, and Defense; and the White House "shelter" where Vice President Cheney was located (the

---

432. 9/11 Commission Staff Report, August 26, 2004. At the same time, FAA Air Traffic Control System Command Center (Herndon) advises FAA headquarters that AA Flight 77 is lost in Indy Center's airspace, that it could not be located on radar.

433. National Park Service, Flight 93, September 11, 2001.

434. NIST Chronology.

435. "The Secret Service timeline reflects an open line with FAA Presidential Operations was also established." 9/11 Commission, Memorandum for the Record, n.d., 2012-042-doc24, partially declassified.

436. Richard A. Clarke, *Against All Enemies: Inside America's War on Terror* (New York: Free Press, 2004), p. 1.

PEOC is not yet occupied).[437] The WHSR conference is unable to link directly with an FAA representative until 9:40; instead, it receives information on the air situation from the Pentagon or NORAD.[438] The CIA also does not join until 9:40 a.m.

The WHSR deputies conference is one of a number of government-wide national security teleconferences that will convene on 9/11. The 9/11 Commission later says: "While important . . . [the teleconference convened at the WHSR] had no immediate effect on the emergency defense efforts," that is, it was not part of any decision-making.[439] Information from the WHSR is passed to the PEOC, where Vice President Cheney is the penultimate decision maker.

9:26 a.m.: The Secret Service orders the evacuation of the Eisenhower Executive Office Building adjacent to the White House. It reports in its logs that "all personnel were departing the building in an orderly but expeditious fashion."[440]

Special Agent Truscott, on his way to the "shelter tunnel" where Vice President Cheney is being held, meets Condoleezza Rice in the WHSR, and he accompanies her to the shelter tunnel as well.[441]

By Rice's account, "the Secret Service came and said, 'Dr. Rice, you must go to the bunker. Now! Planes are hitting buildings all over Washington. The White House has got to be next.'"[442]

---

437. 9/11 Commission Report, p. 38.

438. "Unable to link directly with [the FAA in] Herndon, and getting little operational information from FAA headquarters, the [White House] Sit Room relied on the North American Aerospace Defense Command and the Pentagon's command center for details." Michael K. Bohn, "Former Staffers Remember the White House Situation Room on 9/11," McClatchy Newspapers, August 29, 2011.

439. "Twelfth Public Hearing," National Commission on Terrorist Attacks upon the United States, June 17, 2004, http://www.9-11commission.gov/archive/hearing12/9-11Commis sion_Hearing_2004-06-17.htm.

440. Secret Service, "Actions of TSD Related to Terrorist Incident," partially declassified.

441. Secret Service, Memorandum, Interview with SAIC Carl Truscott, October 1, 2001, partially declassified.

442. *No Higher Honor*, p. 72.

9:26 a.m.: FAA Cleveland Center engages in conversations with several aircraft about the prospects for additional flights to be allowed to land in Philadelphia.[443]

9:26 a.m.: UA Flight 93. Capt. Jason Dahl asks for confirmation of the ACARS warning message he received at 9:24 a.m.: "Ed confirm latest mssg plz—Jason."[444]

Two minutes later, the hijackers will begin their takeover of the plane.

9:26 a.m.: At the World Trade Center, NYPD says emergency units are set up at Vesey and West Streets and are prepared to enter the towers.[445]

9:27 a.m.: NORAD's situational awareness is summarized on the NEADS watch floor as follows: "Three planes unaccounted for. American Airlines 11 [sic] may still be airborne . . . United 175 to the World Trade Center. We're not sure who the other one is."[446]

9:28 a.m.: UA Flight 93 is hijacked. While traveling at 35,000 feet above eastern Ohio, UA Flight 93 suddenly drops 685 feet. Eleven seconds into the descent, FAA Cleveland Center receives the first of two radio transmissions from the aircraft. During the first broadcast, the captain or first officer can be heard declaring "Mayday!" amid the sounds of a physical struggle in the cockpit. FAA Cleveland Center replies over the radio: "Somebody call Cleveland?" There is no reply.

9:28:19 a.m.: Radio transmission of unintelligible sounds of possible screaming or a struggle from an unknown origin is heard over the FAA Cleveland Center radio.

---

443. 9/11 Commission Staff Report, August 26, 2004.
444. 9/11 Commission Report, p. 10. 9/11 Commission Staff Report, August 26, 2004, says 9:27 a.m.
445. NIST Chronology.
446. 9/11 Commission Staff Report, August 26, 2004.

A second radio transmission, 35 seconds later, indicates that the fight is continuing. The captain or first officer can be heard shouting: "Hey, get out of here—get out of here—get out of here."

9:28:54 a.m.: Second radio transmission, mostly unintelligible, again with sounds of possible screaming or a struggle and a statement, "Get out of here, get out of here!"

The hijackers wield knives (reported by at least five callers); engage in violence, including stabbing (reported by at least four callers and indicated by the sounds of the cockpit struggle transmitted over the radio); relocate the passengers to the back of the plane (reported by at least two callers); threaten use of a bomb, either real or fake (reported by at least three callers); and engage in deception about their intentions (as indicated by the hijackers' radio transmission received by FAA air traffic control).[447]

The FBI later discovers that a passenger aboard the flight left a voice mail on his home number at about the time that the flight had been hijacked and said that "they have a bomb."[448]

9:28 a.m.: At the World Trade Center, there are reports that a third hijacked airliner is approaching New York City, briefly disrupting rescue efforts.

9:29 a.m.: President Bush leaves the holding room at Emma E. Booker Elementary School to go to the media center to give a public statement.[449]

9:29 a.m.: AA Flight 77. The autopilot is disengaged. The flight is now flying at 7,000 feet and is approximately 38 miles west of Washington.[450]

9:29 a.m.: UA Flight 93. FAA Cleveland Center pings UA Flight 93: "United ninety-three, verify three-five-zero [35,000 feet]." There is no reply.

447. 9/11 Commission Report, p. 11; 9/11 Commission Staff Report, August 26, 2004.

448. FBI Working Draft Chronology. The passenger's name has been deleted from the Chronology for privacy reasons.

449. Presidential Daily Diary, partially declassified.

450. 9/11 Commission Report, p. 9; 9/11 Commission Staff Report, August 26, 2004.

At 9:29:50 a.m., Cleveland Center begins moving other aircraft away from UA Flight 93 due to the lack of acknowledgment of any radio transmissions. Several other aircraft on the frequency confirm unusual sounds of an unknown origin heard over the radio.

Cleveland Center makes several attempts to contact UA Flight 93 but receives no acknowledgment.

9:29 a.m.: At the World Trade Center, casualty collection points are established at West and Vesey Streets. The FDNY recalls off-duty firefighters.[451]

9:30 a.m.: President Bush makes his first statement on the attack on the World Trade Center.

Remarks by the President after Two Planes Crash into World Trade Center

Ladies and gentlemen, this is a difficult moment for America. I, unfortunately, will be going back to Washington after my remarks. Secretary Rod Paige and the Lt. Governor will take the podium and discuss education. I do want to thank the folks here at Booker Elementary School for their hospitality.

Today we've had a national tragedy. Two airplanes have crashed into the World Trade Center in an apparent terrorist attack on our country. I have spoken to the Vice President, to the Governor of New York, to the Director of the FBI, and have ordered that the full resources of the federal government go to help the victims and their families, and to conduct a full-scale investigation to hunt down and to find those folks who committed this act.

Terrorism against our nation will not stand.

And now if you would join me in a moment of silence. May God bless the victims, their families, and America. Thank you very much.

Rice later writes: "Looking back, I can see that the first statement by the President, which Karen Hughes cobbled together with Ari Fleischer, was neither informative nor reassuring. But at the time no one wanted to say too much or too little about what might happen next."[452]

---

451. NIST Chronology.
452. *No Higher Honor*, p. 75.

President George W. Bush delivers remarks from Emma E. Booker Elementary School in Sarasota, Florida, at 9:30 a.m., September 11, 2001, following terrorist attacks on the World Trade Center. (Source: George W. Bush Presidential Library and Museum / Eric Draper [P7058-31A])

9:30 a.m.: At about this time, at 9:30 a.m., President Bush speaks privately with Condoleezza Rice.[453]

At the White House, inside the shelter tunnel, "Cheney and the [Secret Service] agents paused in an area of the [ZP] tunnel that had a secure phone, a bench, and television."[454]

Truscott, the Secret Service chief at the White House, arrives at the ZP shelter tunnel. There are about 10 people present, including Cheney and Rice. The vice president is completing a call "at the base of the stairs," and

453. No such conversation is listed in the Presidential Daily Diary, partially declassified. Rice, in *No Higher Honor*, conflates a number of her conversations with the president and other times, saying that she talked to the president after the Pentagon was hit, which would have been after 9:30 a.m. The diary lists a conversation at 9:40 a.m., on his way to the airport. Michael Morell (*The Great War of Our Time*, p. 49) also says that the president spoke to Rice at 9:30 a.m.

454. 9/11 Commission Report, pp. 39–40.

upon completion of the call, Truscott requests that the group proceed down the tunnel to the PEOC underneath the East Wing of the White House.[455]

9:30 a.m.: At the World Trade Center, telephone calls from the upper floors of the North Tower cease as smoke and fire overtakes those in the interior. An assistant fire chief makes the decision that the building is no longer safe. Most of the evacuees from below the impact zone have now evacuated.[456]

9:30 a.m.: AA Flight 77. On the floor at NORAD NEADS, the ID technicians continued to attempt to locate AA Flight 11, mistaking it for AA Flight 77.[457]

At the NMCC, the Significant Event Conference log states that the DDO summarizes the situation: "2 aircraft into WTC; also been 1 aircraft confirmed hijacking—AA11. It's just been confirmed that the aircraft is still airborne and heading to DC. Is FAA in the conference?"[458]

Gen. Myers later writes that "a communications glitch mak[es] it impossible to speak directly to the Federal Aviation Administration on the secure conference call."[459]

At the Pentagon and NORAD, there is still confusion between the two American Airlines flights, undoubtedly caused by (or at least made worse by) poor direct communications between the FAA and the Defense Department.

9:30 a.m.: Air Force F-16 fighters out of Langley AFB, Virginia, are airborne.[460]

Lt. Col. Kevin J. Nasypany, NEADS MCC, says "the fighters were given a 010 [north] heading even though they scrambled to a 090 for 60 [east] heading. . . . He commented that the traffic at Norfolk Approach would explain the initial trajectory, but once it became clear the fighters were out of Norfolk

---

455. Secret Service, "Actions of TSD Related to Terrorist Incident," partially declassified.
456. NIST Chronology.
457. 9/11 Commission Staff Report, August 26, 2004; NORAD 9/11 Timeline, n.d., prepared for the 9/11 Commission.
458. Air Threat Conference Call log, "DJH Notes," Top Secret, partially declassified.
459. *Eyes on the Horizon*, p. 153.
460. According to radar data collected by NORAD and local base air traffic control.

Approach air traffic the NEADS Weapons desk noticed the fighters were not turning per the scramble order, and became immediately involved."[461]

`9:30 a.m.:` FAA Herndon Command Center issues Advisory 031 concerning the nationwide ground stop.[462]

The "nationwide ground stop" order is promulgated via radio and ACARS messages, with US airlines directing their flights to land. Some 120 inbound overseas flights are diverted to Canada.[463]

`9:30 a.m.:` UA Flight 93. FAA informs United Airlines headquarters that UA Flight 93 is not responding to attempted radio contacts.

FAA Cleveland Center begins to poll the other flights in the vicinity to determine if they heard the screaming on board UA Flight 93; several said they had.

`9:30 a.m.:` The New York Stock Exchange does not open at its scheduled time; its employees in the building evacuate.

`9:31:57 a.m.:` UA Flight 93. A third radio transmission, mostly unintelligible, sounding like an individual out of breath, with more unintelligible words and what sounds like "bomb on board," is heard at FAA Cleveland Center.

United Airlines sends two ACARS text messages to the flight asking it to establish radio contact with air traffic control. There is no response to these or any subsequent ACARS messages.[464]

`9:31 a.m.:` FAA DC log: "Military working on setting up COMM war room,"[465] hoping to improve communications.

---

461. 9/11 Commission Memorandum for the Record, Interview with NEADS Alpha Flight Mission Crew Commander (MCC), Lt. Col. Kevin J. Nasypany, January 22, 2004, and January 23, 2004.

462. FAA Chronology.

463. Roger A. Mola, "Shutdown of National Airspace System Was 'Organized Mayhem,'" AIN Online, October 8, 2007.

464. 9/11 Commission Staff Report, August 26, 2004.

465. DCC Timeline.

9:31 a.m.: At the World Trade Center, FDNY receives reports of a third plane incoming and threatening, again temporarily disrupting rescue efforts.[466]

9:32 a.m.: President Bush gets into his limousine to drive to the Sarasota-Bradenton Airport and Air Force One, roaring down Route 41. White House Chief of Staff Andrew Card accompanies him in his limo. It is a 13-minute drive.[467]

9:32 a.m.: UA Flight 93. The flight is now 30 miles east of "Dryer" remote communications outlet (RCO) (a ground communications transceiver) in Ohio, with hijacker pilot Ziad Jarrah evidently in control in the cockpit four minutes after the hijacking begins. Jarrah attempts to make the following announcement to the passengers: "Ladies and gentlemen: Here the captain, please sit down; keep remaining sitting. We have a bomb on board. So, sit."[468]

FAA Cleveland Center overhears the transmission.[469]

The cockpit voice recorder also indicates that a woman, most likely a flight attendant, is being held captive in the cockpit. At 9:32:31, a fourth radio transmission from an unknown origin, "Did you hear that transmission that reported a bomb on board?" is heard over the Cleveland Center radio. Moments after hearing the transmission, Cleveland Center reports to FAA Herndon Command Center that the flight may have a bomb on board.

United Airlines dispatcher Ed Ballinger begins sending a new set of ACARS messages to flights ("High security alert. Secure cockpit."). This communication is transmitted to now-hijacked UA Flight 93 at 9:33 a.m.[470]

---

466. FDNY Report; NIST Chronology.

467. Presidential Daily Diary, partially declassified.

468. 9/11 Commission Report, p. 12.

469. "FAA DC logs (at 1332Z): "On National Telcon ZOB [Cleveland Center] reports that UAL 93 may have a bomb on board. UAL 93 is out of EWR-SFO. He is 30 East of DJB. ZOB does have a transponder and is in radar contact. DCC asked why ZOB believes there is a bomb on board. ZOB responds that this is what he is screaming on the frequency." DCC Timeline.

470. 9/11 Commission Staff Report, August 26, 2004.

9:32 a.m.: At the World Trade Center, because elevators are ceasing operations in the North Tower and because of extensive flooding in the concourse, orders are given for all units to come down to the lobby. No response is received from this order; it is either unheard or ignored.

Firefighter Danny Suhr is killed soon after his Brooklyn Engine Company 216 arrives at the scene, hit by a person who jumps from the South Tower.[471]

---

471. NIST Chronology.

CHAPTER 8

WASHINGTON ATTACKED

Was the White House or the US Capitol the target for UA Flight 93? There is much speculation about the destination of the flight that crashed near Shanksville, Pennsylvania. The consensus now seems to be, based on subsequent intelligence and the interrogations of al Qaeda planners, that it was the Capitol building.[472]

To this day, though, 9/11 holds some mysteries as to what might have been targeted, as to what al Qaeda wanted, what Khalid Sheikh Mohammed communicated to Mohammed Atta, what Atta himself wanted, what he thought most possible in terms of the location of the target or the flying skills of the pilots, and perhaps even what Atta personally wanted (i.e., to die together with Marwan al-Shehhi, the hijacker pilot of the plane that hit the South Tower). After he was captured, Khalid Sheikh Mohammed told interrogators that he was surprised that the South Tower was hit and that the White House was intended to be the fourth target. We also know that in an intercepted call between Atta and Ramzi bin al-Shibh—the intended fourth pilot, also now a prisoner at Guantanamo—the two spoke (in code) about the four impending targets: the North Tower, the Pentagon, the White House, and the Capitol.

If only the North Tower had been hit, it might not have collapsed entirely. We know that the fire, fuel, debris, and heat from the two towers combined to weaken both structures, leading to their collapse. The combination effect is seen most clearly in the collapse of 7 World Trade Center, a third building in the World Trade Center that wasn't directly hit. That's how intense the conflagration from the two strikes was.

---

472. Michael Morell, in *The Great War of Our Time* (p. 52), says the US Capitol building definitively.

And imagine, too, what would have happened if the White House were attacked: not just the deaths that would have occurred or how many would have been saved at the World Trade Center but also what the aftermath and recovery to the country would have been like if that symbolic building had been destroyed.

We don't know the reason for Atta's decision to substitute the South Tower instead of the White House. We do know that Atta and Marwan al-Shehhi visited Washington, scouting the Pentagon, White House, and Capitol. Intelligence and FBI experts who have dealt with the reconstruction of the plot, and who are familiar with Atta's thinking through the interrogations of KSM and Ramzi Bin al-Shibh, think that there is so much more to the story, particularly in the relationship of the two (that they were inseparable) and that perhaps they defied al Qaeda because they wanted to die together.[473]

We will probably never have a complete accounting of the attackers' motives and decision-making: 20 years later we still do not truly know who these men were or what drove them to take their own lives on behalf of a cause and their beliefs. A lot of bitter condemnation was directed at them. Aside from simply labeling them as "evil," voices in the media declared that they were bad Muslims and even bad pilots—the stories abounded of what bad students the hijacker pilots were, of how their teachers thought they weren't qualified to fly airliners. Yet, when Hani Hanjour steered American Airlines Flight 77 into the Pentagon, he executed an almost 360-degree turn over the Potomac River and then brought the plane in at 530 miles per hour, flying in at treetop level and hitting the west face of the Pentagon just at the ground level. The force of that attack pushed through three of the building's five concentric rings (each separated by large air shafts), causing the entire structure to collapse. It was a newly renovated "wedge," and the only reason more people were not killed was that it was partly occupied. The shock of the Pentagon itself being attacked was lasting. And perhaps, in the anger and indignation that Washington was itself attacked, we lost the will to understand the reasons why.

9:32 a.m.: (Approximate time) AA Flight 77. Dulles Terminal Radar Approach Control (TRACON) "observed a primary radar target tracking

---

473. I explore Mohammed Atta's motivations and the reason why the South Tower was ultimately chosen as a target of attack in *History in One Act: A Novel of 9/11.*

eastbound at a high rate of speed" and notifies National Airport of an approaching aircraft.[474]

9:33 a.m.: AA Flight 77. "At 9:33 the Ronald Reagan Washington National Airport [DCA] tower [through an internal DC-only 'hotline'] passes to the Secret Service that 'an aircraft [is] coming at you and not talking with us.'"

DCA tower logs: "IAD controller advises DCA controller on 462 line that there is a primary target 10 west of DCA heading for P56, fast moving. Subsequently, DCA has radar contact on fast moving target."[475]

"The Dulles Tower Operations Supervisor also provides continuous updates on the 'critical event' teleconference established at FAA Headquarters."[476]

9:33 a.m.: Vice President Cheney enters the PEOC, a bunker deep underneath the east wing of the White House; the Secret Service is now concerned that the building might be directly targeted as a result of the tip-off of the fast-moving target.

There is much confusion about when Cheney actually enters the PEOC, but the best evidence indicates it is at 9:33 a.m.[477] The 9/11 Commission conflates the ZP shelter, the basement holding area and the "tunnel" leading to the PEOC, with the bunker itself and states that the vice president entered the "underground tunnel" at 9:37 a.m.[478] It is possible that Cheney was in the ZP shelter tunnel and in the staff area outside the PEOC until 9:58 a.m. and that even many of those inside the White House were unaware that there were separate facilities.

474. 9/11 Commission Report, p. 9; 9/11 Commission Staff Report, August 26, 2004.

475. Department of Transportation/FAA Report of Aircraft Accident, ZDC-ARTCC-212, AAL 77, Washington National (DCA) ATCT, November 13, 2001.

476. Defense Studies Series, Pentagon 9/11.

477. Secret Service, "Actions of TSD Related to Terrorist Incident," partially declassified. The White House PEOC shelter log places Vice President Cheney in the shelter at 9:58 a.m., 25 minutes later. See 9/11 Commission, MFR, "Status of WH 'Day of' Investigation," March 2, 2004.

478. 9/11 Commission Report, pp. 39–40.

A military officer describes the "shelter" as plain and functional, with a large conference room at its center and living accommodations for the chief executive off to one side. Adjacent to it, and accessed from a separate entrance, is the emergency apparatus of the White House Military Office, a 30-by-20-foot operations center with desks, computers, telephones, and televisions.[479]

In the PEOC, an operations section day shift is on duty. This includes a White House communications team and various military officers of the White House Military Office and the National Security Council (NSC) staff who had gone to the PEOC bunker after the Pentagon was hit and who serve as a literal go-between with the WHSR overhead.[480]

Among those who will join Cheney in the PEOC during the day at various times are the following:

- Condoleezza Rice
- Stephen Hadley[481]
- I. Lewis "Scooter" Libby
- David Addington
- Eric Edelman
- Mary Matalin
- Josh Bolten
- Lawrence Lindsey
- Tucker Eskew
- Nick Calio
- Secretary of Transportation Norman Mineta[482]

---

479. Lt. Col. Robert J. Darling, USMC (Ret.), *24 Hours Inside the President's Bunker: 9-11-01 The White House* (Bloomington, IN: iUniverse, 2010), pp. 49–50.

480. See, in particular, the account of one WHMO Marine Corps officer, Lt. Col. Robert J. Darling, in *24 Hours Inside the President's Bunker*.

481. Hadley stays in the WHSR for most of the day, going to the PEOC later in the afternoon or evening.

482. *No Higher Honor*, p. 70; Barton Gellman, *Angler: The Cheney Vice Presidency* (New York: Penguin, 2009), pp. 116–118; Dick Cheney, *In My Time: A Personal and Political Memoir* (New York: Threshold, 2011), pp. 1–10; Robert Draper, *Dead Certain: The Presidency of George W. Bush* (New York: Free Press, 2007), p. 139; *A Pretext for War*, p. 46.

Cheney says that at one point, the oxygen in the overcrowded bunker drops to such a dangerous level that all but the most essential senior officials are asked to leave.[483]

When he first arrives at the PEOC, Cheney asks to speak to the president, but he cannot be immediately connected.[484] Secret Service White House Chief Truscott opens a line of communication from the PEOC with the Secret Service director, located in the director's crisis center across town. The Secret Service says: "For several hours . . . security issues were passed from SAIC Truscott through the Vice President to the President."[485]

What orders were passed from Bush to Cheney through this channel remain a mystery. Clearly the Secret Service's direct channel to the president's protective detail in Sarasota, on Air Force One, and then later at the Barksdale and Offutt AFBs was used to discuss COG and other security decisions.

Cheney says, "The two sort of major concerns that occupied most of our time . . . getting all the airplanes down out of the sky and the other was guaranteeing that there would be somebody in the line of succession in a position to be able to take over." Subsequently, Cheney says that he makes sure that he, Bush, and the third in line to the presidency, then–Speaker of the House Dennis Hastert, are all in secure locations and never together.[486]

9:33 a.m.: NORAD calls for an Air Threat Conference Call, and the NMCC concurs, transitioning the Significant Event Conference to an Air Threat Conference.[487]

---

483. Stephen F. Hayes, *Cheney: The Untold Story of America's Most Powerful and Controversial Vice President* (New York: HarperCollins, 2007), p. 343; *No Higher Honor*, p. 75.

484. 9/11 Commission Report, pp. 39–40.

485. Secret Service, Memorandum, Interview with SAIC Carl Truscott, October 1, 2001, partially declassified.

486. "9/11 Tenth Anniversary Interview with Former Vice President Cheney," AP, September 9, 2011.

487. 9/11 Air Threat Conference Call Transcription, partially declassified; 9/11 Commission, Memorandum for the Record, n.d., 2012-042-doc24, partially declassified. The Air Threat Conference Call log states: "NORAD proceeding w/ air threat conference." At 9:34 a.m., the SEIC was dropped.

Capt. Leidig, the DDO in the NMCC, says he thought an Air Threat Conference had "cold war implications and brought a different group of people to a conference," including nuclear commands.[488]

Air Threat Conference Call log: "Two Otis fighters airborne and awaiting tasking; concern that hijacked is still airborne heading toward DC."[489]

NORAD reports that there is a KC-135 aerial tanker airborne out of Bangor, Maine, and a second tanker out of McGuire AFB, New Jersey, to refuel fighter interceptors in the air.[490]

9:34 a.m.: President Bush telephones Vice President Cheney from his limousine, but the call cannot be completed.[491]

9:34 a.m.: AA Flight 77 turns south toward Alexandria, Virginia, and then circles back to the northeast, making a 330-degree right turn west-south-west of the Pentagon.[492]

"DCA Tower Controllers visually observe the fast-moving target, a B757, completing a right 360 turn just south of the Pentagon. Subsequently, IAD Controller informs IAD Operations Supervisor, whom in turn advises the DCA Operations Supervisor. The DCA Operations Supervisor advised the United States Secret Service (USSS) via the 'Hotline' of the aircraft."[493]

At the same time, FAA advises NORAD NEADS that AA Flight 77 is missing, the first notice to the military that AA Flight 77 was missing,[494] just minutes before it hits the Pentagon.

---

488. 9/11 Commission Memorandum for the Record, Interview, Captain Charles Joseph Leidig, USN, April 29, 2004.

489. Air Threat Conference Call log, "DJH Notes," Top Secret, partially declassified.

490. 9/11 Air Threat Conference Call Transcription, partially declassified.

491. Presidential Daily Diary, partially declassified.

492. 9/11 Commission Staff Report, August 26, 2004; Defense Studies Series, Pentagon 9/11.

493. Department of Transportation/FAA Report of Aircraft Accident, ZDC-ARTCC-212, AAL 77, Washington National (DCA) ATCT, November 13, 2001.

494. NORAD NEADS only finds out about AA Flight 77 when a technician makes a call to inquire about AA Flight 11. If NEADS had not placed that call, they would have received no information whatsoever that the flight was even missing, although the FAA had been searching for it. The NEADS identification technician—who, at 9:21 a.m., had been told by FAA Boston Center that AA Flight 11 was still airborne and heading south—contacted the operations manager at FAA Washington Center to provide an update on the evolving

NORAD: "0934—FAA reports AA 77 'lost.'"[495]

9:34 a.m.: UA Flight 93. FAA Herndon Command Center relays reports it has received on the UA Flight 93 hijacking to FAA HQ.[496]

Between 9:34 a.m. and 9:38 a.m., FAA Cleveland Center observes UA Flight 93 climbing to 40,700 feet and moves several aircraft out of its way. The Center continues to try to contact UA Flight 93 and asks whether the pilot can confirm that he has been hijacked. There is no response. As the flight continues to climb and turn to the southeast, Cleveland Center moves to clear other flights in the sector out of the way.[497]

9:35 a.m.: In Sarasota, White House staffers traveling with President Bush leave the Emma E. Booker School in five armored Secret Service cars and Suburban support vehicles. The Secret Service tells the staff that the motorcade will wait for no one.[498]

In the vans are senior staffers Karl Rove, Harriet Miers, Dan Bartlett, Ari Fleischer, Gordon Johndroe, Navy Capt. Deborah Loewer, Brig. Gen. Mark Rosenker (director of the White House Military Office), CIA officer Michael Morell (Bush's intelligence briefer), and two military aides to the president, one a Marine Corps officer who will soon be replaced by Lt. Col. Thomas Gould.[499]

---

situation. In the course of the conversation, the operations manager informs NEADS that AA Flight 77 was lost. 9/11 Commission Staff Report, August 26, 2004. According to the Air Force: "Less than four minutes before American Airlines Flight 77 crashed into the Pentagon, the FAA told the NEADS air defenders that the flight was missing." See *The First 109 Minutes: 9/11 and the US Air Force*, 2011.

495. NORAD 9/11 Timeline, n.d., prepared for the 9/11 Commission.

496. 9/11 Commission Staff Report, August 26, 2004.

497. 9/11 Commission Staff Report, August 26, 2004.

498. *The Great War of Our Time*, p. 50.

499. One interesting fact is that Gould was actually off duty that day. The five aides leapfrog, some heading to a site of a future visit. A Marine Corps officer who had scouted Florida locales for the presidential visit was the aide during Bush's time at the school. See Janene Scully, "Vandenberg Officer at Bush's Side During Attacks," *Santa Maria Times*, September 11, 2011.

Representatives Dan Miller and Adam Putnam of adjacent Sarasota districts are also with the traveling party, as is Matt Kirk, the White House congressional liaison.[500]

9:35 a.m.: AA Flight 77. NORAD: "0935–0940: Discussion between NEADS ID and FAA (Indy Center) about location of AA [Flight] 77."[501]

9:35 a.m.: UA Flight 93 flight attendant is heard over the radio pleading for her life. "I don't want to die. I don't want to die. I don't want to die."[502]

9:35 a.m.: At the World Trade Center, the NYPD orders no roof rescue to be attempted. The mayor's office reports that there is another plane in the area.[503]

9:36 a.m.: AA Flight 77. National Airport Tower asks an Air National Guard C-130H aircraft (GOPHR06) that had departed Andrews AFB en route to Minnesota to ID an unknown airplane flying near the Pentagon in Washington airspace. The C-130H pilot is able to identify the suspicious aircraft as a commercial Boeing 757.[504] Secret Service is advised.[505]

9:36 a.m.: NORAD NEADS MCC Lt. Col. Nasypany "directs that fighters airborne from Langley go straight to Washington; based on aircraft reported 6 miles west of White House."[506]

FAA Boston Center tells NORAD NEADS: "Latest report. Aircraft VFR [Visual Flight Rules, that is, observed] six miles southeast of the White House. . . . Six, southwest. Six, southwest of the White House, deviating away."[507]

500. *24 Hours Inside the President's Bunker*, p. 35; "Voices of 9-11: 'A Cacophony of Information,'" *National Journal*, August 31, 2002.

501. NORAD 9/11 Timeline, n.d., prepared for the 9/11 Commission.

502. National Park Service, Flight 93, September 11, 2001.

503. NIST Chronology.

504. 9/11 Commission Staff Report, August 26, 2004.

505. Department of Transportation/FAA Report of Aircraft Accident, ZDC-ARTCC-212, AAL 77, Washington National (DCA) ATCT, November 13, 2001.

506. NORAD 9/11 Timeline, n.d., prepared for the 9/11 Commission.

507. NORAD 9/11 Timeline, n.d., prepared for the 9/11 Commission; 9/11 Commission Staff Report, August 26, 2004.

Shortly afterward, Lt. Col. Nasypany discovers, to his surprise, that the Langley-based fighters have not headed north as the scramble order had instructed but instead went east over the ocean. His response is emotional: "I don't care how many windows you break," he says he ordered the unit. "Damn it. . . . Okay. Push them back."[508]

It is at this point that Lt. Col. Nasypany orders "AFIO" (Authorization for Interceptor Operations).[509]

AFIO is a term used when military aircraft invoke the right to deviate from ATC clearances to intercept targets of interest. Upon declaring AFIO, NORAD assumes responsibility for the interceptor to see all known aircraft and avoid any interfering civilian flight paths to ensure safe intercept conduct. FAA still provides traffic advisories to nearby aircraft.

9:36 a.m.: UA Flight 93 alters course to the southeast (from radar data).[510]

FAA Cleveland Center advises FAA Herndon Command Center that they are still tracking UA Flight 93 and inquire specifically whether someone has requested the military to launch fighter aircraft to intercept. They add that they are prepared to contact a nearby military base to request fighter aircraft assistance. Herndon Center tells Cleveland Center that FAA personnel above them in the chain of command have requested military assistance.[511]

The first discussions of the hijacking of UA Flight 93 take place in NORAD channels after this point.[512]

---

508. 9/11 Commission Staff Report, August 26, 2004. Another version is as follows: He then orders the fighters to proceed directly toward Washington, DC: "Okay, we're going to turn it . . . crank it up. . . . Run them [the fighters] to the White House." See NORAD 9/11 Timeline, n.d., prepared for the 9/11 Commission.

509. NORAD 9/11 Timeline, n.d., prepared for the 9/11 Commission; 9/11 Commission Staff Report, August 26, 2004.

510. NORAD 9/11 Timeline, n.d., prepared for the 9/11 Commission.

511. 9/11 Commission Staff Report, August 26, 2004.

512. NORAD states: "0916–0922: NEADS Commander stated, 'The time that the FAA notified NEADS of the hijacking of UAL 93 is described as being unknown, part of open line conversations with the FAA that were established while discussing AA 77. Some briefings describe the time that the UAL 93 hijacking was announced as being 0916L [this is impossible]. Any of these times are educated guesses based upon the wide range of information, most of it inaccurate, which was coming into NEADS at the time. The Mission Crew Commander log describes hijacking information at 0916L, but further research indicates

Also at 9:36 a.m., the United Airlines manager of flight dispatch operations advises United dispatcher Ed Ballinger that UA Flight 93 is "off track, heading for DC." By this point, United headquarters believes the aircraft has been hijacked. Another UAL dispatcher, assisting Ballinger, sends an ACARS message to Flight 93, asking, "How's the wx [weather]? Can dispatch be of any assistance?"[513]

The first of many calls from flight attendants and passengers on board are received:

- UA Flight 93 flight attendant contacts United Airlines maintenance facility in San Francisco. Her call is first answered by a United maintenance employee and is subsequently taken over by a manager at the facility. The manager describes the flight attendant as "shockingly calm." The flight attendant, reporting from the back of the plane, tells the maintenance employees that hijackers are in the cabin behind the first-class curtain and in the cockpit. They had announced they have a bomb on the plane. The hijackers had pulled a knife. They had killed a flight attendant. The manager reports the emergency to his supervisor, who passes the information to the United Airlines crisis center. The manager then instructs the air phone operator to try and reestablish contact with the plane, but the effort is unsuccessful.[514]
- UA Flight 93 passenger calls his mother. He tells her that he is on UA Flight 93, and it is being hijacked, that the plane has been taken over by three guys, and that they said they have a bomb.[515]

that this information is most likely related to the previous hijackings that impacted the World Trade Center. It is most likely that the first report of UAL 93 came into the Battle cab via a conference call (DEN line which was not recorded) that established with the FAA that morning. [NORAD then incorrectly speculates that] . . . it is most likely that the UAL 93 hijacking was originally discussed over the FAA conference line as a possibility sometime between 0916L and 0922L (allowing for an estimated two minutes processing time from the direction to scramble Langley fighters to the time the scramble order was actually transmitted at 0924L)." NORAD 9/11 Timeline, n.d., prepared for the 9/11 Commission.

513. 9/11 Commission Staff Report, August 26, 2004.
514. 9/11 Commission Staff Report, August 26, 2004.
515. 9/11 Commission Staff Report, August 26, 2004.

9:36 a.m.: FAA DC logs: "Command Center NTMO [national traffic management officer] informs ZSE/ZOA/ZLC watch desk to watch for unusual flights/happenings. ZOA asks about Oceanic traffic. Talking about Guam and places like that. Island depts. Into the USA or going west into Australia or the Far East. DCC checks and states that ZOA [Oakland Center] should stop all island traffic coming to the US."[516]

9:37:19 a.m.: American Airlines Flight 77 strikes the Pentagon.[517]

At the end of its 330-degree right turn, the plane descends through 2,200 feet, and over the next 30 seconds, power is increased to near maximum. "The airplane accelerated to approximately 460 knots (530 miles per hour) at the point of impact with the Pentagon."[518]

The plane comes in so low that it clips five lamp posts and hits a portable generator outside before impact. The plane strikes the side of the Pentagon at the first-floor level, just inside Wedge 1 near the fourth corridor, and proceeds diagonally at an approximate 42-degree angle toward the fifth corridor in the mostly vacant and unrenovated part of Wedge 2. After the nose of the plane hits the Pentagon, a huge fireball bursts upward and 200 feet above the roof. Multiple explosions occur as the plane smashes through the building. The front part of the relatively weak fuselage disintegrates, but the midsection and tail end continue moving for another fraction of a second, progressively destroying segments of the building farther inward. The chain of destruction results in parts of the plane ending up inside the Pentagon in reverse of the order they had entered it, with the tail end of the airliner penetrating the greatest distance into the building.[519]

Deputy FAA Administrator Monte Belger later says that "everyone was very confused about which aircraft hit the Pentagon. Nether United nor American Airlines were sure."[520]

---

516. DCC Timeline.

517. The 9/11 Commission Report (p. 10) again strangely reports that AA Flight 77 hit the Pentagon at 9:37:46, slightly off from the NORAD and FAA logs.

518. NTSB, Flight Path Study.

519. Defense Studies Series, Pentagon 9/11.

520. 9/11 Commission Memorandum for the Record, Interview Monte Belger, former Deputy Administrator of the Federal Aviation Administration, November 24, 2003.

American Airlines Flight 77 (AA 77)
Washington, D.C., to Los Angeles

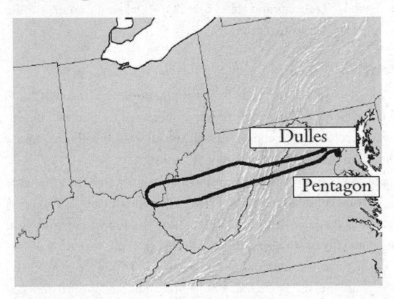

(Source: 9/11 Commission)

Surveillance video from a Pentagon security camera shows a fireball rising from the southwestern side of the building as American Airlines Flight 77 crashes into it at 9:37:19 a.m. (Source: Department of Defense)

PATH OF PLANE INTO BUILDING

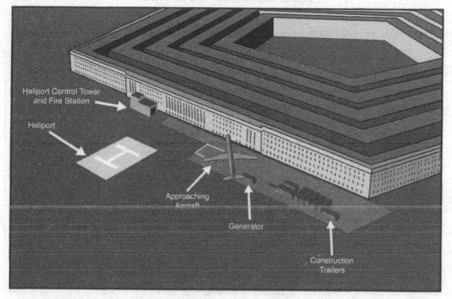

(Source: Department of Defense)

Moments after the crash, before the Pentagon building collapses onto the impact area. (Source: FBI)

Witnessing the crash from above is the crew of the Air National Guard C-130H (GOPHR06). As AA Flight 77 descends toward the Pentagon, it crosses the C-130H's flight path. Pilot Lt. Col. Steve O'Brien watches in disbelief as the flight smashes into the building. He is ordered to leave the area immediately because fighter aircraft are approaching; he flies on to his destination of Minneapolis–St. Paul.[521]

At the Pentagon Heliport, 150 feet from the west side of the building, preparations are underway for the expected arrival of President George Bush around noon. "The president was scheduled to return from a trip to Florida. On occasion he used the Pentagon Heliport instead of the White House grounds for his helicopter when going to and from Air Force One at Andrews AFB, Maryland. . . . The helipad at the White House was not available for use because of preparations for a social function on the grounds."[522]

Secretary Rumsfeld is at his desk when he says he feels the building shake. He immediately leaves his office, moving along the E Ring, the Pentagon's outer corridor, until he finds himself in heavy smoke on the opposite side of the building. He heads down the stairs to an exit. "For the first time I could see the clouds of black smoke rising from the wide side of the building. I ran along the Pentagon's perimeter, and then saw the flames."[523]

The Navy Command Center is one of the elements destroyed: "Explosions and fire quickly destroyed the Navy Command Center on the 1st

---

521. Defense Studies Series, Pentagon 9/11.

522. Defense Studies Series, Pentagon 9/11.

523. *Known and Unknown*, pp. 335–337. According to the official DOD history: "In his office listening to an intelligence briefing at the moment Flight 77 struck the Pentagon, Rumsfeld recalled, 'The plane hit the building, and the building shook and the tables jumped.' Thinking bomb, the secretary opened his office door and asked Vice Adm. Edmund Giambastiani, his three-star military aide, 'What the hell's happening?' On peering out the window and seeing nothing unusual he went into the hallway and asked his plainclothes security guards, Officers Aubrey Davis and Gilbert Oldach, what was going on. Listening to Pentagon police communication traffic via his radio earpiece, Davis stated that there was a report of an explosion at the Mall side of the building. Rumsfeld immediately hastened down the E Ring in that direction, accompanied by his two guards, his communications officer, and the deputy director of security for the secretary's office. At the undamaged 2nd Floor Mall Entrance, after Davis relayed new reports of a plane crash at the Heliport, Rumsfeld pressed on through the smoke and down the stairs to the 1st Floor, where he exited the building just north of the Heliport." See Defense Studies Series, Pentagon 9/11.

Floor and killed many of its people, confronting the Navy with the urgent need to improvise a functioning operations center."[524]

At the NMCC, Capt. Leidig, the DDO, remembers a call from Vice Adm. Giambastiani, Rumsfeld's three-star aide, who asks if he felt the explosion in the building and asks Leidig to investigate, saying that it might be a terrorist attack. Up to this point, Leidig says, he had "no awareness" of AA Flight 77 coming back to Washington, DC.[525]

In the Army Operations Center in the Pentagon basement, Brig. Gen. Peter Chiarelli is told by "the INTEL folks" that an aircraft is headed for DC, and "it is right about then that we heard the noise and the building had been hit."[526]

In the Air Force Operations Center on the mezzanine level of the Pentagon, members of the Air Force Crisis Action Team have already begun to assemble for a 10:00 a.m. briefing; one of their responsibilities is to work with the Army to provide assistance to civil authorities in New York. With the attack on the Pentagon, Chief of Staff Gen. John Jumper and Secretary of the Air Force James Roche go to the Operations Center. The center soon activates a team to focus on continuity of operations, specifically movement of national leaders.[527]

At some point between 9:12 a.m. and the crash of AA Flight 77 into the Pentagon, flight attendant Renee May's parents reach an American Airlines employee at National Airport, providing the information from their daughter, including her phone number on board and the flight number. Initially, the American Airlines employee thinks they are talking about the aircraft that had crashed into the World Trade Center. May's mother reiterates that she is speaking of Flight 77, still in the air. At some point after completing the call, the American Airlines employee is told to evacuate the building. On her way out, she hears explosions from the direction of the Pentagon, though she is not sure that it is the crash of an aircraft. She

524. Defense Studies Series, Pentagon 9/11.
525. 9/11 Commission Memorandum for the Record, Interview, Captain Charles Joseph Leidig, USN, April 29, 2004.
526. Defense Studies Series, Pentagon 9/11.
527. Defense Studies Series, Pentagon 9/11.

then informs a flight services manager at the airport about her conversation with May's parents.[528]

Of the 125 fatalities in the Pentagon, 92 occur on the first floor, 31 on the second floor, and 2 on the third floor, all between corridors four and five. The dead include 70 civilians (60 civil servants and 10 contractor employees) and 55 uniformed military.[529]

9:37 a.m.: Langley-based F-16 fighter jets are about 100–150 miles away from the Pentagon when the attack occurs.[530]

The official DOD history states that "the fighters had flown over the ocean in accordance with standing instructions and did not turn toward Washington until ordered to do so at almost the same time that the Pentagon was struck."[531]

(The fighters had actually been ordered north by NORAD NEADS to impose interceptors between New York and Washington. Plus, Lt. Col. Nasypany told the 9/11 Commission that there was no prior notification of AA Flight 77 heading for the Pentagon and that there had been "no change in the ROE or specific orders from higher authority that changed the engagement regulations" for the fighters prior to the attack on the Pentagon, meaning that they were still operating under an order to "tail" any hijacked airliners.)[532]

528. 9/11 Commission Staff Report, August 26, 2004.

529. Defense Studies Series, Pentagon 9/11. The Marine Corps was fortunate in that no Marines were killed or seriously injured in this attack. The weekend before, most of the Department of Marine Aviation, located directly above the site of impact, had been relocated to another area of the Pentagon during building renovation. Immediately following the attack, Marines set up a "command center" under an overpass of Interstate 395, which runs beside the Pentagon. Working alongside fellow servicepeople and civilians for hours, days, and weeks after the tragedy, Marines played a large role in the rescue and recovery effort.

530. "Langley Air Force Base . . . three F-16's . . . were still about 150 miles away from Washington when Flight 77 crashed into the Pentagon seven minutes later." Defense Studies Series, Pentagon 9/11. See also Hart Seely, "Amid Crisis Simulation, 'We Were Suddenly No-Kidding Under Attack,'" Newhouse News Service, January 25, 2002; 9/11 Commission Staff Report, August 26, 2004.

531. Defense Studies Series, Pentagon 9/11. "The NMCC chronology notes that the DDO entered the ATC, possible threat to CONUS." 9/11 Commission, Memorandum for the Record, n.d., 2012-042-doc24, partially declassified.

532. 9/11 Commission Memorandum for the Record, Interview with NEADS Alpha Flight Mission Crew Commander (MCC), Lt. Col. Kevin J. Nasypany, January 22, 2004, and January 23, 2004.

9:37 a.m.: A UA Flight 93 passenger makes the first of several calls to his wife. During these calls, he reports that the plane had been hijacked, the hijackers claimed to have a bomb, and a passenger had been knifed. He thought one of them had a gun. He didn't think they had a bomb because he couldn't see it. The passenger asked his wife if she had heard about any other planes. His wife informed him about the World Trade Center. The passenger asked if the planes that crashed into the towers were commercial.

In one of the later calls to his wife, the passenger reports that the passenger who had been knifed has died, that "they" are in the cockpit, and that a group of passengers is getting ready to do something.

Between 9:37 and 9:57 a.m., a passenger is in contact with his wife and his mother-in-law, who immediately calls 911 on her cell phone. The passenger tells his family that Flight 93 has been hijacked by three "Iranian-looking" males, with dark skin and bandannas; one of the males has stated that he is in possession of a bomb in a red box, and one is armed with a knife; the captain has not made any announcements; the hijackers have herded the passengers into the rear of the plane; the three hijackers have entered the cockpit. He and other passengers are contemplating "rushing" the hijackers; he does not observe any guns in the possession of the hijackers; the passengers are voting on whether to storm the cockpit and try to retake control of the airplane.[533]

According to one news media report: "At least four other planes were behaving strangely, according to the FAA. Each might be another hijacking. Most notably, United Airlines Flight 93 had turned off its transponder in Ohio."

"We're thinking: Where's he going? To Chicago?" a NEADS technician says. "Where is he going?"[534]

9:37 a.m.: At the World Trade Center, PAPD order an evacuation of people in and around the concourse.[535]

---

533. 9/11 Commission Staff Report, August 26, 2004.

534. Hart Seely, "Amid Crisis Simulation, 'We Were Suddenly No-Kidding Under Attack,'" Newhouse News Service, January 25, 2002.

535. NIST Chronology.

9:37 a.m.: Australian Prime Minister Howard is in the middle of a press conference at his hotel in Washington when the Pentagon is hit.[536]

Howard is then taken to a "cellar" under the Australian embassy.[537] Though it is unclear when, "the Australian [prime minister] and his staff were whisked off to an underground bunker in the Washington area."[538]

9:38:47 a.m.: UA Flight 93 altitude indicates 40,700 feet.

9:39 a.m.: News media begins reporting that an explosion has taken place at the Pentagon.

9:39 a.m.: Air Threat Conference Call log:[539]

> NMCC (DDO): "Report of crash into small [sic, mall] side of Pentagon."
> NMCC (DDO): "An air attack against North America may be in progress. NORAD, what's the situation?"
> NORAD: "This is NORAD. We have radar and visual indication of a possible threat to CONUS. Unknown country of origin. We have a possible hijack situation. We are receiving conflicting reports regarding the hijack. Latest information says that we have a possibly hijacked aircraft taking off out of JFK currently en route to Washington, DC."[540]
> NMCC (DDO): "We are receiving conflicting reports regarding the hijack. Latest information possible hijacked aircraft taking off out of JFK en route to DC. No assessment given for this event. No

---

536. James Grubel, "Australia's Howard a Surprise 9-11 Witness," Reuters, September 4, 2011.

537. Sarah Collerton, "John Howard 'Saved My Life on 9/11,'" ABC (Australia) News, September 6, 2011.

538. *All Roads Lead to Baghdad: Army Special Operations Forces in Iraq* (Army Special Operations Command History Office, 2007), p. 49.

539. Air Threat Conference Call log, "DJH Notes," Top Secret, partially declassified; Defense Studies Series, Pentagon 9/11.

540. 9/11 Air Threat Conference Call Transcription, partially declassified. See also Defense Studies Series, Pentagon 9/11; 9/11 Commission, Memorandum for the Record, n.d., 2012-042-doc24, partially declassified.

assessment for overall air situation. CINC NORAD not declaring air defense emergency at this point."[541]

The NMCC requests that Secretary Rumsfeld be added to the conference, but he is outside at the crash site.[542]

9:39 a.m.: UA Flight 93. FAA Cleveland Center overhears another radio transmission from hijacker pilot Ziad Jarrah, indicating that there is a bomb on board and that the plane is returning to the airport: "Uh, is the captain. Would like you all to remain seated. There is a bomb on board and are going back to the airport, and to have our demands [unintelligible]. Please remain quiet." The announcement is not heard by the passengers but mistakenly broadcast over external radio.[543]

Cleveland Center notifies FAA Great Lakes Regional Operations Center of the screams and statements.

Passenger Lauren Grandcolas calls her husband and leaves a message that the flight has been hijacked.[544]

9:39 a.m.: At the World Trade Center, 33 Manhattan firehouses are recorded responding (12 of the 33 responding with multiple units), and 18 Brooklyn firehouses are responding (2 of the 18 responding with multiple units).[545]

9:39 a.m.: FAA reports:

"DCA Controller advises IAD Controller that the B757 crashed into the Pentagon."[546]

---

541. An Air Defense Emergency is defined as follows: "An emergency condition that exists when an attack on CONUS, Alaska, Canada, or US installations in Greenland by hostile aircraft or missiles is considered probable, is imminent, or is taking place." It is the equivalent of DEFCON 1, maximum readiness, for air defense assets.

542. Air Threat Conference Call log, "DJH Notes," Top Secret, partially declassified; Defense Studies Series, Pentagon 9/11.

543. 9/11 Commission Report, p. 12; 9/11 Commission Staff Report, August 26, 2004.

544. 9/11 Commission Staff Report, August 26, 2004.

545. NIST Chronology.

546. Department of Transportation/FAA Report of Aircraft Accident, ZDC-ARTCC-212, AAL 77, Washington National (DCA) ATCT, November 13, 2001.

FAA DC logs: "Command Center NTMO [national traffic management
   officer] informs ZLA [Los Angeles Center] watch desk to watch for
   unusual flights."

"ZAU [Chicago Center] advises COA [Continental Airlines] 321, three
   updates showing hijack, CLE-DEN, landed PIA [Peoria, IL]."[547]

Continental Airlines Flight 321 seems to be the first of a dozen flights identified on 9/11 as being potentially a hijacked airplane in addition to the
four actual hijacked flights.

9:40 a.m.: President Bush speaks with Condoleezza Rice from his limousine en route to the Sarasota-Bradenton airport.[548] She tells him that a third
plane hit the Pentagon. He says he thought, *The first plane could have been
an accident. The second was definitely an attack. The third was a declaration
of war.*[549]

"I'm coming back," the president tells Rice.

"Mr. President," Rice responds, "stay where you are. You cannot come
back here."

I then did something that I never did again. I raised my voice with the President and in a tone as firm as I could possibly muster, I said, "Mr. President,
you cannot come back here. Washington, I mean the United States, is under
attack."[550]

9:40 a.m.: NORAD commander Gen. Eberhart, for the second time, has
the authority to order scrambled air defense assets to shoot down hijacked
planes under Joint Chiefs of Staff Standing Rules of Engagement but "took
positive action not to do so."[551]

NMCC chronology contains a NORAD-related entry: "Conflict-
ing FAA reports on hijacks, one out of JFK enroute DC, no assessment.

---

547. DCC Timeline.
548. Presidential Daily Diary, partially declassified.
549. *Decision Points*, p. 128.
550. *No Higher Honor*, pp. 72–73.
551. 9/11 Commission, Memorandum for the Record, n.d., 2012-042-doc24, partially
declassified.

CINCNORAD *not* declaring Air Defense Event, recommends reconvene when more info available."[552]

According to NORAD, this is the second of three occasions where Gen. Eberhart is given an opportunity—in discussions with his command center—to order aircraft to shoot down civilian airliners but declines to issue any such order.[553]

9:40 a.m.: At the World Trade Center, there are reports that the floor of the South Tower is buckling and that more WTC buildings (including Building 7) could collapse. WTC security still reporting victims jumping from the upper floors.[554]

9:40 a.m.: (Approximate time) Speaker of the House Hastert, observing "smoke rising above the Mall [in the direction of the Pentagon]," deliberates about whether he can shut down Congress. He is unable to reach the Senate side to determine their status, so he asks Rep. Porter Goss to serve as Speaker pro tempore.[555]

Soon after the Pentagon is hit, at about 9:45 a.m., the House Sergeant at Arms, the senior security officer, orders evacuation of the US Capitol and adjacent office buildings. Members and staff congregate outside without additional guidance as to what to do.

9:40 a.m.: Arlington Police dispatch emergency response and fire assets to the Pentagon.

9:40 a.m.: FAA and CIA join the WHSR teleconference that began at 9:25 a.m.[556]

552. 9/11 Commission, Memorandum for the Record, n.d., 2012-042-doc24, partially declassified.

553. 9/11 Commission, Memorandum for the Record, n.d., 2012-042-doc24, partially declassified.

554. NIST Chronology.

555. Whereas: Stories from the People's House.

556. 9/11 Commission Report, p. 38.

9:40 a.m.: UA Flight 93. United Airlines coordinator for West Coast flights notifies FAA Herndon Command Center that UA Flight 93 is off course and not responding to the airline's attempts to contact it.[557]

FAA DC logs: "ZBW [Boston Center] calls to advise the DCC that UAL 93 has started to descend. There has been no contact with the aircraft for some time."[558]

United Airlines dispatcher Ed Ballinger sends the following ACARS transmission to Flight 93: "High security alert. Secure cockpit. Two airliner hit NY Trade Center. And one aircraft in IAD missing. And one in EWR [Newark] missing . . . too. UAL 175/93 missing."[559]

9:41 a.m.: News media report that a second hijacked airplane has hit the Pentagon.[560]

9:41 a.m.: Air Threat Conference Call log: "DDO: Confirms crash, 'You can see smoke emitting from the Pentagon.'"[561]

Vice President Cheney, now in the PEOC, learns that the Pentagon has been hit, and he watches television coverage.[562]

9:41 a.m.: UA Flight 93 secondary radar returns, indicating aircraft speed, altitude, and flight information, become intermittent and eventually fail on FAA Cleveland Center displays.[563] Cleveland Center locates the aircraft on primary radar and matches his reading with visual sightings from other aircraft to follow UA Flight 93 as it turns east and, ultimately, south.

FAA Herndon Command Center notifies FAA headquarters that the flight has reversed course from its intended flight path.[564]

---

557. 9/11 Commission Staff Report, August 26, 2004.

558. DCC Timeline.

559. 9/11 Commission Staff Report, August 26, 2004.

560. Secret Service, "Actions of TSD Related to Terrorist Incident," partially declassified.

561. Air Threat Conference Call log, "DJH Notes," Top Secret, partially declassified.

562. 9/11 Commission Report, pp. 39–40.

563. The transponder on the plane of UA Flight 93 was turned off "from RADES radar data"; NORAD 9/11 Timeline, n.d., prepared for the 9/11 Commission.

564. 9/11 Commission Staff Report, August 26, 2004.

United Airlines dispatcher Ed Ballinger sends an ACARS message to UA Flight 93, with the following at the end: "UAL 175/93 found."[565]

9:41 a.m.: NORAD: "0941–0958: Discussion between NEADS . . . and FAA (Indy and Cleveland Centers) about Delta 89 [Delta Flight 1989] being hijacked near Cleveland."[566]

NORAD: "We have indications from the continental NORAD region there's a possible fourth hijacking in progress, Delta Flight 89. Original flight plan from Boston to Las Vegas. No further information available at this time."[567]

Air Threat Conference Call log: "NORAD Update: Possible fourth hijacking in progress—Delta 89."[568]

NEADS MCC Lt. Col. Nasypany says that they tried to get fighters based in Duluth, Minnesota, to scramble fighters toward Delta Flight 1989, "but Duluth was unable to respond."[569]

Delta Flight 1989 is the second plane that the FAA and NORAD suspect of being a hijacking. It is also one of the most significant. Though the FAA will notify NEADS at 9:45 a.m. that the flight is following instruction to land in Cleveland and inform NORAD at 9:58 a.m. that it is "not a hijacking," speculation about a bomb aboard persists until 12:14 p.m., when, after having been held in a secure area on the ground for more than an hour, the FBI enters the plane to search for a bomb.[570]

---

565. 9/11 Commission Staff Report, August 26, 2004.

566. NORAD 9/11 Timeline, n.d., prepared for the 9/11 Commission. The 9/11 Commission later stated that at 9:44 a.m., the DOD Significant Events Conference, now discontinued, logs: "At 9:44, NORAD briefed the [Air Threat] conference on the possible hijacking of Delta Flight 1989." See "Twelfth Public Hearing," National Commission on Terrorist Attacks upon the United States, June 17, 2004, http://www.9-11commission.gov/archive/hearing12/9-11Commission_Hearing_2004-06-17.htm.

567. 9/11 Air Threat Conference Call Transcription, partially declassified.

568. Air Threat Conference Call log, "DJH Notes," Top Secret, partially declassified.

569. 9/11 Commission Memorandum for the Record, Interview with NEADS Alpha Flight Mission Crew Commander (MCC), Lt. Col. Kevin J. Nasypany, January 22, 2004, and January 23, 2004.

570. DCC Timeline; NORAD 9/11 Timeline, n.d., prepared for the 9/11 Commission; National Archives Chronology.

9:42 a.m.: President Bush's limo arrives at the Sarasota-Bradenton airport, and he boards Air Force One. (The plane will not take off until about 9:45 a.m.)[571]

"Take care of my wife and daughters," Bush reportedly snarls at his Secret Service supervisory agent as he boards Air Force One.[572]

As the presidential motorcades get to Air Force One, Lt. Col. Tom Gould takes over as military aide to the president, relieving the Marine Corps aide who was on duty. "We don't know the scope of this attack and what's in front of us," Gould recalls, anticipating that he might be with the president for days, the other aides dispersing to locations to take over wherever the president was anticipated to end up.[573]

President Bush's "military aide" is the officer with the nuclear "football" and one of five aides who is always by his side. The coveted assignment, shared by representatives of the Air Force, Army, Navy, Marines, and Coast Guard, has one main task. The aide is the emergency action officer for the president, explaining not just the nuclear codes but also Pentagon emergency procedures and war plans. Lt. Col. Thomas Gould is the relevant aide for 9/11, taking over from a Marine Corps aide who was also with the president that morning. He boards Air Force One, anticipating multiple days away from Washington. Gould is thus another link between the moving presidency, the White House, and the Pentagon on that day. We know virtually nothing about his counsel other than that he is at the president's side and in touch with the Pentagon, through the SIEC, with the Secret Service, and probably with the White House Military Office in the PEOC. "I was there to ensure that the commander in chief had direct access to his military commanders, specifically in the realm of if we were under a nuclear attack I would present the president with his options," Gould says in an interview on the 10th anniversary of 9/11.[574]

571. Presidential Daily Diary, partially declassified. The Air Threat Conference Call log for 9:42 a.m. states: "White House (PEOC) reports: 'POTUS not yet left FLA; planning to depart and head to DC.'" See Air Threat Conference Call log, "DJH Notes," Top Secret, partially declassified.

572. *Dead Certain: The Presidency of George W. Bush*, p. 141.

573. Janene Scully, "Vandenberg Officer at Bush's Side During Attacks," *Santa Maria Times*, September 11, 2011.

574. The president's aide is also the military representative for official functions and, on weekends, is the personal aide to the president.

Michael Morell recounts: "Dire speculation took hold: how many planes had been hijacked and how many more targets might there be?"[575]

9:42 a.m.: UA Flight 93. FAA Herndon Command Center continues to give FAA headquarters updates on the progress and location of UA Flight 93.[576]

Deputy FAA Administrator Monte Belger says that after the crash into the Pentagon, he and Administrator Garvey got on the phone with Secretary Mineta, "who decided to bring everything down."[577]

At about this time, FAA national traffic management officer Ben Sliney orders all FAA facilities to instruct all aircraft to land at the nearest airport. The 9/11 Commission report says: "This was an unprecedented order. The air traffic control system handled it with great skill, as about 4,500 commercial and general aviation aircraft soon landed without incident."[578]

9:42: a.m.: At the World Trade Center, WTC Security tells police and fire to send volunteers away because of the danger around the buildings. "We are not letting anybody come close."[579]

9:42 a.m.: NMCC chronology contains an entry: "[Deleted] asks PEOC for instructions, is told to prepare to evacuate VP [vice president]."[580]

Air Threat Conference Call log says that Cheney was to have evacuated the White House.[581] A minute later, one of the NAOC secondary aircraft (call sign "Sword One") is reported airborne out of Andrews AFB, Maryland.[582]

575. *The Great War of Our Time*, pp. 50–51.

576. 9/11 Commission Staff Report, August 26, 2004.

577. 9/11 Commission Memorandum for the Record, Interview Monte Belger, former Deputy Administrator of the Federal Aviation Administration, November 24, 2003.

578. 9/11 Commission Report, p. 29.

579. NIST Chronology.

580. 9/11 Commission, Memorandum for the Record, n.d., 2012-042-doc24, partially declassified.

581. 9/11 Air Threat Conference Call Transcription, partially declassified.

582. 9/11 Commission, Memorandum for the Record, n.d., 2012-042-doc24, partially declassified.

9:43 a.m.: Secret Service headquarters informs White House Chief Truscott "that the Intelligence Division (ID) duty desk was reporting . . . a suspicious aircraft [another suspicious aircraft] . . . was coming toward Washington, DC."[583]

9:43 a.m.: UA Flight 93 passenger Joe DeLuca in row 26 contacts his father via Airfone to inform him that the flight has been hijacked.[584]

9:43 a.m.: FAA DC logs: "Canadians advised to keep all aircraft."[585]

9:44 a.m.: "NMCC chronology shows that the PEOC instructed [deleted] to remain on alert."[586]

This could refer to Night Hawk, the primary E-4 NAOC at Offutt AFB, Nebraska, or it could be one of the other airborne command centers operated by the military.

9:44 a.m.: Air Threat Conference Call log: "Still trying to track down the SecDef [Rumsfeld]."[587]

Since rushing to the scene of AA Flight 77's crash zone, Rumsfeld has been out of touch since the crash, now for seven minutes.

9:44 a.m.: UA Flight 93 passenger Todd Beamer in row 32 contacts an Airfone operator. His connection lasts for the remainder of the flight. He says:

583. Secret Service, Memorandum, Interview with SAIC Carl Truscott, October 1, 2001, partially declassified.

584. 9/11 Commission Staff Report, August 26, 2004.

585. DCC Timeline.

586. 9/11 Commission, Memorandum for the Record, n.d., 2012-042-doc24, partially declassified.

587. Air Threat Conference Call log, "DJH Notes," Top Secret, partially declassified. The 9/11 Commission would report that the "DOD Significant Events Conference" log stated at 9:46 a.m.: "The Office of the Secretary of Defense and the Office of the Vice Chairman of the Joint Chiefs of Staff reported that they were still trying to track down the secretary [Rumsfeld] and vice chairman [Myers], and bring them into the conference." It appears that Myers was on the call already. See "Twelfth Public Hearing," National Commission on Terrorist Attacks upon the United States, June 17, 2004, http://www.9-11commission.gov/archive/hearing12/9-11Commission_Hearing_2004-06-17.htm.

The flight had been hijacked, and the captain and first officer were lying on the floor of the first-class cabin and were injured or possibly dead. One of the hijackers had a red belt with a bomb strapped to his waist. Two of the hijackers, who had knives, entered the cockpit and closed the door behind them. At some point the hijackers closed the curtain between first class and coach so that passengers could not see into first class; those in the rear of the plane were not being monitored by the hijackers. The plane was going up and down and had turned or changed direction. He and some other passengers were planning something and he was going to put the phone down.[588]

Before UA Flight 93 crashes, at least 10 passengers and two crew members contact family, friends, colleagues, or others on the ground and report on the status of the flight.[589]

9:44:31 a.m.: UA Flight 93. FAA Cleveland Center notifies Pittsburgh Terminal Radar Approach Control of the unanticipated turn of the flight over Ohio and its eastern trajectory. There has been a loss of secondary radar (from the transponder), and there is an absence of any radio communications with the flight. Cleveland Center speculates that the projected flight path would result in UA Flight 93 passing in close proximity to, if not directly over, the Greater Pittsburgh IAP.[590]

9:44 a.m.: At the World Trade Center, Building 7 (WTC 7) is evacuated, and the NYC Command and Control Center is relocated to One Police Plaza.[591]

Mayor Giuliani later says on CNN at 12:26 p.m. that the New York City command center located in WTC 7, where he had initially relocated to, "was located close enough to it so that it was affected by it, it's not in one of the [twin tower] buildings. But it was located right in that area, as is city hall, the police department, and all of them had to be evacuated. . . . I was in a building at the time that we were using as command center, and we

588. 9/11 Commission Staff Report, August 26, 2004.
589. 9/11 Commission Report, p. 13.
590. National Park Service, Flight 93, September 11, 2001.
591. NIST Chronology.

were trapped in the building for a while, for about 20 minutes, not able to get out, different exits that were overcome with smoke and debris."[592]

9:45 a.m.: President Bush, aboard Air Force One, makes a rapid departure from the Sarasota-Bradenton airport.[593] The decision is made to get up in the air and then decide where to go. The plane has about six hours of fuel.[594]

"The pilot, after conferring with the lead Secret Service agent on board, flew the plane as high and fast as possible for better security."[595]

"[Secret Service] DSAIC [Deputy Special Agent in Charge Eddie] Marinzel [President Bush's head of protection for that day] advised that in short succession, they had been told of attacks on the Pentagon and Camp David. A discussion among the President, Mr. Card, Mr. Gould [Lt. Col. Gould], and DSAIC Marinzel focused on the question, 'Where they should go?' DSAIC Marinzel opined that given the series of attacks on the East Coast, and the apparent state of instability, Air Force One should head west. Mr. Card, Mr. Gold [*sic*, Gould], and the President agreed."[596]

Col. Mark Tillman, the Air Force One pilot for Mission No. 3480 that day, says:

592. "CNN Breaking News: Mayor Talks of Damage in New York City," September 11, 2001, CNN http://transcripts.cnn.com/TRANSCRIPTS/0109/11/bn.12.html.

593. Presidential Daily Diary, partially declassified. The time is incorrectly listed at "Twelfth Public Hearing," National Commission on Terrorist Attacks upon the United States, June 17, 2004, http://www.9-11commission.gov/archive/hearing12/9-11Commission_Hearing_2004-06-17.htm, and Defense Studies Series, Pentagon 9/11 as 9:55 a.m. Aboard Air Force One are Andrew Card, Ari Fleischer, Harriet Miers, Karl Rove, Gordon Johndroe, Deborah Loewer, Brian Montgomery, Ellen Eckert, Eric Draper, Dan Bartlett, Richard J. Tubb (White House physician), and additional classified White House and Air Force One personnel.

594. Secret Service unlabeled document, released under FOIA Appeal (File Numbers 20080330 and 20080331), in Letter, April 23, 2010.

595. Defense Studies Series, Pentagon 9/11.

596. Secret Service unlabeled document, partially declassified, and released under FOIA Appeal (File Numbers 20080330 and 20080331), in Letter, April 23, 2010. "The lead Secret Service agent, the president's military aide, and the pilot were conferring on a possible destination for Air Force One. The Secret Service agent felt strongly that the situation in Washington was too unstable to return. [White House Chief of Staff] Card agreed." "Twelfth Public Hearing," National Commission on Terrorist Attacks upon the United States, June 17, 2004, http://www.9-11commission.gov/archive/hearing12/9-11Commission_Hearing_2004-06-17.htm.

The jet roared down the runway, "a rather steep takeoff," Tillman recalls. He heard from air controllers in Gainesville that an unidentified plane was descending toward them. He asked for fighter jets to protect the plane.

"I didn't know the capabilities of the terrorists, so just err to the worst case," Tillman says. "It wouldn't be bad to have fighter support in the event that airliners were tracking us. Maybe that airliner was coming to crash into us over Sarasota, saw us take off and was coming after us. In reality, it was just like many of the threats that day. It was not an actual threat. It was an airliner whose transponder had failed."[597]

Col. Tillman, according to Ari Fleischer, was told that there was a sniper at the end of the runway.[598]

Michael Morell later writes: "The aircraft accelerated down the runway and began a rapid climb—one steeper than I had ever imagined a wide-bodied aircraft could achieve. . . . I asked the president's military aide—the keeper of the nuclear 'football' . . . where we were going. He responded, 'We are just flying around for a bit.'"[599]

President Bush calls Vice President Cheney as the plane is climbing. "I told him that I would make decisions from the air and count on him to implement them on the ground."[600] According to the notes of Ari Fleischer, President Bush tells Cheney: "Sounds like we have a minor war going on here, I heard about the Pentagon. We're at war . . . somebody's going to pay."[601] Fleischer said Bush was told that three more aircraft were "missing," that there could be three more hijackings or attacks.[602]

597. Tom Vanden Brook, "Air Force One Pilot Remembers 9/11," *Chicago Sun Times*, August 26, 2011; 9/11 Commission Report, pp. 325–326, 554, n1; and Defense Studies Series, Pentagon 9/11.

598. Ari Fleischer (@AriFleischer), "AF One took off like a rocket. Years later, the pilot, Col. Mark Tillman, told me he was told there was a sniper at the end of the runway," Twitter, September 11, 2015, 6:59 a.m., https://twitter.com/AriFleischer/status/642336574286524416.

599. *The Great War of Our Time*, p. 51.

600. *Decision Points*, p. 129.

601. 9/11 Commission Report, p. 39.

602. Ari Fleischer (@AriFleischer), "Bush was told 3 aircraft were 'missing,' meaning we thought there might be 3 more hijackings and 3 more attacks," Twitter, September 11, 2015, 6:50 a.m., https://twitter.com/AriFleischer/status/642334446994227201.

Aboard Air Force One, staffers and press are told to keep their cell phones turned off because the signal might allow terrorists to locate the airplane.[603]

9:45 a.m.: FAA orders all civil aircraft to land at the nearest airport as soon as is practical, in what is the first ever unplanned shutdown of US airspace. At this time, there are more than 4,500 aircraft in the air on instrument flight rules (IFR) flight plans.

NORAD: "The airspace over the District of Columbia was closed by the FAA at 0945 EDT when the FAA ordered all aircraft over the United States to land at the nearest suitable airfield."[604]

9:45 a.m.: Secret Service orders a mandatory evacuation of the White House.[605]

The evacuation turns to panic as Secret Service personnel yell for people to run. Women are told to take off their heels to run faster. Staffers are told to pull off their White House badges to avoid being targeted by snipers and suicide bombers. A uniformed Secret Service guard is heard shouting "Incoming, incoming, get out of here!"

Vice President Cheney is already in the PEOC with the head of his protective detail, Tony Zotto, head of the Vice Presidential Protective Division.[606]

Cheney's counsel David Addington flees the White House only to be called back by the vice president.[607]

The vice president gives authorization for Karen Hughes to be brought in by military drivers. She is late for work on 9/11 because she was with her son Robert at his school.[608]

---

603. Tom Vanden Brook, "Air Force One Pilot Remembers 9/11," *Chicago Sun Times*, August 26, 2011; Defense Studies Series, Pentagon 9/11.

604. 9/11 Commission, NORAD Questions for the Record, partially declassified.

605. It is interesting to note that at 9:43:59 a.m., the Associated Press reports that the West Wing of the White House is being evacuated. AP, "A Stunning 48 Hours of News," timeline document, n.d. (September 12, 2001).

606. Secret Service, Memorandum, Interview with SAIC Carl Truscott, October 1, 2001, partially declassified.

607. *Angler: The Cheney Vice Presidency*, p. 129; *Cheney: The Untold Story of America's Most Powerful and Controversial Vice President*, pp. 333–334.

608. *Dead Certain: The Presidency of George W. Bush*, p. 142.

In the WHSR:

The senior duty officer, Rob Hargis, took a call from a National Security Council official, who urged the team to leave. Hargis turned to the others in the room and said evenly, "We have been ordered to evacuate. If you want to go, go now." The room fell silent. No one moved. "We're staying," Hargis said on the phone, and moved to another call.

"I guess we're expendable," Don Gentile, the Situation Room's senior analyst at the time, joked darkly. Senior White House staffer Franklin Miller quietly collected everyone's names and gave them to the watch team's communications technician, Scott Heyer, for transmission to the CIA operations center. If an aircraft hit the White House, the agency would know everyone who was in the Situation Room. The duty officers called it the "Dead List."

According to a news media report:

For hours, Hargis and his team [at the WHSR] had constant contact with Cheney and Rice, who struggled with limited communications in the Presidential Emergency Operations Center, and with Air Force One. Calls streamed in from members of Congress, evacuated staff and one agitated aide to New York Mayor Rudy Giuliani, whose thick accent challenged Sherman, a Texas native. "Everyone viewed us as the only all-source center," Padinski said. "We saw most everything, whether classified or media reporting."

The Sit Room faced another anxious moment when Clarke's team had sent for a few gas masks. When it became clear that there weren't enough masks for everyone, some questioned the apparent lottery, while others wondered what they didn't know.[609]

At around this time, the Secret Service independently contacts the 113th Wing of the DC National Guard. The Wing commander, initially Brig. Gen. Wherley, calls the JOC on a special internal Washington line while watching television coverage of the White House being evacuated. He speaks to Special Agent Ken Beauchamp of the presidential protection division. "Beauchamp asked the commander to send up aircraft to protect

---

609. Michael K. Bohn, "Former Staffers Remember the White House Situation Room on 9/11," McClatchy Newspapers, August 29, 2011.

Washington. Wherley wanted to help but asked, with all respect, to "speak to someone a little higher up the food chain."[610]

9:45 a.m.: The news media report a fire on the National Mall as well as at the USA Today building in Arlington, Virginia.

Secret Service agent Paul Nenninger later recalls: "We first heard that a plane had gone down on the Washington Mall near the Lincoln Memorial. As with most fast breaking events, watching any of the major networks or the cable news channels provided about as much information as any other source."[611]

Gen. Myers later writes: "Fractured, unconfirmed reports reached us from the intelligence community and the Secret Service. A civil aircraft was down near Camp David (false report) . . . a car bomb had exploded near the State Department, raising the question of where the nearest bio-chemical protection team was located (false report) . . . three commercial aircraft were 'squawking' Mayday distress calls (false report)."[612]

9:45 a.m.: (Approximate time) George Tenet orders the evacuation of the CIA complex in McLean, Virginia. The operations center and counterterrorism specialists largely remain behind. The executive suite moves to the CIA's print shop, "a non-descript two-story building."[613]

According to Michael Morell: "In a meeting in his conference room, Tenet was reminded that years earlier, Ramzi Yousef, the mastermind of the first World Trade Center bombing in 1993, had developed a plan to crash a plane into CIA headquarters."[614]

---

610. 9/11 Commission Memorandum for the Record, Interview, BG David Wherley, on September 11, 2001, Commander of the 113th Wing of the USAF, August 28, 2003.

611. Paul L. Nenninger, "One Secret Service Agent's Experience," *Southeast Missourian,* August 29, 2011.

612. *Eyes on the Horizon,* p. 155.

613. Ron Suskind, *The One Percent Doctrine: Deep Inside America's Pursuit of Its Enemies* (New York: Thorndike, 2006), p. 3.

614. *The Great War of Our Time,* p. 51.

CHAPTER 9

"LET'S ROLL"

The UA Flight 93 passenger revolt began at 9:57 a.m. The passengers were now aware, through calls to family, friends, and officials, that the World Trade Center had been attacked and that the buildings had already collapsed. Over the last 20 minutes of the flight, more than half a dozen passengers and flight attendants had been on Airfones and cell phones with friends and relatives, with airline authorities, and even with phone company representatives, reporting on what was going on on board the intended Newark–to–San Francisco flight.

Those phone calls and the voices on the cockpit voice recorder, recovered in Pennsylvania, tell a still harrowing story of courage and desperation: how a couple dozen passengers on the plane banded together to storm the cockpit and force the plane down.

It all began at 9:28 a.m., when the true pilot made a "mayday" call over the radio. The hijackers then entered the cockpit, killing the pilot and copilot and taking over the plane in less than four minutes. At 9:36 a.m., a flight attendant contacted United Air Lines maintenance in San Francisco.

A minute later, passenger Jeremy Glick said that he and others were contemplating "rushing" the hijackers, that they were voting on whether to storm the cockpit. Passenger Todd Beamer was able to speak to Airfone representative Lisa Jefferson for about 15 minutes until the end, until his famous last words were said to nearby passengers: "Let's roll."

One flight attendant who called her husband at 9:50 a.m. abruptly ended her phone call at 9:57 a.m. "Everyone is running up to first class," she said. "I've got to go. Bye." The sounds of the passenger uprising captured by the cockpit voice recorder suggest a great struggle, one that continued until the flight plowed into the ground six minutes later near Shanksville, Pennsylvania.

`9:45 a.m.:` UA Flight 93. FAA DC logs: "ZOB [Cleveland Center] advises that they think they have located the primary [radar return] for UAL 93. They believe it is heading for Washington, 29 minutes out. 'DCC states that . . . track shows 50 [miles] south of CLE [Cleveland].'"[615]

`9:45 a.m.:` At the World Trade Center, officials seek to relieve radio congestion on the city radio channel—dedicated solely for communications among chief officers and supervisors—by moving units and ambulances to other channels.[616]

`9:45 a.m.:` UA Flight 93. At some point between 9:45 a.m. and 9:50 a.m., United Airlines receives a report from San Francisco maintenance about a call from a UA Flight 93 flight attendant advising that the aircraft has been hijacked. The information is passed on to United Airlines dispatcher Ed Ballinger and the crisis center. Ballinger attempts to initiate a lockout of UA Flight 93. The United computer system, however, is not set up at that time to deal with two such procedures simultaneously. United has already locked out UA Flight 175.[617]

`9:45 a.m.:` American Airlines headquarters calls United Airlines headquarters to inform them that an aircraft has hit the Pentagon and that American believes it was a US Airways turbojet.[618]

`9:45 a.m.:` FAA notifies NEADS that Delta Flight 1989 has acknowledged air traffic control instructions to land in Cleveland "and may not be hijacked."[619]

`9:46 a.m.:` UA Flight 93. FAA Herndon Command Center updates FAA HQ that UA Flight 93 is tracking toward Washington, DC, and is 29 minutes away from the city.[620]

---

615. DCC Timeline.
616. FDNY Report.
617. 9/11 Commission Staff Report, August 26, 2004.
618. 9/11 Commission Staff Report, August 26, 2004.
619. NORAD 9/11 Timeline, n.d., prepared for the 9/11 Commission. At 9:50 a.m., the FAA logs: "DAL 1989, B767, BOS [Boston Logan] . . . LAX [Los Angeles IAP] divert to CLE [Cleveland] due to bomb threat."
620. 9/11 Commission Staff Report, August 26, 2004.

United Airlines San Francisco sends the following ACARS message to UA Flight 93: "Heard report of incident. Plz confirm all is normal."[621]

At about this time, passenger Linda Gronlund contacts her sister and leaves a voice mail message: "Apparently, they, uh, flown a couple of planes into the World Trade Center already and it looks like they're going to take this one down as well," she says. "Mostly, I just wanted to say I love you, and I'm going to miss you."[622]

9:46 a.m.: Air Threat Conference Call log: "NORAD: Please confirm FAA on [the] line. . . . Get them on."[623]

9:46 a.m.: At the World Trade Center, FDNY requests an additional fifth alarm.[624]

9:47 a.m.: FAA reports: "UAL 93 descending in ZOB [Cleveland Center] airspace south of Akron, OH."[625]

9:47 a.m.: The Associated Press reports that the White House has been threatened with a direct terrorist attack.[626]

9:47 a.m.: Secretary Rumsfeld is still outdoors at the crash site, the opposite side of the building from his office and out of touch, some 10 minutes after the Pentagon has been hit.[627]

"Oh, my Lord, the whole place was burning," Rumsfeld later remembers. He smells jet fuel and sees hundreds of pieces of metal on the lawn. He picks up a piece and examines it. Hearing someone shout, "We need help!" he runs over to assist in carrying a severely burned victim on a stretcher

---

621. 9/11 Commission Staff Report, August 26, 2004.
622. 9/11 Commission Staff Report, August 26, 2004.
623. Air Threat Conference Call log, "DJH Notes," Top Secret, partially declassified.
624. NIST Chronology.
625. National Archives Chronology.
626. AP, "A Stunning 48 Hours of News," n.d. (September 12, 2001).
627. 9/11 Commission Report, p. 43, has Rumsfeld arriving at 9:47 a.m., but that would have meant it took him 9–10 minutes to walk there.

to the sidewalk by Route 27. From there he has a direct view of the inferno and destruction before the floors collapse.[628]

9:47 a.m.: At the World Trade Center, all five FDNY rescue companies have now arrived, including one from Staten Island.[629]

9:48 a.m.: UA Flight 93 flight attendant CeeCee Lyles calls her husband using an Airfone and leaves a message: "The aircraft had been hijacked; there were three hijackers; the plane had turned around." She's heard that planes have flown into the World Trade Center. "We've turned around, and I've heard that there's planes that's been, been flown into the World Trade Center. I hope to be able to see your face again."[630]

9:48 a.m.: Air Threat Conference Call log:[631]

> NMCC (DDO): "NORAD drop off [the conference]."
> NMCC (Duty Director of Intelligence): "DDO, this is the DI. We just got a hard-line call from NORAD, said that they had dropped out of the conference and wanted to know if we were still up."
> NMCC (DDO): "Summarizing for PEOC . . . NORAD just reported possible Delta [Flight 1989] hijack. That would be fourth."

NMCC DDO Capt. Leidig remembers discussions about Delta Flight 1989. "He recalled that he thought at that time that D1989 was still a threat,"[632] even though the FAA is reporting that it is cooperating in landing.

9:48 a.m.: NORAD commander Gen. Eberhart, for the third time, has the authority to order scrambled air defense assets to shoot down hijacked

628. Defense Studies Series, Pentagon 9/11.
629. NIST Chronology.
630. 9/11 Commission Staff Report, August 26, 2004.
631. Air Threat Conference Call log, "DJH Notes," Top Secret, partially declassified; 9/11 Air Threat Conference Call Transcription, partially declassified.
632. 9/11 Commission Memorandum for the Record, Interview, Captain Charles Joseph Leidig, USN, April 29, 2004.

planes under Joint Chiefs of Staff Standing Rules of Engagement, but he "took positive action not to do so."[633]

"NORAD Missile Warning Center Log . . . Cheyenne MT [Mountain] is in force protection bravo [FPCON Bravo], worldwide force protection Alpha."[634]

There were earlier rumors that all military bases in the United States had been ordered to shift to Force Protection Threat Condition (FPCON) Delta at 9:26 a.m., but there is no evidence that such an order was made yet.

9:49 a.m.: NORAD commander Gen. Eberhart directs all air defense aircraft to go to battle stations (to be prepared to launch) and to be fully armed with air-to-air missiles for potential future missions.[635]

At NEADS in Rome, New York: "We were trying to figure out departure destination [of hijacked aircraft], how many people were on board, how big the aircraft actually was, and factoring all of that stuff in. That way the [F-15 and F-16] fighters, when they got airborne, would know that they had the right plane in sight," Senior Airman Stacia Rountree recalls. "I stayed on the phone for 12–14 hours, just calling all the bases and asking how quick the fighters could get armed, get airborne, and if they could go to a certain location," Jeremy Powell adds.[636]

Air Threat Conference Call log:[637]

> NORAD: "CINC NORAD [Gen. Eberhart] directed all air sovereignty aircraft to go to battle stations fully armed."[638]

633. 9/11 Commission, Memorandum for the Record, n.d., 2012-042-doc24, partially declassified.

634. 9/11 Commission, Memorandum for the Record, n.d., 2012-042-doc24, partially declassified.

635. 9/11 Commission, Memorandum for the Record, n.d., 2012-042-doc24, partially declassified; also "Twelfth Public Hearing," National Commission on Terrorist Attacks upon the United States, June 17, 2004, http://www.9-11commission.gov/archive/hearing12/9-11Commission_Hearing_2004-06-17.htm.

636. Katie Lange, "8 Things You May Not Know about Our Air Defense on 9/11," DOD News, September 11, 2019.

637. 9/11 Air Threat Conference Call Transcription, partially declassified.

638. Air Threat Conference Call log, "DJH Notes," Top Secret, partially declassified.

NORAD: "That has been ordered at this time. NORAD will notify
　　upon attainment."

9:49 a.m.: UA Flight 93 passenger Marion Britton calls her husband, telling him that her plane has been hijacked and that the hijackers have cut
two passengers' throats.[639]

Her husband tells her he is watching television and confirms to her
that two planes have crashed into the World Trade Center. She tells him
that the plane has been hijacked by three men. She says the hijackers are
carrying knives and had put on red headbands as they were hijacking
the plane. She says that the passengers have been moved to the rear of
the plane and that the hijackers are up front. She says that she thinks the
plane may be over the Mississippi because they are passing over a large
river. She says that the passengers are discussing how to overpower the
hijackers, including preparing hot water to throw on the hijackers and
then rush them.[640]

9:49 a.m.: Thirteen minutes after FAA Cleveland Center requests military
help, FAA Herndon Command Center suggests to FAA HQ that someone
should decide whether to request military assistance.

Herndon Command Center: "Do we want to think, uh, about
　　scrambling aircraft?"
FAA Headquarters: "Oh, God, I don't know."
Herndon Command Center: "Uh, that's a decision somebody's gonna
　　have to make, probably in the next ten minutes."
FAA Headquarters: "Uh, ya know everybody just left the room."[641]

9:50 a.m.: FAA DC logs: "Launched 2 [more] F-15s from Otis. [Aerial
refueling] tankers available."[642]

639. 9/11 Commission Staff Report, August 26, 2004.
640. 9/11 Commission Staff Report, August 26, 2004.
641. 9/11 Commission Staff Report, August 26, 2004.
642. DCC Timeline.

9:50 a.m.: "NORAD Command Director log notes that Exercise Global Guardian was cancelled."[643]

Global Guardian is a STRATCOM exercise. It is scheduled to run from August 20 through September 30; the annual nuclear war exercise, called Global Guardian 01-2, has been going on for more than a week. "Dozens of nuclear weapons had been loaded aboard strategic bombers at US air bases in Louisiana, North Dakota and Missouri. Ballistic-missile crews in the western Great Plains were on alert. So were several Trident submarine crews."[644]

9:50 a.m.: United Airlines dispatcher Ed Ballinger continues to send ACARS messages to transcontinental flights, advising them to "land ASP [as soon possible] at nearest UAL airport. . . . No one into cockpit. . . . Land asp." He sends a second message advising aircraft to land anywhere. He sends the same message again one minute later.[645]

9:50 a.m.: FBI WFO Special Agent Christopher Combs, a member of the National Capital Response Squad (NCRS), heads to the Pentagon, reporting to Assistant Chief James Schwartz, the Arlington County Fire Department (ACFD) incident commander.[646]

The FBI declares the area a crime scene. "Still, for a few more hours some military and civilians persisted in their desperate rescue efforts, evading FBI and other guards. Some slipped into the building hoping to account for colleagues for whom they felt responsible or to salvage records and even equipment. Others helped injured Pentagon workers outside."[647]

Later, the US Marshals Service Special Operations Group arrives and secures the area.[648]

643. 9/11 Commission, Memorandum for the Record, n.d., 2012-042-doc24, partially declassified.

644. Steve Liewer, "On 9/11, StratCom Leaders Were Practicing for a Fictional Threat When Real, Unprecedented Catastrophe Struck," *Omaha World Herald*, September 8, 2016.

645. 9/11 Commission Staff Report, August 26, 2004.

646. Arlington County: After-Action Report on the Response to the September 11 Terrorist Attack on the Pentagon; Defense Studies Series, Pentagon 9/11.

647. Defense Studies Series, Pentagon 9/11.

648. The USMS provided investigative support by gathering evidence at the scene and subsequently tracking down witnesses.

9:50 a.m.: Secret Service reports that First Lady Laura Bush is at the US Capitol, awaiting escort to Secret Service headquarters.[649]

9:50 a.m.: At the World Trade Center, the FDNY is still receiving radio communications of firefighters high up in the towers.[650]

9:51 a.m.: At the World Trade Center, FDNY Battalion Chief Orio Palmer reaches the South Tower's 78th-floor sky lobby along with Fire Marshal Ronald Bucca. Palmer reports that there are pockets of fire and numerous dead bodies.[651]

9:51 a.m.: UA Flight 93. Greater Pittsburgh IAP tower is evacuated after a warning from the FAA that the flight could be headed there. Controllers hand off their flights to adjacent facilities.[652]

9:52 a.m.: At the House of Representatives. "Speaker Hastert told Representative Porter Goss of Florida [Speaker pro tempore] to reconvene for a quick prayer and then immediately recess the House. According to the House Parliamentarian, Charles Johnson, however, there was no 'explicit authority to reconvene' before 10 a.m.—meaning that technically the House could not yet come back into session. Under normal circumstances, House parliamentarians would have scoured their records to determine whether the House had ever taken such an action, since, as Johnson said, it was important to 'have some semblance of authority for having reconvened the House.' But on September 11, evacuation was paramount. Representative Goss called the House to order early at 9:52 a.m.

"Representative Goss confirmed with House Chaplain Reverend Dan Coughlin that they still had to give the daily invocation, which typically precedes the opening of House proceedings. . . . Father Gerry Creedon was

---

649. Secret Service, Timeline Report, Current as of September 12, 2001, partially declassified.
650. NIST Chronology.
651. FDNY Report; NIST Chronology.
652. National Park Service, Flight 93, September 11, 2001.

scheduled to be the guest chaplain. 'I had a prayer about welcome, because a few weeks before, the president of Mexico was visiting our country, and talked about the immigration issues, and I thought that I would reflect the church's concern about immigrants and having an attitude of human rights and welcome,' Father Creedon remembered in his oral history.

"After learning of the attacks . . . Father Creedon deemed his original message 'totally inappropriate.' Instead, he quickly wrote a new prayer, using Reverend Coughlin's shoulder as an impromptu desk. Beforehand Representative Goss had told Creedon, 'I don't care what your prayer is, as long as it's brief, because we need to dismiss.' In the revised version, the priest spoke of leadership, consolation for the injured, and peace. Congressman Goss then recessed the House, 'subject to the call of the Chair.' After a total of one minute on the floor, the officials evacuated."[653]

9:52 a.m.: Air Threat Conference Call log: "NORAD: Suggest the [NMCC] DDO consider that the aircraft south . . . of Cleveland heading west [believed to be UA Flight 93] may have as its objective the Sears Tower in Chicago. Information on the location of the aircraft is limited. But it seems prudent that we might take measures to evacuate that facility."[654]

At the NMCC, staff speculate about an attack on the Sears Tower in Chicago. DDO Capt. Leidig "is certain that the Vice Chairman [Gen. Myers] was in the room at the time. He recalled looking at him and saying there is a recommendation to evacuate the tower. He remembered General Meyers [sic] saying that was a good idea, the military supports it. It makes sense to him, today, that there was a threat to Chicago."[655]

NORAD commander Gen. Eberhart also says he believes the Sears Tower in Chicago is a likely target.[656]

653. Whereas: Stories from the People's House.

654. 9/11 Air Threat Conference Call Transcription, partially declassified.

655. 9/11 Commission Memorandum for the Record, Interview, Captain Charles Joseph Leidig, USN, April 29, 2004.

656. 9/11 Commission Memorandum for the Record, Interview with CINC NORAD (Commander in Chief NORAD), General Edward "Ed" Eberhart, March 1, 2004.

9:52 a.m.: FAA reports: "Military scrambling fighters to Washington and New York area. [FAA] CARF advised ATP-200 [FAA Special Military Operations Office] can't get through."[657]

9:52 a.m.: At the World Trade Center, NYPD helicopters report "large pieces" are falling from the South Tower.[658]

9:53 a.m.: Air Threat Conference Call log: "NORAD Command Center: Please confirm FAA is in conference and request that FAA poll all airborne aircraft to determine if [additional] hijack is underway."[659]

9:53 a.m.: According to a later report by CBS News, at 9:53 a.m., the National Security Agency (NSA) "intercepted a phone call from one of Osama bin Laden's operatives in Afghanistan to a phone number in the former Soviet Republic of Georgia." The caller says that he has "heard good news" and that more is still to come.[660]

According to CBS News, George Tenet tells Rumsfeld about the intercepted conversation at 12:05 p.m.

9:53 a.m.: FAA HQ informs Herndon Command Center that the Deputy Director for Air Traffic Services was talking to FAA Deputy Administrator Monte Belger about scrambling military aircraft.[661]

This isn't the first time that the FAA logs reflect discussions about scrambling (or directing) military aircraft, an authority that the FAA does not have.

9:54 a.m.: President Bush, aboard Air Force One, makes a two-minute phone call to an unidentified person.[662]

---

657. DCC Timeline.

658. NIST Chronology.

659. Air Threat Conference Call log, "DJH Notes," Top Secret, partially declassified.

660. CBS News, "Plans for Iraq Attack Began on 9/11," September 4, 2002, reporting on a David Martin story. See also *A Pretext for War*, p. 284.

661. 9/11 Commission Staff Report, August 26, 2004.

662. Presidential Daily Diary, partially declassified.

President Bush talks on the telephone during his flight from Sarasota, Florida, to Barksdale Air Force Base in Louisiana. (Source: George W. Bush Presidential Library and Museum / Eric Draper [P7071-29])

This is one of only a few remaining deletions still in the president's mostly declassified diary from that day. As calls are logged to the vice president, to other officials, and to his family (and according to Michael Morell, the president had not yet spoken to the CIA directly), the deletion is particularly odd. But coming at a time when the NSA received its first intercept regarding the attacks, it might have been some call with NSA or the CIA or some other intelligence watch center.

9:54 a.m.: UA Flight 93 passenger Honor Elizabeth Wainio calls her stepmother and tells her that the plane has been hijacked. The call lasts approximately four and a half minutes. Before hanging up, Wainio says she has to go because passengers are trying to break into the cockpit. "I have to go. I love you. Goodbye," she says.[663]

---

663. 9/11 Commission Staff Report, August 26, 2004.

9:55 a.m.: Air Threat Conference Call log:[664]

> Air Force: "The White House is requesting fighter coverage for
>   protection overhead White House."
> NORAD: "NORAD will process that request, and we'll give you an
>   ETA when they will be on station."

9:55 a.m.: UA Flight 93 hijacker pilot Ziad Jarrah dials the navigational code for Washington National Airport into the flight computer (according to the recovered cockpit recorder) in order to fly the aircraft toward the nation's capital.[665]

9:55 a.m.: At the World Trade Center, FDNY radio communications reports that Ladder 15 is trapped on the South Tower's 78th floor.[666]

9:56 a.m.: Greater Pittsburgh IAP tower employees return. A small contingent voluntarily return to their positions.[667]

9:56 a.m.: Secretary Rumsfeld heads back inside the Pentagon from the crash site outside.[668]

Rumsfeld has now been away from his desk and the command center—and out of communications—for 19 minutes since the Pentagon attack occurred.

"Rumsfeld reentered the building on the Mall side, went directly to his office, and tried without success to telephone the president. Then proceeding to the Executive Support Center ('Cables') on the 3rd Floor, he joined

---

664. 9/11 Air Threat Conference Call Transcription, partially declassified. See also Air Threat Conference Call log, "DJH Notes," Top Secret, partially declassified. The 9/11 Commission writes, "NMCC chronology notes that AFOPS [Air Force operations] reported that the White House requested fighter coverage, NORAD will process and provide ETA." See 9/11 Commission, Memorandum for the Record, n.d., 2012-042-doc24, partially declassified.

665. 9/11 Commission Staff Report, August 26, 2004.

666. NIST Chronology.

667. National Park Service, Flight 93, September 11, 2001.

668. 9/11 Commission Report, p. 43. The report states incorrectly that Rumsfeld went to the National Military Command Center.

a White House [Situation Room] video teleconference [involving the 'deputies'] in progress."[669]

At about the same time (10:00–10:10 a.m.), Gen. Myers arrives back to the Pentagon from Capitol Hill, instructing his driver to go to the River entrance. He then goes to the NMCC.[670]

9:56 a.m.: At the World Trade Center, WTC security reports that the North Tower is still not completely evacuated. FDNY units are trapped, and some are reported still ascending.[671]

9:57 a.m.: UA Flight 93 passenger revolt begins.

An Airfone operator, who has been on the line with passenger Todd Beamer since 9:44, hears someone say at about 9:55 a.m.: "Are you guys ready? Okay! Let's roll!" Shortly thereafter she hears screaming, followed by silence.[672]

One flight attendant who had called her husband at 9:50 a.m. ends her phone call at about this time. She says, "Everyone is running up to first class. I've got to go. Bye." She hangs up the phone.[673]

At 9:57, several passengers terminate phone calls with loved ones in order to join the revolt.[674]

Passenger Edward Felt calls 911 in Westmoreland County, Pennsylvania, from his cell phone, reporting for 70 seconds, also about a passenger revolt.[675]

The sounds of the passenger uprising captured by the cockpit voice recorder suggest that the revolt begins at the back of the airplane and progresses toward the front. The evidence from the cockpit voice recorder indicates that a struggle continues for the duration of the flight.[676]

---

669. Defense Studies Series, Pentagon 9/11.

670. Memorandum for the Record, Interview of General Richard Myers, February 17, 2004, partially declassified; Defense Studies Series, Pentagon 9/11.

671. NIST Chronology.

672. 9/11 Commission Staff Report, August 26, 2004.

673. 9/11 Commission Staff Report, August 26, 2004.

674. 9/11 Commission Report, p. 13.

675. 9/11 Commission Staff Report, August 26, 2004.

676. 9/11 Commission Staff Report, August 26, 2004.

FAA Herndon Command Center informs FAA HQ they have lost track of the flight over the Pittsburgh area.[677]

9:57 a.m.: At the World Trade Center, dozens of firefighters are gathered at the South Tower lobby command post, awaiting orders to go up.[678]

9:57 a.m.: The roof line of the Pentagon building begins to collapse.

9:58 a.m. UA Flight 93. FAA reports: "UAL 93 heading SE to Washington Area."[679]

In response to the passenger revolt, hijacker pilot Ziad Jarrah begins to roll the airplane to the left and right, attempting to knock the passengers off balance. At 9:58:57 a.m., Jarrah tells another hijacker in the cockpit to block the door. Jarrah continues to roll the airplane sharply left and right as the assault continues.[680]

9:58 a.m.: "NMCC chronology notes that WHCA [White House Communications Agency] broke into conference and told DDO to stand by . . . PEOC relays request from Deputy NSA Hadley: [deleted] fighter escort for President, fighter CAP over DC."[681] Air Threat Conference Call log:[682]

> NORAD: "No update at this time . . . we'll provide an ETA when fighters will be on CAP over WH [White House]."
> FEMA: "In conference."
> NMCC (DDO): "To FEMA, Vice Chairman [Myers] recommends evacuating Chicago [Sears] Tower [based on erroneous information that Delta Flight 1989 was hijacked and was heading west]."
> FEMA: "Copy."

---

677. 9/11 Commission Staff Report, August 26, 2004.
678. NIST Chronology.
679. National Archives Chronology.
680. 9/11 Commission Report, p. 13; 9/11 Commission Staff Report, August 26, 2004.
681. 9/11 Commission, Memorandum for the Record, n.d., 2012-042-doc24, partially declassified.
682. Air Threat Conference Call log, "DJH Notes," Top Secret, partially declassified.

9:58 a.m.: Lynne Cheney arrives at the White House and joins her husband in the PEOC.[683]

She has been at a hair salon just a block away from the White House. "I was so naive," she later recalls. "At the first one [AA Flight 11 hitting the North Tower] I thought, 'Gee, that's odd.' And then the second one—now this is really naive—I thought, 'That's really odd.'"[684]

9:59 a.m.: The South Tower (WTC 2) collapses approximately 56 minutes after UA Flight 175 hit the building.

Millions of pounds—200,000 cubic yards—of metal, concrete, glass, and other debris fall with a sudden ear-splitting din, the collapse killing everyone remaining in the building, a number of people below on the concourse, occupants and firefighters in the adjacent Marriott Hotel, and people on surrounding streets.[685] The tower's north side buckles; the building seems to list and then begins collapsing, floor by floor, pancaking on top of each other as fast as momentum allows, a cloud of dust and debris propelling out from the ground, the dust finding its way down the narrow streets and alleyways of lower Manhattan.

An AP reporter on the scene writes, "People walked around like ghosts, covered in dirt, weeping and wandering dazed."

The North Tower shakes violently, and the lobby is further inundated with water, debris, and fire from the South Tower, causing additional damage. Firefighters and police officers inside the North Tower are initially unaware of precisely what is happening next door. Many believe that a partial collapse has occurred in their own tower. As the lobby fills with blinding dust and debris, the first battalion chief, who is at the operations post inside WTC 1, immediately issues an evacuation order over his portable radio. Some hear it; others don't. Some firefighters still inside the North Tower as high as the 36th floor hear an urgent order over their radios to

---

683. Secret Service log. Secret Service Memorandum, White House Events on 9/11/01 (Special Agent James O. Scott), September 12, 2001, partially declassified, says 9:52 a.m.

684. White House Transcript, Telephone Interview of Mrs. Cheney by *Newsweek* magazine, November 9, 2001.

685. At the Marriott Hotel (WTC 3), some firefighters in the lobby and directing evacuations on the upper floors are killed when the South Tower (WTC 2) collapses. Others are trapped.

evacuate. It is heard over the command radio channel. Multiple companies start down the stairs.[686]

The collapse of the South Tower destroys the ICP and EMS command post, both across West Street, and weakens the command-and-control hierarchy as fire and EMS chiefs at the post seek shelter in surrounding structures. The FDNY Field Communications Unit is destroyed.[687]

9:59:52 a.m.: UA Flight 93 hijacker pilot Ziad Jarrah pitches the nose of the airplane up and down to continue to try to disrupt the passenger assault. The cockpit voice recorder captures the sounds of loud thumps, crashes, shouts, and breaking glasses and plates.[688]

A native English-speaking male voice (or voices) says, "Stop him!" and "Let's get them."[689]

9:59 a.m.: NORAD commander Gen. Eberhart declares an Air Defense Emergency, the highest air defense alert and a state that provides the authority for scrambled air defense assets to shoot down hijacked planes. This order finally comes after NORAD receives "White House interest." Previously (at 9:13 a.m., 9:40 a.m., and 9:48 a.m.), Eberhart had declined to issue any such order.[690]

---

686. NIST Chronology.

687. WTC 2's collapse at 9:59 a.m. destroyed the EMS command post, which was next to the incident command post on West Street. The EMS divisions and sectors that had been established prior to the collapse were dispersed as personnel evacuated the area and sought shelter in surrounding structures. Chief officers at the ICP also sought shelter in nearby structures. In the absence of ranking chief officers, the EMS communications officer, previously located at the ICP, recommended to EMS Dispatch that command be transferred until resources could regroup. However, EMS Dispatch was unable to immediately act on this for two reasons: (1) it is not a normal procedure to transfer command via Dispatch and (2) it was unclear at that point in time who was available to assume command; FDNY Report.

688. 9/11 Commission Report, p. 14; 9/11 Commission Staff Report, August 26, 2004.

689. National Park Service, Flight 93, September 11, 2001.

690. 9/11 Commission, Memorandum for the Record, n.d., 2012-042-doc24, partially declassified.

Air Threat Conference Call log: "NORAD already taken CAP [combat air patrol] issue [over DC, requested by the White House]."[691]

DDO NMCC Capt. Leidig says he did not know that there were fighter aircraft in CAP over DC before discussions at the national level about the need.[692]

691. Air Threat Conference Call log, "DJH Notes," Top Secret, partially declassified.

692. 9/11 Commission Memorandum for the Record, Interview, Captain Charles Joseph Leidig, USN, April 29, 2004.

CHAPTER 10

CONTINUITY OF GOVERNMENT

Then and now, the apparatus of COG is a multibillion-dollar-a-year government operation, carried out in the strictest secrecy. There are bureaucracies that wait for disaster. There are the bunkers, special communications, and transportation assets on standby to evacuate Washington. Before 9/11, full COG had never been declared. Even during the darkest days of the Cold War—during the Cuban Missile Crisis—President Kennedy and his advisers stayed and deliberated in the White House. And though there is a constant pretense of continuity preparations—such as when the "designated survivor" sits out a State of the Union address—other than in exercises, the system had never really been tested.

So it should come as no surprise that although the White House felt the need to implement COG measures at 9:59 a.m., almost every aspect of it failed. Here was a crisis where Vice President Cheney and others thought that Washington and even the White House would be attacked—and even that Air Force One was being targeted—and yet only one of the five individuals in the constitutional line of succession actually followed the existing plans. That person was then–Speaker of the House Dennis Hastert.

It is a miserable record, especially given the vast sums that have been spent on the program. But as bad as the record might be, it's not as though some aspect of essential government function was unavailable because COG wasn't implemented. Neither is it the case—as it is with nuclear deterrence, for which the COG system was created—that some instant federal government decision was needed to ensure the survival of the nation. In some odd way, the fact that two of the most senior Cabinet members designated to assume the presidency—Secretary of State Colin Powell and Secretary of the Treasury Paul O'Neill (fourth and fifth in line)—were both outside the country was even a good thing.

What isn't comforting is that 20 years later, the same internal contradictions of COG persist—both the difficulty of evacuating a select few and the imperial quality of the program (the Bush and Cheney families were protected and moved on 9/11). A deeper issue is confusion with regard to who was in charge and what authority was or wasn't passed down from the president. We saw some of the same issues at play during the first few months of COVID-19 (and then again in the last days of the Trump administration): about whether the president and vice president should be separated, about whether Congress could muster a virtual rather than physical quorum, about who had authority to do what, about what should be done when the president was not carrying out his duties. When the insurrection at the Capitol occurred on January 6, 2021, and the Twenty-Fifth Amendment was being discussed, the apparatus of "continuity"—built for wartime—was also ignored and glossed over. Washington evidently felt that a working presidency was less important than confronting Donald Trump, and part of the system—Vice President Pence's survival—was pursued while other parts were ignored.

If it had merely been the case that the national security functions of government worked on 9/11 while the civil functions were ignored, it would at least point to a need for a rebalance. But hardly any aspect of national security

Vice President	Dick Cheney	Stayed at the White House
Speaker of the House	Dennis Hastert	Evacuated to Mount Weather
Senate President *pro tem*	Robert Byrd	Went to his home on Capitol Hill
Secretary of State	Colin Powell	Flying back from Peru
Secretary of the Treasury	Paul O'Neill	Flying back from Japan
Secretary of Defense	Donald Rumsfeld	Stayed at the Pentagon
Attorney General	John Ashcroft	Flying back from Wisconsin
Secretary of the Interior	Gale A. Norton	Forgotten; never received orders
Secretary of Agriculture	Ann Veneman	Forgotten; never received orders
Secretary of Commerce	Donald Evans	Never received orders; went home*
Secretary of Labor	Elaine Chao	Forgotten; never received orders
Secretary of HHS	Tommy Thompson	Forgotten; never received orders
Secretary of HUD	Mel Martinez	Forgotten; never received orders
Secretary of Transportation	Norman Mineta	Summonsed to the White House
Secretary of Energy	Spencer Abraham	Forgotten; never received orders
Secretary of Education	Rod Paige	Traveling with POTUS; left in Florida
Secretary of Veterans Affairs	Anthony Principi	Forgotten; never received orders

*Evans says he sat in his office all morning waiting for some kind of order, even after continuity of government measures were implemented, until finally going home to McLean, Virginia, where he watched television. *Dead Certain: The Presidency of George W. Bush*, p. 143.

Successors to the presidency on September 11.

worked either, raising questions of why such an elaborate system is even maintained or why it is still predominantly designed around an obsolete Cold War architecture. In the end it is the continuing lack of transparency with regard to what would happen (or truly happens) in a disaster involving the death or incapacitation of the president and vice president that is the greatest problem. The rules should be crystal clear and made public, for that is the only way to ensure constitutional government and instill public confidence when indeed it might matter.

9:59 a.m.: COG procedures are officially ordered into effect.

At 9:59 a.m., the White House Military Office (WHMO) tells various WHSR teleconference attendees that Deputy NSA Hadley orders:

(1) the implementation of COG measures,

(2) fighter escorts for Air Force One, and

(3) a fighter combat air patrol over Washington, DC.[693]

On the Air Threat Conference Call, the WHSR participant says: "Just talked to the NSC, Mr. Hadley up there [*sic*]. We have a couple requests. We're going to go ahead and execute continuity of government. We would

---

693. 9/11 Commission Report, pp. 35–36. "At 9:59, an Air Force lieutenant colonel working in the White House Military Office joined the conference and stated that he had just talked to Deputy National Security Adviser Steve Hadley [in the WHSR]. The White House requested: one, the implementation of continuity of government measures; two, fighter escorts for Air Force One; and three, the establishment of a fighter combat air patrol over Washington, DC." See "Twelfth Public Hearing," National Commission on Terrorist Attacks upon the United States, June 17, 2004, http://www.9-11commission.gov/archive/hearing12 /9-11Commission_Hearing_2004-06-17.htm.

Air Threat Conference Call log: "PEOC: Col Irwin just talked to Hadley couple of requests:

1. Execute continuity of government.
2. Request fighter escort for AF 1.
3. Sit Room any possibility of getting any kind of fighter CAP over DC?" (See DOD Air Threat Conference Call log, "DJH Notes," Top Secret, partially declassified.)

Richard Clarke later claims that he implemented COG, but he seemed to be embellishing his importance. See *Against All Enemies*, p. 8.

like to get somebody up at either [deleted location, probably Site R] or Camp David. I imagine you're already working [deleted].[694]

"Lawrence Di Rita, special assistant to Rumsfeld, also states that the White House directed that federal departments activate alternate command sites as a precaution."[695]

According to Gen. Myers: "The measure included establishing a survivors' core of key federal government members. A rotating staff of around 150 senior officials from every cabinet department would be sent to two security underground bunkers [Site R and Mount Weather] within driving or helicopter-flight distance of Washington. Their families and loved ones could only contact them through a 'sterile' toll-free phone number."[696]

An aide informs Cheney that he is to evacuate from the White House. Cheney says he looked at him like he was insane and said he wasn't going anywhere.[697]

According to the 9/11 Commission: "NMCC chronology [at 9:59 a.m.] contains a cryptic entry, without explanation: 'EA goes to box, ADDO confirms, then holds. Box is not opened.'"[698]

Though COG plans call for the vice president and the secretary of defense to evacuate from Washington, neither Cheney nor Rumsfeld agrees to leave. Cheney and Rumsfeld don't move, but special government jets are ordered to return former President George H. W. and Mrs. Bush from Wisconsin to their home in Maine. Similarly, former President Clinton is flown to the United States from a private trip in Australia. The two young adult daughters of President Bush are taken by their Secret Service details to secure locations in Austin, Texas, and New Haven, Connecticut. The adult daughters of Vice President Cheney are also moved. Daughter Mary has been scuba diving in the Caribbean and is returned to the United States on a government jet on September 13 while airspace is still closed.

---

694. 9/11 Air Threat Conference Call Transcription, partially declassified.

695. 9/11 Commission Report, p. 38; Defense Studies Series, Pentagon 9/11, p. 240, n. 6.

696. *Eyes on the Horizon*, p. 153.

697. *In My Time: A Personal and Political Memoir*, p. 4.

698. 9/11 Commission, Memorandum for the Record, n.d., 2012-042-doc24, partially declassified.

Daughter Elizabeth ("Liz") and her family, including her husband, children, and nanny, are taken to a relocation site outside Washington.

10:00 a.m.: (Approximate time) After the declaration of COG, probably sometime between 10:00 and 11:00 a.m., Speaker of the House Dennis Hastert, third in line to the presidency, is taken from Capitol Hill.

The Secret Service JOC takes a call from a US Capitol Police intelligence analyst, and they discuss a report that a plane has circled the Capitol. A Secret Service agent says: "I told him that we were still monitoring another suspect flight out of Newark and would keep them advised. He said they (USCP) were considering the relocation of the members, but 'they did not want to go out west (Mt. Weather).'"[699]

Hastert recalls: "He was escorted out through the tunnels to an SUV waiting outside the Rayburn building."

On the Senate side, 83-year-old Sen. Robert Byrd (D-WV), fourth in line to the presidency as the president of the Senate pro tempore, refuses to move anywhere. Instead, he goes to his Capitol Hill home, where he spends the day watching television.[700]

"The Speaker boarded a helicopter to [go to] . . . a secure location [Mount Weather in Bluemont, Virginia]. He recalled an eerily quiet city usually bustling on a weekday—no traffic on the streets, no planes taking off or landing at Reagan National Airport, and only 'blue-black smoke just belching out of the Pentagon.'"[701]

---

699. Secret Service unlabeled document, partially declassified, and released under FOIA Appeal (File Numbers 20080330 and 20080331), in Letter, April 23, 2010.

700. *In My Time: A Personal and Political Memoir*, p. 6; *Disaster: Hurricane Katrina and the Failure of Homeland Security*, p. 45. According to an account by then Sen. Joe Biden: "I heard that some congressmen and senators were over at the police headquarters by the Monocle restaurant. I asked where [Tom] Daschle was, where the leadership was. I got a private briefing upstairs. They had already briefed Daschle and others, and said they should go to a secure bunker. I called and said, 'Tom, don't go. Don't do that. Stay here.' He explained that he felt that since others were doing it, he was obliged to. He didn't think he should. Byrd refused to go, God love him, which I loved." "Voices of 9-11: 'A Cacophony of Information,'" *National Journal*, August 31, 2002. A few sources report incorrectly that Byrd was also evacuated when he was not; see, e.g., *Angler: The Cheney Vice Presidency*, p. 156.

701. "Hastert Recalls Sept. 11, 2001 Evacuation of the Capitol," *Roll Call*, October 21, 2014.

(It is unclear where Hastert was initially taken to and when he actually boarded a helicopter for Mount Weather, though the FAA will report at 12:50 p.m. that Congress "relocated." It is unclear if that refers to the secondary leaders, because it is believed that Hastert—as a key COG principal—was immediately evacuated to separate him from Vice President Cheney should Washington be destroyed.)

10:00 a.m.: UA Flight 93. FAA reports: "East southeast PIT [Pittsburgh] 40 miles squawking 7500."[702]

Squawking 7500 means a hijacking. The IFF transponder on the dashboard has a four-digit code that the pilot can dial that uniquely identifies the aircraft, with numbers zero to seven. All codes beginning with 7 signify an emergency and set off alarms at air traffic control centers. The pilot can covertly dial a 7 code to communicate with ATC: 7700 means "Help! Mayday!" 7600 means lost communication with ATC, and 7500 means "I've been hijacked." When a plane squawks 7500, the air traffic controller will covertly respond, "Confirm you are squawking 7500." It is unclear if UA Flight 93 was squawking 7500 or the FAA merely used the well-known code to communicate that the plane had been hijacked.

According to the cockpit voice recorder:

- 10:00:03 a.m.: Hijacker pilot Ziad Jarrah stabilizes the airplane.
- 10:00:05 a.m.: Hijackers discuss final actions. One of the hijackers asks Jarrah, "Is that it? Shall we finish it off?" A hijacker voice responds, "No. Not yet. When they all come, we finish it off." Sounds of fighting continue outside the cockpit. Jarrah pitches the nose of the aircraft up and down.
- 10:00:14 a.m.: English-speaking voices are captured by cockpit voice recorder. A native English-speaking male shouts, "Ah!" Another native English-speaking male says, "I'm injured." Another native English-speaking male shouts, "In the cockpit! If we don't, we'll die!" A command is shouted, in the distance, by a native English-speaking male: "Roll it!"[703]

---

702. National Archives Chronology.
703. National Park Service, Flight 93, September 11, 2001.

FAA Cleveland Center's statement indicates that Bill Wright, pilot of a small private plane in the area, reports sighting a United Airlines aircraft (UA Flight 93) at approximately 8,000 feet in the vicinity of Latrobe, Pennsylvania. The aircraft's landing gear is down, he says, the wings are rocking, and the aircraft appears to be in distress.[704]

FAA Herndon Command Center advises FAA HQ that "United ninety-three was spotted by a VFR [Wright's plane] at eight thousand feet, eleven, eleven miles south of Indianhead, just north of Cumberland, Maryland."[705]

10:00 a.m.: (Approximate time) At the Pentagon, back in his office, Rumsfeld says he briefly speaks with President Bush on Air Force One. "He was anxious to learn what damage had been done by the attack on the Pentagon. I reported what information I had," Rumsfeld later writes.[706]

This seems to be the first direct conversation of the day between President Bush and Rumsfeld. The Pentagon official history of 9/11 includes this promotional passage: "Despite the explosion, fire, and smoke hazard, Secretary Rumsfeld remained in the Pentagon continuing to direct departmental operations and exercise control of the US armed forces. The attack did not prevent him from communicating with President Bush, a critical need because the president and the secretary comprise the National Command Authority from which overall direction of military operations emanates."[707] This is complete obfuscation. Three hijacked planes had all already hit their targets. If 9/11 had been any sort of nation-state attack,

---

704. National Park Service, Flight 93, September 11, 2001.

705. 9/11 Commission Staff Report, August 26, 2004.

706. *Known and Unknown*, p. 337. Though the 9/11 Commission Report states that Secretary Rumsfeld speaks to President Bush shortly after 10:00 a.m. after an earlier unsuccessful attempt to contact him (9/11 Commission Report, p. 43), according to the Presidential Diary, no such call is logged (Presidential Daily Diary, partially declassified). According to the official DOD history: "Based on his account, it seems that Rumsfeld had not previously talked with the president, so Rumsfeld's attempt to call Air Force One from his Pentagon office was not successful. The president told the commission that 'he could not reach key officials, including Secretary Rumsfeld, for a period of time.'" Defense Studies Series, Pentagon 9/11, p. 240, n. 6. See also 9/11 Commission Report, pp. 40, 43, 465, n. 232 (quote, 40).

707. Defense Studies Series, Pentagon 9/11.

the president and secretary of defense would have been out of touch for an hour and 24 minutes after the initial strike.

10:00 a.m.: (Approximate time) Langley F-16 fighters reach the skies over Washington.[708]

NORAD CONR chat transcript "records that White House has directed fighter coverage over the White House."[709]

10:00 a.m.: At the World Trade Center, moments after the South Tower falls, FDNY Battalion Chief Joseph Pfeifer (inside of the North Tower) says on the radio, at least twice, that everyone should "evacuate the building. . . . All FDNY, get the fuck out!"[710] The NYPD also says that all its personnel are now ordered out of the buildings.[711]

10:00 a.m.: The Associated Press reports that an explosion has hit another building near the World Trade Center.[712]

10:01 a.m.: UA Flight 93 hijacker pilot Ziad Jarrah stops his violent maneuvers. The sounds of fighting continue.

Jarrah says, "Allah is the greatest! Allah is the greatest!" He then asks another hijacker in the cockpit, "Is that it? I mean, shall we put it down?" to which the other replies, "Yes, put it in it, and pull it down."[713]

FAA Herndon Command Center (Herndon) updates FAA HQ that UA Flight 93 is "rocking its wings."[714]

---

708. 9/11 Commission Staff Report, August 26, 2004.

709. 9/11 Commission, Memorandum for the Record, n.d., 2012-042-doc24, partially declassified.

710. FDNY Report.

711. NIST Chronology.

712. AP, "A Stunning 48 Hours of News," n.d. (September 12, 2001).

713. 9/11 Commission Report, p. 14; 9/11 Commission Staff Report, August 26, 2004.

714. 9/11 Commission Staff Report, August 26, 2004. At 10:01 a.m., the FAA logs: "UAL 93, B757, EWR [Newark IAP] . . . SFO [San Francisco] bomb aboard, 40 miles SE PIT headed eastbound spotted by a VFR at 075."

`10:01 a.m.:` Air Threat Conference Call log: "NORAD: . . . This is NORAD with an update. At this time, CINC NORAD has declared 'concern.' I say again, CINC NORAD has declared an assessment of 'concern.'"[715]

`10:01 a.m.:` The FAA and Secret Service report that the White House, US Capitol building, State Department, and Department of the Treasury are being evacuated.[716] Over the course of the day, museums and other public monuments in Washington are closed, and the UN, the Empire State Building, the Kennedy Space Center, Disney World, and the Mall of America are all reported evacuated.

`10:02:23 a.m.:` UA Flight 93. The flight heads down, the control wheel turning hard to the right. The airplane rolls onto its back. The hijackers continue to shout: "Allah is the greatest! Allah is the greatest!"[717]

NORAD log states: "Radar contact regained [for UA Flight 93] from RADES radar data."[718]

`10:02 a.m.:` FAA reports a false alarm: "AGL [FAA Great Lakes Region] reports a Hijack/Bomb threat—unknown call-sign type."

`10:02 a.m.:` CNN announces that the Sears Tower in Chicago has been evacuated.

`10:02 a.m.:` At the World Trade Center, FDNY reports that a civilian has called for assistance when he gets trapped inside a fire truck covered in debris.[719]

`10:03:11 a.m.:` UA Flight 93, flying at 580 miles per hour, crashes into an empty field near Shanksville, Pennsylvania. The last sound, according

---

715. 9/11 Air Threat Conference Call Transcription, partially declassified. See also 9/11 Commission, Memorandum for the Record, n.d., 2012-042-doc24, partially declassified.

716. DCC Timeline; Secret Service, Timeline Report, Current as of September 12, 2001, partially declassified.

717. 9/11 Commission Report, p. 14; 9/11 Commission Staff Report, August 26, 2004.

718. NORAD 9/11 Timeline, n.d., prepared for the 9/11 Commission.

719. NIST Chronology.

United Airlines Flight 93 (UA 93)
Newark to San Francisco

(Source: 9/11 Commission)

to the cockpit voice recorder (at 10:03:07 a.m.) is the sound of a native English-speaking man shouting loudly, "No!"[720] The plane is about 20 minutes' flying time from Washington.[721]

Area residents call 911 to report the crash. Drawn onto the front porch of her house on Lambertsville Road by an unexplained loud noise, Paula Pluta sees a silver streak in the sky, followed by a massive fireball and a plume of smoke coming from behind the trees. The plane has crashed half a mile from her house. She dials 911 and reports, "Oh my God! There was an airplane crash here!" A few seconds later, another caller to the 911 Center reports, breathlessly, "There was an airplane just went down over by Diamond T. . . . It was a big airplane, a big jet . . . it went down nose first, upside down."

Shanksville residents see, hear, and feel the crash. In Shanksville, three miles from the crash site, residents feel the impact of the crash, hear the explosion, rush outdoors, and see a cloud of black smoke rising above the trees.

---

720. National Park Service, Flight 93, September 11, 2001.
721. 9/11 Commission Report, p. 14; 9/11 Commission Staff Report, August 26, 2004.

GOVERNMENT
EXHIBIT
P200057
01-455-A

M-CSP-00009957

Aerial view of the impact site and debris field taken in the early stages of the investigation in Shanksville, Pennsylvania, in September 2001. The white specks are debris. (Source: FBI)

Rick King, assistant chief of the Shanksville Volunteer Fire Company, as well as the owner of Ida's Store, hears the sound of a large plane approaching and then crashing just over the hill from Shanksville. King runs to the store to tell his wife and employees that a plane has crashed; he then runs to the fire station to answer the radio call from Somerset County 911 Center. When he learns that only three volunteer fire companies have been dispatched, King, breathing hard, informs the dispatcher that "this is a large jetliner, probably related to what's going on," and requests that additional companies be dispatched for assistance.

When the airliner crashes, students at Shanksville-Stonycreek School feel the building shake and hear the windows rattle. Some teachers tell their students to take shelter under their desks. Other students run to the windows and see a large cloud of black smoke rising from the crash site.[722]

---

722. National Park Service, Flight 93, September 11, 2001.

10:03 a.m.: FAA reports a false alarm of "a fast moving twin [*sic*] from Pougipsee [*sic*, Poughkeepsie] towards World Trade Center."

10:03 a.m.: At NORAD NEADS in Rome, New York: "In the Ops Room, scopes now searched for [another United flight], which had turned toward Cleveland. Was it a hijacking? NEADS and Cleveland Center watched until it landed. The pilot simply wanted to get down. 'I was actually expecting to hear about more (hijackings) from other parts of the country,' a technician says. 'Los Angeles, Dallas that's what I was expecting.'"[723]

10:04 a.m.: At the Pentagon, Army Brig. Gen. Montague Winfield takes over from Capt. Leidig as the DDO in the NMCC.[724] The Air Threat Conference Call log for 10:04 a.m. is now showing multiple new reports of additional hijacked aircraft:[725]

> White House (PEOC): "Understand we have inbound [toward Washington] twenty-five minutes out [referring to UA Flight 93, which has already crashed]. We have assets at Andrews [of the DC National Guard]. Has anybody contacted those?"
>
> NMCC (DDO): "PEOC say again your request. I'm not sure we have the same information you do."
>
> White House (PEOC): "From the [Secret Service] JOC we just heard that we have an inbound that's twenty-five minutes out, and my question is, the fighter assets out at Andrews—have we given them the word?"
>
> Air Force: "Is that confirmed that they're coming to DC? Copy."
>
> NMCC (DDO): "That's the word that we got from the JOC, but we haven't got a confirmation yet."
>
> Air Force: "If you can, type aircraft?"

---

723. Hart Seely, "Amid Crisis Simulation, 'We Were Suddenly No-Kidding Under Attack,'" Newhouse News Service, January 25, 2002.

724. 9/11 Commission Memorandum for the Record, Interview, Captain Charles Joseph Leidig, USN, April 29, 2004.

725. 9/11 Air Threat Conference Call Transcription, partially declassified.

This is the first mention of the DC National Guard F-16 unit, stationed at Andrews AFB, Maryland. The wing is not an air defense unit, and it is not under NORAD control. But it will become involved in protecting the skies over Washington, initially receiving orders that ultimately come from the White House rather than the Pentagon.

10:05 a.m.: Air Threat Conference Call log:[726]

> NMCC (DDO): "We understand 767 from United, but I can't confirm that. NORAD?" [Crosstalk and confusion follows]
> NORAD: "NORAD has no indication of a hijack heading to Washington at this time."

10:05 a.m.: Secret Service reports that the Eisenhower Executive Office Building (adjacent to the White House) has now been fully evacuated except for the Secret Service JOC.[727] Secret Service agents armed with automatic rifles are deployed into Lafayette Park across from the White House.[728]

10:05 a.m.: FAA DC logs: "Fighter coverage over White House reported by military."[729]

10:06 a.m.: FAA reports a false alarm: "TWA [Flight] 315 refused to go to PIT [Pittsburgh] diverting to IAD [Dulles], altitude 160."[730]

10:07 a.m.: White House PEOC shelter log places Secretary of Transportation Norman Mineta in the shelter.[731]

---

726. 9/11 Air Threat Conference Call Transcription, partially declassified; Air Threat Conference Call log, "DJH Notes," Top Secret, partially declassified.

727. Secret Service, Timeline Report, Current as of September 12, 2001, partially declassified.

728. Secret Service, Timeline Report, Current as of September 12, 2001, partially declassified.

729. DCC Timeline.

730. At 10:08 a.m., the FAA reported: "TWA 315 [was] diverting to ORD [Chicago]." At 10:10 a.m., it reports: "TWA 315 [is] responding to clearances."

731. 9/11 Commission, MFR, "Status of WH 'Day of' Investigation," March 2, 2004.

(Acting Secretary Mineta later testified before the 9/11 Commission that he entered the PEOC at 9:20 a.m., but the PEOC wasn't occupied by senior officials yet, so he probably meant that was the time he entered the White House. Responsible for the FAA, Mineta was at his office at the Department of Transportation before that. He may have played a role as adviser to Cheney, but otherwise his presence ends up being perfunctory, given that all four of the aircraft had crashed by the time he arrived.)

10:07 a.m.: Air Threat Conference Call log: "P[EOC]: Update on CAP [combat air patrol over Washington]?"[732]

10:07 a.m.: UA Flight 93. FAA reports: "Lost radar with UAL 93 south Johnstown, PA."[733]

In response to a request from FAA Cleveland Center, a Fairchild Falcon 20 business jet, already descending to land at the Johnstown-Cambria County Airport, is instructed to drop down to look for a crash. The pilot spots smoke and flames and reports the position of the UA Flight 93 crash site and a description of the area.[734]

Cleveland Center notifies NORAD NEADS that UA Flight 93 had a bomb on board and passes along the aircraft's last known latitude and longitude.

NEADS is not able to locate UA Flight 93 on radar because it has already crashed. The call is the first notification the military—at any level—receives about UA Flight 93. No one from FAA HQ, which was informed of the hijacking at 9:34 a.m., contacts the DOD. In fact, the executive-level managers at FAA headquarters do not forward to the military any of the information they receive from FAA Herndon Command Center regarding the flight.[735]

---

732. Air Threat Conference Call log, "DJH Notes," Top Secret, partially declassified.

733. At 10:04 a.m., FAA Cleveland Center indicates that its primary radar target (UA Flight 93) terminated in the vicinity of Somerset, Pennsylvania.

734. National Park Service, Flight 93, September 11, 2001.

735. 9/11 Commission Staff Report, August 26, 2004; NORAD 9/11 Timeline, n.d., prepared for the 9/11 Commission.

According to the Air Force: "NEADS personnel were not aware that United Airlines Flight 93 had been hijacked until just over four minutes after it had slammed into an abandoned strip mine in Pennsylvania. Word of United Flight 93's last known latitude and longitude came during a telephone call from an FAA military liaison who was himself unaware that the aircraft had crashed. Twelve minutes after the crash, in the course of a telephone call initiated by NEADS staff, the FAA informed the air defenders that United Flight 93 had gone down at an unknown location northeast of Camp David."[736]

10:07 a.m.: "FBI NCRS and JTTF [Joint Terrorism Task Force] were dispatched to the Pentagon, with the Crime Scene Team onsite 30 minutes after the attack. Special Agent John Adams began organizing the FBI Evidence Recovery Team on a grassy site about 30 yards from the ACFD ICP [Arlington County Fire Department Incident Command Post] . . . FBI agents began searching for aircraft parts and other evidence . . . being careful not to interfere with fire and rescue."[737]

10:07 a.m.: At the World Trade Center, NYPD helicopter Aviation 6 warns that collapse of the North Tower is likely and further advises immediate evacuation. "About fifteen floors down from the top, it looks like it's glowing red," the helicopter pilot reports.

NYPD helicopter Aviation 14 also radios at 10:07 a.m. "It's inevitable." Seconds later, the other pilot (Aviation 6) reports: "I don't think this has too much longer to go. I would evacuate all people within the area of that second building."[738]

10:08 a.m.: FAA reports bomb threat: "CLE [Cleveland] AFSS evacuated bomb threat."

---

736. *The First 109 Minutes: 9/11 and the US Air Force*, 2011.
737. Arlington County: After-Action Report on the Response to the September 11 Terrorist Attack on the Pentagon.
738. NIST Chronology.

10:08 a.m.: In Shanksville, Pennsylvania, the fire department requests all available emergency medical units. Rick King, en route to the crash site with three other firefighters in Shanksville's engine, radios to request all available emergency medical service units in Somerset and Cambria Counties. He phones his wife at Ida's Store and tells her to get their children out of school.[739]

10:08 a.m.: NYPD Chief of Department Terence Monahan orders that no traffic be allowed to enter Manhattan.[740]

10:09 a.m.: Air Threat Conference Call log:[741]

> White House (PEOC): "Word from [Secret Service] JOC is UAL 93 out of Pitt about twenty minutes out [from Washington]. FAA has not made contact with it yet but has tried." [The flight has already crashed.]
>
> Air Force: "Destination or heading?"
>
> White House (PEOC): "That's why I am asking about [fighter aircraft out of] Andrews."
>
> NMCC (DDO) to Air Force: "Have any aircraft been scrambled in response to UAL 93, and what is status of CAP?"
>
> Air Force: "Stand by."

10:10 a.m.: Air Force One changes direction and heads west.[742] "Joint Surveillance System radar files show that AF One diverted to the west."[743]

After flying for just 25 minutes, but for what seems like an eternity on the morning of 9/11, the president's plane banks in the direction of Barksdale AFB, Louisiana, where it will land, refuel, and replenish with supplies, food, and water. There the president will record a statement.

---

739. National Park Service Flight 93 National Memorial, Timeline, Flight 93, September 11, 2001.

740. NIST Chronology.

741. Air Threat Conference Call log, "DJH Notes," Top Secret, partially declassified.

742. Defense Studies Series, Pentagon 9/11.

743. 9/11 Commission, Memorandum for the Record, n.d., 2012-042-doc24, partially declassified.

CHAPTER 11

"CLEARED TO ENGAGE"

In hindsight, some think it scandalous that on 9/11, the airspace of the northeastern United States was defended by only two air defense posts—one at Otis Air National Guard Base on Cape Cod, Massachusetts, and the other at Langley AFB in Virginia. Each site had two fighter jets on alert 24 hours a day, seven days a week, a legacy of Cold War days when hundreds of fighters—some armed with nuclear air-to-air missiles—guarded US skies from a Soviet enemy.

Additionally, some think it a blunder that the US military was focused outward, not just because the national security community lacked imagination in anticipating 9/11-like hijackings but also somehow suggesting that inwardly focused aircraft could have prevented the attacks, which, as should now be clear, was never the case.

The two F-15 fighters on alert at Otis took off at 8:52 a.m., 15 minutes after NORAD's NEADS was initially contacted by FAA Boston Center. What followed from the initial request for help was a series of calls, from NEADS to the continental command in Florida and from Florida to NORAD Central in Colorado Springs. "Go ahead and scramble them," Maj. Gen. Larry Arnold at continental headquarters told NEADS, saying that they'd get authorization later.

By the time fighters were in the sky, AA Flight 11 had already struck the North Tower (at 8:46 a.m.), and UA Flight 175—barely yet recognized as another hijacking—hit the South Tower 17 minutes later. This was just 11 minutes after the Cape Cod planes were airborne, not enough time for the fighters to cover the distance from Massachusetts to New York City. To further punctuate this point, it wouldn't have been enough time even—as some critics assert—for fighters, even had they been on alert in the New York area, to intervene.[744] That is, even if the military pilots had had enough time to take off, had gotten to Manhattan, and had been able to find a nonsquawking airliner among heavy air traffic, hijacker pilot Mohammed Atta had switched off the airliner's transponder—the device that actively tells the air control system where the plane is. Without a transponder, the FAA and NORAD had to physically "find" the flight in and among thousands of objects in the sky. Radar technicians frantically looked.

Once in the air, there was still a huge question as to what the fighter pilots were expected to do. Had interceptors managed to reach AA Flight 11, everyone thought at the time that they were dealing with a standard hijacking, and the military jets would escort the airliner to John F. Kennedy Airport or some other location, where it would land, and hijackers would make their demands. And later, when it became clear that more planes were being hijacked, that this wasn't a normal situation—even then, what were the interceptors to do? Shoot planes out of the skies over Manhattan or the District of Columbia to fall into those cities?

At 10:12 a.m., more than an hour after the World Trade Center was hit, the White House conveyed verbal orders from Vice President Cheney that fighters could shoot down civilian airliners. NORAD commander Gen. Eberhart later said that the initial order conveyed to pilots was location-based (that planes had to be over the nation's capital) and not that a hijacked airliner would have to display a "hostile act." Eberhart considered this "an extreme act," and he modified the White House order to say that pilots should still look for a hostile act on the part of suspect planes. He later said he viewed his direction as specificity, not countermanding.[745] Countermanding or not, by the time Eberhart modified the order (and after President Bush approved "the military to use force if necessary" at 10:25 a.m.[746]), the Pentagon had also already been hit, and UA Flight 93 had already gone down in Pennsylvania.

By then, the first F-16 fighters from Langley AFB in Virginia had established a combat air patrol over the skies of Washington. "If a plane ignored warnings,

---

744. There was an Air National Guard F-16 unit in Atlantic City, New Jersey, but it had ceased 24-hour status in 1998. The two planes are actually in the air at the time, but unarmed. Shortly after UA Flight 175 hits the South Tower, they are ordered back to base to arm and sent to Washington, arriving at around 11:00 a.m.

745. 9/11 Commission NORAD MFR.

746. Presidential Daily Diary, partially declassified.

they would fire on it, on orders from the president," one report says.[747] On orders from the president, the report says, but NORAD's own logs say that fighter pilots over DC were told that they had "negative clearance to shoot."

Secretary Rumsfeld says that as a former naval aviator, he was particularly concerned about the orders being given to the pilots. "There were no rules of engagement on the books about when and how our pilots should handle a situation in which civilian aircraft had been hijacked. . . . [Gen.] Myers was troubled too. 'I'd hate to be a pilot up there and not know exactly what I should do,' I said to him."[748] And yet that ambiguity persisted throughout the rest of the day. All during this time, NORAD deliberated about "what" authority pilots were actually flying under and what rules of engagement (ROE) applied. It was never fully resolved.

F-16s from the DC National Guard join the Langley-based fighters over the skies of Washington at 11:09 a.m. Their ROE were even more jumbled, as the planes were not assigned to NORAD, and they seemed to be getting their instructions from the Secret Service. More military jets—now armed with long-range air-to-air missiles—gathered in the afternoon, planes from Richmond, Virginia, and Atlantic City, New Jersey. At one point as many as 12 fighters—including Navy and Marine Corps aircraft—were flying patrols over the capital region.[749] "By the afternoon," the National Guard says in its history, "34 Air National Guard fighter units had generated aircraft around the nation ready to fly combat missions. Fifteen of those units flew 179 fighter missions during the first 24 hours, refueled in the air by 18 Guard wings generating 78 aircraft."[750] Like the planes of the DC National Guard, many of these units were not part of NORAD's normal pool and had never even practiced any kind of domestic air defense mission.

10:10 a.m.: Langley-based F-16 fighter pilots, now over Washington, inquire as to what orders they are to follow with respect to potential targets. NORAD NEADS emphatically tells pilots: "Negative clearance to shoot."

747. Hart Seely, "Amid Crisis Simulation, 'We Were Suddenly No-Kidding Under Attack,'" Newhouse News Service, January 25, 2002.

748. *Known and Unknown*, pp. 339–340.

749. Defense Studies Series, Pentagon 9/11. F-1s from the Marine Fighter Attack Squadron 321 flew over DC skies later in the day as well. Navy fighters flew just off the Atlantic coast, near New York.

750. National Guard Bureau, *A Chronological History of the Air National Guard and Its Antecedents, 1908–2007*, compiled by Dr. Charles J. Gross, NGB-PAH, April 2, 2007.

Lt. Col. Nasypany, the MCC, and his weapons director discuss the current ROE, agreeing that they do not have permission to shoot down targets; their task is to identify aircraft by type and tail number.[751]

10:10 a.m.: UA Flight 93. Even after the flight has crashed, United Airlines dispatcher Ed Ballinger sends an ACARS message: "Don't divert to DC. Not an option." He sends the same message one minute later.[752]

FAA reports: "Receiving 911 calls from UAL 93, 40 SE Johnston, PA and black smoke."

10:10 a.m.: At the World Trade Center, fire chiefs in front of the Marriott Hotel (WTC 3) work to reestablish operations as firefighters try to find their way down from the upper floors while others try to free people trapped in the lobby of the hotel.[753]

10:10 a.m.: First Lady Laura Bush is evacuated from the Russell Senate Office Building to Secret Service headquarters in downtown Washington, DC.

Mrs. Bush was on Capitol Hill to give remarks on early reading before the Senate Education Subcommittee. Senators Edward Kennedy (D-MA) and Judd Gregg (R-NH) meet her as her limo pulls up, making small talk in Kennedy's office as they wait to either carry on with the hearing or implement some kind of emergency procedure.

After the Pentagon is hit, Mrs. Bush's Secret Service detail moves her to Senator Gregg's hideaway office on the lower-level interior of the Capitol building. The head of her protective detail wants to take her to the secure location, leaving the staff behind, but the First Lady stands firm that they have to accompany her. As the First Lady later recalls it, they all run behind black-clad men with guns drawn through the Capitol basement and the Russell Senate Office Building garage to waiting limos and vans, to be taken to the Secret Service building less than a mile away. There, the First

751. 9/11 Commission Memorandum for the Record, Interview with NEADS Alpha Flight Mission Crew Commander (MCC), Lt. Col. Kevin J. Nasypany, January 22, 2004, and January 23, 2004; 9/11 Commission Staff Report, August 26, 2004.

752. 9/11 Commission Staff Report, August 26, 2004.

753. NIST Chronology.

Lady waits in an underground conference room for most of the day, watching television and trying to get her husband, daughters, and parents on the phone. One of her aides is sent back to retrieve a few days of clothes for her from the White House just in case she won't be going back. Her advance man retrieves Spot, Barney, and India, the Bushes' two dogs and cat.[754]

Noelia Rodriguez, press secretary to the First Lady, recalls: "We left the Capitol at 10:10. Mrs. Bush had a lot of staffers there and some of us were in the limo, which was parked in the portico at the Capitol, and we were talking excitedly: 'What could this be? Where are we going? What's next?' . . . just chatter, you know. Then the driver said something like, 'Ladies, this is a time to pay attention.' He meant it was a time to be quiet. I think he wanted to hear the instructions he was getting in his earpiece. Just then, what seemed like two dozen of these ninja guys surrounded the car . . . Secret Service agents all dressed in black. Mrs. Bush then got in the car, and they took us to the 'secure location' you've heard about.

"Many of the women on our staff are quite young. Some were crying; others, you could see the shock on their faces. Mrs. Bush was worried about them. She was trying to show by example that everything was going to be OK. She was also concerned about the staff we'd left behind at the White House."[755]

10:11 a.m.: Deputy NSA Hadley informs the WHSR: "By executive order of the President of the United States, Continuity of Government and Continuity of Presidency programs are now in effect."[756]

---

754. *Spoken from the Heart*, pp. 197–203. Some of the others with Laura Bush were Andi Ball, the First Lady's chief of staff; White House Domestic Policy Adviser Margaret Spellings; Noelia Rodriguez, press secretary to Laura Bush; Ashleigh Adams, deputy press secretary to Laura Bush; John Meyer, advance man; and Sarah Moss, the First Lady's personal aide. See "Voices of 9-11: 'A Cacophony of Information,'" *National Journal*, August 31, 2002; *Dead Certain: The Presidency of George W. Bush*, p. 141.

755. See "Voices of 9-11: 'A Cacophony of Information,'" *National Journal*, August 31, 2002; *Dead Certain: The Presidency of George W. Bush*, p. 141.

756. "At 10:11 a.m., on the morning of September 11, 2001, Deputy National Security Adviser Stephen Hadley notified the White House Situation Room that 'Continuity of Government and Continuity of Presidency programs' were in effect"; *24 Hours Inside the President's Bunker*, p. 57. See also 9/11 Commission Report, pp. 35–36.

Though COG is declared at 9:59 a.m., it appears that at 10:11 a.m., the WHSR affirms not just that continuity has been declared but also that participants have acknowledged that they have received the order. There is no record of an actual executive order issued to the effect that COG is authorized by President Bush. The proclamation of continuity of the presidency (COP) at 10:11 a.m. is more specific. "By executive order of the President," though, was a verbal order. No paper order was ever produced.

10:11 a.m.: Air Threat Conference Call log:[757]

> 10:11 a.m.: NORAD: "Currently have two [fighter] aircraft airborne out of Atlantic City. Additional scramble . . . standby for ETA to DC."
>
> 10:11 a.m.: White House (PEOC): "FAA in conference?"
>
> 10:11 a.m.: NMCC (DDO): "No, we've been unable to get them. We have them on separate lines in NMCC."
>
> 10:11 a.m.: White House (PEOC): "Can you clarify with them information on UAL 93?"
>
> 10:12 a.m.: NMCC (DDO): "We're doing it."
>
> 10:13: a.m.: White House (PEOC): "We've got confirmation of a place sixty miles out. We think it's 93. Apparently we're hearing weapons free right now. Status of Atlantic City?"
>
> 10:13 a.m.: NORAD: "We have confirmation that Atlantic City aircraft are airborne; we're querying destination."
>
> 10:14 a.m.: NMCC (DDO): "Assets out of Andrews launched?"
>
> 10:14 a.m.: NORAD: "No info on that."

The NORAD CONR chat transcript also "reflects that WADS [NORAD Western Air Defense Sector] asked 'What ROE are we working under?'"[758]

The White House seems more in control of aircraft over Washington than the Pentagon, even inquiring about whether the FAA has the right

---

757. Air Threat Conference Call log, "DJH Notes," Top Secret, partially declassified. At 10:11 a.m., the FAA reports again: "UAL 93 heading to Washington," after the plane had already crashed. See National Archives Chronology.

758. 9/11 Commission, Memorandum for the Record, n.d., 2012-042-doc24, partially declassified.

information that UA Flight 93 has already crashed. But its belief that the fighter jets have some "weapons free" order is incorrect, and the Pentagon seems not to answer their assertion over the teleconference.

10:12 a.m.: NORAD receives verbal orders from Vice President Cheney that fighters can shoot down civilian airliners.[759]

"White House (PEOC): DDO, this is PEOC. The Vice President has just confirmed fighters are cleared to engage the aircraft inbound if we can verify that it is, in fact, the hijacked aircraft."[760]

Capt. Leidig, then in the NMCC, says, "Concerning the first registering of the vice president's shoot down language. He recalled that it was more specific than what is registered in the transcript at this point. It is more of a question than an order. He doesn't think that they have given the order at that point." Later, he says he recalls a modification of the order, "that when a plane got 15 minutes" from Washington, "they had authority to engage." He calls it a "pin drop" moment, "when the '15 minutes' language came over the speaker phone. All heads in the room turned toward the speaker."[761]

"By 1012 EDT, JCS, and by extension NORAD, had verbal authority from the VP to take out aircraft threatening Washington DC. Prior to that, at least one CONR Sector (Western) asked for ROE clarification. CJCS and NORAD standing rules-of-engagement were written with an external threat in mind. Internal language, however, appears to give CINC NORAD latitude apart from the National Command Authority (NCA)."[762]

Gen. Myers is later asked by the 9/11 Commission whether this guidance from the PEOC—from Cheney—was sufficient for him "from a chain

759. There are contradictory times, whether this occurred at 10:12 or 10:14 a.m.

760. 9/11 Air Threat Conference Call Transcription, partially declassified. This is a slightly different formulation reached by the 9/11 Commission and one that was far more restrictive. "NMCC chronology records that PEOC . . . states 'VP has directed that fighters can confirm A/C is hijacked they are cleared to take it out.'" See 9/11 Commission, Memorandum for the Record, n.d., 2012-042-doc24, partially declassified.

761. 9/11 Commission Memorandum for the Record, Interview Captain Charles Joseph Leidig, USN, April 29, 2004.

762. 9/11 Commission, Memorandum for the Record, n.d., 2012-042-doc24, partially declassified.

of command perspective." Myers says yes: "You make several assumptions; that he's [Cheney] in contact with the people he needs to be in contact with."[763]

Despite Cheney's order, NEADS MCC Lt. Col. Nasypany says his command center received "no engagement orders or change in ROE."[764]

NORAD commander Gen. Eberhart had ordered an Air Defense Emergency at 9:59 a.m., the needed authority under contingency plans to order scrambled air defense assets to shoot down attacking planes. It is still unclear, though, if the declared Air Defense Emergency could be applied to a hijacking. Despite Gen. Eberhart's order, no apparent change is made to the ROE, that is, no new order is issued. And Cheney's order probably has no lawful basis—unless it is transmitting President Bush's authority as commander in chief. The reality is that there is so much uncertainty about what pilots are authorized to do, as reflected in the many entries in NMCC, NORAD, White House, Secret Service, and FAA logs.

10:12 a.m.: "NMCC chronology notes that the PEOC directs NAOC airborne."[765]

Two National Airborne Operations Center E-4Bs are evidently already airborne, a primary and a secondary, at least one out of Andrews AFB. Later, in the Air Threat Conference Call, it is reported that three NAOCs are involved: a primary "in the primary survival orbit"; a secondary, at Offutt AFB, Nebraska, for the "north area"; and a tertiary, in the "NAOC survival orbit."[766] The origins and location of the third plane are unknown.

10:12 a.m.: FAA DC logs: "Air Force One has fighter escort [according to] ZJX [Jacksonville Center]."[767]

---

763. 9/11 Commission, MFR 04019757, Richard Myers Interview, n.d. (2003), partially declassified.

764. 9/11 Commission Memorandum for the Record, Interview with NEADS Alpha Flight Mission Crew Commander (MCC), Lt. Col. Kevin J. Nasypany, January 22, 2004, and January 23, 2004.

765. 9/11 Commission, Memorandum for the Record, n.d., 2012-042-doc24, partially declassified.

766. 9/11 Air Threat Conference Call Transcription, partially declassified.

767. DCC Timeline.

10:12 a.m.: At the World Trade Center, NYPD says all emergency vehicles are ordered to pull back away from the buildings.

10:12 a.m.: The news media reports an explosion on Capitol Hill.

10:14 a.m.: Air Threat Conference Call log:[768]

> White House (PEOC): "The VP has just confirmed fighters are cleared to engage the aircraft inbound if we can verify they are hijacked. Can you confirm with FAA?"
> NMCC (DDO): "Checking with FAA."
> White House (PEOC): "Just talked to the mil aide (AF1) [military aide Lt. Col. Gould]; we'd like AWACS over Louisiana. We'd like fighter escort."

10:14 a.m.: NORAD CONR chat transcript "reflects that WADS [NORAD Western Air Defense Sector] requested an ATO (Air Tasking Order) change real world requesting to load 'slammers' [air-to-air missiles]."

CONR chat transcript reflects that the CONR told WADS to "bring up with live missiles, cleared to load slammers."[769]

10:14 a.m.: FAA reports false alarm: "Fast-moving A/C 60 [miles] NW DC southeast bound headed towards DC."

10:15 a.m.: At the Pentagon, after buckling since 9:57 a.m., the roof of the E Ring area (the outer ring of the Pentagon) collapses above the hole carved by the penetration of AA Flight 77, pulling down the second through fifth floors. Narrower than the swath of damage created by the plane crash, the collapse zone is about 95 feet at its widest point along the building's outer wall and approximately 50 feet at its deepest point, reaching to the E Ring's inner wall, which remains standing.[770]

---

768. Air Threat Conference Call log, "DJH Notes," Top Secret, partially declassified.

769. 9/11 Commission, Memorandum for the Record, n.d., 2012-042-doc24, partially declassified.

770. Defense Studies Series, Pentagon 9/11.

10:15 a.m.: At the Pentagon, Gen. Myers is again trying to locate Secretary Rumsfeld, who is now in his third-floor Executive Communications Center ("Cables") rather than at the NMCC.[771]

With the collapse of the Pentagon roof, the building begins general evacuation. "Myers' staff evacuated the building and relocated to an alternate site; only his executive assistant stayed with Myers in the NMCC."[772]

When Arlington Fire Department Battalion Chief Dale Smith arrives in the Pentagon Center Court and establishes an auxiliary command post, he thinks the entire building is being evacuated. He relays an order to close down all air handlers, not knowing that many in command centers intended to remain. The incident commander and subordinates later direct the manipulation of the air handlers to reduce the amount of smoke in certain undamaged sections of the Pentagon.[773]

10:15 a.m.: (Approximate time) Defense officials start leaving the Pentagon for Site R ("Raven Rock"), the underground Alternate Joint Communications Center and backup NMCC on the Maryland-Pennsylvania border in Liberty Township, Pennsylvania.

"Rumsfeld says he was unwilling to be out of touch during the time it would take to relocate me to the safe site. I asked a reluctant Paul Wolfowitz . . . and my special assistant, Larry Di Rita, to leave immediately for Site R."[774]

(Gen. Myers later tells the 9/11 Commission that he spoke to Wolfowitz outside the Pentagon when he arrived from Capitol Hill and that Wolfowitz said "he was relocating for continuity reasons."[775] That conversation probably didn't happen as Myers recollects, because COG hadn't yet been invoked when Myers arrived at the Pentagon.)

---

771. Memorandum for the Record, Interview of General Richard Myers, February 17, 2004, partially declassified.

772. Memorandum for the Record, Interview of General Richard Myers, February 17, 2004, partially declassified.

773. Defense Studies Series, Pentagon 9/11.

774. *Known and Unknown*, p. 338. See also Defense Studies Series, Pentagon 9/11.

775. Memorandum for the Record, Interview of General Richard Myers, February 17, 2004, partially declassified.

Paul Wolfowitz remembers: "We told Rumsfeld to get out of the Building, but he didn't pay any attention. Again, after five or ten minutes we told him he ought to get out of the Building, that there might be something in the smoke. But he ignored it. After another ten minutes I also told him he ought to get out, and he said no, that I should get out and go up to Site R. They arranged helicopters to take a bunch of us up to Site R."[776]

According to the DOD history: "When the secretary [Rumsfeld] chose not to follow emergency plans that called on him to move to an alternate command site outside Washington, most other Defense leaders also stayed in the Pentagon, or close to it."[777]

Though the Pentagon COG plan calls for the vice chairman of the Joint Chiefs of Staff to also move to Site R, Gen. Myers (vice chairman and acting chairman) stays in the Pentagon as well. "[Chairman] Hugh Shelton was airborne on his way to Europe for a NATO meeting and couldn't be back for hours," Myers later writes.[778]

Other officials traveling to Site R under the continuity plans include Secretary of the Army Thomas White, the Defense Department executive agent responsible for implementing continuity as well as the official responsible for military support to civil authorities, the provision of military support for everything from disaster response to civil unrest. According to the Army's official history, White at first insists on staying at the Pentagon but is "forcibly" herded out of the building to Site R, leaving Army Vice Chief of Staff Gen. Jack Keane in charge (the chief of staff is in Asia). Once White is evacuated, the very people who insisted he evacuate realize that they have operated contrary to their own plans and bring White back from Site R. Under the law, a civilian is needed to implement COG and to broker support to the states.[779]

---

776. Office of the Secretary of Defense (OSD), "Pentagon Attack, Interview with Paul Wolfowitz," April 19, 2002, https://history.defense.gov/Portals/70/Documents/oral_history/OH_Trans_WolfowitzPaul4-19-2002.pdf.

777. Defense Studies Series, Pentagon 9/11.

778. *Eyes on the Horizon*, p. 10.

779. Army Brig. Gen. Peter Chiarelli, then head of the Army Operations Center, recalls:

We got word that a specific stage [of continuity] . . . had been ordered. And at this time, the Secretary of the Army was up with the Vice [Chief of Staff Gen. Keane]. We informed the Secretary that it was time for him to leave. He indicated he was

10:15 a.m.: The Navy evacuates its Pentagon command center.

"Deprived of his command center [with the evacuation of the Pentagon], Chief of Naval Operations Admiral Vernon Clark . . . told his vice chief, Admiral William Fallon, and Vice Admiral Patricia Tracey, director

---

not leaving. He was staying in the building. We knew by the regulation that he had no choice.

The NCO [in charge of continuity] looked at me and said, "Sir, he has no choice at this time. This has been directed, and he must immediately proceed and leave here. This is bigger than him. This is continuity of the government of the United States."

I remember looking at him and saying, "Are you sure of this?"

And he said, "Yes, I'm sure. Sir, you need to go up and tell him that he needs to get up and go."

And I remember—I had been in the job for less than a month, and having heard just a few minutes ago that there was a CAP [combat air patrol] over the building, I was about to leave my desk, walk upstairs to the balcony, walk down to the Secretary of the Army, and basically order him out of the building, along with my NCO—I was thinking, "My God, when is somebody going to wake me up. When is this horrible, horrible dream going to end!" But it didn't end, as we all know.

I left with the good sergeant. . . . We went upstairs and I basically leaned over between the Vice and the Secretary of the Army, who were sitting next to each other, and so informed the Secretary that he had no choice. He was bound to do this. We had gotten word that this portion of the implementation plan was in effect and that he must proceed directly to a specified place in the building where he would get in a helicopter and leave.

He said, "Well, how do I get there?"

I said, "The sergeant will lead."

Sure enough, he said, "All right," and off he goes.

Only to find out later on, like most reports go—this was the phenomena of the first report, something I know very, very well, but it was one of those where you couldn't take a chance, where we had verified the information and were told yes—we found out that it wasn't required for him to leave at that particular point in time, because the level of evacuation did not reach his level. It was, in reality, a splitting of some key and critical people in the national command authority to go to a different site, but it was not a requirement, and the person who had told us had misspoke over the phone, only to find out that we kicked the Secretary of the Army out of the building to get into a helicopter to fly to a location, when he, in fact, really didn't have to.

See *Then Came the Fire*. See also Defense Studies Series, Pentagon 9/11.

Perhaps another reason they brought him back was that the Secretary of the Army was second in the Defense Department line of succession, after the deputy secretary of defense, to assume responsibilities as the acting secretary of defense, and it made no sense to have the second and third in line in the same place.

of the Navy staff, that he would not relocate to the Pentagon's alternate command post [at Site R]. Instead he would move to the Washington Navy Yard, a few miles away . . . some staff members had already left to prepare accommodations there in the headquarters building of the Naval Criminal Investigative Service (NCIS). Secretary of the Navy Gordon England joined Clark at the temporary site."[780] NCIS agents keep them informed of efforts to account for missing personnel, a top priority.

Earlier, Fallon had moved to the Navy Annex building on Columbia Pike (and adjacent to the Pentagon) to establish a command center that would allow Navy leaders to operate in close proximity to the Pentagon. By the time Fallon arrived, the Annex had been evacuated. The building has electrical power but has lost its air conditioning, a condition that can cause computerized communication systems to overheat and shut down. Still, the Marine Corps Command Center in the building is functioning. After its director, Maj. Gen. Gordon Nash, offers space to the Navy, Fallon makes arrangements for the Navy's leadership to move there. Maintenance crews begin to set up portable air conditioners and exhaust fans for the center. Because of fear of another attack, however, only mission-essential personnel are allowed to enter.[781]

10:15 a.m.: At the Pentagon, FBI Special Agent Combs passes a warning to Assistant Chief Schwartz, the incident commander, that a fourth hijacked airliner is on a direct flight path to Washington (from the 10:14 a.m. FAA alert).[782]

Schwartz orders evacuation. Rescue workers withdraw to what are thought to be safe areas.[783]

---

780. England had flown to Fort Worth, Texas, the previous day to deliver a speech and was flying back to Washington in a Navy plane when he heard of the terrorist attacks. He was escorted by F-16s to Andrews AFB, Maryland. He went to the improvised Navy command center set up at the Washington Navy Yard. See Donna Miles, "Deputy Secretary: 9/11 Changed America Forever," American Forces Press Service, September 7, 2006.

781. Defense Studies Series, Pentagon 9/11.

782. Defense Studies Series, Pentagon 9/11.

783. Defense Studies Series, Pentagon 9/11.

The order to evacuate is broadcast repeatedly on fire, police, Defense Protective Service, and other radio channels. The DOD history says: "Portable radios, however, were not always fully functional, cell phones did not work, and there were few of the more reliable Nextel radio phones available. Consequently, evacuation orders were passed by word of mouth, shouted out through bullhorns, or sounded by air horns and honking fire trucks to clear the area rapidly. But it took time to disseminate the command and even longer for everyone in and around the building to respond. Every five minutes or so radios announced the time remaining until the [hijacked] aircraft was expected to arrive."[784]

10:15 a.m.: UA Flight 93. FAA reports: "UAL 93 is down, confirmed . . . [at] site, in mountains SE Johnstown-Somerset, PA."

10:15 a.m.: At the World Trade Center, units from the outer boroughs arrive. Firefighters are still in the North Tower, "in no apparent hurry to get out."[785]

10:16 a.m.: NORAD CONR chat transcript "records that CONR DCO [Defense Coordination Officer] declared that 'Peacetime ROE [rules of engagement] still [in effect].'"[786]

But peacetime ROE are definitely not in effect, neither for aircraft over Washington nor for those flying nationwide. According to NORAD, Gen. Eberhart's declaration of an Air Defense Emergency at 9:59 a.m. has automatically transitioned the peacetime ROE to a new set of authorities, allowing subordinate commanders to make independent decisions. And though the Washington-area planes are in more direct contact with the White House (either directly or through the Secret Service), the vice president's order (at 10:12 a.m.) has also provided new ROEs.

---

784. Defense Studies Series, Pentagon 9/11.

785. NIST Chronology.

786. 9/11 Commission, Memorandum for the Record, n.d., 2012-042-doc24, partially declassified.

10:17 a.m.: FAA joins the Air Threat Conference Call hosted by the NMCC.[787] The 9/11 Commission later reports:

> Operators worked feverishly to include the FAA in this teleconference, but they had equipment problems and difficulty finding secure phone numbers. NORAD asked three times before 10:03 to confirm the presence of FAA on the conference, to provide an update on hijackings. The FAA did not join the call until 10:17 a.m.
>
> The FAA representative who joined the call had no familiarity with or responsibility for a hijack situation, had no access to decision-makers, and had none of the information available to senior FAA officials by that time. We found no evidence that, at this critical time, during the morning of September 11th, NORAD's top commanders in Florida or Cheyenne Mountain ever coordinated with their counterparts at FAA headquarters to improve situational awareness and organize a common response. Lower-level officials improvised—the FAA's Boston Center bypassing the chain of command to contact NORAD NEADS in Rome, NY directly. But the highest level Defense Department officials relied on the NMCC's Air Threat Conference, in which the FAA did not meaningfully participate.[788]

The Air Threat Conference Call log (for 10:17 a.m.) records the following:[789]

NMCC (DDO): "FAA, are you in conference?"

FAA: "Yes."

NMCC (DDO): "Vice Chairman [Gen. Myers] would like to know
    who's controlling aircraft over DC."

FAA: "The Washington Center [FAA Herndon Command Center],
    if any. FAA has implemented nationwide ground stop to DC and
    NY. If any aircraft cover [sic, actually over] DC, being controlled
    by Wash Center. We understand that there are some, and fighters
    launched to patrol the DC area."

---

787. "Twelfth Public Hearing," National Commission on Terrorist Attacks upon the United States, June 17, 2004, http://www.9-11commission.gov/archive/hearing12/9-11Commission_Hearing_2004-06-17.htm.

788. "Twelfth Public Hearing," National Commission on Terrorist Attacks upon the United States, June 17, 2004, http://www.9-11commission.gov/archive/hearing12/9-11Commission_Hearing_2004-06-17.htm.

789. Air Threat Conference Call log, "DJH Notes," Top Secret, partially declassified.

NMCC (DDO): "Yes. We have reports of two aircraft currently over DC."

"Myers was informed [by the 9/11 Commission staff] that . . . there was no evidence NORAD was effectively tracking aircraft inbound to Washington at that time. He replied, 'I was not aware of that . . . I have in my mind that in fact we could pair fighters against the inbound from the north, northwest . . . whether the FAA was there or not I don't know; they were there later.'"[790]

10:16 a.m.: FAA reports false alarm: "Fast westbound [aircraft headed] to Boston 16,000 [feet] reported by ZNY [New York Center]."[791]

10:17 a.m.: FAA reports on bomb threat clearing Cleveland Center: "ZOB [Cleveland Center] bomb threat, evacuating the building."

10:18 a.m.: President Bush, aboard Air Force One, talks with Vice President Cheney, now in the PEOC.[792]

During this call, at 10:25 a.m., President Bush authorizes the use of force to shoot down threatening commercial airliners (see 10:25 a.m.).

Bush is urged not to return until Cheney and Rice can "find out what the hell was going on."[793]

---

790. Memorandum for the Record, Interview of General Richard Myers, February 17, 2004, partially declassified.

791. National Archives Chronology.

792. Presidential Daily Diary, partially declassified.

793. *Cheney: The Untold Story of America's Most Powerful and Controversial Vice President*, p. 335. See also *Dead Certain: The Presidency of George W. Bush*, p. 139; *No Higher Honor*, pp. 72–73; *Known and Unknown*, p. 338. The 9/11 Commission writes: "All witnesses agreed that the president strongly wanted to return to Washington and only grudgingly agreed to go elsewhere. The issue was still undecided when the president conferred with the vice president at about the time Air Force One was taking off. The vice president recalled urging the president not to come back to Washington." See "Twelfth Public Hearing," National Commission on Terrorist Attacks upon the United States, June 17, 2004, http://www.9-11com mission.gov/archive/hearing12/9-11Commission_Hearing_2004-06-17.htm.

Vice President Dick Cheney talks with President Bush as senior staff listen from the National Presidential Emergency Operations Center. (Source: White House)

Col. Tillman, the Air Force One pilot, recalls: "We had the president who didn't want to follow our plans for a nuclear attack, which is hide him, keep him safe and allow continuity of government."[794]

The original plan, once the Pentagon was hit, was to fly directly to Offutt AFB in Omaha, but Andrew Card feels that this will take too long. "It was very important to the President to address the nation and make sure that the people could see that he was safe and in total control of the situation," Brig. Gen. Rosenker (head of the White House Military Office) later says.[795]

Eddie Marinzel, head of Bush's Secret Service detail that day, says that after consultations with White House Secret Service Chief Truscott in the PEOC and with director Stafford at Secret Service headquarters, everyone recommends that the president should continue traveling in a westerly

794. Tom Vanden Brook, "Air Force One Pilot Remembers 9/11," *Chicago Sun Times*, August 26, 2011.

795. The White House, Office of the Press Secretary, Internal Transcript, Interview of Gen. Mark V. Rosenker, Director of the White House Military Office by CBS, August 29, 2002.

direction. "DSAIC Marinzel was advised by Mr. Card that the President desired to land so that he could make a statement to the press."[796]

Lt. Col. Thomas Gould, the president's military aide, recalls President Bush saying: "I need to address the American people in the next hour." Bush is adamant. "He was concerned from his perspective that the leader of the United States shouldn't be in an airplane talking to the American people over a radio, which is the only capability we had at the time."[797]

They decide to go to nearby Barksdale AFB in Louisiana so that the president can make a public statement.[798]

At some point during the flight, President Bush summons CIA briefer Michael Morell to his airborne office and asks him about news media reports that the Democratic Front for the Liberation of Palestine (DFLP) is responsible. Morell says he tells Bush that they "do not possess the capability to do this." Bush tells Morell that he is to be informed as soon as the CIA knows anything. "The president said, 'Michael, I want to be the first to know. Got that?' He said it in a tone that meant he was deadly serious. 'Yes, sir,' I replied."[799]

10:18 a.m.: FAA reports false alarm: "Aircraft 160 [miles] east of Nantucket westbound high rate of speed headed toward BOS [Boston]."

10:19 a.m.: Air Threat Conference Call log:[800]

> White House (PEOC): "Unconfirmed we have an aircraft ten miles out from DC right now? FAA, can you confirm?"

796. Secret Service unlabeled document, partially declassified, and released under FOIA Appeal (File Numbers 20080330 and 20080331), in Letter, April 23, 2010. "Secret Service timeline reflects a collective decision to not return POTUS [Bush] to WH until conditions in WDC stabilize." 9/11 Commission, Memorandum for the Record, n.d., 2012-042-doc24, partially declassified.

797. Janene Scully, "Vandenberg Officer at Bush's Side During Attacks," *Santa Maria Times*, September 11, 2011.

798. National Museum of the United States Air Force, Wings and Things Guest Lecture Series, "Air Force One: Zero Failure," presentation of Col. (Ret.) Mark W. Tillman, n.d. (2009).

799. *The Great War of Our Time*, p. 52.

800. 9/11 Air Threat Conference Call Transcription, partially declassified.

FAA: "That I don't know. I'm back in secure area in Command Center. I'd have to go out on the floor to find out which is out there at this time. It would probably be as far as I know. Washington Center controlling all the aircraft in DC area at this time."[801]

White House (PEOC): "The vice president has cleared fighter aircraft engage any aircraft inbound to Washington, DC, area without authority."

NMCC (DDO): "Roger, understood. It can engage any aircraft without authority."

Why the vice president would be passing an order to the FAA is puzzling. And engage "without authority" could mean that the commercial aircraft is in DC airspace without authority, thus authorizing the pilot to engage. Or it could mean that the pilot is authorized to engage without higher authority.

10:19 a.m.: The Associated Press reports that the State Department is being evacuated due to a possible explosion.[802]

The Pentagon history states: "About 10:30 a.m. a report in official channels, repeated through the rumor mill, mistakenly stated that a car bomb had exploded at the State Department. Reports about truck bombs at the Capitol, fires on the Mall, and a 'suspicious' rental truck near the Pentagon, possibly loaded with explosives, added to the confusion. Sergeant Keith Bohn of the Park Police recalled, 'There were a lot of things coming up. All of a sudden, everything was just unbelievable—to check bridges for abandoned cars which were believed to be packed with explosives. So, we were running from one report of things to another report. Actually, in the city nothing else, in essence, happened that day, but . . . lots of fear was running rampant.'"[803]

Maj. David McNulty, an intelligence officer in the 113th Wing, says that once DC National Guard F-16 aircraft were launched, "they erased the white board on which they were noting information and turned off the TV" because, according to him, "at that point they [news media and Secret

---

801. Air Threat Conference Call log, "DJH Notes," Top Secret, partially declassified.
802. AP, "A Stunning 48 Hours of News," n.d. (September 12, 2001).
803. Defense Studies Series, Pentagon 9/11.

Service] were reporting crap," such as that the State Department had been blown up and so on.[804]

10:20 a.m.: The White House inquires as to whether a fighter plane has shot down UA Flight 93. Condoleezza Rice writes from the PEOC: "'You must know if you engaged a civilian aircraft,' the Vice President kept saying. 'How could you not know if you engaged a civilian aircraft?' It took what seemed like an eternity to get an answer: no, the air force had not shot down a civilian aircraft."[805]

Air Threat Conference Call log:[806]

AFOPS [Air Force operations]: "Questions about escort of AF1."

White House (PEOC): "Confirmed (escort required). Put that request in via the president, and also Dr. Rice is [in] the PEOC now. We'd like an update on aircraft that's supposedly ten miles out, probably closer now from Washington."

NMCC (DDO): "What type?"

White House (PEOC): "No confirmation. Airline from [Secret Service] JOC."

NMCC (DDO): "If you mean 93, FAA reported unidentified aircraft crashed sixty miles south of PA—we think that is 93."

White House (PEOC): "Yes. We know about that one—our question from the VP is whether that was the result of the fighters."

NORAD: "No info on that."

---

804. 9/11 Commission Memorandum for the Record, Interview, Major David McNulty, Chief of Intelligence, 121st Fighter Squadron, Air National Guard, Andrews AFB, March 11, 2004.

805. *No Higher Honor*, p. 74.

806. Air Threat Conference Call log, "DJH Notes," Top Secret, partially declassified; 9/11 Air Threat Conference Call Transcription, partially declassified. The 9/11 Commission later simplified this exchange, stating at 10:18 a.m.: "NMCC chronology records DDO telling PEOC UA93 is reported crashed in PA. PEOC asks that VP wants to know if it is a result of fighter engagement. DDO asked NORAD to confirm how A/C went down. NORAD has no info on engagement. FAA has no info." See 9/11 Commission, Memorandum for the Record, n.d., 2012-042-doc24, partially declassified.

10:20 a.m.: FAA reports false alarm: "N84048 departed from Orange County, NY without authorization."

10:20 a.m.: FAA reports: "ZNY [New York Center] reports sterilizing domestic airspace."

10:20 a.m.: At the World Trade Center, an NYPD helicopter (Aviation 14) reports that the North Tower is leaning. Firefighters inside the Marriott Hotel (WTC 3) are still ascending to answer mayday calls from trapped occupants.[807]

New York Metropolitan Transit Authority decides to halt all subway service in Manhattan.

10:20 a.m.: Secret Service in Washington attempts to reach the protective detail of Vice President Cheney's daughter Mary Cheney in Bonaire at her hotel and by cell phone, with no success.[808]

Mary Cheney, the vice president's youngest daughter, is scuba diving with her partner Heather Poe on the Caribbean island of Bonaire. As she tells the story, the two later emerge from an "amazing dive" to a minivan tearing down the beach road filled with Secret Service agents, one of her protective detail jumping out and saying something had happened, and "we've got to go." They are taken back to their hotel under a protective screen of agents.[809]

(A little more than 24 hours later, Mary and Heather are exclusive passengers on a specially laid on US Customs Service jet, allowed to fly though US airspace even though it is otherwise closed.)[810]

10:21 a.m.: FAA reports more bomb threats: "ZOB [Cleveland Center] reports two more."

---

807. NIST Chronology.

808. Secret Service Memorandum, White House Events on 9/11/01 (Special Agent James O. Scott), September 12, 2001, partially declassified.

809. *Cheney: The Untold Story of America's Most Powerful and Controversial Vice President*, p. 334.

810. Linda Kramer, "Mary Cheney Opens Up on Dad, Gay Marriage," *People*, May 4, 2006, https://people.com/celebrity/mary-cheney-opens-up-on-dad-gay-marriage/.

10:22 a.m.: WTOP radio, the all-news radio station in Washington, reports: "A plane went overhead . . . some sort of jet, maybe it was a military plane. But everywhere you looked, people were looking up into the sky with concern and fear on their faces that this might be another incoming terrorist attack. Just mind-boggling."

Air Threat Conference Call log for 10:22 a.m.:[811]

> NMCC (DDO): "AF, who has tactical control of the fighter aircraft flying over DC? Also questions to NORAD."
> Air Force operations: "We assumed NORAD."
> NORAD: "Confirmed, CONR has control."

10:22 a.m.: Department of the Army Operations Center at the Pentagon formally raises the worldwide Force Protection level to Delta (FPCON Delta).[812]

Unlike DEFCONs that apply to the readiness of US military forces, "Force Protection Conditions" govern a system of protective measures to reduce vulnerability of bases and forces to terrorist attacks (and civil disturbances, and in 2020, to COVID). Local commanders may increase the FPCON based on local factors and may apply additional protection measures to reduce the risk of attack. Delta is the highest level, required, according to DOD regulations, when "intelligence indicates that some form of terrorist action against personnel or facilities is imminent." It is an internal order relating to the security of military bases and personnel, not an alert per se. The conditions are as follows:

- Delta: Threatening action imminent.
- Charlie: Targeting imminent.
- Bravo: Predictable threat activity exists.
- Alpha: Possible threat activity.
- Normal: Routine security posture.

---

811. Air Threat Conference Call log, "DJH Notes," Top Secret, partially declassified.

812. Email, Global Command and Control System (US Joint Forces Command), "Force Protection Delta Ordered in CONUS," TCRM #12, September 11, 2001, and email from Major Scott Vendenbroek to Major James Anderson, "Threatcon Guidance," TCRM #13, September 11, 2001.

10:23 a.m.: FAA report clears up false alarm: "Westbound aircraft [reported as suspect at 10:16 a.m.] is Coast Guard from Nantucket."

Air Force fighters have been diverted to try to identify the aircraft.

10:23 a.m.: In Shanksville, Pennsylvania, Somerset County Coroner learns of the crash of UA Flight 93. Coroner Wally Miller calls Somerset County Emergency Management for confirmation. The EMA director advises him, "If I were you, I'd find a place to set up a temporary morgue somewhere."[813]

10:23 a.m.: At the World Trade Center, fires are now rapidly spreading throughout the North Tower. There are still dozens of firefighters in the building.[814]

10:24 a.m.: Air Threat Conference Call log:

Air Force: "Any info on aircraft ten miles out [from DC]?"
NORAD: "No."
White House (PEOC): "Unofficial word from [Secret Service] JOC is
        that aircraft is down."[815]

The NORAD CONR chat transcript "records the WADS Director of Operations telling CONR he got the word on armament, more than guns. Can you please help us with ROE?"[816]

10:24 a.m.: FAA logs report:

"All inbound transatlantic aircraft flying into the United States are now
        being diverted to Canada."
"UA 93 [UA Flight 93] down, 3959N/07846W (reported by military)
        (NE of Camp David)."[817]

---

813. National Park Service Flight 93 National Memorial, Timeline, Flight 93, September 11, 2001.

814. NIST Chronology.

815. Air Threat Conference Call log, "DJH Notes," Top Secret, partially declassified.

816. 9/11 Commission, Memorandum for the Record, n.d., 2012-042-doc24, partially declassified.

817. FAA, 11 Sep 01 Catastrophic Crisis (all times given in EDT).

10:24 a.m.: At the World Trade Center, dozens of people trapped in a North Tower stairway on and above the third floor are directed out by a firefighter who has broken through an office wall with an ax, allowing access to the mezzanine and the street. He lights the path with his flashlight. He stays behind to direct others out of the building and does not exit with people who have been trapped.

Final count of firehouse units reporting before the North Tower collapse: 35 Manhattan firehouses (13 of the 35 reporting multiple units), 30 Brooklyn firehouses (6 of 30 reporting multiple units), 7 Queens firehouses, 7 Bronx firehouses (1 of the 7 reporting multiple units), and 1 Staten Island firehouse.[818]

10:25 a.m.: President Bush, aboard Air Force One, authorizes the military to use force, if necessary, to bring down a commercial airplane.[819]

"I told Dick that our pilots should contact suspicious planes and try to get them to land peacefully. If that failed, they had my authority to shoot them down," Bush says.[820]

Bush says he had one call with Cheney that started at 10:18 a.m. and then another "a few minutes later," probably at 10:33 a.m. The order to use force, though, had already been issued by Cheney, most accounts agree, even if those orders related only to threats to Washington, DC.

"Secret Service timeline shows that the VP protection detail [was] notified that VP has directed military to shoot down the A/C if it gets too close to the WH."[821]

Brig. Gen. Wherley, commander of the 113th Wing of the DC National Guard, speaks directly to Secret Service agent Becky Editor, whom Wherley says is speaking for the vice president. He learns that the White House wants him to put aircraft over DC "with orders to intercept any aircraft that approached within any [sic] 20 miles of the city and turn the aircraft

---

818. NIST Chronology.

819. Presidential Daily Diary, partially declassified, states explicitly that at 10:25 a.m.: "NOTE: The President authorized the use of force."

820. *Decision Points*, p. 129.

821. 9/11 Commission, Memorandum for the Record, n.d., 2012-042-doc24, partially declassified.

around. If the aircraft would not change course, the interceptor should use 'any force necessary' to keep the aircraft from crashing into a building. Wherley asked if there was anybody in a uniform around there he could talk to. The Secret Service agent alluded to a Navy captain who was busy on other matters, but said no one was available. Wherley felt the instructions were not in military terms, but were understandable enough."[822]

Gen. Eberhart later notes that the order from Vice President Cheney is "an extreme act" and says that pilots should still look for a hostile act, not just for the fact that an airliner is approaching Washington.[823] Eberhart later tells the 9/11 Commission that he "assumed that the order was passed to the level of the fighter pilot. Rules of engagement are only good if those engaged know the rules."[824]

The order, according to the Secret Service, now contains the condition "too close" to the White House, though this is not what President Bush says he told Cheney in their first conversation. This further muddies the waters as to what Cheney and Bush's actual orders mean. As indicated in the logs of both the NMCC and NORAD, shoot-down authority had already been passed by the PEOC earlier, as a "White House" order.

Secretary Mineta later tells the 9/11 Commission that "probably about five or six minutes" after he entered the PEOC, he observed a conversation between Dick Cheney and a young aide.

During the time that the airplane coming into the Pentagon. There was a young man who had come in and said to the vice president, "The plane is 50 miles out. The plane is 30 miles out." And when it got down to, "The plane is 10 miles out," the young man also said to the vice president, "Do the orders still stand?" And the vice president turned and whipped his neck around and said, "Of course the orders still stand. Have you heard anything to the contrary?"[825]

822. 9/11 Commission Memorandum for the Record, Interview, BG David Wherley, on September 11, 2001, Commander of the 113th Wing of the USAF, August 28, 2003.

823. 9/11 Commission Memorandum for the Record, Interview with CINC NORAD (Commander in Chief NORAD), General Edward "Ed" Eberhart, March 1, 2004; 9/11 Commission NORAD MFR.

824. 9/11 Commission Memorandum for the Record, Interview with CINC NORAD (Commander in Chief NORAD), General Edward "Ed" Eberhart, March 1, 2004.

825. Testimony of Secretary of Transportation Norman Y. Mineta before the National Commission on Terrorist Attacks upon the United States (9/11 Commission), Public

10:25 a.m.: Air Threat Conference Call log alludes to DOD-wide FPCON Delta declaration, three minutes after the Army declares an increase to maximum vigilance. The STRATCOM rep says, "Break, break, this is STRATCOM controller. DOD has directed force protection condition Delta [FPCON Delta] immediately." A few moments later, NORAD asks if this applies to US assets worldwide, and the NMCC DDO states, "That's correct. DOD directed force protection level Delta worldwide."[826]

10:25 a.m.: FAA reports: "NOTAM issued: Washington-area airports closed."[827]

10:26 a.m.: "NORAD Air Warning Center log reflects that CONR said [that the] present set of A/C [aircraft in the air over Washington] has guns, next set will have missiles. The CONR chat transcript records that CONR DCO [defense coordination officer] told WADS, 'Still peacetime ROE, NCA working modifications.'"[828]

10:27 a.m.: UA Flight 93. Air Threat Conference Call log: "CONR. We just got a call from [FAA] Cleveland Center. That the aircraft that went down in PA was they believe to be a military aircraft. Call sign GOPHR 06."[829]

This report is wrong (GOPHR 06 was the C-130 flying to Minnesota) but again demonstrates how muddled the information in the possession of the FAA was and, by extension, highlights the confusion at the Pentagon, NORAD, and the White House.

Hearing, May 23, 2003. Bush later says (*Decision Points*, p. 130) that "Josh Bolten had pushed for clarification to ensure that the chain of command was respected."

826. 9/11 Air Threat Conference Call Transcription, partially declassified.

827. National Archives Chronology. FAA Logs state: "DC/NY area small [VFR] airports closed."

828. 9/11 Commission, Memorandum for the Record, n.d., 2012-042-doc24, partially declassified.

829. Air Threat Conference Call log, "DJH Notes," Top Secret, partially declassified.

10:27 a.m.: FAA reports another false alarm: "ZDC [Washington Center] reports loss of radar contact with MWE 411 (Midwest Express MD80) over Bucko, WV."[830]

10:28 a.m.: Twenty-nine minutes after the South Tower falls, the North Tower (WTC 1) collapses in approximately 11 seconds.

The building collapses, a column of metal, concrete, and debris, and another titanic dust cloud is released. The collapse destroys the adjacent 22-story Marriott Hotel (WTC 3) and adds to the wreckage and damage of other surrounding buildings. The site of the Twin Towers is transformed into Ground Zero, a 16-acre ruin containing two billion pounds of debris and rubble and surrounded by a knee-deep sea of ash.

The *New York Times* reports, "The area around the World Trade Center resembled a desert after a terrible sandstorm. Parts of buildings, crushed vehicles and the shoes, purses, umbrellas and baby carriages of those who fled lay covered with thick, gray ash, through which weeping people wandered in search of safety, each with a story of pure horror."

The collapse killed FDNY Chief of Department Ganci and other officers, temporarily leaving the rescue effort without a commander.

10:29 a.m.: Air Threat Conference Call log:

> White House (PEOC): "Latest update on escort for AF1? Be aware we have received threats."
> NMCC (DDO): "Understand. We have received threats?"
> White House (PEOC): "That's correct. But we cannot confirm where they came from. It was a telcon."[831]

10:30 a.m.: New York Gov. George E. Pataki declares a state of emergency.

10:30 a.m.: (Approximate time) Secretary Rumsfeld arrives at the NMCC, almost an hour after the Pentagon is attacked,[832] with Vice Adm. Giambastiani;

830. FAA, 11 Sep 01 Catastrophic Crisis (all times given in EDT). FAA Logs says 10:29 a.m.

831. Air Threat Conference Call log, "DJH Notes," Top Secret, partially declassified.

832. Gen. Myers "stated he had only been in the NMCC for a short period of time when the Secretary arrived." See Memorandum for the Record, Interview of General Richard Myers, February 17, 2004, partially declassified.

A Coast Guard rescue team from Sandy Hook, New Jersey, races to the scene as the World Trade Center tower falls. (Source: US Coast Guard / PA2 Tom Sperduto)

Jim Haynes, the Pentagon's general counsel; Steve Cambone, the deputy undersecretary for policy; and Torie Clarke, the Pentagon spokesperson.[833]

"Because the [Secretary's] Executive Support Center ['Cables'] had too few phones, desks, and computers and its teleconference screens were small, shortly before 10:30 a.m. the secretary and his staff moved one floor down to the National Military Command Center. The spacious, compartmented center, although smoky and without air conditioning, had electrical power, and its communication and computer systems were operating adequately."[834]

"Soon after arriving at the [national military] command center the secretary participated in an air threat conference call with officials from the North American Air Defense Command, a representative from the Federal

833. *Known and Unknown*, p. 337. Rumsfeld says that his special assistant Lawrence Di Rita was with him, but this might be an error, as Di Rita was dispatched to Site R with Wolfowitz.

834. Defense Studies Series, Pentagon 9/11.

Aviation Administration, and Vice President Cheney and others in the White House shelter conference room."[835]

Air Threat Conference Call log:

NORAD CONR: "Re GOPHR 06—he reported the crash north of
   Camp David. And it appears to be an airliner."
NMCC (DDO): "Repeat—N/E of Camp David."[836]

Northeast of Camp David could connote the vicinity of Site R. Shanksville, Pennsylvania, is west of Camp David. But the entry is incorrect. GOPHR 06 is the call sign of the C-130 that confirms a B757 airliner hitting the Pentagon, not the crash of UA Flight 93.

10:30 a.m.: Secret Service agents are en route to County Day School and Potomac School to pick up the children of Liz Cheney, Vice President Cheney's adult daughter.[837]

10:31 a.m.: Air Threat Conference Call log:[838]

NORAD CONR: "I have that lat-longs for the crash site—3951 North
   7846 West.
White House (PEOC): "Are those coordinates for UAL 93?"
NMCC (DDO): "We're not sure of the identification of the airliner, but
   we know it was a civilian aircraft."

10:32 a.m.: At this time, the NORAD CONR chat transcript again "records that VP has cleared us to intercept tracks of interest and shoot them down if they do not respond, per CONR."[839]

---

835. Defense Studies Series, Pentagon 9/11.
   836. Air Threat Conference Call log, "DJH Notes," Top Secret, partially declassified.
   837. Secret Service Memorandum, White House Events on 9/11/01 (Special Agent James O. Scott), September 12, 2001, partially declassified.
   838. Air Threat Conference Call log, "DJH Notes," Top Secret, partially declassified.
   839. 9/11 Commission, Memorandum for the Record, n.d., 2012-042-doc24, partially declassified.

Air Threat Conference Call log: Deputy NSA Hadley: "I need to get word to Dick Myers that our reports are, there's an inbound aircraft flying low five miles out. The Vice President's guidance was we need to take them out."[840]

"NMCC chronology reflects that Hadley added that any information about the A/C that can be gathered before you have to take it out would be useful."[841]

Though there is by now presidential authorization, NORAD commander Gen. Eberhart's guidance regarding the rules of engagement are contradictory, and the DC National Guard is operating under its own rules, as are the other aircraft over Washington.

At the Pentagon, the NMCC asks NORAD to facilitate the return of the chairman of the Joint Chiefs of Staff, Army Gen. Henry "Hugh" Shelton, who is inbound to the United States returning from Europe and needs permission to enter US airspace.

10:33 a.m.: President Bush, on Air Force One, speaks over a secure voice line with Vice President Cheney.[842] Bush says that the PEOC "had been informed that an unresponsive plane was headed toward Washington. Dick asked me to confirm the shootdown order I had given. I did. . . . 'I cannot imagine what it would be like to receive this order,' I told Andy Card. I sure hoped no one would have to execute it."[843]

Sometime before 10:29 a.m., the PEOC also receives word from the Secret Service that there has been an anonymous call received threatening "Angel" (the code name for Air Force One) as another target of attack.[844] Bush later writes: "The caller had used the plane's code name, Angel, which few people knew."[845]

---

840. 9/11 Air Threat Conference Call Transcription, partially declassified. See also Air Threat Conference Call log, "DJH Notes," Top Secret, partially declassified. "NMCC chronology reflects that [Deputy NSA] Steve Hadley wants to get word to VCJCS [Gen. Myers] that there is an aircraft 5 miles out and that the VP's guidance is to take it out." See 9/11 Commission, Memorandum for the Record, n.d., 2012-042-doc24, partially declassified.

841. 9/11 Commission, Memorandum for the Record, n.d., 2012-042-doc24, partially declassified.

842. Presidential Daily Diary, partially declassified.

843. *Decision Points*, p. 130.

844. 9/11 Air Threat Conference Call Transcription, partially declassified.

845. *Decision Points*, p. 131.

"Air Force One was being targeted," Col. Tillman, the Air Force One pilot, recalls.[846]

Bush's Secret Service head Eddie Marinzel "discusses possible defensive measures with [deleted]" (likely Lt. Col. Gould).[847]

Michael Morell writes that White House Chief of Staff Card takes him aside to tell him that they've received word of a threat to their airplane. "I thanked Card for sharing the information with me, but my instinct was that this was not a major concern."[848]

Later, the official DOD history reports, "The notion of a threat to Air Force One stemmed from a misunderstood communication."[849]

Soon thereafter, Morell calls the CIA to convey the president's request to be the first to know about who is responsible for the attacks. Unable to get George Tenet on the phone, he speaks with Cofer Black, head of the Counterterrorist Center. "I relayed the president's request that he be informed instantly if and when information came in regarding responsibility for the attacks and asked him to get word to the director. When I hung up, I somehow knew it wasn't going to happen."[850]

10:34 a.m.: "JCS chronology reflects that MG [Maj. Gen. William E.] Ward discussed 'authority' and 'decision made by [unknown]' with an . . . [unidentified] person. General Arnold, CONR, was mentioned."[851]

10:34 a.m.: FAA reports a resolved false alarm: "MWE [Midway Express]/ MEP 411 on final to CMH [Columbus, OH] (original MWE-DCA) . . . landed without incident."

846. Tom Vanden Brook, "Air Force One Pilot Remembers 9/11," *Chicago Sun Times*, August 26, 2011.

847. Secret Service unlabeled document, released under FOIA Appeal (File Numbers 20080330 and 20080331), in Letter, April 23, 2010.

848. *The Great War of Our Time*, p. 53.

849. DOD, Defense Studies Series, Pentagon 9/11.

850. *The Great War of Our Time*, p. 53.

851. 9/11 Commission, Memorandum for the Record, n.d., 2012-042-doc24, partially declassified.

10:35 a.m.: (Approximate time) Deputy Secretary of Defense Wolfowitz is at Site R. At around 10:15, Wolfowitz boards a helicopter to travel the 75 miles.[852]

The Blackhawk helicopter ride would take about 20 minutes at full throttle, making Wolfowitz's arrival at Site R at about 10:35–11:00 a.m.

Wolfowitz recalls at Site R: "One of the first people I remember seeing was [Secretary of the Army] Tom White, who had been ordered up there also. He was looking almost green, I could really see the tension in his face. I didn't realize at the time just how bad the Army had been hit. One of their three-stars was killed, and Tom was unhappy at being up there when he thought he should be down . . . [in Washington]. When we got into the cavernous place I was able to get Rumsfeld's approval to send White back down, which we did quickly."[853]

According to the official DOD history: "Wolfowitz reported that the computer and communication systems there functioned poorly or not at all. He could, however, participate in video teleconference calls."[854] Wolfowitz recounts, "The rest of the afternoon was kind of nutty. Equipment didn't work, communications didn't work, and in any case the people weren't particularly interested in communicating. They had their hands full with plenty of other things to do. . . . The sense of isolation up there was powerful, reinforced by the windowless cavernous atmosphere and, I suppose, also the fact that we were isolated and learning next to nothing."[855]

It is interesting to note that a suspected hijacked plane coming down the Potomac River, one that caused the DC National Guard to send an F-16 to

852. Rumsfeld says that Wolfowitz was driven to Davison Army Airfield not far from the Pentagon (at Fort Belvoir) where he was then helicoptered to Site R. *Known and Unknown*, p. 338.

853. OSD, "Pentagon Attack, Interview with Paul Wolfowitz," April 19, 2002. "Amid the hectic activity and confusion," the official Army history reads, "the Army Operations Center staff removed Secretary White, despite his objection, to a remote location. Later, the staff realized that his relocation had not been required by the situation in accordance with contingency plans. The evacuation of Secretary White left General Keane in charge [of the Army] at the Pentagon for the remainder of the day." Department of the Army Historical Summary, Fiscal Year 2001, p. 57.

854. Defense Studies Series, Pentagon 9/11.

855. OSD, "Pentagon Attack, Interview with Paul Wolfowitz," April 19, 2002.

check on it, ended up being one of the helicopters based out of Davison Army Airfield at Ft. Belvoir, flying to or from Site R.[856]

`10:36 a.m.:` FAA reports: "Regions advised not to release essential personnel."

`10:37 a.m.:` Vice President Cheney asks Secretary Rumsfeld if military forces are on a heightened state of alert, and he confirms that they are.[857]

The actual transcript of the conversation shows that Cheney, as former secretary of defense, is asking about the alert status of US forces (DEFCON), but Rumsfeld is referring to the FPCON level, the status of base security.

The Air Threat Conference Call contemporaneous recording for five minutes, from 10:34 a.m. to 10:39 a.m., shows that Rumsfeld and Cheney did not start speaking to each other until 10:37 a.m.:[858]

10:34 a.m.: Deputy NSA Hadley: "This is Steve Hadley again. I've just confirmed from the vice president, if the inbound aircraft looks threatening, his instruction was to take it out."

10:34 a.m.: NMCC (DDO): "Roger. If it looks threatening, the vice president has directed that we take it out."

10:35 a.m.: Deputy NSA Hadley: "That's correct . . . any additional info you can get about that aircraft, obviously, is useful before you get [to] the point where you have to make a takeout decision. Do you copy?"

10:35 a.m.: NMCC (DDO): "Last calling station, relaying the message from the vice president. Please identify yourself."

10:35 a.m.: PEOC: "That was Mr. Hadley, NSC."

10:35 a.m.: NMCC (DDO): "Mr. Hadley. Roger, thank you much."

856. 9/11 Commission Memorandum for the Record, Interview, Major David McNulty, Chief of Intelligence, 121st Fighter Squadron, Air National Guard, Andrews AFB, March 11, 2004.

857. 9/11 Commission, Memorandum for the Record, n.d., 2012-042-doc24, partially declassified.

858. 9/11 Air Threat Conference Call Transcription, partially declassified.

10:35 a.m.: Deputy NSA Hadley: "Is Myers on conference?"

10:35 a.m.: NMCC (DDO): "Sir, he's standing right here."

10:35 a.m.: Deputy NSA Hadley: "Can you put him on conference."

10:35 a.m.: NMCC (DDO): "Roger, sir."

10:35 a.m.: SECDEF [Rumsfeld]: "Steve, General Myers and I are here. This is Don Rumsfeld."

10:36 a.m.: Deputy NSA Hadley: "Mr. Secretary, good. I talked briefly with the vice president, and his guidance was, if there was an aircraft inbound that close, and it looked threatening, his guidance was to take it out. Do you copy?"

10:36 a.m.: Gen. Myers: "We copy, Steve."

10:36 a.m.: Deputy NSA Hadley: "Do you want to speak directly to the vice president about it? Over."

10:36 a.m.: Gen. Myers: "Secretary Rumsfeld would like to speak to the vice president."

10:36 a.m.: Deputy NSA Hadley: "Let me see if I can bring him to the phone. Hold on."

10:37 a.m.: Cheney: "Hello."

10:37 a.m.: Rumsfeld: "Mr. Vice President, this is Don Rumsfeld and Gen. Myers in the NMCC."

10:37 a.m.: Cheney: "You guys are in the NMCC?"

10:37 a.m.: Rumsfeld: "We are."

10:37 a.m.: Cheney: "I've been in touch with the president. I know he is trying to reach you as well. Have you had a chance to talk to him yet?"

10:37 a.m.: Rumsfeld: "I did, but it was very early. It was right after the airplane hit the Pentagon."

10:37 a.m.: Cheney: "Okay. He's going to relocate to another site. They haven't found it yet. We received an anonymous call over here that Angel [Air Force One] . . . was the next target, and I assume he thought steps had been taken to provide protection for Air Force One."

10:37 a.m.: Rumsfeld: "That's true. That's been ordered."

10:37 a.m.: Cheney: "All right. Then our forces are on a heightened state of alert worldwide?"

10:38 a.m.: Rumsfeld: "They are. They're on THREATCON Delta."

10:38 a.m.: Cheney: "Now, there's been at least three instances here where we've had reports of aircraft approaching Washington. In a couple of those cases, they were confirmed as hijacked aircraft. And pursuant to the president's instructions, I gave authorization for them to be taken out." (Pause) "Hello?"

10:38 a.m.: Rumsfeld: "Yes, I understand. And who did you give that direction to?"

10:38 a.m.: Cheney: "It was passed from here through the OP center at the White House, from the PEOC."

10:38 a.m.: Rumsfeld: "Okay. Let me ask the question here, has that directive been transmitted to the aircraft?"

10:38 a.m.: Cheney: "Yes, it has."

10:38 a.m.: Rumsfeld: "So, we have a couple of aircraft up there that have those instructions at the present time?"

10:38 a.m.: Cheney: "That is correct. And it's my understanding they've already taken a couple of the aircraft out."

10:39 a.m.: Rumsfeld: "We can't confirm that. We're told that one aircraft is down, but we do not have a pilot report that they did it."

10:39 a.m.: Cheney: "Okay. Well, as soon as you get more info let me know . . . we're . . . because we're getting fragments here as well, too."

10:39 a.m.: Rumsfeld: "The report is that one is down north of Camp David, but—"

10:39 a.m.: Cheney: "Don, can you hold for a minute? The president is trying to reach me. Stand by."

10:37 a.m.: UA Flight 93. The Associated Press reports that a large plane has crashed in Pennsylvania; officials at Somerset County airport confirm.[859]

10:37 a.m.: FAA reports: "Medevacs authorized into New York airspace."

---

859. AP, "A Stunning 48 Hours of News," n.d. (September 12, 2001).

10:38 a.m.: The first of two F-16s of the DC National Guard take off. Based on direct discussions between the Secret Service JOC and the unit, F-16 fighters of the 113th Wing of the DC National Guard are alerted and prepared and then, under the tactical control of NORAD, launch out of Andrews AFB, Maryland.[860] The planes are effectively unarmed except for "training bullets" that would be used on a shooting range.[861]

"After a call with the White House operations center, the 113th Wing commander [Brig. Gen. David Wherley] issued a scramble order to set up a combat air patrol over DC and deter all aircraft within 20 miles with 'whatever force is necessary . . . to keep from hitting a building downtown.'"[862]

According to one of the F-16 pilots, Maj. John Daniel Caine, "Caine and Lt Col Marc Sasseville [CAPS 1 flight lead] knew coming out of their preflight brief that they lacked ROE and that they needed them. General Wherley gave them succinct rules that he had gotten from somewhere. [Note: General Wherley recalls briefing Sasseville but not Caine. Sasseville does not remember getting ROE until later, while in the air.] General Wherley got the ROE from one of two entities, Caine speculated, the Secret Service or NEADS. He knew that General Wherley did not make them up. . . . Caine agreed that the ROE likely came through the Secret Service."[863]

10:38 a.m.: Secret Service at the White House logs that a plane has crashed near Camp David, Maryland.[864]

---

860. 9/11 Commission Report, p. 48.

861. 9/11 Commission Memorandum for the Record, Interview, BG David Wherley, on September 11, 2001, Commander of the 113th Wing of the USAF, August 28, 2003.

862. "9/11 Response," District of Columbia National Guard, accessed July 30, 2020, https://dc.ng.mil/About-Us/Heritage/History/9-11-Response/.

863. 9/11 Commission Memorandum for the Record, Interview with Major John Daniel Caine, USAF, Supervisor of Flying at 121st Squadron, 113th Wing, Andrews Air Force Base on September 11, 2001, March 8, 2004.

864. Secret Service, Memorandum, Interview with SAIC Carl Truscott, October 1, 2001, partially declassified.

10:38 a.m.: NORAD CONR chat transcript "records that VP has cleared us to intercept tracks of interest and to shoot them down if they do not respond, per CC [Maj. Gen. Arnold]."[865]

10:38 a.m.: FAA reports: "Controllers ending shifts at ZBW [Boston Center] not to be released."

10:39 a.m.: The Associated Press reports a fourth explosion at the World Trade Center.[866]

10:39 a.m.: FAA issues a Notice to Airmen (NOTAM) reaffirming earlier orders and halting takeoffs and landings at all airports.

10:39 a.m.: Vice President Cheney interrupts his conversation with Secretary Rumsfeld (see transcript at 10:34 a.m.) to tell him that the president is trying to reach him.

10:40 a.m.: President Bush, aboard Air Force One, attempts to call the First Lady, but the call cannot be completed.[867]

"I couldn't believe that the president of the United States couldn't reach his wife in the Capitol Building," Bush later writes. "'What the hell is going on?' I snapped at Andy Card."[868]

10:40 a.m.: At the Pentagon, after evacuating the rescue site at about 10:00 a.m. because of rumors of another plane heading toward Washington, firefighters and other emergency responders return "only after about 25 minutes (shortly after 10:40 a.m.) when they received the all clear signal."[869]

---

865. 9/11 Commission, Memorandum for the Record, n.d., 2012-042-doc24, partially declassified.

866. AP, "A Stunning 48 Hours of News," n.d. (September 12, 2001).

867. Presidential Daily Diary, partially declassified.

868. *Decision Points*, p. 132.

869. Defense Studies Series, Pentagon 9/11.

(Source: US Coast Guard / Telfair Brown)

10:40 a.m.: Air Threat Conference Call log: "NORAD Update [for Washington DC]. 2 fighters, a single E-3 [AWACs, an airborne radar plane and command center] as well as a tanker currently inbound. Estimate time 10 minutes overhead at CAP pt north of Langley Field for protection of Washington DC area."[870]

It is unclear where the Langley F-16s are at this point, but it is thought that they are closer to the city itself.

10:40 a.m.: FAA reports: "N4 [Attorney General Ashcroft] over Toledo, Ohio; refuses to land in accordance with FAA orders; wants to continue to ADW [Andrews AFB, MD]."

At 10:57 a.m., the FAA reports that the attorney general's plane is diverted to Washington National instead, with an ETA of noon. He is authorized to land at 11:12 a.m., but the plane waits for an escort through 11:50 a.m.[871] Ashcroft later tells the 9/11 Commission: "As they approached DC, they were put in a holding pattern outside of DC until a fighter jet could escort

---

870. Air Threat Conference Call log, "DJH Notes," Top Secret, partially declassified.
871. DCC Timeline; National Archives Chronology.

them in. Ashcroft speculated that the fighter was there to shoot them down in case their plane started to veer off course."[872]

Attorney General John Ashcroft is in the air flying to Milwaukee, Wisconsin, on the morning of 9/11 to participate in an event to promote reading when he learns of the attacks. He orders his government plane to turn around and return to Washington. Ashcroft seemingly can't clear his own way through to the capital, and he has to wait for a military fighter escort to come and accompany him before proceeding into Washington airspace.[873] He later says that "the attacks came as a 'complete surprise' to him."[874]

10:41 a.m.: NORAD writes: "At 1041 EDT . . . the Vice President of the United States authorized the intercept and engagement of tracks of interest, if an aircraft was unresponsive. At the time, NORAD was at Peacetime Rules of Engagement (ROE), which meant the Commander, NORAD . . . retained the authority to order engagement of hostile forces and Region Commanders [e.g., NEADS, CONR] had emergency authority as defined in NORAD CONPLAN 3310-96 change 2."[875]

(The NORAD version here is incorrect. The vice president's order did not come at 10:41 a.m., and neither was his order the definitive executive decision at that time, as President Bush had already given his consent. But there are also numerous contradictory orders that had already been issued, and what pilots perceived they were authorized to do isn't clear.)

10:41 a.m.: President Bush is first officially told that Osama bin Laden is most likely behind the attacks.

"[Ari] Fleischer was keeping careful notes that day, and the first time he recorded bin Laden's name was at 10:41 a.m., when Chief of Staff Andy Card said to Bush on Air Force One, 'It smells like Osama bin Laden to me.'"

872. 9/11 Commission Memorandum for the Record, Interview with Attorney General John D. Ashcroft, December 17, 2003.

873. "John Ashcroft on September 11, 2001," Salem Radio Network, September 9, 2011, video, 3:30 ("John Ashcroft reflects with Janet Mefferd on his experiences the day the United States came under attack by al-Qaeda"), http://www.youtube.com/watch?v=GC-GytLiDQ4.

874. 9/11 Commission Memorandum for the Record, Interview with Attorney General John D. Ashcroft, December 17, 2003.

875. 9/11 Commission, NORAD Questions for the Record, partially declassified.

10:41 a.m.: AA Flight 77. FAA reports: "AAL 77 holding in middle ZKC's [Kansas City] airspace."

This is incorrect information, as the plane had crashed into the Pentagon more than an hour earlier.

10:42 a.m.: NORAD CONR chat chronology "clarifies that clearance to shoot from VP is to save lives on the ground if A/C do not respond."[876]

("To save lives on the ground" appears to be yet another condition fighter pilots would have had to now consider in deciding to shoot down an airplane, that is, if they received word of each of these new versions of the supposed shootdown order.)

10:42 a.m.: FAA reports a false alarm: "Preliminary report of fire at Camp David, Maryland."

---

876. 9/11 Commission, Memorandum for the Record, n.d., 2012-042-doc24, partially declassified.

CHAPTER 12

DEFENSE CONDITION 3

At 10:41 a.m., after four planes had hit their targets or crashed, Secretary Rumsfeld told Vice President Cheney that he was recommending increasing the worldwide readiness of US armed forces to Defense Readiness Condition 3 (DEFCON 3). Cheney told Rumsfeld that he agreed but thought that Rumsfeld should confer with the president before doing so.[877] Two minutes later, before Rumsfeld had spoken to the president, the NMCC announced that Rumsfeld had directed that US forces go to DEFCON 3—"and be prepared to go to Level 2," one step below maximum readiness and hair trigger alert.[878] Then, two minutes after that, the NMCC directed that forces "hold off on DEFCON 3" so that the president could be informed.[879] And yet despite that order, a minute later, at 10:46 a.m., acting Chairman of the Joint Chiefs Gen. Myers declared DEFCON 3.

In a post-9/11 interview, Myers said he did not recall if the DEFCON 3 move was run by the president before the decision was made.[880] With those four different timestamps in mind, DEFCON 3 was officially declared at 10:53 a.m.[881] There is no record of Secretary Rumsfeld having spoken to the president between 10:41 and 10:53 a.m. There are questions as to whether DEFCON 3 should have been declared at all. But clearly a system that could have caused World War III was on autopilot.

---

877. 9/11 Commission, Memorandum for the Record, n.d., 2012-042-doc24, partially declassified.

878. 9/11 Commission, Secretary Rumsfeld "Day of" 9/11 Questions, Draft, June 9, 2004, partially declassified.

879. 9/11 Commission NORAD MFR.

880. Memorandum for the Record, Interview of General Richard Myers, February 17, 2004, partially declassified.

881. Defense Studies Series, Pentagon 9/11. The order went out at 10:53 a.m., according to the DOD.

Defense Readiness Conditions (DEFCONs) were established in 1960 to have a universal system of military readiness and gradual escalation—including for nuclear forces—in the face of a crisis. There are five levels, from lowest to highest:

- DEFCON 5 (normal, peacetime readiness).

- DEFCON 4 (normal, peacetime readiness, but with increased intelligence and strengthened security measures).

- DEFCON 3 (increase in force readiness above normal readiness and air defense readiness conditions 1 or 2 based on tensions existing "which may have serious and adverse effects, and the possibility of force involvement exists").

- DEFCON 2 (further increase In force readiness that is less than the maximum readiness; air defense readiness conditions 3 or 4 based on "heightened tensions and or indications that an enemy force is taking actions which increase their readiness for attack").

- DEFCON 1 (maximum force readiness; air defense emergency).

In 2001 and now, all US military forces are at DEFCON 5, the lowest level—though US forces on the Korean Peninsula are always at DEFCON 4. It is believed that DEFCON 3 has been implemented two other times in the past 65 years—once in 1962 during the Cuban Missile Crisis and once during the 1973 Arab-Israeli War.[882] And to make matters more complicated, an air defense emergency had never been declared except on 9/11, and that state of emergency matches DEFCON 1.

At 11:15 a.m. on 9/11, 14 minutes after DEFCON 3 was declared, US Ambassador to Russia Alexander Vershbow called the White House to say that the Kremlin called and that Russian President Vladimir Putin wanted to speak to President Bush.[883] Russia had detected some movement in the United States (or intercepted the order). The declaration was destabilizing because the United States was in the middle of its annual nuclear war exercise (involving

---

882. On October 22, 1962, NORAD's Continental Air Command increased its weapons readiness status and declared DEFCON 3 for its forces. This caused dispersal of interceptor forces. Two days later, NORAD declared DEFCON 3 for all forces, a condition that persisted until November 27, 1962. North American Aerospace Defense Command Office of History, "A Brief History of NORAD, as of 31 December 2013."

883. Michael K. Bohn, "Former Staffers Remember the White House Situation Room on 9/11," McClatchy Newspapers, August 29, 2011.

live nuclear weapons). In fact, both countries were—Russia was carrying out its major autumn nuclear war exercise as well. In all of this, President Bush never spoke to Putin.

With the DEFCON 3 declaration now an irritant, Deputy Secretary of State Richard Armitage evidently spoke to his counterpart in Moscow, and later in the afternoon, Rumsfeld called Russian Defense Minister Ivanov as well. But it fell to National Security Adviser Condoleezza Rice (who could speak Russian) to call Putin, which she did around noon. She says she reassured him that US forces "were standing down" and that the United States would be happy to have Russia's cooperation on counterterrorism. There is no record to indicate that the DEFCON was then countermanded, though the Global Guardian exercise was suspended.

Exactly what US military forces did to implement DEFCON 3 is still unknown, and the reason for a change in the DEFCON is baffling. There was no threat to the United States from Russia or any other country. Behind the scenes, Rumsfeld and Myers did discuss whether the attacks were carried out by a state (Iraq or Iran), but even there such an act wouldn't have necessarily provoked a worldwide DEFCON change, as it never had before (and hasn't since). Rumsfeld ruminated that a defense of Saudi Arabia should be undertaken (even that a combat air patrol over Saudi skies be created). Gen. Myers later said that he thought the DEFCON 3 move to increase the readiness posture of US global forces was prudent "in light of the possibility that the CONUS attacks would be followed by attacks on US forces abroad."[884]

Given that the "force protection" condition (FPCON) of US forces worldwide was raised to "maximum," the DEFCON change was the wrong move to merely protect US forces. It is really meant to place nuclear and conventional forces on a greater level of alert, that is, a preparation to use those forces. It is alarming that neither Rumsfeld nor Myers understood what DEFCON really triggered or what it was for. And perhaps what is most alarming is that clearly some intermediary (or different) step was and is required to respond to terrorism. And yet the DEFCON change has received little attention, and no real change has been made to the system of DEFCON and FPCON since 2001. In fact, the FPCON system, intended for terrorism, was invoked during COVID-19, with the "protection" of US forces applied to the threat of a virus.

884. 9/11 Commission NORAD MFR.

10:43 a.m.: Secretary of Defense Rumsfeld directs that US military forces raise their alert level to DEFCON 3 and be prepared to transition to DEF-CON 2.[885]

NMCC (DDO): "This is the DDO. Secretary of Defense has directed that we go to worldwide DEFCON 3 and be prepared to go to [DEFCON] 2. Please acknowledge."[886]

According to the 9/11 Commission, "Rumsfeld believed the matter was urgent and, having consulted DOD directives, concluded he had the authority to issue the order and would [then] brief the President."[887]

Rumsfeld says he and Gen. Myers "discussed raising America's threat level . . . an increased state of alert for the nation's armed forces, two levels short of full-scale war. 'It's a huge move,' Myers said, 'but it's appropriate.'"[888]

Gen. Myers later tells the 9/11 Commission: "Regarding the decision to go to DEFCON 3, Myers stated he did not recall if that issue was run by the President before the decision was made to go to Level 3. He stated that they 'got out the book' and reviewed the various levels, and the Secretary spoke to the Vice President about the issue."[889]

Rumsfeld's declaration comes just three minutes after he gets off the call with Cheney (see 10:34 a.m.), during which the vice president asks if the readiness of US forces has been increased. Evidently Cheney's question precipitates Rumsfeld's decision. Though Rumsfeld says (and the record reflects) that DEFCON 3 is ordered at 10:43 a.m., it isn't immediately implemented. The NMCC chronology reflects that the DDO directed conferees at 10:45 a.m. to "hold" on implementing Rumsfeld's DEFCON 3 order "until POTUS [Bush] is consulted."[890]

885. 9/11 Commission, Secretary Rumsfeld "Day of" 9/11 Questions, Draft, June 9, 2004, partially declassified.

886. 9/11 Air Threat Conference Call Transcription, partially declassified.

887. 9/11 Commission Report, p. 554, fn. 8.

888. *Known and Unknown*, p. 338.

889. 9/11 Commission, MFR 04019757, Richard Myers Interview, n.d. (2003), partially declassified.

890. 9/11 Commission, Memorandum for the Record, n.d., 2012-042-doc24, partially declassified.

`10:43 a.m.:` FAA reports another false alarm but also clarifies that there is no fire at Camp David: "A/C [aircraft] northeast on fire, but Camp David now reported OK."

At some point, President Bush's Secret Service agent Eddie Marinzel aboard Air Force One says he "learned that Camp David had in fact, not been attacked, and that 'things were settling down.'"[891]

`10:43 a.m.:` The Departments of State and Justice are already reported as evacuated, along with the World Bank; the remaining federal office buildings in Washington are evacuated, with some 250,000 federal employees, contractors, and visitors pouring into the streets and onto public transportation, the city paralyzed by massive gridlock.

`10:44 a.m.:` Air Threat Conference Call contemporaneous recording for 10:44–10:45 a.m.:[892]

> 10:44 a.m.: Cheney: "Yeah, Cheney here, Don. The president would like to hear from you, and needless to say, he's still trying to decide where to locate."
>
> 10:44 a.m.: Rumsfeld: "I beg your pardon?"
>
> 10:44 a.m.: Cheney: "I say, the president would like to talk to you and would appreciate a call. Just brief him on the status of US forces. He may want to consult with you also about location, where he can go to. And any information you can tell him about the interception of the aircraft that were coming to Washington also would be helpful."[893]
>
> 10:44 a.m.: Rumsfeld: "Okay. Apparently, you're on a conference, a video conference that does not come into the NMCC."

---

891. Secret Service unlabeled document, released under FOIA Appeal (File Numbers 20080330 and 20080331), in Letter, April 23, 2010.

892. 9/11 Air Threat Conference Call Transcription, partially declassified.

893. Air Threat Conference Call log, "DJH Notes," Top Secret, partially declassified, has a slightly different version: Cheney (to Rumsfeld): "Spoke to POTUS. He'd like to hear from you and he's still trying to decide where to locate—brief him on status of forces, he may want to consult w/you about locations. And any information about the interception of aircraft would be helpful."

10:44 a.m.: Cheney: "I can't believe it."

10:44 a.m.: Rumsfeld: "Well, now we know. We think . . . we're recommending going to DEFCON 3."

10:44 a.m.: Cheney: "All right. I'll have to run that by him and let him make the call. But I think that's a good idea."[894]

10:44 a.m.: Rumsfeld: "And what I'll do is pull together some notes here and be ready to talk to him and give him a call shortly."

10:45 a.m.: Cheney: "All right."

10:45 a.m.: Rumsfeld: "Are you going to be on the call too maybe?"

10:45 a.m.: Cheney: "I don't need to be. The communications . . . I wouldn't make a prediction at this point."

10:45 a.m.: Rumsfeld: "Where are you?"

10:45 a.m.: Cheney: "I'm in the PEOC over in the east wing."

10:45 a.m.: AA Flight 77. FAA reports: "Possible crash site in vicinity of York, KY—possible [sic] AAL 77."

10:45 a.m.: Air Threat Conference Call log: "This is the DDO back in the conference. Again, hold off on DEFCON 3. I say again, we need to go to the POTUS before we actually execute. All stations, I say again. This is the DDO. Please hold on DEFCON 3."[895]

Brig. Gen. Montague, the JCS deputy director of operations, is back directing the conference since the crash of UA Flight 93 in Pennsylvania. After Rumsfeld speaks to Cheney about the move to DEFCON 3, and

---

894. For some reason, the NMCC chronology provided to the 9/11 Commission incorrectly reflects this conversation with Cheney taking place at 10:41 a.m., which is contrary to the timestamp of the log: "NMCC chronology reflects that SECDEF [Rumsfeld] told VP [Cheney] he is recommending DEFCON 3. VP told SECDEF he should confer with POTUS and let him make decision, but he [Cheney] agrees [that the move should be made]." 9/11 Commission, Memorandum for the Record, n.d., 2012-042-doc24, partially declassified.

895. 9/11 Air Threat Conference Call Transcription, partially declassified. Still, some report that DEFCON 3 was issued at 9:45 a.m., but this is incorrect. "At 10:45 a.m., Defense Secretary Donald Rumsfeld ordered the US military to assume Defense Condition 3 (DEFCON 3), a heightened state of readiness last implemented during the 1973 Arab-Israeli War." Michael K. Bohn, "Former Staffers Remember the White House Situation Room on 9/11," McClatchy Newspapers, August 29, 2011.

Cheney advises him that it should be the president's call, Rumsfeld's order is suspended.

10:45 a.m.: Secret Service reports that Liz Cheney and her children are en route to her Washington residence, she from her office at the State Department and her children from their schools.[896]

10:45 a.m.: According to news media reports, in the West Bank town of Nablus, some 3,000 people are reportedly celebrating the attacks and chanting, "God is great." NBC News shows footage from "earlier this morning" of what it says are Palestinians celebrating the terrorist attacks on America. The footage is repeatedly aired.

It is later shown that the footage was filmed during an earlier funeral.

10:46 a.m.: President Bush, aboard Air Force One, talks over a secure voice line with Vice President Cheney.[897] This conversation probably relates to UA Flight 93 going down in Pennsylvania and the move to DEFCON 3.

Learning of the fourth plane down in Pennsylvania, Bush says he asked Cheney: "Did we shoot it down, or did it crash? . . . Nobody knew. I felt sick to my stomach. Had I ordered the death of those innocent Americans?"[898]

Ari Fleischer says that President Bush "said two things that 'sent a chill' down his spine," aboard Air Force One. "First, that he authorized the military to shoot down commercial planes if necessary. And second, that he put the military on DEFCON 3, the highest alert status since the 1973 Yom Kippur War."[899]

---

896. Secret Service Memorandum, White House Events on 9/11/01 (Special Agent James O. Scott), September 12, 2001, partially declassified.

897. Presidential Daily Diary, partially declassified.

898. *Decision Points*, p. 131.

899. Ari Fleischer tweeted his own timeline of 9/11. See particularly Ari Fleischer (@AriFleischer), "He authorized the military to shoot down commercial planes if necessary," Twitter, September 11, 2015, 7:26 a.m., https://twitter.com/AriFleischer/status/642343562823208960; and Ari Fleischer (@AriFleischer), "Ari Fleischer (@AriFleischer), "AF One took off like a rocket. Years later, the pilot, Col. Mark Tillman, told me he was told there was a sniper at the end of the runway," Twitter, September 11, 2015, Twitter, September 11, 2015, 7:27 a.m., https://twitter.com/AriFleischer/status/642343771141705728.

10:46 a.m.: The NMCC officially declares the shift of all US forces to DEF-
CON 3.⁹⁰⁰ A minute after the DDO issues a hold, Vice Chairman of the Joint
Chiefs of Staff Gen. Richard Myers authorizes the order.

Air Threat Conference Call log:

> NMCC (DDO): "All conferees, this is the DDO. We have an update
> on the declaration of DEFCON 3. Again, we are overriding the
> last given. DEFCON 3 has been declared. We are now directing
> worldwide DEFCON 3. That's being directed by the vice chairman.
> I say again, it's being directed by the vice chairman. Time, 10:46
> EDT. All stations acknowledge DEFCON 3 worldwide, effective
> 10:46 EDT. Acknowledge. . . . Roger, that's 14:46 Zulu. Also be
> advised we are drafting the EAM [Emergency Action Message],
> and it will follow shortly."⁹⁰¹

"Regarding the decision to go to DefCon 3, [Gen.] Myers stated he did
not recall if that issue was run by the President before the decision was
made to go to Level 3. He stated that they 'got out the book' and reviewed
the instructions and actions for the various levels, and the Secretary spoke
to the Vice President about the issue. He did not recall anything after that."⁹⁰²

Capt. Leidig, who has reverted to deputy for Command Center Operations with the handover of the DDO to Brig. Gen. Montague, says: "There
was a historical discussion about how the move to DEFCON 3 went during
previous crises, Cuba specifically. He recalled that they showed General
Meyers [sic] that he had approval authority to go to DEFCON 3. Their
reference was a book on the shelf which they used and showed to the Vice
Chairman."⁹⁰³

Fleischer says in his tweets that this occurred at 10:20 a.m., but the declaration of DEFCON
3—or at least President Bush's agreement—hadn't yet occurred.

900. 9/11 Commission, Memorandum for the Record, n.d., 2012-042-doc24, partially
declassified.

901. 9/11 Air Threat Conference Call Transcription, partially declassified.

902. Memorandum for the Record, Interview of General Richard Myers, February 17,
2004, partially declassified.

903. 9/11 Commission Memorandum for the Record, Interview, Captain Charles Joseph
Leidig, USN, April 29, 2004.

The following organizations promptly acknowledge receipt of the order: Air Force, Marines, NORAD, STRATCOM, SPACECOM, National Military Joint Intelligence Center (NMJOC), Night Hawk (Presidential and COG aircraft and helicopter control), Pacific Command, FAA, and FEMA.[904]

The shift automatically changes the ROE for NORAD. "At 1046 EDT, . . . DEFCON 3 Defense Readiness Condition 3 . . . changed NORAD's status to [the] Transition ROE . . . [deleted]."[905] This means: "By 1046 EDT General Eberhart had clear shootdown authority by virtue of JCS declaration of DEFCON 3 which, by policy, put Transition ROE in place."[906]

There is still great confusion regarding this declaration, whether Gen. Myers had any authority as informal acting chairman in the chain of command, or whether he was merely passing along Rumsfeld's 10:43 a.m. order. Rumsfeld, as half of the "National Command Authority," would have had to have ordered the shift, and though it is clear that he was involved in the decision-making, the authority to make the shift should have been articulated as an order from Rumsfeld and not from Myers.

And to add even more to the confusion, the official Defense Department history later says that DEFCON 3 wasn't declared until 10:53 a.m. But then that history also has Rumsfeld fully engaged ("focused on immediate questions relating to control of US airspace: the status of the fourth hijacked aircraft, grounding of all civilian flights, tracking of unidentified aircraft, the possibility of more hijackings and attacks, possible orders for launching intercept aircraft, maintaining combat air patrols, and providing rules of engagement for fighter pilots"),[907] when in fact he didn't arrive at the NMCC until 10:30 a.m. and didn't even appear to talk to President Bush directly until 12:13 p.m.

NORAD Commander Gen. Eberhart later explains to the 9/11 Commission "that there was a debate over the advantages and disadvantages

904. Air Threat Conference Call log, "DJH Notes," Top Secret, partially declassified. See also 9/11 Commission NORAD MFR.

905. 9/11 Commission, NORAD Questions for the Record, partially declassified.

906. 9/11 Commission, Memorandum for the Record, n.d., 2012-042-doc24, partially declassified.

907. Defense Studies Series, Pentagon 9/11.

of declaring DEFCON 3. . . . Eberhart commented that DEFCON 3 was not intended for the attacks of 9/11, and thus could have complicated the response to the attacks. Eberhart did not think it would have 'done anything for us' within CONUS."[908]

10:46 a.m.: CNN reports that Secretary Powell has cut short his trip to Latin America to return to the United States. Powell was attending an Organization of American States General Assembly meeting in Lima, Peru, and leaves his hotel after the second attack. He cancels a visit to Colombia. Before leaving Peru, he publicly says that terrorists "will never be allowed to kill the spirit of democracy. They cannot destroy our society. They cannot destroy our belief in the democratic way."

10:48 a.m.: Air Threat Conference Call log: "Air Force One to divert to Barksdale AFB, LA."[909]

"NORAD: Update: Verification scrambled 2 fighters out of Ellington Field (Texas) to escort AF1—standby for intercept time."[910]

Air Force One pilot Col. Tillman "reported that the fighter escorts had been dispatched and were traveling from the west to join Air Force One. Their estimated time of rendezvous with the escort aircraft was unknown but in order to decrease that time, Air Force One assumed a westbound flight path."[911]

10:49 a.m.: Air Threat Conference Call log: NMCC (DDO): "Emergency Action Message [regarding official movement to DEFCON 3] released at 1452 Zulu."[912]

---

908. 9/11 Commission NORAD MFR.

909. Air Threat Conference Call log, "DJH Notes," Top Secret, partially declassified. See also 9/11 Commission NORAD MFR.

910. Air Threat Conference Call log, "DJH Notes," Top Secret, partially declassified. See also 9/11 Commission NORAD MFR.

911. Secret Service unlabeled document, released under FOIA Appeal (File Numbers 20080330 and 20080331), in Letter, April 23, 2010.

912. 9/11 Air Threat Conference Call Transcription, partially declassified.

President Bush, aboard Air Force One, watches television coverage of the terrorist attacks from his office. (Source: George W. Bush Presidential Library and Museum / Eric Draper)

Though the FAA is noted as earlier acknowledging the DEFCON 3 declaration, the logs state that "FAA asks what it means."[913]

10:50 a.m.: President Bush, aboard Air Force One, is called by the First Lady, but the call cannot be completed.[914]

10:50 a.m.: At the World Trade Center, FDNY Engine 33 advises that the water pressure is lost in lower Manhattan and requests a fireboat to augment the water supply.[915]

10:51 a.m.: FAA reports:

FAA DC logs: "VP [Cheney] notified [FAA] CARF, Defcon Level 2 [*sic*] . . . reviewing necessary actions will advise when complete."

913. Air Threat Conference Call log, "DJH Notes," Top Secret, partially declassified. See also 9/11 Commission NORAD MFR.
914. Presidential Daily Diary, partially declassified.
915. NIST Chronology.

FAA DC logs: "DCC says they are showing 460 targets in domestic airspace."[916]

FAA reports: "CLE [Cleveland] has two unidentified A/C circling in upstate NY at FL350."

10:52 a.m.: President Bush, aboard Air Force One, talks over a secure phone line with the First Lady for the first time since the attacks. Laura Bush is being held at Secret Service headquarters in downtown Washington.[917]

Eddie Marinzel says he had just spoken to Secret Service director Brian L. Stafford (who was with the First Lady). Stafford assures him that the First Lady is safe and has been relocated and that Barbara and Jenna Bush have also been safely relocated. "DSAIC Marinzel advised the President of that information. The President requested and was provided a direct contact telephone number for the first lady."[918]

10:52 a.m.: Air Threat Conference Call log:[919]

White House (PEOC): "Able to confirm final status of UAL 93? Plane that went down north? Was it the result of fighter engagement?"

NMCC (DDO): "Can't confirm."

NORAD: "No reports of intercept on civilian aircraft."

This is the second time the PEOC asks whether a fighter plane shot down UA Flight 93 (see 10:20 a.m.).

10:53 a.m.: New York's primary elections, scheduled for Tuesday, are postponed.

---

916. DCC Timeline, logged as 1451Z.

917. Presidential Daily Diary, partially declassified.

918. Secret Service unlabeled document, released under FOIA Appeal (File Numbers 20080330 and 20080331), in Letter, April 23, 2010.

919. Air Threat Conference Call log, "DJH Notes," Top Secret, partially declassified. See also 9/11 Commission NORAD MFR.

10:53 a.m.: Air Threat Conference Call log:[920]

> NORAD: "Two fighters out of Ellington [Texas] to escort AF1 [Air Force One] . . . Ellington also ordered four aircraft as backup. Also we have two F-16s scrambling out of Andrews AFB. No airborne cap at this time."
>
> White House (PEOC): "Understand two out of Ellington, two out of Andrews; and that will make the total cap over Washington at four right now or six?"
>
> NMCC (DDO): "My count is a total of eight once we get them all—two Andrews, four addition [*sic*] aircraft coming in, and there are two out of Ellington [with Air Force One]. NORAD, if that is wrong, tell me."
>
> NORAD: "That is the correct number."

10:54 a.m.: Sen. Hillary Clinton (D-NY) calls President Bush aboard Air Force One. The president's personal aide, Logan M. Walters, takes the call.[921]

Former President Bill Clinton is in Cairns, Australia, giving a speech. According to one news media report, he gets his Secret Service detail to falsely invoke a threat to him so that he can get clearance (and a government plane) to fly home that night.[922]

The Secret Service at the White House merely says: "We were also answering inquiries from the Director's Crisis Center reference the location of the Secretary of the Treasury [Paul O'Neill] and former President Clinton. Requests were relayed directly to the PEOC for military aircraft to pick them up respectively in Tokyo and Australia."[923]

10:54 a.m.: FAA reports: "AWP [FAA Western Pacific in El Segundo, California] . . . confirms no controllers to be released."

---

920. Air Threat Conference Call log, "DJH Notes," Top Secret, partially declassified. See also 9/11 Commission NORAD MFR.

921. Presidential Daily Diary, partially declassified.

922. *24 Hours Inside the President's Bunker*, pp. 84–86.

923. Secret Service unlabeled document, partially declassified, and released under FOIA Appeal (File Numbers 20080330 and 20080331), in Letter, April 23, 2010.

10:55 a.m.: FAA reports: "ZBW [Boston Center] evacuated when Coast Guard flight reported heading toward BOS (will try to get controllers back in building)."

10:55 a.m.: Secret Service reports that Liz Cheney and her children are at their residence.[924]

10:56 a.m.: FAA reports: "AEA [FAA Eastern Region in Jamaica, New York] to release controllers with relatives who work at World Trade Center."

10:57 a.m.: NORAD Air Warning Center log reflects: "CINC NORAD [Gen. Eberhart] reviewing for appropriate actions [to take with declaration of DEFCON 3]."[925]

10:57 a.m.: New York Gov. George Pataki says that all state government offices are closed.

10:58 a.m.: Air Threat Conference Call log: "PEOC, DDO and NORAD have conversation about current location of Air Force One."[926]

10:58 a.m.: FAA reports false alarm: "ZOB [Cleveland Center] local police reports A/C circling ZOB . . . will release personnel if needed."

10:59 a.m.: AA Flight 77. FAA reports: "AAL 77 down Ashland, KY unconfirmed."[927]

FAA Western Pacific Region in El Segundo, California, is asked how many aircraft are inbound to the Los Angeles area.

---

924. Secret Service Memorandum, White House Events on 9/11/01 (Special Agent James O. Scott), September 12, 2001, partially declassified.

925. 9/11 Commission, Memorandum for the Record, n.d., 2012-042-doc24, partially declassified.

926. Air Threat Conference Call log, "DJH Notes," Top Secret, partially declassified. See also 9/11 Commission NORAD MFR.

927. National Archives Chronology.

10:59 a.m.: News media reports say that an ambulance at the World Trade Center has exploded.

11:00 a.m.: CNN reports that a second plane (in addition to UA Flight 93) went down around 80 miles or so southeast of Pittsburgh.[928]

11:00 a.m.: At the World Trade Center, the "overall incident command remained unclear for nearly another half hour. . . . During this time, several senior fire chiefs took the initiative to restore overall command, sometimes leading to multiple incident commanders. Overall command was restored at 11:28 a.m. by Citywide Tour Commander 4C, who replaced Chief of Department Ganci [who had died in the collapse of the North Tower]."[929]

11:00 a.m.: Air Threat Conference Call log: "NORAD: Unknown track on the east coast—not threat to DC."[930]

11:00 a.m.: FAA DC logs: "Now at DEFCON 3 . . . building evacuated."[931]

11:00 a.m.: Transport Canada halts all aircraft departures until further notice, except for police, military, and humanitarian flights. The operation is well underway as international flights headed for the United States have already started to land at Canadian airports, beginning at CFB Goose Bay, Newfoundland and Labrador. Fourteen other airports follow, including Halifax, Lester B. Pearson in Toronto, Montréal-Dorval, and Vancouver.

11:00 a.m.: Commandant of the Marine Corps Gen. Jim Jones returns to the Pentagon from a funeral he had been attending in DC, going to the office he maintains at the Navy Annex.[932]

---

928. "CNN Breaking News: America Under Attack," CNN, September 11, 2001, http://transcripts.cnn.com/TRANSCRIPTS/0109/11/bn.11.html.

929. FDNY Report; NIST Chronology.

930. Air Threat Conference Call log, "DJH Notes," Top Secret, partially declassified. See also 9/11 Commission NORAD MFR.

931. DCC Timeline.

932. The Navy Annex was a building on Columbia Pike in Arlington near the Pentagon, mainly used as overflow offices for the Navy and Marine Corps. The buildings were demolished in 2013 to make room for an expansion of Arlington National Cemetery.

Later in the day, CNO Adm. Clark and his staff move from the Washington Navy Yard to the Annex and join Jones for meetings in the commandant's conference room.[933]

11:00 a.m.: Federal law enforcement personnel from the Bureau of Alcohol, Tobacco, and Firearms (ATF) arrive at the Pentagon to assist Arlington police with site security.[934]

By 11:00 a.m., more than 100 law enforcement personnel have reported, representing Arlington County police, sheriff's office, and park rangers; Fairfax County Police Department, Alexandria Police Department, the FBI, US Marshals Service, ATF, and the Immigration and Naturalization Service (INS).[935]

11:00 a.m.: (Approximate time) News media reports a plane crashing into Camp David and another crashing in Kentucky. There are also reports of a third plane landing in Rockford, Illinois, with a bomb on board (see 12:13 p.m.).

11:02 a.m.: New York City mayor Giuliani orders the evacuation of all of Lower Manhattan below Canal Street. Giuliani urges resident New Yorkers to stay at home.

11:02 a.m.: FAA reports: "AEA [FAA Eastern Region in Jamaica, New York] confirms US inbounds diverted to Canada."

11:03 a.m.: AA Flight 77. FAA reports: "AAL 77 suspected down near Ashland, KY."

11:04 a.m.: Air Threat Conference Call log: "White House (PEOC): Let us know intercept time for Ellington fights [on Air Force One].... Also from

---

933. Defense Studies Series, Pentagon 9/11.
934. Defense Studies Series, Pentagon 9/11.
935. Arlington County: After-Action Report on the Response to the September 11 Terrorist Attack on the Pentagon.

Dr. Rice, for NATO make sure we maintain a good log of disposition of assets."[936]

11:04 a.m.: FAA reports: "ZID [Indy Center, reports that it] does not know about crash in Ashland [Kentucky] area."

11:05 a.m.: Jamie McIntyre, CNN Pentagon correspondent, reports an eyewitness account from outside the building: "I'm looking at the charred facade of the Pentagon, a huge gaping hole on the side where the Pentagon heliport is located, the side that faces Arlington Cemetery. . . . You can see exposed five floors of the Pentagon offices just ripped apart."

He continues: "A short time after this attack there were urgent announcements made over the loudspeakers [in the Pentagon] telling people to quickly get away from the building because they had reports of a second plane heading this way just two minutes away. F-16 jets were scrambled over the Pentagon. I saw several of them go by, but no second plane ever materialized."[937]

11:05 a.m.: FAA issues Advisory 036 suspending operations in the National Airspace System.[938]

DUE TO EXTRAORDINARY CIRCUMSTANCES AND FOR REASONS OF SAFETY. ATTENTION ALL AIRCRAFT OPERATORS, BY ORDER OF THE FEDERAL AVIATION COMMAND CENTER ALL AIRPORTS/AIRDROMES ARE NOT AUTHORIZED FOR LANDING AND TAKEOFF. ALL TRAFFIC INCLUDING AIRBORNE AIRCRAFT ARE ENCOURAGED TO LAND SHORTLY, INCLUDING ALL HELICOPTER TRAFFIC.

AIRCRAFT INVOLVED IN FIREFIGHTING IN THE NORTHWEST US ARE EXCLUDED. PLEASE READ THIS NOTICE OVER THE EMERGENCY FREQUENCIES, AND VOR [VHF Omnidirectional Radio Range] VOICE.

936. Air Threat Conference Call log, "DJH Notes," Top Secret, partially declassified. See also 9/11 Commission NORAD MFR.

937. "CNN Breaking News: America Under Attack," CNN, September 11, 2001, http://transcripts.cnn.com/TRANSCRIPTS/0109/11/bn.11.html.

938. FAA Chronology.

11:05 a.m.: Air Threat Conference Call log: Discussion of unidentified track off east coast. NORAD: "Otis fighters are in route."[939]

11:05 a.m.: FAA reports false alarm: "Low-flying aircraft, ZOB [Cleveland Center] evacuation."[940]

11:06 a.m.: FAA DC logs: "SCATANA requested [by] acting ANE 500 [FAA New England Region in Burlington, Massachusetts] referred [to] [redacted]."[941]

This is the first mention of SCATANA (Security Control of Air Traffic and Air Navigation Aids), the Cold War plan providing national security priority for the use of the air control system. The plan is officially implemented at 12:06 p.m.

11:08 a.m.: Air Threat Conference Call log:[942]

> NORAD: "Need to confirm the ROE . . . on [sic] unidentified track in vicinity of Mass."
> FAA: "I need a beacon code. Do you have a beacon code for your scrambled aircraft that tends to separate them from other aircraft?"
> NORAD: "Stand by."

11:09 a.m.: DC National Guard launches a second flight of F-16s (Wild 01 and 02)—the original planes taking to the skies being low on fuel and unarmed.

Once the DC National Guard F-16s are over Washington, they establish contact with the Langley AFB fighters for deconfliction. The Guard planes, still not formally under NORAD operational control, fly at a low altitude while the NORAD F-16s from Langley fly at a higher altitude. Brig. Gen.

---

939. Air Threat Conference Call log, "DJH Notes," Top Secret, partially declassified. See also 9/11 Commission NORAD MFR.

940. DCC Timeline.

941. DCC Timeline.

942. Air Threat Conference Call log, "DJH Notes," Top Secret, partially declassified. See also 9/11 Commission NORAD MFR.

Wherley later tells the 9/11 Commission: "The NORAD planes had the advantages of being properly armed and they had good situation awareness because of their altitude. But the Guard planes had the advantage of solid, reasonably clear information on the rules of engagement, while NORAD had different, unclear information on ROEs that NORAD was still sorting out. The Guard planes also had better communications with Washington Approach, which was the best source of radar data on possible threats. . . . Wherley felt the Guard and NORAD pilots actually in the air did a good job of interacting directly with each other so that either pair of aircraft could be ready for any contingency."[943]

The DC National Guard history says: "As the first F-16 crew returned due to fuel, the next crew went out. There was no time to arm them with missiles, so each fighter went out with only 500 training bullets—just enough for a five-second burst. At the time, they believed that there may be more hostile aircraft. Each committed to doing whatever necessary to stop any hostile aircraft they encountered—up to and including ramming the airliner."[944]

A news media report later recounted: "Word came to them that they had shoot-to-kill orders. Knowing that they had taken off with unarmed aircraft, that could mean only one thing. They would be flying a kamikaze mission, ramming into [UA] Flight 93, a Boeing 757 aircraft, nearly 7 times the weight of their F-16 fighter jets."[945]

In the words of NEADS technician Stacia Rountree: "In case their weapons were out, and if we would have had to use force, they were discussing whether or not those guys would have to go kamikaze," she says, meaning some pilots were considering risking their own lives by using their planes to stop hijacked jetliners. "It was scary, when you thought about the possibility of them having to do that."[946]

---

943. 9/11 Commission Memorandum for the Record, Interview, BG David Wherley, on September 11, 2001, Commander of the 113th Wing of the USAF, August 28, 2003.

944. "9/11 Response," District of Columbia National Guard, accessed July 30, 2020, https://dc.ng.mil/About-Us/Heritage/History/9-11-Response/.

945. Greg Timmons, "On 9/11, Heather Penney Tried to Bring Down Flight 93 in a Kamikaze Mission," History Channel, September 9, 2020.

946. Katie Lange, "8 Things You May Not Know About Our Air Defense on 9/11," DOD News, September 11, 2019.

11:10 a.m.: FAA DC logs: "Military asked flights authorized to fly, i.e. police helicopters, to be on discrete codes, not 1200."[947] Air Threat Conference Call log:[948]

> NMCC (DDO): "We need the ROE for aircraft in vicinity of Mass. Again it is important that we just escort it to the ground but not fire on it."
> NORAD: "Acknowledges [sic]."

Now, even with presidential and vice-presidential orders, and with implementation of DEFCON 3, the Pentagon is still cautioning intercepting unidentified aircraft— at least those not over Washington—to escort them rather than shoot at them.

11:10 a.m.: FAA reports a false alarm:

> FAA DC logs: "DOT—PA-to-DC [airplane] not squawking [a beacon code]."[949]
> FAA reports: "NTSB told ORD [Chicago] controllers not to return to facility . . . FAA countermanded NTSB order."

11:11 a.m.: FAA reports:

> "Military advised that they need to work with FAA to release medevac aircraft in NY/DC area."
> FAA DC logs: "Two hundred flights airborne."[950]
> "Security requesting [Michael A. Canavan, FAA Associate Administrator for Civil Aviation Security] (ACS-1) to be picked up in Puerto Rico."[951]

---

947. DCC Timeline.

948. Air Threat Conference Call log, "DJH Notes," Top Secret, partially declassified. See also 9/11 Commission NORAD MFR.

949. DCC Timeline.

950. DCC Timeline.

951. National Archives Chronology. At 11:14 a.m., the FAA reports: "Attempting to get General Cavanaugh [sic, actually Michael A. Canavan, FAA head of security (N1A)] from

Though never publicized, a number of aircraft are dispatched during the day to retrieve minor government officials, making exceptions to the ground stoppage (and requiring fighter interceptor escorts to enter DC airspace). These officials include retired Army Gen. Michael A. Canavan, head of Civil Aviation Security (who is in Puerto Rico), Assistant FBI Director Ike Nakamoto (at Hilton Head, South Carolina),[952] some unidentified Navy official,[953] and an unnamed FAA Associate Administrator for Air Traffic (in New Orleans).[954] Other government or contractor aircraft fly with supposed VIPs aboard.[955]

11:12 a.m.: FAA reports: "FBI on site in LAX [Los Angeles airport] . . . observing."

11:13 a.m.: Air Threat Conference Call log: NMCC (DDO): "SECDEF [Rumsfeld] interested in getting situation . . . worldwide. We need to know the status of any events that are going on and also whether we have a CAP over sensitive areas such as Saudi and others."[956]

Puerto Rico back to US." An Army plane (60180 (PAT 108) is dispatched and lands at West Palm Beach, Florida, before heading to Andrews AFB, Maryland, landing at 5:30 p.m.

952. At 12:05 p.m., the FAA reports: Assistant Director of the FBI "requesting release of Ross 72, Cessna Citation (Ike Nakamoto) from Manassas, VA to Hilton Head then back." At 12:30 p.m., FAA DC logs: "MEK called to release [Ross 72 (N172CV), Cessna Citation] aircraft on ground at Manassas to pick up Asst. Director of FBI." DCC Timeline. At 3:07 p.m., FAA reports: "Ross 72 [Deputy FBI Director, *sic*] beacon code 0573 IAD to HEF [Hilton Head] is approved."

953. At 11:31 a.m., that FAA reported: "Southwest of Nashville: G3 with Secretary of the Navy [*sic*] requests permission to land . . . referred to ATCSCC." At 11:57 a.m., FAA DC logs: "Col. Cruise military assistant to Secretary of Navy JRB [Port Authority Downtown Heliport, New York] to ADW [Andrews AFB, Maryland]. Told him to call military." DCC Timeline.

954. At 10:50 a.m., the: FAA reports: "N2 [G3] to be released from DCA [Washington National] . . . N2 Leaving DCA cleared to MSY [New Orleans, Louisiana]." The plane is released to go from Washington to New Orleans to pick up the FAA Associate Administrator for Air Traffic (AAT-1), who is out of town. He is picked up at 3:14 and escorted by DC National Guard F-16s to land at Washington National at 4:57 p.m. See FAA, 11 Sep 01 Catastrophic Crisis (all times given in EDT).

955. At 11:49 a.m., FAA DC logs: "N2164L [an apparent FBI contracted plane], DIA [Denver] to Manassas BE90." See DCC Timeline.

956. Air Threat Conference Call log, "DJH Notes," Top Secret, partially declassified. See also 9/11 Commission NORAD MFR.

The DEFCON 3 order, in theory, shifts the readiness of forces worldwide, but there is no evidence that CENTCOM in the Middle East took any immediate actions. A no-fly zone was already being enforced over Iraqi skies—from aircraft partially flying out of bases in Saudi Arabia—that would have detected and responded to any other hostile acts in the Gulf region. There is no evidence that they changed their operations or schedules.

11:13 a.m.: FAA reports: "Military scrambled fighters to A/C circling ZOB [Cleveland Center]."

11:15 a.m.: Secretary Rumsfeld, according to the 9/11 Commission report, briefs President Bush on the move of the US armed forces to DEFCON 3.[957]

(There is no evidence—from President Bush's diary—that Rumsfeld spoke to the president at this time, but he could have communicated through Bush's military aide.)

"A few minutes" after DOD declares DEFCON 3 (probably around 11:00–11:15 a.m.), discussions begin with Russia.

"The US ambassador to Moscow, Alexander Vershbow, called the [White House] Sit Room, saying that [Russian President] Putin wanted to speak with Bush."[958] At around this time, Deputy Secretary of State Richard Armitage reportedly speaks to his Russian counterparts about the DEFCON change.

Condoleezza Rice says she thought about contacting the Russians:

"As it turned out, Putin had been trying to reach the President . . . ," she says.
    She called the Kremlin, she says, asking to speak to Russian Defense Minister Sergei Ivanov, but Putin got on the phone. "Mr. President," I said, "the President is not able to take your call right now . . . I wanted to let you know that American forces are going up on alert."

---

957. 9/11 Commission Report, p. 554, fn. 8. The footnote reads: "See DOD transcript, Air Threat Conference Call, Sept. 11, 2001; Stephen Cambone interviews (July 8, 2004; July 12, 2004); DOD notes, Stephen Cambone notes, Sept. 11, 2001."
    958. Michael K. Bohn, "Former Staffers Remember the White House Situation Room on 9/11," McClatchy Newspapers, August 29, 2011.

"We already know, and we have canceled our exercises and brought our alert levels down," he said. "Is there anything else we can do?"

I thanked him, and for one brief moment the thought flashed through my head: the Cold War really is over.[959]

In the afternoon, Rumsfeld says, he spoke with Ivanov. By Rumsfeld's account, they discussed neither the DEFCON change nor any ongoing US nuclear exercise. "He sounded sad as we discussed the casualties. He pledged Russia's cooperation. As it happened, I already had a request to make. The Russian military was conducting an aircraft exercise near Alaska, and our forces were understandably sensitive now about any intrusions into American airspace. So I asked Ivanov if he would have his military stand down. He promptly agreed to halt the exercise."[960]

Gen. Myers says, however, that Rumsfeld called to discuss the DEFCON change.[961]

According to one news media account, Rice's call takes place at 11:50 a.m. That account says that the Kremlin requested to speak to President Bush about the purpose of the DEFCON 3 declaration. Rice (who could speak Russian) told Putin that US forces had gone on alert; Putin responded, "I know, I've seen them." That account glosses over the gravity: "Putin understood that the US DEFCON 3 status wasn't a threat to his nation. He told Rice that Russian forces were standing down, forestalling any tensions between the two countries, and offered his country's help."[962]

11:15 a.m.: Secret Service reports that Liz Cheney and her family are en route to a relocation site.[963]

959. *No Higher Honor*, pp. 74–75.
960. *Known and Unknown*, p. 344.
961. *Eyes on the Horizon*, p. 159.
962. Michael K. Bohn, "Former Staffers Remember the White House Situation Room on 9/11," McClatchy Newspapers, August 29, 2011.
963. Secret Service Memorandum, White House Events on 9/11/01 (Special Agent James O. Scott), September 12, 2001, partially declassified. Some logs incorrectly say that Liz is evacuated at 9:52 a.m.

Liz Cheney, her husband, her toddler children, and their nanny are whisked away from their upper Northwest Washington home by the Secret Service and taken to Mount Weather (and later to Camp David).[964]

11:16 a.m.: CNN reports that the Centers for Disease Control and Prevention (CDC) is preparing emergency response teams as a precautionary move against the possibility of some biological attack event.

11:16 a.m.: FAA reports: "SCATANA Procedures for ANE [FAA New England Region in Burlington, Massachusetts]/AEA [FAA Eastern Region in Jamaica, New York] by Military. Military will confirm."[965]

11:17 a.m.: The Associated Press reports an expert as saying: "I would name at the top of the list Osama Bin Laden."[966]

11:17 a.m.: FAA reports: "Reconfirm ground stop exceptions include military, Coast Guard, medivac [sic], and law enforcement."

11:18 a.m.: American Airlines publicly states that it has lost two aircraft. The first is AA Flight 11, a Boeing 767 flying from Boston to Los Angeles, with 81 passengers and 11 crew aboard. The second is AA Flight 77, a Boeing 757 en route from Dulles IAP to Los Angeles, with 58 passengers and 6 crew members aboard.

11:18 a.m.: FAA reports false alarms: "USCG out of Norfolk reports receiving distress calls from three aircraft (UA 947/COA 57/Air Canada 065)."

11:20 a.m.: David Ensor, national security correspondent, reports on CNN about the perpetrators of the attacks:

---

964. *In My Time: A Personal and Political Memoir*, p. 4. Secret Service, Interview with SA Michael Seremetis, October 1, 2001, partially declassified, mentions Mount Weather specifically.

965. National Archives Chronology.

966. AP, "A Stunning 48 Hours of News," n.d. (September 12, 2001).

I'm talking to US officials who are obviously working on who is responsible for this. They're [*sic*] working thesis is that this is overseas terrorism, not domestic. They cannot rule out additional attacks yet to come. In terms of claims of responsibility so far, there is an Agence France Press report, in which a group with a [*sic*] word Palestine in the name claims responsibility. There is also a report quoting "personnel close to Osama bin Laden." The fugitive Saudi accused terrorist denying that that group was involved. But again, US officials say they can't add—shed any light on whether these reports are correct or incorrect. Usually when this kind of attack occurs, you have claims of responsibility from all sorts of people who have nothing to do with it. So it's a very fluid situation at this point.

He goes on to say: "Attention will quickly turn to the bin Laden group, because it has long tentacles, has connections with all sorts of other groups. We saw at the millennium, a group of Algerians apparently involved in trying to arrange bombing in the United States, and now there is evidence being produced in court sessions that those Algerians were working for the bin Laden group. So that group certainly will come under immediate suspicion. There are very few others that could have pulled this off."[967]

11:20 a.m.: After evacuation of John F. Kennedy IAP is ordered by the PAPD,[968] three supposedly Middle Eastern men refuse to deplane from UA Flight 23, scheduled to fly to Los Angeles.

FAA DC reports: "Three Arabs refused to exit aircraft at gate 27. Unknown locations. UAL 23 at JFK."[969]

At 11:28 a.m., the FAA reports: "JFK: three alleged Middle Eastern persons refuse to debark from UAL 23 at Gate 2, Terminal 7."[970]

The incident is pointed to by some as another possible hijacking, now known to be false, even though a NORAD general later speculates that at least one other hijacking was avoided.

---

967. "CNN Breaking News: America Under Attack," CNN, September 11, 2001, http://transcripts.cnn.com/TRANSCRIPTS/0109/11/bn.11.html.

968. National Archives Chronology.

969. DCC Timeline.

970. FAA, 11 Sep 01 Catastrophic Crisis (all times given in EDT).

`11:21 a.m.:` AA Flight 77. FAA reports: "AAL 77 according to ZID [Indy Center] . . . no wreckage reported on ground near Ashland [Kentucky]."[971]

`11:23 a.m.:` FAA reports bomb threats: FAA DC logs: "LAX/ONT/PBI bomb threats per FBI."[972]

`11:26 a.m.:` FAA reports false alarm: "COA 57 [Continental Airlines Flight 57] (B777) in Moncton (Canada) . . . airspace, inbound to EWR [Newark IAP]."

NEADS MCC Lt. Col. Nasypany later tells the 9/11 Commission that "an aircraft headed south from Canada was the 'fifth aircraft' NEADS became concerned with,"[973] presumably this flight.

Maj. McNulty, intelligence officer in the DC National Guard, says, "Around 11:30-ish it seemed like another wave of hijacks were coming from overseas because a whole other series of planes squawking emergency. Later it was determined the emergency squawk was because they were all diverted to Canada."[974]

`11:27 a.m.:` FAA DC logs: "Air Force One to S93."[975]

`11:28 a.m.:` FAA DC logs: "President of Uganda lands . . . in ZJX [FAA Jacksonville Center]."[976]

`11:28 a.m.:` Retired Army Gen. Wesley Clark says on CNN: "There is only one group that has ever indicated that it has this kind of ability, and that's Osama bin Laden's. So obviously, that will be the first suspicion."

---

971. National Archives Chronology.

972. DCC Timeline.

973. 9/11 Commission Memorandum for the Record, Interview with NEADS Alpha Flight Mission Crew Commander (MCC), Lt. Col. Kevin J. Nasypany, January 22, 2004, and January 23, 2004.

974. 9/11 Commission Memorandum for the Record, Interview, Major David McNulty, Chief of Intelligence, 121st Fighter Squadron, Air National Guard, Andrews AFB, March 11, 2004.

975. DCC Timeline.

976. DCC Timeline.

On the US military, he says: "There are command centers in various places of the Pentagon and there are many other alternate command centers. So I don't think there's really any issue about the command and control of the United States armed forces. I'm sure that's very solid right now."[977]

11:29 a.m.: FAA reports false alarm: "UAL 947/Air Canada 65, no info."

11:30 a.m.: US Joint Forces Command (JFCOM), the command responsible for the United States (and a predecessor to today's NORTHCOM), directs subordinates to implement FPCON Delta, an hour and 10 minutes after it was declared by the Pentagon.

Maj. Gen. Craig Bambrough, the deputy commanding general at Army Forces Command (FORSCOM), one of JFCOM's subordinate commands, later says:

I can't remember the Army ever going to Delta, at least not in my career. . . . The Army's focus has always been outward. We've always been concerned about a threat outside the country.[978]

11:30 a.m.: At NORAD Cheyenne Mountain Center, the three-foot-thick, 25-ton steel blast doors are closed for the first time in history.[979]

NORAD commander Gen. Eberhart is now inside the mountain, again in communication with Gen. Myers. Eberhart notes that it had "quieted down" before he made the decision to travel from Peterson AFB to the Mountain, where he arrived at about 11:30 a.m.[980]

977. "CNN Breaking News: America Under Attack: Gen. Wesley Clark Discusses Ongoing Terrorist Situation," CNN, September 11, 2001, http://transcripts.cnn.com/TRANSCRIPTS/0109/11/bn.10.html.

978. Email, "Force Protection Delta Ordered in CONUS," Global Command and Control System (US Joint Forces Command), THREATCON Research material; hereafter referred to as TCRM #12, September 11, 2001.

979. Lynn Spencer, "9/11: The Saga of the Skies, Chaos and Control over Washington, While the Pentagon Burned," *Air & Space* magazine, March 14, 2008.

980. 9/11 Commission NORAD MFR.

Medical personnel and volunteers work the first medical triage area set up outside the Pentagon after a hijacked commercial airliner crashed into the southwest corner of the building. (Source: US Navy Photo / Journalist First Class Mark D. Faram)

11:30 a.m.: At the Pentagon, at around 11:30 a.m., Arlington County Manager Ron Carlee declares a local state of disaster. Working with the Virginia state government, "Carlee cut through the cumbersome process for obtaining state and federal assistance, facilitating rapid deployment of FEMA Urban Search and Rescue Teams that [Arlington Fire Chief] Schwartz urgently needed."[981]

11:30 a.m.: At the World Trade Center, NYPD Chief of Department Monahan returns to One Police Plaza.[982]

11:30 a.m.: FAA reports: "NWA 51 [Northwest Airlines Flight 51] from FRA [sic], Germany . . . Canada will not allow to land in Canadian airspace . . . originally inbound for DTW [Detroit]."

981. Defense Studies Series, Pentagon 9/11.
982. NIST Chronology.

`11:34 a.m.:` FAA reports: "UAL 947 over BANKS [a fixed point over the Atlantic Ocean] heading toward Gander, Nova Scotia, [*sic*] Canada (worked by Gander ACC)."

`11:35 a.m.:` FAA reports: "Life Parts (Medevac) flights will be coordinated with military case-by-case."

`11:38 a.m.:` At the World Trade Center, recalled firefighters on city buses are awaiting deployment.[983]

`11:42 a.m.:` New York authorities request state and federal assistance to include the Disaster Medical Assistance Team and the Disaster Mortuary Operational Response Team.[984]

`11:42 a.m.:` FAA DC logs: "Unidentified aircraft circling/possible [violation of] SCATANA."[985]
SCATANA is not formally declared until 12:06 p.m.

`11:44 a.m.:` FAA DC logs: "Cape Approach reported large aircraft overflying MVY [Martha's Vineyard]. Non-transponder."[986]

`11:45 a.m.:` FAA reports: "Some controllers working some of the crisis aircraft are traumatized and need [to be] relieved."

`11:46 a.m.:` FAA reports resolve earlier false alarm:

"All three A/C that USCG reported [at 11:18 a.m.] hearing distress calls from are accounted for (all OK)."
"ZNY request release personnel . . . case by case basis."

---

983. NIST Chronology.
984. FDNY Report.
985. DCC Timeline.
986. DCC Timeline.

11:47 a.m.: FAA reports: "Some controllers in NY area are refusing to report to work (to be ordered to work)."

11:50 a.m.: In the Air Threat Conference Call, there is an exchange from around this time (not stamped with a specific time):

> Air Force operations: "We have a request from Air Combat Command to the Russian government to stand down their exercise in the Siberian region to alleviate any confusion with that particular defense sector."
>
> NMCC (DDO): "Which area are we working at? What area are you interested in having them stand down?"
>
> Air Force operations: "Basically, anything west of Alaska."
>
> NMCC (DDO): "Roger. We've been told that two hours ago, they were directed to do that."
>
> Air Force operations: "Air Force copies."[987]

11:50 a.m.: FAA DC logs: "Concurrence to SCATANA."[988]

11:52 a.m.: The Associated Press reports that the Federal Reserve says it is prepared to provide additional money to the nation's banking system as needed following terrorist attacks.[989]

11:52 a.m.: FAA reports: "COA 57 est. 60W at 1515Z and no confirmation on UAL 947 from Moncton [Canada]."

987. 9/11 Air Threat Conference Call Transcription, partially declassified.
988. DCC Timeline.
989. AP, "A Stunning 48 Hours of News," n.d. (September 12, 2001).

CHAPTER 13

A PRESIDENT MISSING IN ACTION

Air Force One left Sarasota at 9:55 a.m. with no destination yet determined, and at 10:10 a.m., the plane changed directions and headed west, away from Washington, at first in a hold pattern and then specifically to Barksdale AFB in Louisiana. President Bush wanted to make another statement to the American people, and Barksdale was chosen both because it was secure and because it had a high-level strategic headquarters (Eighth Air Force) from which the president would also be able to connect securely to his team in Washington. Probably unknown to those who decided to land at Barksdale was the fact that the base was at the center of the ongoing nuclear war exercise—Global Guardian—and that B-52 bombers loaded with live nuclear weapons were in the alert area adjacent to the very runways the president's plane would use. Airmen quickly unloaded the nuclear bombs and cruise missiles as the president's plane waited. The reason for the unloading wasn't necessarily because the president was coming. STRATCOM commander Adm. Richard Mies had pulled the plug on the exercise five minutes before Air Force One left Florida, at 9:50 a.m.

While all of this was going on, an anonymous call came into the Secret Service threatening "Angel," the code name for Air Force One. The White House panicked, based on the false belief that that name was so secret that anyone who could have known it must have been a true terrorist. And yet any national security specialist knew the code name. Fearful of being tracked by terrorists, reporters aboard Air Force One were told to turn off their cell phones and asked to refer to Barksdale as an "unidentified location." The secrecy didn't last long; local news stations reported Bush's arrival in Louisiana, and CNN was soon announcing where he was.

After the message to the American people was recorded from an Eighth Air Force conference room, Bush got back on Air Force One—which had been loaded with days' worth of food and pallets of bottled water. They didn't know how long the attacks would go on for, and they didn't know when he could return to the capital city. Given the uncertainty of the day and the threat to "Angel," another Air Force base was chosen—Offutt AFB in Omaha, Nebraska—for Bush to land. He needed reliable communications. There, from the underground nuclear war command center, he did have an opportunity to speak to his advisers and convened an impromptu NSC meeting. Cheney and Rice, at the White House, still urged the president to stay away from Washington, but Bush insisted that he return. He not only thought he had to be in Washington but also was frustrated and angry that his communications aboard the plane were so restricted. "This ass is going back to Washington," Bush told them.

Out of sight and seemingly out of touch, the rumors began almost immediately that President Bush was AWOL, derelict, or even a coward for not returning to Washington immediately upon hearing of the hijackings. Conservative commentator William Bennett said on 9/11: "It cannot look as if the president has been run off, or it will look like we can't defend our most important institutions." A Republican fundraiser was quoted as worrying: "I am stunned that he has not come home. It looks like he is running. This looks bad."

The day of 9/11 seemed like an eternity, and Bush's wandering the skies for eight hours is one of the most criticized elements of government action (or inaction). Billions were spent after 9/11 to improve airborne communications (and television reception) for Air Force One, but no one was ever held accountable for why the plane proved to be so isolating or for why the president's communications were so deficient. Aboard the hijacked planes, flight attendants and passengers managed to get through on cell phones and the installed Airfones, but the president of the United States couldn't always communicate. Technological advances have resolved most of the connectivity issues, but undoubtedly, when the next earth-shattering crisis looms, some new flaw in a supposed fail-safe system will be revealed.

11:55 a.m.: Air Force One, with President Bush aboard, arrives at Barksdale AFB, Louisiana.[990]

---

990. Presidential Daily Diary, partially declassified.

Bush remembers: "The taxiway was lined with bombers."[991] Air Force One reportedly waits until live nuclear weapons are unloaded from B-52 bombers parked in the alert area at the base, part of the ongoing Global Guardian strategic nuclear war exercise. The *Omaha World Herald* will later report:

> The Air Force was especially concerned . . . that a hijacked jet might try to crash into the bomb-laden B-52's on the tarmac at Barksdale Air Force Base . . . [Adm. Mies, STRATCOM commander] said such an act wouldn't have set off a nuclear blast, though it might have caused a large explosion.
>
> "You would destroy half of Bossier City, Louisiana, with the explosions," [STRATCOM adviser] Buckles said. "That would have been a way to really cripple us. All these nuclear weapons were exposed."
>
> Airmen had begun to unload nuclear bombs from the B-52's.[992]

11:55 a.m.: FAA reports false alarm: "ORF [Norfolk, VA]: Coast Guard station reporting Alitalia Cell #EICRL distress call."

11:56 a.m.: FAA reports false alarm: "F-16 intercepted N22CJ intruder A/C 35 NM west of PIT [Pittsburgh]."

11:57 a.m.: FAA reports: "Canada now refusing to allow any A/C to land in Canadian airspace ([FAA Herndon Command Center] . . . will try to turn A/C around)."

11:58 a.m.: President Bush is driven from the tarmac at Barksdale AFB to the Eighth Air Force Dougherty Conference Center, accompanied by Andrew Card.[993]

11:58 a.m.: Secretary Powell boards his government jet in Lima, Peru, to head back to the United States.[994]

---

991. *Decision Points*, p. 132.

992. Steve Liewer, "On 9/11, StratCom Leaders Were Practicing for a Fictional Threat When Real, Unprecedented Catastrophe Struck," *Omaha World Herald*, September 8, 2016.

993. Presidential Daily Diary, partially declassified.

994. *24 Hours Inside the President's Bunker*, p. 70.

11:58 a.m.: FAA reports: "NMCC still determining that medevacs, USCG, and law enforcement to be released."

11:59 a.m.: United Airlines publicly confirms that UA Flight 175, from Boston to Los Angeles, with 56 passengers and nine crew members aboard, is one of the hijacked airplanes.

12:00 p.m.: President Bush is greeted at the Eighth Air Force headquarters by Lt. Gen. Tom Keck and is taken to his office.[995]

12:00 p.m.: At the Pentagon, a small meeting convenes via video teleconference with Deputy Secretary Wolfowitz (from Site R), Gen. Myers, and head of the Defense Intelligence Agency (DIA) Vice Adm. Tom Wilson. Rumsfeld is in and out of the call.[996]

According to Gen. Myers, Vice Adm. Wilson "confirmed what everybody at the conference table had already surmised: The attacks had undoubtedly come from al Qaeda."

Gen. Myers also recalls: "In the first small meeting at the Pentagon at about noon with all the principals, Secretary Rumsfeld asked loudly enough for everybody to hear, 'What else could the enemy do?' He was thinking ahead, engaging in Rumsfeld's well-known outside-the-box speculation. 'NBC,' I said. I didn't mean the National Broadcasting Corporation. I meant nuclear, biological, and chemical—weapons of mass destruction."[997]

This might be the first explicit high-level discussion of weapons of mass destruction on 9/11, though CDC had activated a task force to deal with a possible biological agent attack and the Secret Service was concerned about a chemical attack on the White House.

---

995. Presidential Daily Diary, partially declassified.

996. At Site R (Raven Rock), Deputy Secretary Wolfowitz joins the DOD video teleconference. "Deputy Secretary Paul Wolfowitz had reached Site R, from where his image appeared in a small box at the upper right hand corner of our [video teleconference] screen." See *Eyes on the Horizon*, p. 155.

997. *Eyes on the Horizon*, p. 156.

`12:00 p.m.:` (Approximate time) At the Pentagon, Maj. Gen. James Jackson, commander of the Military District of Washington, says he saw "the need to 'get some kind of cohesive unit in here [at the Pentagon], specifically the Old Guard' (3rd Infantry Regiment) from Fort Myers [to assist in the rescue efforts] and to move the volunteers out of the way.'"[998]

`12:00 p.m.:` John King says on CNN: "I am told by Secret Service and administration sources that all of the principles [*sic*], all of the protectees, meaning the President, the Vice President, and the first lady and Mrs. Cheney, are safe. They do not want us disclosing their locations, but I am told by a senior administration official that the plan and the priority is to get President Bush back to the White House as soon as they believe it is safe.

"And in the past half-hour or so, we have seen security precautions on the street, checks being taken out on the street on the grounds around the White House. There are snipers up on the roofs of the White House itself including buildings around it. And a military helicopter gunship flew over the premises not that long ago."[999]

`12:00 p.m.:` (Approximate time) Attorney General Ashcroft lands at Washington National. Ashcroft later tells the 9/11 Commission "that his wife was found and that they were sent to the remote location where other DOJ people had gone. The city was deadlocked and he was stuck in traffic. After a while, it became useless and he ordered the car to turn back and he went straight to the SIOC [the Strategic Information Operations Center at FBI headquarters]. He told his staff at the remote location to come in.

"The SIOC was a chaotic setting, Ashcroft says. Earlier it was thought that one of the planes might be headed for the FBI headquarters building. He . . . guessed that he arrived at the SIOC between 1:00–2:00 p.m."[1000]

`12:00 p.m.:` The news media reports a plane crash in Chicago.

---

998. Defense Studies Series, Pentagon 9/11.

999. "CNN Breaking News: White House Personnel and Officials Are Safe," CNN, September 11, 2001, http://transcripts.cnn.com/TRANSCRIPTS/0109/11/bn.14.html.

1000. 9/11 Commission Memorandum for the Record, Interview with Attorney General John D. Ashcroft, December 17, 2003.

12:00 p.m.: After being offline for nearly three hours because of massive internet traffic congestion, CNN.com manages to get a stripped-down version of its news website back up and running.

12:01 p.m.: FAA reports: "[FAA Deputy Administrator] Monte Belger contacting NAV Canada (Mr. Creighton) regarding ability of Canada to receive divert A/C."

12:03 p.m.: President Bush arrives at the conference room at Eighth Air Force headquarters at Barksdale AFB.[1001]

12:04 a.m.: Los Angeles IAP (LAX), the intended destination of three of the now-crashed airplanes, is evacuated and shut down.

12:04 p.m.: FAA reports: "NMCC and AF/CC confirm medevacs released at TEB [Teterboro, New Jersey]."

12:05 p.m.: CIA Director George Tenet tells Secretary Rumsfeld about an intercepted conversation collected by the NSA from "one of Osama bin Laden's operatives in Afghanistan" speaking of the "good news" to a phone number in the former Soviet republic of Georgia and saying that another target was still to come.[1002]

Rumsfeld receives a call from Tenet shortly after noon. "George, what do you know that I don't know?" he asks.[1003]

12:05 p.m.: At the World Trade Center, the NYPD says the Verizon building at 140 West Street is flooded.[1004]

12:06 p.m.: Security Control of Air Traffic and Air Navigation Aids (SCAT-ANA) is implemented by the FAA, grounding all air traffic over the United

---

1001. Presidential Daily Diary, partially declassified.

1002. CBS News, "Plans for Iraq Attack Began on 9/11," September 4, 2002, reporting on a David Martin story.

1003. *Known and Unknown*, p. 341.

1004. NIST Chronology.

States and diverting any incoming traffic to alternate destinations.[1005] FAA reports: "Order 7610.41, SCATANA procedures page 6–31, dated 11/98."

A declaration of SCATANA is far more stringent than the earlier FAA ground stop. The SCATANA plan outlines responsibilities, procedures, and instructions for the security control of civil and military air traffic and navigational aids (NAVAIDs) in order to provide national security priority for the use of the air control system and airspace under emergency conditions. This is an unprecedented order that prescribes the joint action to be taken by DOD, the FAA, and the FCC—in essence, a preparation for war that gives the military sole access to airspace.[1006] The Cold War plan actually calls for all civil navigational aids to be shut down to deny enemy bombers the ability to use them for beaconing and to operate in US airspace. Despite the proscribed measure, on 9/11, no such restriction is ever implemented. The actual plan implemented is Emergency Security Control of Air Traffic (ESCAT), which allows for the continuation of the use of navigational aids. Also, though SCATANA and ESCAT put the US military (NORAD) in sole charge of US airspace, this never really happens.

12:07 p.m.: FAA reports: "Nine aircraft over oceanic airspace inbound to US . . . OK to divert to Canada."

12:07 p.m.: At the World Trade Center, the EMS staging area is moved to Chelsea and Piers Division as a result of a gas leak.[1007]

12:10 p.m.: At the World Trade Center, three new casualty collection points are established at the Javits Center, Brooklyn Navy Yard, and the Yankees minor league stadium on Staten Island.[1008]

1005. SCATANA is promulgated in furtherance of the Federal Aviation Act of 1958, as amended, the Communications Act of 1934, and Executive Order 11490, as amended. The governing DOD regulation on 9/11 was DOD Instruction (DODI) 5030.36, "Plan for the Security Control of Air Traffic and Air Navigation Aids (Short Title: SCATANA)," April 24, 1980.

1006. 9/11 Commission Staff Report, August 26, 2004.

1007. NIST Chronology.

1008. NIST Chronology.

12:13 p.m.: President Bush, in Gen. Keck's office, speaks privately with Secretary Rumsfeld.

"Don had been hard to track down," Bush later writes. Bush says in this call that he approves Rumsfeld's decision to raise the military readiness level to DEFCON 3.[1009]

Though it has been reported that CIA Director Tenet told Rumsfeld that al Qaeda has been implicated in an NSA intercept, evidently Rumsfeld does not pass this information on to the president (see 1:45 p.m.).

12:13 p.m.: FAA reports false alarm: "AGL [FAA Great Lakes Region] reports UAL 809 (B767) on ground at Rockford [Illinois] (UPS area) potential bomb threat."

12:15 p.m.: San Francisco International Airport, the original destination of UA Flight 93, is evacuated and shut down.

12:15 p.m.: INS says that the borders with Canada and Mexico are on the highest state of alert, but no decision has yet been made about closing them.

12:16 p.m.: FAA reports that the airspace over the 48 contiguous states is clear of all commercial and private traffic. Only a small number of law enforcement or emergency operations, as well as a few international arrivals, are in the air.[1010]

12:16 p.m.: FAA reports: "ZBW [Boston Center] back in operation with skeleton crew."

12:17 p.m.: FAA DC logs: "15N of Boston, [transponder] code 4402, unknown aircraft flight level 290. Military not aware. Military will sight."[1011]

1009. *Decision Points*, p. 133. Presidential Daily Diary, partially declassified, says the call took place in the Eighth Air Force conference room. Bush says Keck's office.

1010. FAA Chronology; 9/11 Commission NORAD MFR.

1011. DCC Timeline.

12:18 p.m.: President Bush, in the Eighth Air Force conference room, speaks for the second time with the First Lady.[1012]

"I was worried people would get the impression that the government was disengaged," Bush writes. "Laura had expressed the same concern."[1013]

12:18 p.m.: FAA reports: "10 Major carriers [the 10 major airlines] accounted for all aircraft."

12:19 p.m.: The NMCC in the Pentagon is evacuated because of growing smoke and carbon monoxide in the ventilation systems.

> Chief Edward Plaugher of the Arlington County Fire Department suggested that the NMCC be evacuated but chose not to press the issue with Rumsfeld who was determined to stay, largely because the communications network enabled him to keep in touch with key government officials and military commanders. Plaugher worried that carbon monoxide, odorless and colorless, would possibly reach the NMCC and render its occupants "irrational" before it killed them. At the same time he appreciated the magnitude of the crisis and the determination to continue operations in the Pentagon. The firefighters provided the NMCC occupants with a carbon monoxide detector and respirators along with instructions for their use, but by 12:19 p.m. their eyes and throats had become so irritated by smoke that the secretary and others returned to the Executive Support Center where the air was better. During the afternoon the secretary again spoke with the president by telephone; later he participated in the president's video teleconference from Offutt Air Force Base.[1014]

12:20 p.m.: President Bush, in the Eighth Air Force conference room, speaks privately with Vice President Cheney.[1015]

He tells Cheney, "It's the faceless coward that attacks."

"The vice president and the Secret Service again advised the president against returning to the nation's capital because of the confused and uncertain conditions there."[1016]

1012. Presidential Daily Diary, partially declassified.
1013. *Decision Points*, p. 133.
1014. Defense Studies Series, Pentagon 9/11.
1015. Presidential Daily Diary, partially declassified.
1016. Defense Studies Series, Pentagon 9/11.

By this time Cheney and the Secret Service believe that the threat against Air Force One still exists, even though the basis for the threat will later prove to be unfounded.

12:20 p.m.: (Approximate time) Air Force leaders leave the Pentagon to move to an alternate command center at Bolling AFB, across the Potomac River in southwest DC. They travel to Bolling AFB by helicopter.[1017]

Like their Navy counterparts, the secretary and the chief of staff choose to stay near the Pentagon and not travel to designated emergency relocation sites well outside Washington (as they are supposed to do in accordance with continuity plans).

12:22 p.m.: FAA reports: "[Herndon Command Center] . . . is moving ATSC into larger room to work on releases of A/C."

12:23 p.m.: FAA reports: "State Police wants to land at TEB [Teterboro, New Jersey]."

12:27 p.m.: FAA reports: "COA 57 [Continental Airlines 57] landed in Gander [Newfoundland, Canada]; seven A/C still airborne over oceanic airspace inbound to US diverting to Canada; UAL 947 returned to Europe."

12:29 p.m.: Nic Robertson of CNN appears on the air from Afghanistan: "Mullah Omar is the spiritual leader of the Taliban here, and he's recently issued a short statement. In that statement he criticizes what he called an act of terrorism. He was very explicit, he said that Osama Bin Laden was not responsible for it. He said that all he wanted for his country was peace, and peace for other countries in the world. But he went on to say that he believes Osama Bin Laden could not have been responsible for such a complex act of terrorism. He also said that Afghanistan is a poor country, and therefore he believes that there's no way Afghanistan could be involved in such a complicated act of terrorism."[1018]

1017. Defense Studies Series, Pentagon 9/11.

1018. "CNN Breaking News: Kabul Claims Osama Bin Laden Had Nothing to Do with Attack," CNN, September 11, 2001, http://transcripts.cnn.com/TRANSCRIPTS/0109/11/bn.39.html.

12:30 p.m.: Secretary Powell's plane takes off in Lima, Peru, heading back to Washington.

"During the flight he had sporadic conversations with Deputy Secretary Armitage but radio transmits were breaking up constantly."[1019]

Andrea Koppell of CNN, traveling with Powell, says on CNN (at 12:07 p.m.): "I would say that Secretary Powell is someone who doesn't show his emotions. . . . This is a man with 35 years of military experience, former Chairman of the Joint Chiefs of Staff, former National Security Adviser himself. He has seen a lot in his day. And so I would say that, obviously, he appeared somber. Very serious, but in terms of any other emotion, I would say that he's able to—to keep that very close to his chest."[1020]

12:30 p.m.: FAA says 50 flights are still flying in US airspace, but none is reporting any problems.

12:35 p.m.: Judy Woodruff reports on CNN: "Government sources tell CNN that President Bush, who had been in Florida for a two-day trip, and who broke that trip off this morning to head back to Washington, will now not return to Washington. Repeating, President Bush will not return to Washington."[1021]

12:35 p.m.: Senator Orrin Hatch of Utah, appearing on CNN, says that he's spoken to government officials about who is responsible for the attack:

> They've come to the conclusion that this looks like the signature of Osama bin Laden, and that he may be the one behind this. I think most authorities agree that this is something that we doubt seriously if Iran, Iraq or Libya would try and do, because they know of the massive response that we'd have to bring down on them. But there was no advance notice at all. They had no way of knowing that this was going to happen. It was carefully planned.

1019. 9/11 Commission, Interview with Colin Powell, January 21, 2004.

1020. "CNN Breaking News: Secretary of State Powell's Reaction to Attack," CNN, September 11, 2001, http://transcripts.cnn.com/TRANSCRIPTS/0109/11/bn.16.html.

1021. "CNN Breaking News: Terrorism Attack on New York City and Washington," CNN, September 11, 2001, http://transcripts.cnn.com/TRANSCRIPTS/0109/11/bn.13.html.

He is asked on what basis he comes to this conclusion and answers: "I just have to say that both the FBI and our intelligence community believe that this is bin Laden's signature."[1022]

Later, Sen. Hatch says that the US government is monitoring Osama bin Laden's communications and that the United States overheard two bin Laden aides celebrating the successful terrorist attack. The AP quotes Hatch as saying: "They have an intercept of some information that included people associated with bin Laden who acknowledged a couple of targets were hit."

Secretary Rumsfeld denounces the report as an unauthorized release of classified information. It is worth noting that NSA intercepts of the bin Laden satellite phone had been compromised in 1998.

Richard Clarke later writes: "Osama bin Laden once routinely communicated over a satellite telephone. The conversations gave us great insight into him and what he was doing (and, interestingly, into his relations with his mother). Then one day someone, who obviously was not thinking, revealed that fact to a newspaper that, exercising no discretion, published it. The calls stopped almost immediately."[1023]

According to the Congressional Joint Inquiry: "Our Intelligence Community's ability personally to track Usama [sic] bin Laden himself was lost in 1998 on account of a senior official's boasting to the media about a certain type of collection capability."[1024] The Joint Inquiry also says: "In the fall of 1998, NSA lost the ability to listen to Bin Ladin [sic] on his satellite phone. This loss was probably the result of, among other things, a media leak."[1025]

1022. "CNN Breaking News: Terrorism Attack on New York City and Washington," CNN, September 11, 2001, http://transcripts.cnn.com/TRANSCRIPTS/0109/11/bn.13.html.

1023. Richard A. Clarke, *Your Government Failed You: Breaking the Cycle of National Security Disasters* (New York: Ecco, 2008), p. 105. On August 21, 1998, the *Washington Times* published an article that stated that bin Laden "keeps in touch with the world via computers and satellite phones." (Martin Sieff, "Terrorist Is Driven by Hatred for US, Israel," *Washington Times*, August 21, 1998, p. 1.)

1024. Senate Select Committee on Intelligence, Joint Inquiry into Intelligence Community Activities Before and After the Terrorist Attacks of September 11, 2001, December 2002, https://www.intelligence.senate.gov/sites/default/files/documents/CRPT-107srpt351-5.pdf, p. 69 (hereafter Joint Inquiry).

1025. Joint Inquiry, p. 377.

Sen. Bob Graham later writes: "Until the late 1990s, the most advanced communication regularly used by terrorist organizations was the satellite telephone. For example, Osama bin Laden seemed to be under the impression that his signal from his satellite phone could not be traced or intercepted; because of his false sense of security, we were sometimes able to pick up his conversation. However, before September 11, this information was accidently leaked; bin Laden promptly stopped using his satellite phone and instead communicated in face-to-face meetings, by written messages, and through personal couriers."[1026]

12:35 p.m.: At the World Trade Center, the EMS dispatcher starts to release units back into the general 911 resource pool because the area cannot accommodate more vehicles.[1027]

12:35 p.m.: AA Flight 77. FAA reports: "AAL 77 IAD LAX Pentagon Still Missing."[1028]

The FAA is still struggling to identify AA Flight 77, uncertain what plane hit the Pentagon at 9:37 a.m.

12:36 p.m.: FAA reports false alarm: "Elkins, WV scramble on air carrier? MD88 being intercepted?"

12:40 p.m.: Rep. Curt Weldon (R-PA) says on CNN: "It's a failure of our intelligence system. I asked the sergeant of arms of the Capitol just forty-five minutes ago in a meeting with seventy senators and house members, how much advance notice did you have. He said, none. There was no intelligence.

"Our FBI and our CIA are there to intercept raw data. This is a massive operation, and it's a failure that was caused by a lack of resources and by a compliancy [sic] that set in America over the past ten years, a compliancy

---

1026. *Intelligence Matters*, p. 85.
1027. FDNY Report.
1028. FAA Logs.

[*sic*] that convinced all of us that with the demise of the Soviet Union there were no more threats."[1029]

12:40 p.m.: FAA reports false alarm: "Unidentified MD 88 over Elkens [*sic*, actually Elkins], WV (possible scramble by military) or may be worked by ZOB [Cleveland Center]."

12:42 p.m.: President Bush, in the Eighth Air Force conference room, attempts to telephone New York mayor Rudy Giuliani, but the call cannot be completed.[1030]

12:45 p.m.: Judy Woodruff reports on CNN: "I want to tell our viewers that we do know now that President Bush has landed near Shreveport, Louisiana, at Barksdale Air Force Base. We're told that he is talking to reporters. There may be a statement from the president, from the White House, there on the ground."[1031]

12:45 p.m.: FAA reports false alarm: "Military intercepted unknown aircraft and ID'd it as military."

12:47 p.m.: FAA reports: "ZNY [New York Center]: N911LV (0476); N116MB (0474); N109UP: Medivacs [*sic*] from ABE [Allentown, PA] to NYC."[1032]

12:48 p.m.: FAA reports: "Commander-in-Chief US Pacific Command (CINCPAC) wants to divert 17 flights inbound to HON [Honolulu]."

12:50 p.m.: FAA reports: "Relocating Congress."

1029. "CNN Breaking News: America Under Attack: Members of Congress Speak Out," CNN, September 11, 2001, http://transcripts.cnn.com/TRANSCRIPTS/0109/11/bn.23.html.
    1030. Presidential Daily Diary, partially declassified.
    1031. "CNN Breaking News: America Under Attack: Members of Congress Speak Out," CNN, September 11, 2001, http://transcripts.cnn.com/TRANSCRIPTS/0109/11/bn.23.html.
    1032. FAA, 11 Sep 01 Catastrophic Crisis (all times given in EDT).

Congressional leaders (House Minority Leader Richard Gephardt, House Majority Leader Tom Delay, and Senate Majority Leader Tom Daschle) arrive at Mount Weather at around midday, and there, Hastert and the others "received updates from the White House and watched television reports."[1033] One evacuee would later describe the atmosphere as something out of *Dr. Strangelove*.

In the Air Threat Conference Call at the Pentagon, there is a discussion (at an unstamped time) of inquiries coming in from members of Congress:

> NMCC (DDO): "We're getting inquiries from members of Congress. That want to know whether we've executed a continuity of government. Can you help out with that?"
>
> White House (PEOC): "Stand by. We're trying to figure out if we can clear that information. That fact is, we have. We just don't know if that information is cleared for all members of Congress or not."
>
> White House (PEOC): [after checking] "In talking to our folks here . . . that's not information we necessarily want to pass to all members of Congress. The members of Congress who are involved in that are already aware."[1034]

12:55 p.m.: FAA reports: "TEB [Teterboro, New Jersey] will be emergency ops center [supporting World Trade Center flights]; Floyd Bennet Field [in Brooklyn] (law enforcement ops center)."

12:56 p.m.: FAA reports: "[FAA Herndon Command Center] . . . working with NORAD for releases."

12:57 p.m.: FAA reports: "SCATANA not in effect; need to reassess capabilities."

1:00 p.m.: President Bush speaks privately for the second time with Secretary Rumsfeld.[1035]

1033. Whereas: Stories from the People's House.
1034. 9/11 Air Threat Conference Call Transcription, partially declassified.
1035. Presidential Daily Diary, partially declassified.

Rumsfeld says he briefed the president on the steps the Pentagon had taken, and he updated him on the attack on the building. "Bush, frustrated at being kept so far from where he felt he belonged—in Washington—blurted out what first sprang to mind. 'The United States will hunt down and punish those responsible for these cowardly acts,' he said."[1036]

Bush says he told Rumsfeld that his first priority was to make it through the immediate crisis. "After that," he later writes, "I planned to mount a serious military response. 'The ball will be in your court and Dick Myer's [*sic*] court to respond,' I told him."[1037]

1:00 p.m.: "By 1:00 p.m. the new [Air Force] operations center was functioning [at Bolling AFB]. Surgeon General Paul Carlton . . . briefed [Secretary] Roche and [Chief of Staff Gen.] Jumper on medical assistance—equipment, people, and air evacuation—that the Air Force could provide. . . . The leaders approved Carlton's plan to send medical personnel and equipment to McGuire Air Force Base, New Jersey, to stand by to assist civilian efforts in New York as needed."[1038]

1:02 p.m.: FAA reports: "Tower evacuations being coordinated in AEA [FAA Eastern Region in Jamaica, New York] and AWP [FAA Western Pacific in El Segundo, California]."

1:04 p.m.: President Bush, at Eighth Air Force headquarters, records his statement to the press.[1039] The "sentiment was right," Bush later writes, "but the setting—a sterile conference room at a military base in Louisiana—did not inspire much confidence. The American people needed to see their president in Washington."[1040]

1:04 p.m.: FAA reports: "USAF/CC at Pentagon ready to help."

1036. *Known and Unknown*, pp. 341–342.
1037. *Decision Points*, p. 133.
1038. Defense Studies Series, Pentagon 9/11.
1039. Presidential Daily Diary, partially declassified.
1040. *Decision Points*, p. 133.

President Bush records remarks on the terrorist attacks from Barksdale Air Force Base in Louisiana before departing for Offutt Air Force Base in Nebraska. (Source: George W. Bush Presidential Library and Museum / Eric Draper [P7078-04])

1:05 p.m.: FAA reports: "AEA-500 advised that AAL 11 [AA Flight 11] voice tapes on intranet web site; will be taken off and no more data put on web sites."

This is the first discussion of controlling the data associated with the hijacked flights. For the rest of the day, various orders go out within the FAA to segregate data about the hijacked flights and to preserve material.

1:09 p.m.: President Bush, in the Eighth Air Force conference room, speaks with White House Counselor Karen Hughes.[1041]

1:10 p.m.: CNN airs President Bush's second set of remarks to the nation, recorded at 1:04 p.m.[1042]

1041. Presidential Daily Diary, partially declassified.

1042. "CNN Breaking News: America Under Attack: Former National Security Adviser Richard Holbrooke and Former U.N. Ambassador Discuss Terrorist Situation," CNN, September 11, 2001, http://transcripts.cnn.com/TRANSCRIPTS/0109/11/bn.19.html. Most histories say that this occurred at 12:36 p.m. EST. The audio is located at http://www.authentichistory.com/2001-2008/1-911/1-timeline1/20010911_1304_Bush_2nd_Response_Louisiana.html.

Remarks by the president at Barksdale AFB:

I want to reassure the American people that the full resources of the federal government are working to assist local authorities to save lives and to help the victims of these attacks.

Make no mistake: The United States will hunt down and punish those responsible for these cowardly acts.

I've been in regular contact with the vice president, the secretary of defense, the national security team, and my Cabinet. We have taken all appropriate security precautions to protect the American people. Our military at home and around the world is on high alert status, and we have taken the necessary security precautions to continue the functions of your government.

We have been in touch with the leaders of Congress and with world leaders to assure them that we will do whatever is necessary to protect America and Americans.

I ask the American people to join me in saying a thanks for all the folks who have been fighting hard to rescue our fellow citizens and to join me in saying a prayer for the victims and their families.

The resolve of our great nation is being tested. But make no mistake: We will show the world that we will pass this test. God bless.

After President Bush finishes his remarks, Aaron Brown of CNN says: "We are also told that national security team members are still in the White House Situation Room. And earlier today, at least, as of a little more than an hour ago, Vice President Cheney, as well, directing operations and monitoring things from there. But the president obviously deciding not to come directly back to Washington. We are told that is for security reasons, delivering the statement you just heard. He has been in touch with congressional leaders, and we are told leadership members of the US Congress are also being taken to undisclosed location[s] for their security."[1043]

1:10 p.m.: CIA analysts find two names of known members of al Qaeda on AA Flight 77's passenger manifest, Khalid al-Mihdhar and Nawaf

---

1043. "CNN Breaking News: America Under Attack: Former National Security Adviser Richard Holbrooke and Former U.N. Ambassador Discuss Terrorist Situation," CNN, September 11, 2001, http://transcripts.cnn.com/TRANSCRIPTS/0109/11/bn.19.html.

al-Hazmi.[1044] Working independently, an FBI team had found a link about three hours earlier.

1:15 p.m.: President Bush departs Eighth Air Force headquarters building and is driven back to the tarmac, where Air Force One has been refueled and reprovisioned.[1045]

Condoleezza Rice later incorrectly writes that the reason Air Force One moved on from Barksdale was that "we had insufficient secure communications there."[1046] The communications in the command center are nearly the same as at Offutt AFB. The difference was that Offutt was inland (and thus considered safer), had secure housing, and had an E-4 NAOC airplane on the ground, ready to receive the president if attacks were to continue or if warnings indicated a broader foreign state-sponsored attack. The NAOC was not just more robust and capable of accommodating the president for longer periods of time but also had built-in communications connecting him to the nuclear forces.

1:17 p.m.: Clinton administration National Security Adviser Sandy Berger says on CNN: "I think this . . . certainly exceeds in scope anything that intelligence community anticipated . . . whoever has perpetrated this, has declared war on the United States, and we will have to respond accordingly. But I would also caution here that we should be careful about jumping to certitude about what happened here. We'll know this soon enough. And we'll also know—be able to find out why this was not detected."[1047]

1:18 p.m.: FAA reports false alarm: "Unconfirmed report Korean Air Flight (KAL) 017 inbound to LAX being hijacked [actually KAL 085]."

1044. *The One Percent Doctrine*, p. 3.

1045. Presidential Daily Diary, partially declassified.

1046. *No Higher Honor*, p. 76.

1047. "CNN Breaking News: America Under Attack: Former National Security Adviser Richard Holbrooke and Former U.N. Ambassador Discuss Terrorist Situation," CNN, September 11, 2001, http://transcripts.cnn.com/TRANSCRIPTS/0109/11/bn.19.html.

Gen. Myers updates Secretary Rumsfeld that an international Korean airliner "was squawking a hijack code."[1048]

The Korean Airlines flight reportedly transmits a hijacking code while flying over southern Alaska. The signal sets off evacuations. The local Alaska NORAD commander will later say that he was prepared to shoot down the airliner.

1:19 p.m.: FAA reports: "All releases currently required to go through NORAD; trying to implement system with bank of codes for medivac [*sic*] releases."

1:20 p.m.: FAA reports false alarm: "KAL 085 flight inbound to LAX reports being hijacked . . . (confirming with AWP [FAA Western Pacific in El Segundo, CA]). ZLA [FAA Los Angeles Center] reports KAL [017] (B747-400) inbound to LAX successfully landed at SFO an hour ago."

1:23 p.m.: FAA reports false alarm: "KAL 017 to LAX . . . trying to confirm [that it went to San Francisco]; . . . [FAA Herndon Command Center] confirms KAL 017 diverted Vancouver . . . diverting into Vancouver, BC."

1:24 p.m.: FAA reports: "AA Flight 11 data removed from intranet."

1:25 p.m.: President Bush, still on the ground at Barksdale AFB, Louisiana, talks with Mayor Giuliani.[1049]

1:27 p.m.: The District of Columbia government declares a state of emergency.

1:28 p.m.: FAA reports: "All data to be placed on AAT-20 [Associate Administrator for Air Traffic] intranet."

1048. *Eyes on the Horizon*, p. 157. Myers incorrectly states that he told Rumsfeld at 12:40 p.m., before the airliner was reported.

1049. Presidential Daily Diary, partially declassified.

1:29 p.m.: FAA reports resolved false alarm: "KAL 085 confirms with ZAN [FAA Anchorage] they are not being hijacked."

1:30 p.m.: Air Force One departs Barksdale AFB en route to US Strategic Command (STRATCOM) headquarters in Omaha, Nebraska.[1050]

According to President Bush's military aide, Lt. Col. Gould, Cheney suggested Offutt AFB. "So much uncertainty led Gould to believe they would remain at Offutt for a couple of days."[1051]

After Air Force One lands at Barksdale, much of the news media and the two Florida congressmen traveling with the president are removed from the presidential entourage.

1:30 p.m.: Noelia Rodriguez, press secretary to the First Lady, recalls: "About 1:30 p.m., we were escorted back to the White House to get our purses and keys. And we got the pets, Spot, Barney, and I think India came too. She's the cat. That was the first time I felt afraid. I remember seeing a couple of empty strollers near the East Wing entrance. They must have belonged to visitors who were on a White House tour that morning."[1052]

1:31 p.m.: FAA DC logs: "DCC West TMO [traffic management officer] . . . asks all TMOs to inventory airborne aircraft and make sure everyone is accounted for. If anyone has an aircraft which is overdue, dropped targets or not accounted for, report the call sign to the [Herndon] Command Center ASAP."[1053]

FAA reports: "NORAD will not allow Medevac aircraft airborne."[1054]

1050. Presidential Daily Diary, partially declassified.

1051. See, in particular, the account of the Air Force One pilot, National Museum of the United States Air Force, Wings and Things Guest Lecture Series, "Air Force One: Zero Failure," presentation of Col. (Ret.) Mark W. Tillman, n.d. (2009). Condoleezza Rice says that the reason Air Force One moved on from Barksdale was that "we had insufficient secure communications there"; *No Higher Honor*, p. 76.

1052. See *Dead Certain: The Presidency of George W. Bush*, p. 141; "Voices of 9-11: 'A Cacophony of Information,'" *National Journal*, August 31, 2002.

1053. DCC Timeline.

1054. FAA Logs.

1:33 p.m.: FAA reports false alarm: "Military Helicopter circling nuclear plant 30 southwest AVP [Wilkes-Barre/Scranton, PA]."

1:35 p.m.: FAA reports: "N876 Governor Pataki on Helicopter . . . to East 34th street need clearance (5601 beacon code) denied due to unable to coordinate. . . . No good system to work individual releases."

1:36 p.m.: FAA reports: "UAL flight from IAD [Dulles] to PIT [Pittsburgh] all have emergency personnel on board tail number N949UA."

1:38 p.m.: FAA reports false alarm: "KAL 85 squawking 7500 [an "I've been hijacked" transponder code]."

At 1:29 p.m., the same plane was reported as being cleared as not a hijacking.

1:40 p.m.: FAA reports false alarms: "AWP [FAA Western Pacific in El Segundo, California] reports five aircraft refuse to divert; will advise Admiral Blair [Commander, US Pacific Command (PACOM) in Hawaii]."

Because of a peculiarity of military command boundaries, PACOM and not NORAD is responsible for the air defense of Hawaii and the Western Pacific (but not Alaska).

1:42 p.m.: FAA reports false alarm: "Alaska region [AAL-530] reports unidentified aircraft circling ANC [Anchorage] and numerous aircraft circling over ANC who are short on fuel."[1055]

1:45 p.m.: Aboard Air Force One, Michael Morell says that White House Chief of Staff Card summons him to talk to the president. "He asked me point-blank, 'Michael, who did this?' I said, 'Sir, I haven't seen any intelligence that would point to responsibility, so what I'm going to say is simply my personal view.' He told me he understood. I said that there were two terrorist states capable of conducting such a complex operation—Iraq and Iran—but that neither had much to gain and both had plenty to lose from

---

1055. FAA logs; FAA, 11 Sep 01 Catastrophic Crisis (all times given in EDT).

attacking the United States. Rather, I said, the culprit was almost certainly a non-state actor, adding that I would bet my children's future that the trail would lead to the doorstep of Usama bin Ladin [sic] and al Qa'ida [sic]."

Bush asks how long it would take to know, and Morell says he doesn't know. He later writes: "I had no way of knowing that analysts at CIA head-quarters had already tied the attack to al Qa'ida [sic]. They had acquired the passenger manifest of the four flights" from the FAA and run the names against databases of known terrorists. He said "three passengers" came up with "known and definitive links" to al Qaeda.[1056]

The reference to three hijackers, though repeated by others, is wrong; it comes from what George Tenet was briefing at the time, including later in teleconferences with President Bush.[1057] There were only two hijackers—Khalid al-Mihdhar and Nawaf al-Hazmi, both on AA Flight 77 that hit the Pentagon—who were already known to US intelligence.

`1:45 p.m.:` Mayor Giuliani talks to Fox News by phone about the city's emergency response.

`1:47 p.m.:` Ari Fleischer speaks to the press pool aboard Air Force One, saying that President Bush has spoken to Vice President Cheney "several times," to Secretary Rumsfeld, and to "several members of the national security team." He says there will be an NSC meeting later in the afternoon. He says that there were no warnings of the attack and that the government is assessing who is responsible.[1058]

`1:53 p.m.:` Maj. Gen. Paul A. Weaver Jr. activates the Air National Guard Crisis Action Team in the Air National Guard Readiness Center at Andrews AFB, Maryland.[1059]

1056. The Great War of Our Time, pp. 55–56.

1057. Author's correspondence with Michael Morell.

1058. Transcript, "Press Briefing to the Pool by Ari Fleischer Aboard Air Force One, 1:47 p.m.," Authentic History, September 11, 2001, http://www.authentichistory.com/2001-2008/1-911/1-timeline1/20010911_1347_Ari_Fleischer_Press_Briefing-AF1.html.

1059. National Guard Bureau, A Chronological History of the Air National Guard and Its Antecedents, 1908–2007, compiled by Dr. Charles J. Gross, NGB-PAH, April 2, 2007.

1:55 p.m.: President Bush speaks with Sen. Charles Schumer, Democrat of New York.[1060]

1:57 p.m.: FAA reports false alarm: "B747 reported by citizens, flying up Hudson [River] (citizen report); F-15s refueling over Long Island will take look; later reported that A/C was probably refueler."[1061]

1:58 p.m.: FAA reports: "Air Force One still displayed on TSD [FAA displays]; may have been removed for security reasons."

2:00 p.m.: CNN says that senior FBI sources say that they are working on the assumption that the four airplanes that crashed were part of a larger terrorist attack.[1062]

2:00 p.m.: At the Pentagon at around 2:00 p.m., Arlington Fire Chief Schwartz receives notice of another unidentified aircraft headed for the building. "The firefighters drop their hoses, climb down high ladders or flights of stairs, and take cover several hundred yards away. When Schwartz learned that the plane bore federal officials, he ordered his men and women back to fight the fire."[1063]

2:00 p.m.: FAA reports false alarm: "Citizens report B747 like aircraft coming down Hudson [River]."

1060. Presidential Daily Diary, partially declassified.

1061. DCC Timeline.

1062. "September 11: Chronology of Terror," CNN, September 12, 2001, http://edition.cnn.com/2001/US/09/11/chronology.attack/.

1063. Defense Studies Series, Pentagon 9/11.

CHAPTER 14

"WEAPONS FREE"

The confusing decision already made to authorize the military to shoot down threatening civilian airliners—first by Vice President Cheney and then affirmed by President Bush and then codified in the move to DEFCON 3 and then in the declaration of an Air Defense Emergency and then by the COG declaration—was followed by an additional modification conveyed at 2:02 p.m., an authorization now issued to individual fighters flying over Washington, DC. The pilots were told that they were now "weapons free," able without any additional permission to engage any aircraft that could not be positively identified as "friendly."

All four hijacked planes had by now hit their targets or crashed, but no one knew what more to expect. The air defense system previously just on Cold War–level warm standby—and facing outward—was now to be and stay on alert, particularly over the nation's capital. But the "weapons free" order was hardly as simple as it sounded, either in military or human terms.

By the afternoon, there had been multiple orders—complex, confusing, and even contradictory—regarding the defense of America's skies. The White House, the Pentagon, NORAD, and its subordinate regional commands all issued situational orders, most of them relating to specific conditions. Those orders then changed through the morning and early afternoon. But with each "system" change—DEFCON 3, Air Defense Emergency, COG—prewritten and automatically implemented measures also were triggered, including NORAD's war plans, which contained their own rules and authorizations.

The day obviously moved quickly, but behind all these do-something orders were also the basic military "rules of engagement" as written and practiced by every unit commander—what to do if a hostile force was encountered, what to do in "self-defense," what constituted a "lawful" order, and how to recognize (and respond to) an unlawful one. In the end, it all boiled down to individual responsibility, the universal code of conduct governing every situation and the moral pact that any military officer follows.

From Washington, then, "weapons free" might have looked like a simple authorization, but as NORAD commander Gen. Eberhart would later say, passing along an order authorizing shooting down a civilian airliner "pales in comparison to the burden on the person who would pull the trigger." Eberhart says that "no one wants to do this [pull the trigger] less than the fighter pilot," to carry out their mission and save the day, but on 9/11, even if a pilot saw an airliner "nose down, no landing gear, high speed," as he says, even if they thought that a hostile act was certain, "no matter what the circumstance, the pilot would look towards his command for an indication of what to do."[1064] Fortunately that circumstance never presented itself, but one thing was clear—no one was content with the notion, even if an intercept were made, that the right decision (or action) would result.

2:02 p.m.: A "weapons free" order authorization, the permission to engage any aircraft inbound to Washington, is passed along via Vice President Cheney's authority in the White House. Under this order, fighters over Washington are authorized to engage any aircraft not positively identified as friendly.[1065]

Secretary Rumsfeld says: "Echoing the earlier instructions from the President, I repeated his orders to Myers: The pilots were 'weapons free,' which authorized them to shoot down a plan approaching a high-value target."[1066]

Brig. Gen. Wherley, commander of DC National Guard 113th Wing, who had been in touch with the White House, asked questions "about rules of engagement and finally talked to an [Secret Service] agent . . . who was standing next to the Vice President and confirmed that the planes were free to engage if the aircraft could not be diverted. Again, this seemed clear enough to Wherley, which he interpreted as 'weapons free.'"[1067]

1064. 9/11 Commission NORAD MFR.
1065. 9/11 Commission, NORAD Questions for the Record, partially declassified.
1066. *Known and Unknown*, p. 340.
1067. 9/11 Commission Memorandum for the Record, Interview, BG David Wherley, on September 11, 2001, Commander of the 113th Wing of the USAF, August 28, 2003.

NORAD commander Gen. Eberhart seems to hold Brig. Gen. Wherley responsible for what he characterizes as an erroneous order. He later tells the 9/11 Commission:

> Eberhart noted that General Worley [*sic*] did not have the authority to give a "weapons-free" order. Eberhart commented that a NORAD pilot is not under Worley's command, and thus would not operate under that order. Further, the Andrews pilots under Worley's command should have known that Worley did not have that authority, and thus would ideally have still looked towards a higher command authority for specificity and direction.
>
> Eberhart commented that a fighter pilot is trained only to become weapons-free after a hostile target is identified.[1068]

NEADS MCC Lt. Col. Nasypany later tells the 9/11 Commission, nevertheless, "that there was no weapons free order on 9/11 to his knowledge. If there was a 'weapons free' declaration, the pilots would still need permission through the chain of command to fire upon a target."[1069]

2:05 p.m.: FAA reports resolves false alarm: "Reported aircraft [over Hudson River] is thought to be KC-135 [Air Force aerial refueler]."

2:10 p.m.: Miles O'Brien reports on CNN that "we have just learned from the Federal Aviation Administration that every domestic airliner that was in the area is now on the ground. This is unprecedented in aviation history in this country. There's not a plane flying right now. At any given moment, typically, there are 4,000 aircraft."[1070]

2:15 p.m.: FAA reports that it is concerned about the security of aircraft in the skies: "CNN is reporting flight paths as displayed on flightexplorer.com."

1068. 9/11 Commission Memorandum for the Record, Interview with CINC NORAD (Commander in Chief NORAD), General Edward "Ed" Eberhart, March 1, 2004.

1069. 9/11 Commission Memorandum for the Record, Interview with NEADS Alpha Flight Mission Crew Commander (MCC), Lt. Col. Kevin J. Nasypany, January 22, 2004, and January 23, 2004.

1070. "CNN Breaking News: America Under Attack: Terrorist Launch Successful Attacks Against Targets in New York and Washington," CNN, September 11, 2001, http://transcripts.cnn.com/TRANSCRIPTS/0109/11/bn.31.html.

2:20 p.m.: Judy Woodruff on CNN reports: "We're told also that Secretary of State Colin Powell, who had been on his way back to the United States from Peru, [is] being taken to an undisclosed location."[1071]

Powell has not yet arrived in the United States, and in any case, upon returning, he goes to the White House.[1072]

2:23 p.m.: The president's diary states that President Bush, aboard Air Force One, speaks over a secure voice line with Vice President Cheney for five minutes at 1:23 p.m. CST (2:23 p.m. EST), but this is most likely a mistake.[1073]

On the plane, "Bush expresses his irritation over being away from the White House. 'I want to go back home ASAP,' he told [White House Chief of Staff] Card, according to notes of the conversation. 'I don't want whoever did this holding me outside of Washington.'

"The senior Secret Service agent aboard Air Force One [Marinzel] told Bush the situation was 'too unsteady still' to allow his return. 'The right thing is to let the dust settle,' Card said. The staff wanted him to stay at Offutt for 12 hours or more. Bush argued with his handlers and with Cheney, who was also urging him to stay away. 'Unless they tell me something I haven't heard,' he seethed, 'this ass is going back to Washington.'"[1074]

2:28 p.m.: FAA DC logs: "Ghost Target 200 NM N Bermuda inbound to KMIA ZNY [New York Center]. Deep Ocean has no record of the aircraft. Likely diverted, ETMS continues to track on last LIFP."[1075]

2:30 p.m.: FAA announces there will be no commercial air traffic over the United States until noon EDT Wednesday at the earliest. FAA reports: "New FDC NOTAM issued. ANS—New Advisory has been issued military/Lifeguard, Police can fly with approval of overlying center."

1071. "CNN Breaking News: America Under Attack: Bush Holds Press Briefing," CNN, September 11, 2001, http://transcripts.cnn.com/TRANSCRIPTS/0109/11/bn.35.html.

1072. 9/11 Commission, Interview with Colin Powell, January 21, 2004.

1073. Presidential Daily Diary, partially declassified.

1074. *Decision Points*, pp. 130–131; *Dead Certain: The Presidency of George W. Bush*, p. 142.

1075. DCC Timeline.

FAA DC logs: "FAA can approve Lifeguard, Medivacs [*sic*], and local law enforcement. All other flights provide flight info to EOR room, will be coordinated with Air Force, who will coordinate with air defense sectors for approval. DCC advisory 041 sent."[1076]

2:30 p.m.: Jamie McIntyre, CNN Pentagon correspondent, reports on CNN: "The Pentagon has dispatched several warships out of port Norfolk, including the . . . carriers, USS *George Washington* and USS *Kennedy*. The sensible reason for that, the movement of those ships and their escort ships, is to move them from more vulnerable positions. But the Navy says they'll also head some of the aircraft carriers up toward New York with the idea that they may be able to render some kind of assistance there, given the magnitude of the tragedy there."[1077]

- USS *George Washington* (CVN 73), accompanied by the hospital ship USNS *Comfort* (AH 20), sails to New York City.
- USS *John F. Kennedy* (CV 67) and USS *John C. Stennis* (CVN 74) position themselves to defend the East and West Coasts, respectively.
- USS *Enterprise* (CVN 65), finishing up a six-month tour, is ordered to turn around and go back to the Arabian Sea.

2:38 p.m.: Mayor Giuliani and Governor Pataki hold a joint news conference at the Police Academy. Mayor Giuliani says that subway and bus service are partially restored in New York City, but little service exists south of 14th Street.

Giuliani says that 1,500 "walking wounded" have been taken to nearby parks, and 600 more are being treated in area hospitals. "I have a sense it's a horrendous number of lives lost." Asked about the number of people killed, Giuliani says, "I don't think we want to speculate about that—more than any of us can bear."

1076. DCC Timeline.

1077. "CNN Breaking News: America Under Attack: Bush Holds Press Briefing," CNN, September 11, 2001, http://transcripts.cnn.com/TRANSCRIPTS/0109/11/bn.35.html.

2:38 p.m.: FAA reports: "Advisory 41 issued—Requests to use national airspace will be authorized for military, law enforcement, lifeguard and med evac flights."

2:40 p.m.: Secretary Rumsfeld is given intelligence that three of the names on the airplane passenger manifests of the hijacked planes are suspected al Qaeda operatives. He either speaks to CIA Director Tenet or receives some other kind of report.

Rumsfeld says that he thinks that the intelligence is "vague." Notes he composes (leaked nearly a year later) show Rumsfeld's state of mind at this time:

> Best info fast. Judge whether good enough hit S. H. [Saddam Hussein] at same time. Not only UBL [Osama bin Laden] Go massive. Sweep it all up. Things related and not.[1078]

According to the 9/11 Commission Report, "Rumsfeld later explained that at the time, he had been considering . . . [bin Laden and Iraq], or perhaps someone else, as the responsible party."[1079]

2:44 p.m.: President Bush, aboard Air Force One, telephones Sen. Joseph R. Biden (D-DE), chairman of the Senate Foreign Relations Committee, but the call cannot be completed.[1080]

2:45 p.m.: President Bush, aboard Air Force One, telephones Mayor Giuliani, but the call cannot be completed.[1081]

2:55 p.m.: President Bush, aboard Air Force One, lands at Offutt AFB in Omaha, Nebraska.[1082]

1078. CBS News, "Plans for Iraq Attack Began on 9/11," September 4, 2002, reporting on a David Martin story. See also *A Pretext for War*, p. 284.

1079. 9/11 Commission Report, pp. 334–335.

1080. Presidential Daily Diary, partially declassified.

1081. Presidential Daily Diary, partially declassified.

1082. Presidential Daily Diary, partially declassified. Most conventional histories don't have Air Force One arriving at Offutt AFB until 3:06 p.m. EST.

Air Force One is escorted by two Texas-based fighters on its way to the base.

According to Adm. Mies, "about a half an hour out," STRATCOM is informed that Air Force One is headed their way. "Only after Bush left Barksdale did military leaders at Offutt find out that the president was headed their way. We knew about half an hour out," Mies said. "I didn't want a lot of pomp and circumstance at that point."[1083]

Mies recalls: "It was a logical place for the President to come, if the Secret Service was not willing to let him go back to Washington at the time, where he could communicate with the appropriate people in the Washington area." STRATCOM implements its Presidential Reception checklist.[1084]

"I had no idea the president was coming until I saw him exiting Air Force One on the flightline," says Kevin Church, a security specialist on the E-4 National Airborne Operations Center that was sitting adjacent to where Air Force One parked. "After we arrived back at Offutt on the E-4 [from the Global Guardian exercise] I ran into the NAOC facility to retrieve a timeline of the events so far," Church says. "It wasn't until I stepped back out of the facility and saw the president exiting Air Force One did I know that he was coming. It really caught me off-guard."[1085]

2:58 p.m.: Adm. Mies meets the president on the tarmac and drives him to the headquarters.[1086] The staff is transported to the headquarters building in buses.[1087]

At STRATCOM headquarters, the president and Adm. Mies take an emergency entryway to access the underground Global Operations Center.[1088] KVNO News will later write:

1083. Steve Liewer, "On 9/11, StratCom Leaders Were Practicing for a Fictional Threat When Real, Unprecedented Catastrophe Struck," *Omaha World Herald*, September 8, 2016.

1084. Bill Kelly, NET News, "Military Insiders Recall Bush's 9/11 Stop at Stratcom," KVNO News, September 7, 2011, http://www.kvnonews.com/2011/09/military-insiders-recall-bushs-911-stop-at-stratcom/.

1085. Ryan Hansen, "Offutt Forever Linked with 9-11," Offutt AFB News, September 6, 2011, https://www.offutt.af.mil/News/Article/311755/offutt-forever-linked-with-9-11/.

1086. Presidential Daily Diary, partially declassified.

1087. *The Great War of Our Time*, p. 56.

1088. Ryan Hansen, "Offutt Forever Linked with 9-11," Offutt AFB News, September 6, 2011, https://www.offutt.af.mil/News/Article/311755/offutt-forever-linked-with-9-11/.

President Bush arrives at Offutt AFB, Nebraska. Note the E-4B National Airborne Operations Center on the tarmac. (Source: Department of Defense)

There is only about ten minutes of footage of the President's stop at Offutt. It shows a grim George W. Bush stepping off Air Force One, saluting the guards. Admiral Meis [*sic*], in his khaki battle flight suit, shakes hands. Bush pats him on the back. You can see the motorcade drive past the elaborate front entrance of STRATCOM's headquarters and stop at a tiny beige brick building with a single door.

"Well, I made the decision that it was senseless to go into the front entrance of our Command headquarters, and then walk into the underground facility," Meis said, "when that really is much more readily accessible by a non-traditional means."

"His entrance into the Command Center was through a spiral staircase that goes straight down for 75 to 80 feet . . . [a STRATCOM staffer said] You're just spiraling down a staircase. He went into it, like a cave."[1089]

According to the *Omaha World Herald*, it was the only time Adm. Mies says he ever used the emergency entrance.[1090]

1089. Bill Kelly, NET News, "Military Insiders Recall Bush's 9/11 Stop at Stratcom," KVNO News, September 7, 2011, http://www.kvnonews.com/2011/09/military-insiders-recall-bushs -911-stop-at-stratcom/.

1090. Steve Liewer, "On 9/11, StratCom Leaders Were Practicing for a Fictional Threat When Real, Unprecedented Catastrophe Struck," *Omaha World Herald*, September 8, 2016.

3:00 p.m.: (Approximate time) At the World Trade Center, a survivor, Pasquale Buzzelli, is rescued from the rubble of the North Tower.

3:00 p.m.: FAA reports false alarm: "USA 930 [USAir Flight 930] hijack from Madrid not verified with PHL [Philadelphia, the destination] or DCA [Washington National]."

3:01 p.m.: FAA DC logs: "HQ: contact Delta. Passengers not being allowed off aircraft at Gander, Halifax, or St. John's [Canada]."[1091]

3:06 p.m.: President Bush enters the STRATCOM underground command center,[1092] and "StratCom leaders briefed Bush while setting up a secure video link for him to meet with the National Security Council and other senior government officials."[1093] According to a KVNO report:

> "The President sat down," [Adm.] Meis [*sic*] recalled, "and I briefed him on each of the screens and what each of [the] screens was displaying."
>
> [A STRATCOM adviser] added, "We had the picture of all the FAA airplanes that's in the air, how many of those they were coming down, what's the state of readiness for all the rest of the [military] forces in the US."[1094]

As he was being briefed, Bush recalls: "Suddenly, a voice crackled over the sound system. 'Mr. President, a nonresponsive plane is coming in from Madrid. Do we have authority to shoot it down?' My first reaction was *When is this going to end?* Then I outlined the rules of engagement I had approved earlier. . . . The voice on the loudspeaker returned. 'The flight from Madrid has landed in Lisbon, Portugal.' *Thank God*, I thought."[1095]

1091. DCC Timeline.

1092. Presidential Daily Diary, partially declassified.

1093. Steve Liewer, "On 9/11, StratCom Leaders Were Practicing for a Fictional Threat When Real, Unprecedented Catastrophe Struck," *Omaha World Herald*, September 8, 2016.

1094. Bill Kelly, NET News, "Military Insiders Recall Bush's 9/11 Stop at Stratcom," KVNO News, September 7, 2011, http://www.kvnonews.com/2011/09/military-insiders-recall-bushs-911-stop-at-stratcom/.

1095. *Decision Points*, pp. 133–134. Rumsfeld incorrectly says (*Known and Unknown*, p. 343) that this conversation took place during the later NSC meeting. "A fresh report came in of still another suspicious plane—this one coming from Madrid and scheduled to land in

After being briefed, the president goes to the Joint Intelligence Center within the command center, a more secure facility. He has a conversation with Rumsfeld in which the Madrid flight was discussed, this time Rumsfeld saying it is "twenty minutes out" from the United States. There is no timestamp, but it occurs before the formal NSC meeting and is broadcast over the Air Threat Conference Call line:

> STRATCOM operator: "Mr. Secretary, here's the president. He's at the STRATCOM command center."
> Rumsfeld: "Oh, good. Thank you."
> Bush: "Hi, Don."
> Rumsfeld: "Hi, Mr. President. Have you been advised that there's a US Air flight coming in from Madrid, uh, that is a possible hijack flight?"
> Bush: "I have, sir."
> Rumsfeld: "Okay. Um, the fighters are being, um, launched to intercept it and, uh, NORAD is involved. It looks like, the last I heard, it's maybe twenty minutes out, and, uh, for whatever reasons the FBI didn't indicate they have reason to believe that it might be a hijacked aircraft. Um, but the reason I called to alert you was just to verify that your authorization for the use of force, uh, would apply as well in this situation."
> Bush: "Uh, it does, but let us make sure that the fighters and you on the ground get all the facts. Uh, is the plane, I was just told that they thought the plane might be heading toward Pittsburgh, um, is that, was it scheduled to go to Philadelphia? Anyway, let's just make sure, uh, that, uh, we get all the facts from the FAA, if possible. Are you in touch with the FAA?"

Philadelphia. Over the secure video, the President authorized the use of force if necessary to bring down the airliner."

Condoleezza Rice writes (*No Higher Honor*, p. 73): "At one point a plane was said to have taken off unauthorized from Madrid, heading for the United States. A few minutes later it was said to have landed in Portugal, then supposedly it was still in the air headed for New York, then inexplicably back in Madrid."

Rumsfeld: "I've been dealing through, uh, the CINC NORAD, [Gen.]
Ed Eberhart, who is, has his own contact to the FAA."

Bush: "Is, uh, Ed on the phone call, I wonder, uh, or up on the
conference?"

Rumsfeld: "Well, there's no conference. I just talked to him directly
from, uh, the National Military Command Center here."

Bush: "Yeah, I know, but I mean—actually, I'm doing two things
at once. I'm speaking to you and sitting in the middle of a
conference."

Rumsfeld: "I see. Well, I'm not in the conference."

Bush: "No, I know that [laughing]. You are in a conference, everybody.
You're speaking in front of about one hundred fine Americans."

Rumsfeld: "Terrific!"

Bush: "So make sure you clean up your language."

Rumsfeld: [laughing] "I'll do it."

Bush: "An old Navy fighter pilot, there's no telling what you're going to
say [laughing]. But obviously the information seems to be shifting
somewhat on US Air 937, that's the name, number of the flight
coming in, so, but you still have permission if they think, um, if
they think it's going to target one of the US cities."

Rumsfeld: "Okay. Fair enough. I was told that it was going to
Philadelphia, but I'll stay in touch with [NORAD commander]
Ed Eberhart, and you're gonna probably have as much up-to-date
information as I am, and if it gets to a point and there's time to, uh,
visit, I will certainly . . . get right back on the horn with you."

Bush: "Yep, and we're going to have our National Security call in about
ten minutes."[1096]

3:07 p.m.: FAA reports resolves false alarm: KAL 085 (previously reported
as hijacked) on the ground at Whitehorse, Canada.[1097]

1096. 9/11 Air Threat Conference Call Transcription, partially declassified. Gen. Myers
later writes (*Eyes on the Horizon*, p. 158) that in the middle of the video teleconference with
President Bush, "the FBI had just forwarded a report of a possible hijacked USAir flight."
1097. FAA logs.

3:12 p.m.: President Bush, at STRATCOM headquarters, talks with Sen. Biden over a secure voice line.[1098]

3:15 p.m.: (Approximate time) President Bush, at STRATCOM headquarters, goes to a small conference room inside the Joint Intelligence Center and joins a secure (and closed) video teleconference with officials from the PEOC, the CIA, the State Department, the Pentagon, the Secret Service, the FBI, FEMA, and the WHSR.[1099]

"Who did this?" Bush asks George Tenet. "George answered with two words: al Qaeda."[1100]

Evidently, Tenet says that the CIA is able to identify three people from the airplane's passenger manifests who are familiar to US intelligence. Rumsfeld writes in his notes, "One guy is associate of *Cole* bomber," referring to the October 2000 attack on the USS *Cole* in Yemen.[1101]

Tenet will later write: "Plenty of intelligence data suggested that this was intended as the opening act of a multi-day sequence. Even at this early point, too, there was a growing fear—one that would spread in the days ahead as fresh reports came in—that the terrorists had somehow secreted a weapon of mass destruction into the United States and were preparing to detonate it."[1102]

Michael Morell, who is in the room with the president and listening, says, "George Tenet walked the president and others through the information that tied three of the hijackers to al Qa'ida [*sic*]. When Tenet finished, the president turned and looked me straight in the eye. He didn't say a word, but his look told me that he felt he had been let down. He hadn't wanted to learn about this after the fact on a conference call." Morell says perhaps his message was never transmitted to Tenet or that the director just forgot in the "intense activity," or, perhaps, he asks himself whether

---

1098. Presidential Daily Diary, partially declassified.

1099. Presidential Daily Diary, partially declassified.

1100. *Decision Points*, p. 134. Defense Studies Series, Pentagon 9/11 says, "At about 3:15 p.m.... Director of Central Intelligence George Tenet reported that evidence pointed to the al Qaeda organization as the mastermind behind the attacks."

1101. CBS News, "Plans for Iraq Attack Began on 9/11," September 4, 2002, reporting on a David Martin story. See also *A Pretext for War*, p. 284.

1102. *At the Center of the Storm*, p. 170.

Tenet "knowingly" held back information "because he wanted to brief it himself."

Morell says he then called the CIA Operations Center to ask for the evidence behind Tenet's statement and was told the information was embargoed from leaving the building. "'Embargoed from the president of the United States?' I shouted. 'Just send it!' I slammed the phone down."[1103]

3:15 p.m.: FAA DC logs: "LAX Tower evacuated due to bomb threat . . . in parking Lot 2."[1104]

3:17 p.m.: FAA reports false bomb threat: FAA Western Pacific in El Segundo, California, "reports confirmed bomb found in parking lot #2 at LAX."[1105]

3:20 p.m.: FAA DC logs: "Advised military scrambling on 'approved' aircraft."[1106]

1103. *The Great War of Our Time*, pp. 56–57.
1104. DCC Timeline.
1105. FAA, 11 Sep 01 Catastrophic Crisis (all times given in EDT).
1106. DCC Timeline.

CHAPTER 15

"WE'RE AT WAR"

"We're at war," President Bush said at the opening of the national security meeting at 3:20 p.m. But what did it mean? Congress is the sole authority able to declare war, but as commander in chief, President Bush can issue orders to US military forces to implement war plans—or, more specifically, to exercise their inherent rights and responsibilities for "self-defense." That inherent right on 9/11 still had to be executed by a duly constituted entity, either the "National Command Authority"—defined as the "President and the Secretary of Defense or their duly deputized alternates or successors"—or by a commander in chief (CINC) of one of the Unified Commands, the four-star commanders affirmed by congressional authorizations and acts to undertake combat on behalf of the United States.

On 9/11, even without additional orders, the approved "standing rules of engagement" established "the inherent right of self-defense" and provided guidance for the application of the use of military force.[1107] Those rules almost exclusively applied to situations "outside the territorial jurisdiction of the United States." But they also stated that the "Commander, US element NORAD" (the overall command is a binational US-Canadian creation) was to be considered a CINC of a Unified Command for the purposes of making command decisions. The rules further state that "peacetime operations . . . within the territorial jurisdiction of the United States are governed by use-of-force rules . . . determined on a case-by-case basis." Air defense "responsibilities" of commanders, including those of NORAD, state that "direct engagement" could be ordered for the immediate protection of US military forces (but say nothing about the protection of New York City or Washington).

1107. Chairman of the Joint Chiefs of Staff Instruction 3121.01A, "Standing Rules of Engagement for US Forces," January 15, 2000.

For the US military on 9/11, as it contemplated taking action against hijacked airliners, the question remained whether the nation was or was not "at war." The NORAD contingency plan for the air defense of the United States—CONPLAN 3310-96, "Aerospace Warning, Aerospace Control and Maritime Warning for North America," dated September 24, 1999—made a distinction between three levels of rules of engagement for the commander of NORAD to declare a force "hostile" and thus order a shootdown.

- Peacetime ROE, existing only during declarations of DEFCONs 5 and 4 (peacetime), when the commander of NORAD declares a force hostile. "Hostile Force" is defined as "any civilian, paramilitary, or military force or terrorist(s), with or without national designation, that has committed a hostile act, exhibited hostile intent, or has been declared hostile by appropriate US authority."
- Transition ROE, existing during DEFCONs 3, 2, or 1, when the commander of NORAD has emergency authority to order an engagement when "airborne objects" participating in or indicating "clear intent to participate in an attack against the US or Canada" if in his judgment an actual attack is underway.
- Wartime ROE, existing during DEFCON 1 (defined as "maximum readiness"), where the commander of NORAD is authorized to "mount a defense against a surprise attack" before anyone has declared war. Wartime ROE are automatically implemented and exist without further authorization from headquarters when the commander of NORAD declares an "Air Defense Emergency."

Sound confusing? It is, even to this day. And the ambiguity about war, about whether America is at war, even when it is bombing multiple countries, has led to perpetual war, the legacy of a 2001 counterterrorism campaign that started with 9/11.

3:20 p.m.: (Approximate time) President Bush, in the command center at STRATCOM headquarters, convenes an NSC meeting via video conference. The meeting lasts for one hour and five minutes.[1108]

Attendees include the following: Andrew Card (with the president); Capt. Deborah Loewer, director of the WHSR (with the president); Adm.

1108. Transcript, "Press Briefing to the Pool by Ari Fleischer Aboard Air Force One en route Andrews Air Force Base, 5:30 p.m. EDT," History on the Net, September 11, 2001.

President Bush, White House Chief of Staff Andrew Card (left of the president), and Adm. Richard Mies (right of the president) participate in the secure video tele-conference at Offutt AFB. The person sitting to the left of Card is a White House Communications Agency technician. In the second photo, the president's military aide Lt. Col. Thomas Gould is shown standing behind. (Photo 1 source: George W. Bush Presidential Library and Museum [P7093-16]; Photo 2: National Archives)

Mies (with the president); Cheney (from the PEOC); Rice (from the PEOC); Deputy NSA Hadley (from the PEOC); Tenet (from the operations center at CIA headquarters); Deputy Secretary of State Richard Lee Armitage (from the State Department operations center); Rumsfeld (from the NMCC); Gen. Myers (from the NMCC); Attorney General Ashcroft (from FBI headquarters); Robert Mueller (from FBI headquarters); Joe Allbaugh (from FEMA headquarters); Richard Clarke (from the WHSR); Deputy Secretary of Transportation Michael P. Jackson (from the WHSR); and Secret Service Agent Truscott (from the WHSR).[1109] Secretary Powell is still in the air on his way back from Peru and does not participate.[1110]

Rice later tells the 9/11 Commission that President Bush began the NSC meeting with the words, "We're at war."[1111]

Bush says, according to Gen. Myers: "I want everyone hearing this teleconference to know that no faceless thug will hold our country at bay. I want you to find out who did it, seek them out, and destroy them."[1112]

According to Rumsfeld, Bush says: "No thugs are going to diminish the spirit of the United States."[1113]

Cheney voices concern that more hijacked planes could be out there. Tenet says that as all the attacks have taken place before 10:00 a.m., that is probably it for the day, but there is no way to be sure. FBI Director Mueller expresses concern that investigators still do not know how the terrorists penetrated airport security. Tenet says it is essential to know this before flights resume.

"I'll announce more security measures, but we won't be held hostage," Bush says. "We'll fly at noon tomorrow," he adds, although it takes three more days for commercial flights to resume—and then only on a reduced schedule.

Someone mentions that New York officials have asked whether they should urge people to go back to work the next day, particularly those

---

1109. Presidential Daily Diary, partially declassified.

1110. *No Higher Honor*, p. 76.

1111. The overall discussion is re-created from *Decision Points*, pp. 135–136; *Dead Certain: The Presidency of George W. Bush*, p. 142; *24 Hours Inside the President's Bunker*, p. 76; and *The Great War of Our Time*, p. 57.

1112. *Eyes on the Horizon*, p. 158.

1113. *Known and Unknown*, p. 343.

working in banks and the financial markets. "Terrorists can always attack," Rumsfeld says. "The Pentagon's going back to work tomorrow."

"People in New York should go back to work," the president says. "Banks should open tomorrow, too."

As the meeting is ending, Bush says, "We will find these people, and they will suffer the consequence of taking on this nation. We will do what it takes."[1114]

During the meeting, "there was a lot of discussion about how to get New York and Washington back to some sense of normalcy," Adm. Mies says.[1115] Though some question Bush coming back to Washington, he has already told his traveling party that he will fly back immediately after the NSC meeting. Cheney suggests the president return and make a statement at Andrews AFB, but Secret Service director Brian Stafford still insists that it is not safe.

"I'm coming back," Bush says. He says he has had enough of "this continuity-of-government thing," as he calls it, which he thinks is "making the country and the presidency look like a horse's ass. Enough with going along with these self-declared rules." Bush tells the White House additionally that he now wants every effort expended to bring the Cabinet home, highest priority. Bush thanks them for their input and announces that he is canceling the executive order for continuity of the presidency. He is returning to Washington.

Bush's military aide, Lt. Col. Gould, says, "Literally, in the middle of this meeting, the president declared very forcefully that 'I will be back in DC in two and a half, three hours.' We had been advising him all morning, 'Sir, we can't go back to DC. We have to fly around for a while.'" Gould slips a note to Chief of Staff Andrew Card, saying they can return but "should relocate Vice President Dick Cheney to ensure that both men weren't in the same area in the event of another attack."[1116]

1114. Transcript, "Press Briefing to the Pool by Ari Fleischer Aboard Air Force One en route Andrews Air Force Base, 5:30 p.m. EDT," History on the Net, September 11, 2001.

1115. Steve Liewer, "On 9/11, StratCom Leaders Were Practicing for a Fictional Threat When Real, Unprecedented Catastrophe Struck," Omaha World Herald, September 8, 2016.

1116. Janene Scully, "Vandenberg Officer at Bush's Side During Attacks," Santa Maria Times, September 11, 2011.

3:22 p.m.: FAA reports: "Individual call signs/beacon codes still required for individual releases."

3:23 p.m.: FAA reports false alarm: "FBI reports US Airways squawking 7700 from Madrid."

3:25 p.m.: FAA reports false bomb threat: "Additional explosive device at LAX found in old terminal."

3:30 p.m.: President Bush talks with Mayor Giuliani over a secure voice line.[1117]

3:35 p.m.: FAA DC logs: "Secret service reported large commercial aircraft sited [*sic*, sighted] southeast-bound towards DC."[1118]

3:36 p.m.: Mike Hanna, in Israel, reports on CNN: "When news of the events started to filter through in Palestinian areas, there were sporadic incidents of celebration in the streets. In East Jerusalem and in various parts of the West Bank, Palestinians took to the streets in small groups celebrating what they said was an attack against the United States, the United States blamed by some Palestinians for its ongoing support, as it is seen, of Israel in this Middle Eastern conflict. However, while some Palestinians were taking to the streets in apparent celebration, one youth was quoted as saying, as he received sweets handed around in celebration, this is sweet from Osama Bin Laden."[1119]

3:40 p.m.: FAA reports: "LGA [La Guardia] personnel returning to tower from emergency site."

1117. Presidential Daily Diary, partially declassified.

1118. DCC Timeline.

1119. "CNN Breaking News: America Under Attack: Key Players in Israel Respond," CNN, September 11, 2001, http://transcripts.cnn.com/TRANSCRIPTS/0109/11/bn.40.html.

3:44 p.m.: President Bush, at STRATCOM headquarters, talks with Solic- itor General Ted Olson. Olson's wife, Barbara, died aboard AA Flight 77, the plane that hit the Pentagon.[1120]

3:44 p.m.: President Bush, at STRATCOM headquarters, reaches his father, former President George H. W. Bush, on the phone. He is in Brook- field, Wisconsin.[1121]

Former President Bush had spent the night of September 10 at the White House and dropped in on a senior staff meeting in the morning to say hi.[1122] He and his wife, Barbara, then boarded a commercial flight to St. Paul, Minnesota, for a speaking engagement; their plane was ordered to the ground in Milwaukee, and the former first family was secured at a nearby motel by their Secret Service detail.

"Where are you?" Bush recalls asking his father. The former president says he and his wife are in Milwaukee, on their way to Minneapolis. "What are you doing in Milwaukee?" Bush asks.

"You grounded my plane," the former president says.

The next morning, George and Barbara Bush get the okay—and a gov- ernment plane—to fly back to Kennebunkport, Maine. "Flying from a totally closed-down airport, through a totally empty sky, to a totally closed- down airport was eerie. But it was nice to be home," the former First Lady recounts.[1123]

3:52 p.m.: FAA DC logs: "Military flying without regard to PCA . . . flying due regard . . . cell advised."[1124]

3:55 p.m.: White House Counselor Karen Hughes conducts a press con- ference and says that the president is at an undisclosed location. She says he is conducting an NSC meeting by phone. Vice President Dick Cheney

---

1120. Presidential Daily Diary, partially declassified.

1121. Presidential Daily Diary, partially declassified.

1122. *Dead Certain: The Presidency of George W. Bush*, p. 135.

1123. Barbara Bush, *Reflections: Life After the White House* (New York: Simon & Schuster, 2004), p. 389.

1124. DCC Timeline.

and National Security Adviser Condoleezza Rice are in a secure facility at the White House, she says. Secretary Donald Rumsfeld is at the Pentagon.

"Your federal government continues to function effectively," she says, but she refuses to answer questions on where the president is.[1125]

3:55 p.m.: FAA reports false alarm: FAA DC logs: "ZDV [FAA Denver Center] advises that sighting of low flying large jet at Garden Grove, Utah headed toward Colorado. USAF and NOM advised."[1126]

4:00 p.m.: (Approximate time) Deputy Secretary of Defense Paul Wolfowitz, at Site R, recalls: "Originally [Gen.] Shelton was to join me up there (he was coming in from Europe), but he sensibly decided that it was no place for him. Around 4:00 in the afternoon I got the idea that I could be useful somewhere else and proposed to the Secretary that I go to Langley [to the CIA] and get briefed on what we knew about what went on, and he said to go ahead. We shipped out by car; my driver was up there [at Site R]."[1127]

4:00 p.m.: David Ensor, CNN national security correspondent, reports that US officials say there are "good indications" that Osama bin Laden is involved in the attacks, based on "new and specific" information developed that day.

4:00 p.m.: At the World Trade Center, the NYPD says the Verizon facility at 140 West Street fails due to flooding.[1128]

4:02 p.m.: FAA Herndon Command Center reports military aircraft "Due Regard" have been operating close to civil flights (one flight is operating 15 miles north of Boston, not in oceanic airspace). "Due Regard is not authorized in the CONUS," the FAA says.[1129]

1125. The audio is located at http://www.authentichistory.com/2001-2008/1-911/1-timeline1/20010911_1555_Couselor_Karen_Hughes_on_Fed_Gov_Action.html.

1126. DCC Timeline.

1127. OSD, "Pentagon Attack, Interview with Paul Wolfowitz," April 19, 2002.

1128. NIST Chronology.

1129. FAA, 11 Sep 01 Catastrophic Crisis (all times given in EDT).

"Due Regard" is defined as "a phase of flight wherein an aircraft commander of state-operated aircraft assumes responsibility to separate his/her aircraft from all other aircraft" over the high seas—that is, outside air traffic control procedures. "Military operational situations may not lend themselves to ICAO flight procedures; e.g., military contingencies, classified missions, politically sensitive missions, routine aircraft carrier operations, and some training activities. Operations not conducted under ICAO flight procedures are conducted under the 'due regard' or 'operational' prerogative of military aircraft."[1130]

4:02 p.m.: FAA DC logs: "ZSE [Seattle Center] advised Command Center that PDT ATCT [Pendleton, Oregon] was evacuated at 1737Z due to a suspicious briefcase."[1131]

4:10 p.m.: FAA reports: "Will ensure . . . feeds shut down to commercial sources but not to NAV CANADA."[1132]

4:12 p.m.: FAA DC logs: "Delta advises nine aircraft on ground in Canada are not allowing passengers to disembark or take off again . . . between Canadian govt and airlines."[1133]

4:15 p.m.: President Bush, at STRATCOM headquarters, talks privately with Vice President Cheney over a secure voice line.[1134]

4:18 p.m.: FAA reports: "Evacuating non-FAA buildings at SFO [San Francisco] airport."[1135]

4:19 p.m.: FAA reports: "Investigators at Johnstown and Pentagon, but not at WTC."[1136]

1130. ICAO Civil/Military Cooperation Symposium, ICMCS 2015—IP/01, April 15, 2015.
1131. DCC Timeline.
1132. FAA, 11 Sep 01 Catastrophic Crisis (all times given in EDT).
1133. DCC Timeline.
1134. Presidential Daily Diary, partially declassified.
1135. FAA, 11 Sep 01 Catastrophic Crisis (all times given in EDT).
1136. FAA, 11 Sep 01 Catastrophic Crisis (all times given in EDT).

4:20 p.m.: Sen. Bob Graham (D-FL), chairman of the Senate Intelligence Committee, has a press conference in which he says he was "not surprised there was an attack (but) was surprised at the specificity." He says he was "shocked at what actually happened—the extent of it."[1137]

4:20 p.m.: FAA reports several helicopters are being told by military that they cannot take off.[1138]

4:25 p.m.: President Bush, at STRATCOM headquarters, telephones Condoleezza Rice, but the call cannot be completed.[1139]

4:25 p.m.: The New York Stock Exchange, American Stock Exchange, and NASDAQ all say they will remain closed on Wednesday.

4:30 p.m.: President Bush leaves the STRATCOM headquarters building and motors back to the tarmac and to Air Force One.[1140]

4:30 p.m.: Noelia Rodriguez, press secretary to the First Lady, recalls: "At about 4:30 p.m., we returned to the White House. . . . After we showed our IDs, the agent said, 'Thank you, ladies, have a nice day!' I know it's just an automatic response, but it didn't make sense. I said, 'I think it's too late for that.' Then it was time to go home."[1141]

4:31 p.m.: The Associated Press reports that President Bush is returning to the White House.[1142]

4:34 p.m.: FAA reports: "Advisory 41 changed to include emergency evacuation aircraft . . . NOTAM requested."[1143]

1137. The audio of his press conference is located at http://www.authentichistory.com/2001-2008/1-911/1-timeline1/20010911_1620_Senator_Bob_Graham_Press_Conference.html.

1138. FAA, 11 Sep 01 Catastrophic Crisis (all times given in EDT).

1139. Presidential Daily Diary, partially declassified.

1140. Presidential Daily Diary, partially declassified.

1141. See "Voices of 9-11: 'A Cacophony of Information,'" *National Journal*, August 31, 2002; *Dead Certain: The Presidency of George W. Bush*, p. 141.

1142. AP, "A Stunning 48 Hours of News," n.d. (September 12, 2001).

1143. FAA, 11 Sep 01 Catastrophic Crisis (all times given in EDT).

CHAPTER 16

A WHITE HOUSE RESTORED, A NATION ON EDGE

President Bush's return to Washington, six hours after the fourth plane crashed in Pennsylvania, was hardly the end of the fear that more was still to come. Even during his national security teleconference in Nebraska, talk of a hijacked international flight coming from Madrid interrupted the meeting. And while he was in the air on his way back, another international flight, from Los Angeles to Sydney, again spooked the watchers after one of the passengers sent a message that ominously said, "Mission failed."

Over the course of the day, that United Airlines flight to Australia, the flight from Madrid, Delta Flight 1989, the Korean Airlines flight coming from Asia, and others created a constant state of alert. More and more phantom aircraft squawked the emergency 7500 transponder code or were not squawking at all. Radar contacts were lost. Planes took off without authorization. Sonic booms were mistaken for explosions. And then there were the miscellaneous bomb threats, real or imagined, forcing air traffic control towers in Pittsburgh and Cleveland to evacuate, as did the Los Angeles and San Francisco airports.

The Secret Service—swamped by news media reports and threatening raw intelligence—was particularly seeing things, and Washington experienced the greatest number of false alerts. Most turned out to be military planes. There was a Coast Guard patrol plane flying over Nantucket (mistaken by FAA Boston Center as another hijacking), an Air Force KC-135 aerial refueler over the Hudson River mistaken for an airliner, and a helicopter returning from Site R mistaken for a "fast mover" closing on Washington. Fear of an attack on the White House drove increasingly tense and overwrought demands for more protection of capital skies. "By the time the day was over," NORAD NEADS technician Stacia Rountree later said, "there were probably 19 or 20 planes" that she and the other ID technicians had to investigate as possible hijackings.[1144]

There weren't many heroes among government officials on 9/11, but in the end, it was the president's insistence, voiced from what now seems like eons ago in Sarasota, that defied the government worrywarts and sticklers. "I've had enough of this continuity-of-government thing," he said in Omaha—had enough of the Secret Service and the underground White House calling the shots. Some might say he broke protocol and the rules, but those in Washington didn't really have any better information on what was to come. It was almost as if, sitting isolated in their bunkers and operations centers, they needed to do something, to implement something—evacuations, COG, orders to shoot down airliners—because otherwise they were inactive and impotent.

And yet still, the eight minutes President Bush sat in the classroom after Andrew Card whispered in his ear that America was under attack has become the iconic moment—the core of Michael Moore's movie *Fahrenheit 9/11*—of Bush's befuddlement and government failure. On balance, given what we now know, and trying to imagine living through that day in real time, President Bush's reactions and instincts look very reasonable. He reluctantly stayed away from the capital, and his instincts in the face of so much uncertainty—to land and make a statement at Barksdale, to retain decision-making authority, even to reject security advice—don't look so bad in hindsight. And Bush's instinct—to get the country back at work, back into the skies, back to normal life—today seems more right than wrong. But none of that can overshadow his desire to make sure that "those who did this" paid. With that, the system of perpetual war kicked in. The rest of this consequential history was evidence of the overreaction of a frustrated and humiliated Washington.

4:35 p.m.: President Bush, on Air Force One, takes off from Offutt AFB to return to Washington.[1145]

Air Force One now has an F-16 guarding it, off the wing.

"STRATCOM provided one last essential service that afternoon. The Command's Airborne Command Post [the National Airborne Operations

1144. Katie Lange, "8 Things You May Not Know About Our Air Defense on 9/11," DOD News, September 11, 2019.
1145. Presidential Daily Diary, partially declassified.

An F-16 escorts Air Force One from Offutt Air Force Base in Nebraska to Andrews Air Force Base in Maryland. (Source: George W. Bush Presidential Library and Museum / Eric Draper [P7099-18])

Center], a plane used in wartime emergencies that looks much like Air Force One, was for the first time ever deployed as a decoy. The President's plane took off a short time later, safely delivering him back to Washington."[1146]

4:40 p.m.: Aboard Air Force One, Michael Morell receives the CIA's "evidence" regarding the attackers, a written communication from George Tenet's executive assistant, that had previously been denied to him. Morell recounts: "On the cover sheet was a short note: 'Michael, sorry. Here's everything we have.'" Morell goes over the material and asks to see the president, going through the intelligence reports with him. "After reading the documents, the president simply handed them back to me and said, 'Thank you, Michael.'"[1147]

1146. Bill Kelly, NET News, "Military Insiders Recall Bush's 9/11 Stop at Stratcom," KVNO News, September 7, 2011, http://www.kvnonews.com/2011/09/military-insiders-recall-bushs-911-stop-at-stratcom/.

1147. The Great War of Our Time, p. 57.

Bush writes that during his flight back to Washington, "Andy [Card] and CIA briefer Mike Morell came to see me. . . . Mike told me that the French intelligence service had provided reports of other operatives—so called sleeper cells—in the United States planning a second wave of attacks. . . . It was one of the darkest moments of the day."[1148]

4:54 p.m.: The Associated Press reports that the federal government now suspects Osama bin Laden of being responsible for the terrorist attacks, according to two US officials.[1149]

4:56 p.m.: FAA reports: "NORAD requesting tracks [of hijacked aircraft] from departure to point of impact."[1150]

5:00 p.m.: At about 5:00 p.m., the FBI settles on Building 405 at Fort Myer, adjacent to Arlington National Cemetery, as the site for a JOC responsible for rescue and investigations at the Pentagon.[1151]

5:03 p.m.: FAA DC logs: "Canadians letting passengers off aircraft."[1152]

5:05 p.m.: FAA reports false alarm: "Report from MIV [Millville, New Jersey] AFSS & ACY [Atlantic City, New Jersey] ATCT that at 1248Z calls reported on 121.5 of yelling and screaming."[1153]

5:15 p.m.: Jamie McIntyre on CNN reports fires are still burning in parts of the Pentagon. No death figures have been released yet.

5:17 p.m.: FAA reports that "passenger on board UAL A/C enroute from LAX to SID [Sidney] between AUS and NZ sent Email message that 'mission failed.'"[1154]

1148. *Decision Points*, p. 136.

1149. AP, "A Stunning 48 Hours of News," n.d. (September 12, 2001).

1150. FAA, 11 Sep 01 Catastrophic Crisis (all times given in EDT).

1151. Arlington County: After-Action Report on the Response to the September 11 Terrorist Attack on the Pentagon.

1152. DCC Timeline.

1153. FAA, 11 Sep 01 Catastrophic Crisis (all times given in EDT).

1154. FAA, 11 Sep 01 Catastrophic Crisis (all times given in EDT).

5:20:33 p.m.: The 47-story Seven World Trade Center building (WTC 7) begins to collapse after burning for hours. It takes less than one minute (until 5:21:10 p.m.) for the unoccupied building to come down.[1155]

The building has been evacuated during the day. The fire and debris that hit the building have created an uncontrollable situation. The penthouse on top crumbles apart only about six seconds before the entire building begins to collapse.

The building contains New York's emergency operations center, originally intended to be a secure facility to be used in disasters such as the 9/11 terrorist attacks. It also houses domestic offices of the CIA and the New York field office of the Secret Service.

5:21 p.m.: UA Flight 93. FAA reports: "UAL 93 plots [positional details] to be faxed . . . AAL 77 was filed to fly from DUL to LAX; checked on UAL 93 track. . . . No problems relayed to ATC."[1156]

5:30 p.m.: John King on CNN reports that US officials say the plane that crashed in Pennsylvania could have been headed for one of three possible targets: Camp David, the White House, or the US Capitol building.

5:30 p.m.: Aboard Air Force One en route to Andrews AFB, Maryland, Ari Fleischer holds a briefing for the remaining press pool. He says that President Bush will address the nation. "The President has also heard today from countless world leaders either who are calling to—back to Washington or have sent him directly communiques. He's heard from Britain, France, Germany, Russia—a host of nations, all of whom have expressed their outrage at this attack, and who have assured the American people that the international community stands with America."[1157]

1155. NIST Chronology.

1156. FAA, 11 Sep 01 Catastrophic Crisis (all times given in EDT).

1157. Transcript, "Press Briefing to the Pool by Ari Fleischer Aboard Air Force One en route Andrews Air Force Base, 5:30 p.m. EDT," History on the Net, September 11, 2001.

5:32 p.m.: President Bush, aboard Air Force One, talks over the secure voice line with the First Lady for three minutes, their third successful call of the day.[1158]

"I'm coming home, see you at the White House," he says. He then works with aides on what will be his prime-time address to the nation.[1159]

5:35 p.m.: FAA reports: "Vice POTUS [Cheney] wants info on UAL 93."[1160]

5:38 p.m.: FAA reports: "[FAA Herndon Command Center] . . . to verify that all A/C on ground except flights authorized by Advisory 41 & exceptions."[1161]

5:40 p.m.: Gen. Henry "Hugh" Shelton, chairman of the Joint Chiefs of Staff, arrives at the Pentagon.

He is flying across the Atlantic on his way to Europe when word comes in of the attacks. He turns around and returns to Washington. He later goes to the White House to attend the evening NSC meeting in the PEOC.[1162]

When he arrives at the Pentagon, Shelton "turned to Vice Adm. Tom Wilson of the DIA and Rear Adm. Lowell 'Jake' Jacoby, the Director of Intelligence for the Joint Staff. 'Have we had any intel "squeaks" on an attack like this—anything at all?' According to Shelton, Tom Wilson spoke up at once. 'The only possible hint of this coming was several months ago when we got a single intercept requesting jumbo jet training. Since then, there's been nothing.'"[1163]

5:45 p.m.: President Bush, aboard Air Force One, talks over the secure voice line with Condoleezza Rice.[1164]

1158. Presidential Daily Diary, partially declassified.

1159. Bill Kelly, NET News, "Military Insiders Recall Bush's 9/11 Stop at Stratcom," KVNO News, September 7, 2011, http://www.kvnonews.com/2011/09/military-insiders-recall-bushs-911-stop-at-stratcom/.

1160. FAA, 11 Sep 01 Catastrophic Crisis (all times given in EDT).

1161. FAA, 11 Sep 01 Catastrophic Crisis (all times given in EDT).

1162. Hugh Shelton, *Without Hesitation: The Odyssey of an American Warrior* (New York: St. Martin's, 2010), pp. 436–437.

1163. *Eyes on the Horizon*, p. 159.

1164. Presidential Daily Diary, partially declassified.

After departing Offutt Air Force Base in Nebraska, President Bush confers on the phone from Air Force One with Vice President Cheney during the flight to Andrews Air Force Base. (Source: George W. Bush Presidential Library and Museum / Eric Draper [P7091-18])

5:47 p.m.: FAA DC logs: "Special Notice—Effective Immediately until further notice. Flight operations in the National Airspace System by United States civil aircraft and foreign civil and military aircraft are prohibited, except in accordance with . . . [Advisory] 043 or as amended and revised."[1165]

6:00 p.m.: The news media reports that explosions are heard in Kabul, Afghanistan. The explosions occur at about 2:30 a.m. local time, the reports say. US officials say later that the United States had no involvement in any attack whatsoever. CNN credits the anti-Taliban Northern Alliance as the source of the news.[1166]

6:00 p.m.: The last international aircraft headed to the United States lands at a Canadian airport (Vancouver IAP).

1165. DCC Timeline.

1166. "September 11: Chronology of Terror," CNN, September 12, 2001, http://edition.cnn.com/2001/US/09/11/chronology.attack/.

6:00 p.m.: UA Flight 93. Pennsylvania Governor Tom Ridge, after assessing the crash site, holds a news conference: "It's difficult to describe the range of emotions everyone feels when they not only learn about these incidents today, but they've actually seen them. The dictionary is inadequate, and there just aren't enough words. But I guess the range of emotions goes from rage and anger to sorrow to horror to, I guess, a sense of nausea that we all feel."

He calls on Pennsylvanians to give their prayers, their blood, and their talent. He is affected most by what he cannot see: "The most telling site is a large, gaping hole. Very little debris is visible." He promises "a forceful and appropriate response" to those responsible for the "irrational, cowardly, despicable, unconscionable, and immoral" actions that caused United Airlines Flight 93 to crash near Shanksville.[1167]

6:00 p.m.: The Justice Department sends federal law enforcement officers (probably US Marshals) to guard the Pentagon perimeter from 6:00 p.m. until 6:00 a.m. for the next few nights.[1168]

6:10 p.m.: Mayor Giuliani urges New Yorkers to stay home Wednesday if they can.

6:10 p.m.: FAA DC logs: "Explosion at hospital in Dayton.[1169] . . . Crash reported into VA Hospital in Dayton Ohio. VA hospital explosion."[1170]

A minute later, FAA Great Lakes Region "reported that citizens had heard an explosion [in Dayton], but aircraft crash not confirmed."[1171]

6:13 p.m.: FAA reports bomb threat: "AGL [FAA Great Lakes Region] confirmed that explosion could not be confirmed [in Dayton] but could be a sonic boom."[1172]

1167. National Park Service, Flight 93, September 11, 2001.

1168. Defense Studies Series, Pentagon 9/11.

1169. DCC Timeline.

1170. The Department of Transportation reported that local Dayton television was reporting that an aircraft crashed into the VA building in Dayton, Ohio. FAA, 11 Sep 01 Catastrophic Crisis (all times given in EDT).

1171. FAA, 11 Sep 01 Catastrophic Crisis (all times given in EDT).

1172. FAA, 11 Sep 01 Catastrophic Crisis (all times given in EDT).

6:27 p.m.: FAA reports: "In AEA [FAA Eastern Region in Jamaica, New York], only six airports will be closing, ten (HPN, POU, CHO, BGM, ILG, RDG, PNE, ISP, MNU, CXY) staying open to support military ops."[1173]

6:29 p.m.: President Bush, aboard Air Force One, talks over the secure voice line with Karen Hughes in the WHSR.[1174]

6:30 p.m.: White House Deputies Committee teleconference chaired by Deputy NSA Hadley convenes at 6:30 p.m.

Gen. Myers later writes: "We verified that counter-NBC decontamination units had been called out and deployed, standing by in case al-Qaida [sic] decided to follow up with WMD attacks on our cities." He says that they then "discussed the draft National Security Presidential Directive on Combating Terrorism that had been presented on September 4, 2001."[1175]

The New York Army National Guard's Second Civil Support Team (CST)—Weapons of Mass Destruction (WMD)—is the first organized unit of any military service or component to arrive at the World Trade Center, sampling the air to see if biological or chemical contaminants are present.

6:32 p.m.: FAA reports: "Special ops flights (N241LA and 242LA-Cessna Citations) released ADW-FAY-DCA [Andrews AFB, Maryland—Fayetteville, North Carolina—Washington National]."[1176]

This is the only reference to the possibility that special operations forces—the military's "black" National Mission Force—are operating, on 9/11, two aircraft dispatched from Andrews AFB to Fayetteville, North Carolina (home of Ft. Bragg). Adding to the mystery, the aircraft registration numbers do not reconcile with military aircraft.

6:34 p.m.: President Bush, aboard Air Force One, lands at Andrews AFB.[1177]

1173. FAA, 11 Sep 01 Catastrophic Crisis (all times given in EDT).
1174. Presidential Daily Diary, partially declassified.
1175. *Eyes on the Horizon*, pp. 160–161.
1176. FAA, 11 Sep 01 Catastrophic Crisis (all times given in EDT).
1177. Presidential Daily Diary, partially declassified.

Air Force One arrives at Andrews Air Force Base, Maryland, on September 11, 2001, with President Bush on board. (Source: US Air Force)

At Andrews, he is met by Joe Hagin, officially deputy chief of staff in charge of White House operations and the official in charge of presidential continuity. On the morning of 9/11, Hagin is with an advance team scouting an upcoming presidential visit in New York City, uncharacteristically separated from Bush and the White House. As a testament to Hagin's abilities (or his power), the NYPD assigns a set of squad cars to rush him across the Hudson River, where they hand off the car to New Jersey State Troopers, who roar them down the Jersey turnpike to Dover AFB in Delaware, where they board a waiting military jet: destination Omaha and President Bush. Halfway to Nebraska in the air over Missouri, Hagin learns that Air Force One is returning to Washington, so he orders his plane turned around as well: destination Andrews AFB in Maryland.[1178]

1178. Howard Wilkinson, "Real-Life 'West Wing' Drama: Indian Hill Native at Bush's Side," *Cincinnati Enquirer*, January 20, 2003; Mike Allen, "Hagin Leaving the White House," *Politico*, July 3, 2008; *Dead Certain: The Presidency of George W. Bush*, p. 144.

President Bush returns to Andrews Air Force Base, Maryland, from Offutt Air Force Base, Nebraska. (Source: US Air Force / Senior Airman Neal X. Joiner)

6:35 p.m.: President Bush, aboard Air Force One (while the plane is landing and taxiing), talks over the secure voice line with Secretary Rumsfeld.[1179]

6:42 p.m.: At the Pentagon, Secretary Rumsfeld speaks to the press. According to the official DOD history: "Confident and reassuring, Rumsfeld held a brief press conference. . . . Sen. Carl Levin, chairman of the Senate Armed Services Committee, and Sen. John Warner, the committee's ranking minority member, had asked to come to the Pentagon to show bipartisan support. Appreciating their concern, Rumsfeld welcomed them. After visiting the crash site the senators participated in the press conference, joined by JCS Chairman General Shelton just arrived from Europe

---

1179. Presidential Daily Diary, partially declassified.

As President Bush returns to the White House, Marine One prepares to land on the South Lawn. (Source: George W. Bush Presidential Library and Museum / Paul Morse)

and Secretary of the Army White, back from the alternate command location. Near the end of his remarks Rumsfeld pointedly declared that the briefing was taking place in the Pentagon and that 'the Pentagon's functioning. It will be in business tomorrow.' He spoke of casualties but said it was too early to have firm figures because roster checks were still under way. In response to a question he stated that the FBI had secured the site."[1180]

1180. Defense Studies Series, Pentagon 9/11. The audio is located at http://www.authentichistory.com/2001-2008/1-911/1-timeline1/20010911_1840_Sec_of_Def_Rumsfeld.html.

6:45 p.m.: President Bush boards a Marine Corps helicopter (Marine One) for the trip from Andrews AFB, Maryland, to the South Lawn of the White House.[1181]

"I looked out on an abandoned, locked-down Washington. In the distance I saw smoke rising from the Pentagon," Bush later writes.[1182]

His military aide, Lt. Col. Tom Gould, traveling with the president, says, "As you can imagine, here's a young (lieutenant colonel) coming into his capital, of the most powerful nation in the world, looking at a building that represents the most powerful military in the world, smoldering. It sort of hit home at that point that things were going to be different from here on out."[1183]

6:54 p.m.: President Bush arrives at the White House aboard Marine One. He is scheduled to address the nation at 8:30 p.m. EST.

John King on CNN reports that First Lady Laura Bush arrived earlier by motorcade from a "secure location."

6:56 p.m.: President Bush is greeted by senior staff as he walks to the Oval Office along the South Colonnade.[1184]

Condoleezza Rice writes: "I walked out toward him and he asked, 'Where's Laura?' She was in the emergency operations center. He headed to the Oval and then immediately down to see the First Lady."[1185]

6:56 p.m.: FAA DC logs: "Light twin prop heading toward LAX."[1186]

6:59 p.m.: FAA reports false alarm: "ZLA [Los Angeles Center] reports unidentified light twin prop heading toward LAX, reported by small towers; checking with military—possible military scramble."[1187]

1181. Presidential Daily Diary, partially declassified.
1182. *Decision Points*, p. 137.
1183. Janene Scully, "Vandenberg Officer at Bush's Side During Attacks," *Santa Maria Times*, September 11, 2011.
1184. Presidential Daily Diary, partially declassified.
1185. *No Higher Honor*, p. 76.
1186. DCC Timeline.
1187. FAA, 11 Sep 01 Catastrophic Crisis (all times given in EDT).

President George Bush returns to the White House followed by White House Counsel Alberto Gonzales and Counselor Karen Hughes. (Source: White House / Paul Morse)

7:00 p.m.: In the private dining room in the West Wing of the White House, President Bush gathers his senior staff for 10 minutes. Meeting with the president are Alberto Gonzales, Karen Hughes, Condoleezza Rice, Ari Fleischer, and Andy Card.

7:00 p.m.: At the Pentagon, at about 7:00 p.m., Arlington County Fire Chief Schwartz briefs participating agencies on the structure of the incident command system.[1188]

7:00 p.m.: In Shanksville, Pennsylvania, residents gather for prayer. About 70 people meet at the United Methodist Church on Main Street. Donations of food and drink for the first responders begin to arrive at the Shanksville Fire Station.[1189]

7:02 p.m.: Paula Zahn of CNN reports that the Marriott Hotel (WTC 3) at the World Trade Center is on the verge of collapse.

1188. Arlington County: After-Action Report on the Response to the September 11 Terrorist Attack on the Pentagon.

1189. National Park Service Flight 93 National Memorial, Timeline, Flight 93, September 11, 2001.

President Bush immediately gathers senior staff in the private dining room after returning to the White House. Meeting with the president from left are Counsel Alberto Gonzales, Counselor Karen Hughes, National Security Advisor Dr. Condoleezza Rice, Press Secretary Ari Fleischer, and Chief of Staff Andrew Card. (Source: George W. Bush Presidential Library and Museum / Paul Morse [P7111-27a])

7:02 p.m.: FAA reports false alarm: "AWP [FAA Western Pacific in El Segundo, California] update Light Twin out of Orange County 2,000' 3,000' AWACS and F-16, watching and LA Approach watching (information from concerned citizen)."[1190]

7:05 p.m.: FAA reports: "ZLA [Los Angeles Center] reports military aware of unidentified A/C."[1191]

7:11 p.m.: President Bush goes to the PEOC underneath the White House East Wing, arriving at 7:11 p.m.[1192]

He sees the First Lady for the first time that day.

1190. FAA logs.

1191. FAA, 11 Sep 01 Catastrophic Crisis (all times given in EDT).

1192. Presidential Daily Diary, partially declassified.

President Bush meets with Cheney, Card, Rice, and Secret Service White House Chief Truscott. He stays in the PEOC until 7:29 p.m.[1193]

`7:15 p.m.:` Press briefing is held by Attorney General Ashcroft, Secretary of Health and Human Services Tommy G. Thompson, acting Secretary of Transportation Mineta, and FEMA Director Allbaugh.

Ashcroft says the FBI is setting up a website for tips and gives out the phone number for friends and family members of victims to leave contact information.

`7:22 p.m.:` FAA reports: "AWP [FAA Western Pacific in El Segundo, California]—twin engine King Air military C-12."[1194]

`7:30 p.m.:` The news media reports that the US government denies any responsibility for reported explosions in Kabul, Afghanistan.

`7:31 p.m.:` President Bush and the First Lady go to the White House second-floor residence.[1195]

`7:36 p.m.:` President Bush speaks with Andrew Card.[1196]

`7:39 p.m.:` President Bush telephones his daughter Barbara P. Bush in New Haven, Connecticut, but the call cannot be completed.[1197]

`7:39 p.m.:` FAA reports: "White House emergency center [deleted]."[1198]

`7:43 p.m.:` President Bush speaks with Karen Hughes.[1199]

1193. Presidential Daily Diary, partially declassified.
1194. FAA, 11 Sep 01 Catastrophic Crisis (all times given in EDT).
1195. Presidential Daily Diary, partially declassified.
1196. Presidential Daily Diary, partially declassified.
1197. Presidential Daily Diary, partially declassified.
1198. FAA, 11 Sep 01 Catastrophic Crisis (all times given in EDT).
1199. Presidential Daily Diary, partially declassified.

President Bush, in the Presidential Emergency Operations Center underneath the East Wing of the White House, speaks with Vice President Cheney as National Security Adviser Condoleezza Rice, White House Chief of Staff Andrew Card, and Secret Service Special Agent Carl Truscott look on. (Source: George W. Bush Presidential Library and Museum [P7152-18])

7:45 p.m.: CNN reports that the NYPD says that at least 78 officers are missing. The city also says that as many as half of the first 400 firefighters on the scene were killed.

7:45 p.m.: Members of Congress gather on the steps outside the east front of the US Capitol and declare that they stand united behind President Bush. After comments by Dennis Hastert and Tom Daschle, they sing "God Bless America."

Additional questions are raised about intelligence warnings. Rep. Bob Barr, Republican of Georgia, says that there is a "tremendous question about why we didn't have some warning." Rep. Dana Rohrabacher, Republican of California, says: "This is not just a day of infamy. . . . It's a day of disgrace. . . . The president needs to clean house and wipe away the senior executives of the intelligence agency."[1200]

1200. Alison Mitchell and Katherine Q. Seelye, "A Day of Terror: Congress; Horror Knows No Party as Lawmakers Huddle," *New York Times*, September 12, 2001.

(Source: George W. Bush Presidential Library and Museum / Paul Morse [P7132-04])

7:53 p.m.: President Bush leaves the residence and returns via the White House South Grounds to the private dining room.[1201]

7:54 p.m.: President Bush meets with Karen Hughes and Ari Fleischer for speech preparation.[1202]

7:56 p.m.: President Bush talks with his daughter Barbara P. Bush, who is in New Haven, Connecticut.[1203]

In the morning, the president's 19-year-old daughter had been shuttled from her classes at Yale University to the New Haven office of the Secret Service.

1201. Presidential Daily Diary, partially declassified.
1202. Presidential Daily Diary, partially declassified.
1203. Presidential Daily Diary, partially declassified.

Jenna Bush, twin sister to Barbara and a freshman at the University of Texas in Austin, was awakened in her dorm room by her Secret Service detail and taken to the downtown Driskill Hotel, where she spent the day.[1204]

8:00 p.m.: At the Pentagon, an incident command structure meeting (involving a smaller number of key agencies) discusses the need to implement a true Unified Command. All agencies will assign a senior representative with decision-making authority to the JOC.[1205]

8:00 p.m.: Senator Hillary Clinton, Democrat of New York, is interviewed by CNN on the steps of Capitol Hill.[1206]

8:05 p.m.: President Bush and Karen Hughes go to the Oval Office.[1207]
There is an 8:05 p.m. entry in the Presidential Diary that is deleted (likely a telephone call with some foreign leader from a "sensitive" country such as Israel or Saudi Arabia).[1208]

8:05 p.m.: FAA reports: (FAA Herndon Command Center) "Advisory #45 solicits info from airlines about how many A/C diverted to where."[1209]

8:06 p.m.: President Bush meets for speech preparation with Andrew Card, Dan Bartlett, James R. Wilkinson, Tucker Eskew, and Karl Rove. The meeting lasts from 8:06 p.m. to 8:25 p.m.[1210]
Karen Hughes writes about the speech: "It had been chaotic in my office as we put the statement together; the president had called with his thoughts; the speechwriters sent a draft; Condi Rice and her deputy Steve

1204. *Spoken from the Heart*, p. 202; Bob Woodward, *Bush at War* (New York: Simon & Schuster, 2002), p. 15; *Dead Certain: The Presidency of George W. Bush*, p. 141.
1205. Arlington County: After-Action Report on the Response to the September 11 Terrorist Attack on the Pentagon.
1206. The audio is located at http://www.authentichistory.com/2001-2008/1-911/1-timeline1/20010911_2000_Interview_Senator_Clinton.html.
1207. Presidential Daily Diary, partially declassified.
1208. Presidential Daily Diary, partially declassified.
1209. FAA, 11 Sep 01 Catastrophic Crisis (all times given in EDT).
1210. Presidential Daily Diary, partially declassified.

Hadley had policy points they wanted to include . . . several other members of the communications team offered ideas."[1211]

8:07 p.m.: FAA reports: "FEMA DOT liaison [deleted] says FEMA team in Montana using military A/C are having trouble getting release—will contact ATSC or ATCSCC."[1212]

8:17 p.m.: FAA reports: "Seeks airlift of Marines to Manhattan [deleted] HMX-1."[1213]

8:20 p.m.: Secretary Rumsfeld, after his press conference at the Pentagon, arrives at the White House and goes to the Oval Office.[1214]

8:25 p.m.: FAA reports: "AAL 9014 landed JFK. FEMA on board."

1211. Karen Hughes, *Ten Minutes from Normal* (New York: Penguin Books, 2004), p. 244.
1212. FAA, 11 Sep 01 Catastrophic Crisis (all times given in EDT).
1213. FAA, 11 Sep 01 Catastrophic Crisis (all times given in EDT).
1214. Presidential Daily Diary; Defense Studies Series, Pentagon 9/11.

CHAPTER 17

"EVIL, DESPICABLE ACTS OF TERROR"

The day was barely over, and for the rescue workers at the World Trade Center and the Pentagon, September 11 would never quite be just one day. And yet despite the shock, the destruction, and the deaths, by the time President Bush returned to the White House in the evening, Washington was already returning to its old ways, with so many grinding axes and political maneuvers already shaping the future. By evening, there was already speculation being bandied about in the news media and expert circles that US intelligence "knew" or should have known about the hijackers and the attacks. When people weren't blaming the intelligence community, or Bush and his administration, they blamed the Clinton administration for leaving the country defenseless. And the conspiracy-minded blamed Israel's Mossad—a theory floated by Arab Middle Eastern leaders. Commentators speculated that the attacks were good for US-Israeli relations and that Palestinians were once again exposed as part of the global terrorism threat.

Raised by Rumsfeld in the early afternoon was the conviction that Iraq needed to be folded into any response, and there was even public talk on 9/11 of implicating Iraq and finishing off Saddam Hussein. And of course there were the many voices insisting that more needed to be spent on national security. "We should now immediately begin building up our conventional military forces to prepare for what will inevitably and rapidly escalate into confrontation and quite possibly war," Robert Kagan wrote in the *Washington Post*.

Sure retaliation against al Qaeda in Afghanistan was clear by the evening "war council" meeting. But it was also clear that war in Afghanistan would be especially difficult.[1215] It wasn't just the distances involved and lack of nearby

---

1215. CENTCOM Deputy Commander Gen. Michael Delong wrote that he directed the staff to review existing counterterrorism contingency plans and pinpoint known terrorist cells.

bases or that the country had proven unconquerable by the Soviet Union in a decade of brutal war. It was also, as Cheney and Rumsfeld cautioned, that the country had been decimated by two decades of conflict and civil war; Afghanistan might prove to be a bad match for a US military that relied so much on airpower, as it would be hard to find anything worthwhile to bomb.

By the end of the day, Gen. Tommy Franks directed his Florida-based staff to initiate strike planning for Afghanistan. He later wrote: "We had built target sets for key Taliban installations, air defense sites, and early warning radars. The time had come when that effort would pay off." CENTCOM told the Pentagon that they could have 80 Tomahawk cruise missiles in range of Afghan targets in 24 hours and up to 200 within 48 hours.[1216] In the evening meeting, Rumsfeld said that major strikes could take up to 60 days to assemble.[1217] Taking a swipe at the military, George Tenet would later write: "The president had been disappointed to learn that the Pentagon had no contingency plan in place for going after al Qaeda and the Taliban."[1218]

As war planning got underway, in the United States, permanent change was emerging. By evening, armed soldiers were guarding key intersections and transportation hubs in Washington and New York. In Florida, the governor declared a state of emergency. Muslims throughout the United States were eyed, attacked, and even arrested. The additional security measures taken, and the transformation of America, were an unstoppable force—not just the obsession with weapons of mass destruction (soon amplified by anthrax attacks in October) and certain war with Iraq (first mentioned on 9/11 itself) but also the domestic changes (from the PATRIOT Act to the creation of the Department of Homeland Security) that would transform the country.

The conspiracies were already being floated: that the hijackers were assisted in boarding the planes and that, after successfully living in the United States for more than a year, they intentionally left clues behind to misdirect the FBI, in the words of one conspiracy site, "to establish a misleading trail and

But he cautioned, "We had no military presence there, no ambassador, and little human intelligence." See Michael DeLong, *Inside Centcom: The Unvarnished Truth About the Wars in Afghanistan and Iraq* (Washington, DC: Regnery, 2004), p. 20.

1216. Tommy Franks, *American Soldier* (New York: Regan Books/HarperCollins, 2004), pp. 243, 245.

1217. 9/11 Commission Report, p. 330. Bob Woodward later writes: "Rumsfeld actually puts Iraq on the table [as well] and says, 'Part of our response maybe should be attacking Iraq. It's an opportunity.'" See *Bush at War*, p. 32.

1218. *At the Center of the Storm*, p. 176.

false identities." The conspiracy theories would quickly multiply: that the government knew or was even culpable in assisting, that there were no planes, that a missile and not an airplane attacked the Pentagon, and on and on. On September 12, one so-called expert was quoted in the *Albuquerque Journal* as saying that "explosive devices" had been planted inside the World Trade Centers. It would be the beginning of a complex conspiracy theory that persists to this day in questioning the "official story."

8:30 p.m.: President Bush addresses the nation from the Oval Office, calling the attacks "evil, despicable acts of terror" and declaring that the United States, its friends, and its allies would "stand together to win the war against terrorism."

Good evening. Today, our fellow citizens, our way of life, our very freedom came under attack in a series of deliberate and deadly terrorist acts. The victims were in airplanes, or in their offices; secretaries, businessmen and women, military, and federal workers; moms and dads, friends and neighbors. Thousands of lives were suddenly ended by evil, despicable acts of terror.

The pictures of airplanes flying into buildings, fires burning, huge structures collapsing, have filled us with disbelief, terrible sadness, and a quiet, unyielding anger. These acts of mass murder were intended to frighten our nation into chaos and retreat. But they have failed; our country is strong.

A great people has been moved to defend a great nation. Terrorist attacks can shake the foundations of our biggest buildings, but they cannot touch the foundation of America. These acts shattered steel, but they cannot dent the steel of American resolve.

America was targeted for attack because we're the brightest beacon for freedom and opportunity in the world. And no one will keep that light from shining.

Today, our nation saw evil, the very worst of human nature. And we responded with the best of America—with the daring of our rescue workers, with the caring for strangers and neighbors who came to give blood and help in any way they could.

Immediately following the first attack, I implemented our government's emergency response plans. Our military is powerful, and it's prepared. Our emergency teams are working in New York City and Washington, DC, to help with local rescue efforts.

President Bush delivers an address to the nation at 8:30 p.m. from the Oval Office, surrounded by photographers and staff. (Source: George W. Bush Presidential Library and Museum / Paul Morse)

Our first priority is to get help to those who have been injured, and to take every precaution to protect our citizens at home and around the world from further attacks.

The functions of our government continue without interruption. Federal agencies in Washington, which had to be evacuated today, are reopening for essential personnel tonight, and will be open for business tomorrow. Our financial institutions remain strong, and the American economy will be open for business, as well.

The search is underway for those who are behind these evil acts. I've directed the full resources of our intelligence and law enforcement communities to find those responsible and to bring them to justice. We will make no distinction between the terrorists who committed these acts and those who harbor them.

I appreciate so very much the members of Congress who have joined me in strongly condemning these attacks. And on behalf of the American people, I thank the many world leaders who have called to offer their condolences and assistance.

America and our friends and allies join with all those who want peace and security in the world, and we stand together to win the war against terrorism. Tonight, I ask for your prayers for all those who grieve, for the children whose worlds have been shattered, for all whose sense of safety and security has been threatened. And I pray they will be comforted by a power greater than any of us, spoken through the ages in Psalm 23: "Even though I walk through the valley of the shadow of death, I fear no evil, for You are with me."

This is a day when all Americans from every walk of life unite in our resolve for justice and peace. America has stood down enemies before, and we will do so this time. None of us will ever forget this day. Yet, we go forward to defend freedom and all that is good and just in our world.

Thank you. Good night, and God bless America.

8:39 p.m.: President Bush, after delivering his address to the nation, returns to the PEOC, accompanied by his senior staff.[1219]

8:40 p.m.: President Bush meets with a full national security team from 8:40 p.m. to 9:48 p.m. in the PEOC.

Present are Bush, Cheney, Powell, Rumsfeld, Paul H. O'Neill, Mineta, Ashcroft, Rice, Assistant for Economic Policy Lawrence Lindsey, FBI Director Mueller, Tenet, Chairman of the Joint Chiefs Gen. H. "Hugh" Shelton, Andrew Card, Karen Hughes, Deputy NSA Hadley, Richard Clarke, Gen. Myers (vice chairman and chairman-designate of the JCS, slated to take over in days), FEMA Director Joe Allbaugh, Secret Service White House Chief Truscott, Alberto Gonzalez, Cheney's National Security Adviser I. Lewis "Scooter" Libby, and Cheney's Communications Director, Mary Matalin.[1220]

Gen. Shelton says of his visit to the PEOC that *he* had never been to the bunker before, despite his rank and 35 years in the military. He writes that Secret Service agents escorted him down from the West Wing "past thick blast doors and through a long underground tunnel that terminated under the East Wing."[1221]

Condoleezza Rice says of Bush: "I was struck that the President didn't even look tired. He was determined to keep everyone focused on what we needed to do with the immediate aftermath."[1222]

1219. Presidential Daily Diary, partially declassified.
1220. Presidential Daily Diary, partially declassified.
1221. *Without Hesitation*, pp. 436–437.
1222. *No Higher Honor*, p. 77.

President Bush meets with his National Security team in the Presidential Emergency Operations Center at 8:40 p.m. (Source: National Archives)

A smaller meeting of top advisers, a group Bush will later call his "war council," follows the larger meeting. This includes Cheney, Powell, Rumsfeld, Shelton, Myers, Tenet, Ashcroft, and FBI Director Mueller. Rice and Card are part of the core group, and they are often joined by their deputies, Stephen Hadley and Josh Bolten.

In this smaller meeting, the president says, "The United States will punish not just the perpetrators of the attacks, but also those who harbored them."

Rumsfeld and Cheney agree that the United States will have to retaliate not just against Osama bin Laden but also against countries that may have helped him. "We have to force countries to choose," Bush says.

CIA Director Tenet says that they must deny Osama bin Laden and his people any sanctuary by targeting the Taliban as well. "Tell the Taliban we're finished with them," he urges.

Secretary Powell says that the United States has to make it clear to Pakistan, Afghanistan, and the Arab states that the time to act is now. He says the United States will need to build a coalition. He describes the immediate diplomatic tasks: dealing with Afghanistan and its ruling Taliban, which harbors bin Laden, and neighboring Pakistan, which has closer ties to the Taliban regime than any other nation. "We have to make it clear to Pakistan and Afghanistan this is showtime," he says.

Secretary Rumsfeld urges the president and the principals to think broadly about who might have harbored the attackers, including Iraq, Afghanistan, Libya, Sudan, and Iran. The countries, he says, "were now on notice: Bush had announced that the costs for state support of terrorism had just gone up." But he also warns that "a major military effort . . . could take as many as several months to assemble."[1223]

"This is a great opportunity," Bush says, that the administration now has—a chance to improve relations with other countries around the world, including Russia and China. It is more than flushing bin Laden out, he concludes.[1224]

By the end of the day, not only have most US allies declared that they stand firmly with the United States, but so have many Middle Eastern countries—including Iraq's Saddam Hussein—and both Russia and Iran have expressed cooperation and condolences.

8:40 p.m.: FAA reports false alarm: "Trying to track 3701 beacon code at 1300—Exec Jet 351."[1225]

8:45 p.m.: In Shanksville, Pennsylvania, 16 volunteer firefighters and three pieces of equipment, on scene for the past 10 hours, return to the fire station. They remain on standby for the next 13 days, assisting the FBI in the recovery and investigation of the crash.[1226]

8:45 p.m.: FAA reports: "ZDC [Washington Center] reports military intercepting departures from ORF [Norfolk, VA] and PHL [Philadelphia]; perhaps new military crews not fully briefed: ATSC and AAT-4 [associate

---

1223. *Known and Unknown*, p. 346.

1224. 9/11 Commission Report, p. 330. Bob Woodward later writes: "Rumsfeld actually puts Iraq on the table [as well] and says, 'Part of our response maybe should be attacking Iraq. It's an opportunity.'" See *Bush at War*, p. 32.

1225. FAA, 11 Sep 01 Catastrophic Crisis (all times given in EDT).

1226. National Park Service Flight 93 National Memorial, Timeline, Flight 93, September 11, 2001.

administrator for air traffic] advised and working . . . no national change in procedures. ZDC will call NORAD with discreet codes on departures out of ZDC airports."[1227]

8:50 p.m.: CNN interviews terrorism expert Peter Bergen, who once interviewed Osama bin Laden.[1228]

9:00 p.m.: Larry King on CNN interviews Senators John Warner (R-VA), John Kerry (D-MA), Dianne Feinstein (D-CA), and Fred Thompson (R-TN).[1229]

9:50 p.m.: President Bush returns to the second-floor residence.[1230] The Secret Service insists that the president spend the night in the PEOC on a fold-out bed, but Bush refuses.[1231]

9:55 p.m.: President Bush leaves the second-floor residence.[1232]

There is a 9:55 p.m. entry that is deleted from the Presidential Daily Diary in which some event occurs that evidently requires him to leave the upstairs residence.

9:57 p.m.: Mayor Giuliani says New York City schools will be closed Wednesday, and no more volunteers are needed for Tuesday evening's rescue efforts. He says there is hope that there are still people alive in the rubble. He also says that power is out on the west side of Manhattan and that health department tests show there are no airborne chemical agents to worry about.

1227. FAA, 11 Sep 01 Catastrophic Crisis (all times given in EDT).

1228. The audio is located at http://www.authentichistory.com/2001-2008/1-911/1-timeline1/20010911_2250_CNN_Author_Peter_Bergen_on_Bin_Laden.html.

1229. The audio is located at http://www.authentichistory.com/2001-2008/1-911/1-timeline1/20010911_2100c_L_King_int_Sen_Warner_Kerry_Feinstein_Thompson.html.

1230. Presidential Daily Diary, partially declassified.

1231. *Decision Points*, p. 138.

1232. Presidential Daily Diary, partially declassified.

Giuliani names some of the high-ranking police and fire officers who are missing.

There are reports (later proven incorrect) of many survivors buried in rubble making cell phone calls. Only three more survivors will be pulled from the rubble.

10:00 p.m.: Attorney General Ashcroft briefs members of Congress. He tells the 9/11 Commission "that he was nominated to brief the House and Senate Members at 10:00 that night after he attended a meeting at the White House. He said the members wanted a lot of details that he did not have yet."[1233]

10:20 a.m.: President Bush returns to the second-floor residence.[1234]

10:30 p.m.: (Approximate time) Sometime after the national security meetings are concluded, Vice President Cheney, his wife, his military aide with a duplicate of the nuclear "football," his vice-presidential communications officer, his doctor, three Secret Service agents, and his two top staffers—"Scooter" Libby and David Addington—get into Marine Two (Marine One is only the call sign used for the president), embarking from the South Lawn, where only the president had ever before taken off from previously, for a helicopter trip to Camp David, Maryland, the "undisclosed location" where he would reside for the next few weeks.[1235]

In his autobiography, Cheney only tersely says that "the Secret Service evacuated Lynne and me to Camp David, a secure location apart from the president."[1236]

1233. 9/11 Commission Memorandum for the Record, Interview with Attorney General John D. Ashcroft, December 17, 2003.

1234. Presidential Daily Diary, partially declassified.

1235. *Cheney: The Untold Story of America's Most Powerful and Controversial Vice President*, pp. 345–346.

1236. *In My Time: A Personal and Political Memoir*, pp. 10, 329.

`10:30 p.m.:` (Approximate time) At the World Trade Center, rescue workers locate two trapped Port Authority officers, William Jimeno and John McLoughlin, injured but alive in the debris. They free Jimeno after three hours of treacherous tunneling work. McLoughlin's rescue will take another eight hours. Workers will extricate another survivor, Genelle Guzman, on the afternoon of September 12. She will be the last person rescued.

`10:45 p.m.:` The last inbound international flights from Asia land in Honolulu, Hawaii.[1237]

`10:49 p.m.:` Jonathan Karl of CNN reports that Attorney General Ashcroft told members of Congress that there were three to five hijackers on each plane, armed only with knives.

`10:56 p.m.:` Paula Zahn of CNN reports that New York City police believe there are people alive in buildings near the World Trade Center.

`11:00 p.m.:` At the Pentagon, Rumsfeld meets with his staff. Assistant Secretary of Defense for Public Affairs Torie Clarke asks if he has talked to his wife during the day. As Rumsfeld recounts, he hasn't—"so engaged that day that I hadn't even thought of calling her."

"Clarke looked at me with a stare of a woman who was also a wife," Rumsfeld writes. "'You son of a bitch,' she blurted out," he says. "She had a point."[1238]

`11:08 p.m.:` President Bush and the First Lady are interrupted by Secret Service agents. "Mr. President, Mr. President, the White House is under attack! Let's go!"

The agents rush them to the PEOC. Bush is in running shorts and a T-shirt as he makes his way down the stairs, through the tunnel, and into the bunker. "I heard the slam of a heavy door and the sound of a pressurized

---

1237. Roger A. Mola, "Shutdown of National Airspace System Was 'Organized Mayhem,'" AIN Online, October 8, 2007.

1238. *Known and Unknown*, p. 348.

lock as we entered the tunnel. The agents rushed us through another door. *Bang, hiss.* We hustled down the final corridor, past the staff seated outside, and into the PEOC."[1239]

Condoleezza Rice is in her office with Hadley and Card, going over tasks for the next day, "when a Secret Service agent burst into the office. 'Go to the bunker! Another plane is headed for the White House!' We jumped up and walked quickly back towards the emergency operations center."[1240]

Military aide Lt. Col. Gould recalls that as he settled into his bunk in the White House, "a knock on the door warned of an inbound plane." He joins the president, the First Lady, and his primary Secret Service agent in heading to the PEOC.

Also in the bunker are Hadley and Card; Bush's two dogs, Barney and Spot; the president's brother Neil, who is staying at the White House; and Maria Galvan, the Bushes' housekeeper.

"It turned out to be a false alarm involving a military aircraft miscommunication with air traffic controllers," Gould writes.[1241] The Secret Service again urges Bush to spend the night in the PEOC, but he refuses and returns to the residence.

There is no record of an alert in FAA logs or the Presidential Daily Diary. It turns out to be a military airplane squawking on the wrong code.

11:32 p.m.: FAA reports: "No data to be released to anyone"—referring to the public release of any information on the flights or FAA operations.

11:50 p.m.: (Approximate time) President Bush and the First Lady return to the White House residence. Like his father, President Bush tries to keep a daily diary of his thoughts and observations. That night, he dictates:

The Pearl Harbor of the 21st century took place today.
We think it's Usama [*sic*] bin Laden.

1239. *Decision Points*, p. 139.
1240. *No Higher Honor*, p. 78.
1241. Janene Scully, "Vandenberg Officer at Bush's Side During Attacks," *Santa Maria Times*, September 11, 2011.

We think there are other targets in the United States, but I have urged the country to go back to normal.

We cannot allow a terrorist thug to hold us hostage. My hope is that this will provide an opportunity for us to rally the world against terrorism.

President Bush then goes back to bed.

MOHAMMED ATTA'S FINAL LETTER

Late in the day on September 11, Mohammed Atta's two pieces of luggage are recovered by Massachusetts State Police and turned over to the FBI. The bags had not been loaded onto his connecting flight in Boston.[1242]

Upon initial examination, the luggage is found to contain a copy of the Qur'an, a pad with flight-planning data, and an instrument for calculating the weight of an aircraft. When the FBI open Atta's luggage, they recover the following:

- Four-page letter in Arabic
- Electronic flight computer with case
- Islamic Finder prayer schedule
- Simulator Check-ride procedures
- Flight planner sheets attached to cardboard
- Videotape of flight procedures for a Boeing 747-4000
- Videotape of flight procedures for a Boeing 757-200
- Plastic device for determining the effect of an aircraft's weight on range
- Large folding knife
- Brand name First Defense cayenne (red pepper) spray

The second suitcase, belonging to Abdul Aziz al-Omari, contained the following:

- Three English grammar books
- Arabic to English dictionary

1242. FBI American Airlines Flight #11 Investigative Summary, FBI 02991.

- Perfume bottle
- Brand name Brylcream antidandruff hair dressing
- Saudi passport for al-Omari
- Hudson United Bank checkbook for Abdul Aziz al-Omari
- Three photographs
- Handkerchief
- Twenty-dollar bill, US currency

Interestingly, the FBI later reported that the two suitcases had a covert tag placed on the bags by US Airways to warn that Atta and his luggage were a security issue.[1243] This may be why the bags were not loaded on the Boston flight.

The four-page handwritten document, once translated, proves to be Atta's spiritual and literal letter of instructions to other hijackers on how to behave during the hijacking operation.[1244] A copy of the same letter is also recovered at the UA Flight 93 crash site and in Nawaf al-Hazmi's car, found at Dulles IAP.

1243. 9/11 Commission Memorandum for the Record, Review of Investigation by the FBI of Atta's Suitcases at Boston, MA; February 10, 2004.

1244. According to the FBI, "On or about September 11, 2001, Mohamed Atta . . . possessed a handwritten set of final instructions for a martyrdom operation using knives on an airplane. Copies of these instructions were in the possession of at least one hijacker on United Airlines #93 and also placed in Nawaf al Hazmi's . . . Toyota Corolla at Washington Dulles International Airport." See OMC, Charge Sheet, May 31, 2011, p. 15.

The Last Night

- Shave off excess hair from the body and wear perfume.
- Bathe

Mutual covenant with death and renewal of awareness.

2. [*sic*, a paragraph numbered 1 is missing] Know the plan well from all angles and expect the response to the action or the resistance of the enemy.

3. Read Surat al-Tawbah and al-Anfal [the ninth and eighth suras in the Qur'an, respectively] and contemplate the its [*sic*] meanings and the fixed blessings that God has prepared for the Believers, for the martyrs. [Inserted note written at the top of the page and evidently referring to this item:] One of the Prophet's Companions said that the Messenger of God commanded us to read it before going into battle, so we read it, won booty, and came through safely.

4. Remind yourself that you must hear and obey this night, for you will be exposed to decisive situations that require hearing and obeying (100 percent), so tame your soul and make it understand, and convince it, and incite it to do that [i.e., to hear and obey].

God the Exalted said [in the Qur'an] "and obey God and his messenger [Muhammad] and do not dispute with one another lest you fail and your strength leave you; but be steadfast. God is indeed with the steadfast." [VIII: 46]

5. Rise at night to pray in earnest for victory, empowerment, a clear triumph, for matters to be eased for us and for us to be protected.

6. Do a lot of remembrance of God (dhikr) and know that the best remembrance of God is reading the Noble Qur'an, according to the consensus of opinion of the scholars [of religion] in what is best known and sufficient for us is the Word of the creator of the heavens and the earth whom you are going to meet.

7. Purify and heal your heart of faults. Forget and become oblivious to a thing called this world, for the time for playing has passed, and the appointment with Truth has come. How much of the times of our lives have we wasted, should we not use these hours to give offerings and obedience.

8. May your breast be opened, for only a few moments separate you from your marriage, whereupon you begin the happy and pleasing life and the eternal blessedness with those who affirm [religious truth] and the virtuous martyrs—excellent comrades are they. We ask God for his bounty. Be optimistic for [the Prophet], may God's peace and blessings be upon him, loved optimism about all his affairs.

9. Then set your sights upon how you will behave when affliction befalls you and how you will affirm and call back, and you know that that which befalls you could not possibly have missed you and that which misses you could not possibly have befallen you, and that this test comes from God, the Glorious and Exalted, to raise you up in rank and to forgive your sins. Then know that moments appear by the grace of God so welcome to him who gains victory and the great reward from God. God the Exalted has said [in the Qur'an], "did you think you would enter Paradise without God knowing those among you who strove, without knowing those who are steadfast?"

10. Then remember what God the Exalted said: "you longed for death before you came to meet it, then you saw it and you are watching." Then remember after that "how many a small group overcame a large group by the grace of God." And God the Exalted said, "If God brings you victory no one can vanquish you, but if He brings you down, who will give you victory after that? and upon God do the Believers rely."

11. Remind yourself and your brothers by using prayers and contemplate their meanings (dhikr [remembrances] in the morning and evening, remembrances of the home town, remembrances of the place, remembrances of meeting the enemy.)

12. Dropping off (yourself, and luggage, and clothing, and the knife, your tools, your ticket, re[member] your passport, all your papers).

13. Review your security before departure, and before departure and (let one of you sharpen his blade, so that the one he butchers will be glad).

14. Tighten your clothes well, for this is the tradition of the upright salaf (early Muslims), may God be pleased with them, for they used to tighten their dress before battle, then tighten your shoes well; wear socks that stay up in the shoes and don't fall out of them.

All these are things we are commanded to take care of. God is our sufficiency and the most excellent patron.

15. Pray the morning prayer as a group; contemplate your reward for it, and remember [God] after it, and don't leave your apartment unless you have performed the ablution, for the angels ask forgiveness for you so long as you have made your ablution and they pray to God. Read what God the Exalted said [in the Qur'an]: "do you think We created you for no purpose?" Sura "al-Mu'minun" [verse 115]. [Note: part of the bottom line on the page is cut off. It is a reference to a statement attributed to the Prophet Muhammad found in a book by the medieval scholar al-Nawawi called "al Mukhtar."]

[Page 2] After that comes the second stage.

When the taxi takes you to the (a)[irport] remember God . . . [top line of page 2 obscure] . . . and other remembrances.

When you have arrived and gotten out of the taxi say a prayer in the place. Say a prayer in all places you go. Smile. Rest assured that God is with the Believers and the angels guard you though you do not perceive them.

[End of straight translated text.] [Note: The author of the document continues on page 2 with various short prayers, some of which are hard to make out in the handwriting. He goes on to tell himself to recite the verse in the Qur'an (III: 173):] ". . . Those to whom the people said, 'People have gathered together against you so fear them,' but [instead] they were increased in faith and said God is sufficient for us and it is He in whom we trust." [He goes on to say:] God had promised His servants who say this prayer that they would:

1. overcome by the beneficence of God and his bounty,

2. not be afflicted by harm,

3. be following the pleasure of God.

4. God said in the Qur'an [III: 174]: "They returned with the grace and favor of God and no harm touched them. They followed the good pleasure of God and God is of infinite bounty." Thus, their apparatuses, their doors [could be read, "their categories"], their technology cannot harm you. Believers do not fear those things, rather it is the followers of Satan who are afraid of those things. You must remember God (dhikr) and I think some of the greatest dhikr. In particular you must not let it be noticed about you that you recite the credo "There is no god but God." For though you recite it a thousand times, no one should be able to distinguish whether you were silent or mentioning God. The greatness of [the phrase] "There is no god but God" is shown by the statement of the Prophet that "he who recites 'there is no god but God' and whose heart believes in it, enters Paradise."

[Page 3: At the top of page 3, the author says:]

And also, don't show any signs of confusion or nervousness. Be joyful, happy, open of heart, and at peace because you are carrying out an act that God loves, an act that pleases Him. And therefore there will be a day, by God's leave, when you will be with the bright-eyed maidens of Paradise. [The author quotes a couple of verses of poetry.]

Smile in the face of doom, young man, for you are passing to the gardens of eternity.

["Stage three" is the stage aboard the airplane.] As soon as you board the (a)[irplane] entering it and setting foot in it, say a prayer and call to mind that this is a battle for the sake [of God].

[Once in your seat you should] busy yourself by mentioning God [and he quotes the Qur'an again]: "Oh you who believe, if you meet a band [of enemies] stand firm and remember God much so that you might be successful."

Then when the (a)[irplane] has begun to move a little towards (q) [Note from translator: the Arabic letter "qaf." I suspect this stands for "iqla'" which means "take off"] recite the prayer of the traveler, for you are traveling to God the Exalted (and what an excellent journey that is!)

Then you will find that it stops and then departs.

This is the hour when characteristics must come together, so pray to God the Exalted as He commanded [in the Qur'an]: "Oh God, grant us steadfastness and make our feet firm and make us victorious over the unbelieving people. . . .

Pray for yourself, for your brothers for victory and triumph. . . .

Ask God to grant you martyrdom. . . .

Then let every one of you prepare to play his role in the way that earns him the pleasure of God, and to grit his teeth as the early Muslims did—may God bless them—when they prepared to enter into battle.

And when the battle is joined, strike with the blows of heroes who do not want to go back to this world.

Shout "Allahu Akbar!" [God is greatest!] for this cry strikes fear in the hearts of unbelievers. God the Exalted said [in the Qur'an] "strike their necks and their fingertips." Know that Paradise has been most beautifully decorated for you and that the maidens of Paradise are calling you to meet them, oh devotee of God, and they have put on their most beautiful clothes.

[The author of the letter says that if one of them has to kill somebody, he is entitled to that person's possessions, in accordance with ancient notions of seizing booty. He warns, however, that they must not fall to fighting among themselves or allow such things to distract them from their mission.]

[Page 4] [*Note: The last page is very hard to make out. Toward the bottom it says*]

Open your heart to death in the path of God and remember God always.

Let your last words be, "There is no god but God, and Muhammad is the messenger of God."

PERSONALITIES MENTIONED IN THE TIMELINE

US GOVERNMENT

- David Addington: Counsel and national security assistant to Vice President Cheney.
- Joe M. Allbaugh: Director, Federal Emergency Management Agency (FEMA).
- John D. Ashcroft: Attorney General.
- Dan Bartlett: Deputy Assistant and Deputy to the Counselor for Communications, part of President Bush's traveling party.
- Joshua Bolten: Deputy White House Chief of Staff, at the White House.
- George W. Bush: the President (POTUS).
- Laura Bush: the First Lady.
- Nick Calio: Assistant to the President.
- Andrew H. Card Jr.: White House Chief of Staff.
- Dick Cheney: Vice President.
- Lynne Cheney: Wife of Vice President Cheney, taken to the PEOC.
- Richard Clarke: Special Adviser for Cyberspace Security, NSC staff, at the White House Situation Room (WHSR).
- Eric Draper: White House presidential photographer, part of President Bush's traveling party.
- Eric Edelman: National Security Adviser to Vice President Cheney.
- Ellen Eckert: White House stenographer, part of President Bush's traveling party.
- Tucker A. Eskew: Deputy Assistant and Director of Media Affairs.
- Ari Fleischer: White House Press Secretary, part of President Bush's traveling party.
- Don Gentile: White House Situation Room senior analyst.
- Alberto Gonzalez: White House Counsel.
- Stephen J. Hadley: Deputy National Security Adviser at the WHSR and PEOC.
- Joe Hagin: White House Deputy Chief of Staff in charge of operations, the man secretly in charge of "continuity of government."
- Rob Hargis, White House Situation Room senior duty officer.
- Scott Heyer: White House Situation Room communications officer.

- Karen Hughes: White House Counselor.
- Michael P. Jackson: Deputy Secretary of Transportation.
- Gordon Johndroe: assistant press secretary, part of President Bush's traveling party.
- Matt Kirk: White House congressional liaison, part of President Bush's traveling party.
- B. Alexander "Sandy" Kress: Senior Adviser for Education, Domestic Policy Council, part of President Bush's traveling party.
- Irving Lewis "Scooter" Libby: Chief of Staff to the Vice President, in the PEOC.
- Lawrence B. Lindsey: Assistant to the President for Economic Policy.
- Eddie Marinzel: Secret Service Deputy Special Agent in Charge, part of President Bush's traveling party.
- Mary Matalin: Assistant to the President and Counselor to the Vice President.
- Harriet Miers: Presidential Staff Secretary, part of President Bush's traveling party.
- Franklin Miller: National Security Council staff, in the WHSR for the day.
- Norman Mineta: Acting Secretary of Transportation, ends up in the PEOC with Cheney for most of the day.
- Brian D. Montgomery: Director of Advance, White House, part of President Bush's traveling party.
- Michael Morell: CIA briefer of President Bush, part of President Bush's traveling party.
- Robert S. Mueller III: FBI director, in his office at FBI Headquarters on Pennsylvania Avenue. He has been on the job a little more than a week. He attends the evening cabinet meeting in the PEOC.
- Paul H. O'Neill: Secretary of the Treasury; he is in Tokyo, Japan, and is put on an Air Force C-17 transport, making it back to Washington by evening to attend the cabinet meeting in the PEOC.
- Roderick Raynor Paige: Secretary of Education, part of President Bush's traveling party, left in Sarasota.
- Colin Powell: Secretary of State. He is in Lima, Peru, at the OAS General Assembly, and returns to Washington to attend the evening cabinet meeting in the PEOC.
- Condoleezza D. Rice: Assistant for National Security Affairs, National Security Adviser.
- Karl Rove: Senior Adviser to the President, part of President Bush's traveling party.
- Donald Rumsfeld: Secretary of Defense.
- George Tenet: Director, Central Intelligence Agency.
- Carl Truscott: Secret Service Assistant Director and Special Agent in Charge (SAIC), Presidential Protective Division in the White House.
- Dave Wilkinson: Secret Service Assistant Special Agent in Charge, part of President Bush's traveling party.
- James R. Wilkinson: Special Assistant and Deputy Communications Director for Planning.
- Paul Wolfowitz: Deputy Secretary of Defense.

US MILITARY

- Larry K. Arnold, Maj. Gen. (US Air Force): Commander, First Air Force and the NORAD Continental NORAD Region (CONR).
- Michael Delong, Gen. (US Marine Corps): Deputy Commander, US Central Command (CENTCOM).
- Ralph "Ed" Eberhart, Gen. (US Air Force): Commander, North American Aerospace Command and US Space Command.
- Tommy Franks, Gen. (US Army): Commander, US Central Command (CENTCOM).
- Thomas F. Gould, Lt. Col. (US Air Force): Military aide to the president on 9/11.
- Joseph Leidig, Capt. (US Navy): Action Deputy Director for Operations (DDO) Operations Team 2, JCS (in the National Military Command Center).
- Deborah Loewer, Capt. (US Navy): Director, White House Situation Room, a member of President Bush's traveling party in Sarasota.
- Robert K. Marr, Col. (US Air Force): Commander, Northeast Air Defense Sector (NEADS).
- Richard Mies, Adm. (US Navy): Commander, US Strategic Command (STRATCOM).
- Richard "Dick" Myers, Gen. (US Air Force): Vice Chairman of the Joint Chiefs; is on Capitol Hill, returning to the Pentagon as acting chairman, attending the evening cabinet meeting in the White House PEOC, his tenure to become chairman just days away.
- Kevin J. Nasypany, Lt. Col. (US Air Force): NORAD NEADS Mission Crew Commander.
- Mark V. Rosenker, Brig. Gen. (US Army): Deputy Assistant to the President and Director of the White House Military Office, a member of President Bush's traveling party in Sarasota.
- Henry "Hugh" Shelton, Gen. (US Army): Chairman of the Joint Chiefs of Staff, is flying across the Atlantic on his way to Europe, instructing his pilot to turn around and return to Washington, where he attends the evening cabinet meeting in the White House PEOC.
- Dr. Richard Tubb, Col. (US Army): Presidential physician, White House Medical Unit, part of President Bush's traveling party.
- David Franklin Wherley Jr., Brig. Gen. (US Air Force): Commander, 113th Wing, District of Columbia National Guard (DCNG).
- Montague Winfield, Brig. Gen. (US Army): Deputy Director for Operations (DDO) Operations Team 2, JCS (in the National Military Command Center after 10:45 a.m.).

AIRLINES AND FAA

- Gerard Arpey: American Airlines Executive Vice President.
- Ed Ballinger: United Airlines dispatcher.
- Monte Belger: FAA Deputy Administrator.

- Terry Biggio: FAA Boston Center air traffic controller.
- David Bottiglia: FAA New York Center air traffic controller.
- Michael A. Canavan (Gen., US Army, Ret.): FAA Associate Administrator for Civil Aviation Security (ACS-1), often listed in FAA logs as Cavanaugh and Kavinidy.
- Nydia Gonzalez: American Airlines supervisor.
- CeeCee Lyles: UA Flight 93 flight attendant.
- Craig Marquis: American Airlines operations center manager.
- Betty Ong: Flight attendant aboard AA Flight 11.
- Marc Policastro: United Airlines maintenance office in San Francisco.
- Ben Sliney: FAA Air Traffic Control System Command Center (Herndon) National Operations Manager.
- Andy Studdert: United Airlines Chief Operating Officer.
- Madeline "Amy" Sweeney: Flight attendant aboard AA Flight 11.
- John Werth: FAA Cleveland Center air traffic controller.
- Peter Zalewski: FAA Boston Center air traffic controller.

AL QAEDA

- Mohammed Atta: Egyptian, pilot of AA Flight 11.
- Fayez Banihammad: Emirati, one of the musclemen on UA Flight 175.
- Hani Hanjour: Saudi, pilot of AA Flight 77.
- Ahmed al-Ghamdi: Saudi, one of the musclemen on UA Flight 175.
- Hamza al-Ghamdi: Saudi, one of the musclemen on UA Flight 175.
- Saeed al-Ghamdi: Saudi, one of the musclemen on UA Flight 93, brother to Hamza.
- Nawaf al-Hazmi: Saudi, one of the musclemen on AA Flight 77.
- Salem al-Hazmi: Saudi, one of the musclemen on AA Flight 77.
- Ahmed al-Haznawi: Saudi, one of the musclemen on UA Flight 93.
- Ziad Jarrah: Lebanese, pilot of UA Flight 93.
- Khalid al-Mihdhar: Saudi, one of the musclemen on AA Flight 77.
- Majed Moqed: Saudi, one of the musclemen on AA Flight 77.
- Ahmed al-Nami: Saudi, one of the musclemen on UA Flight 93.
- Abdul Aziz al-Omari: Saudi, one of the musclemen on AA Flight 11.
- Marwan al-Shehhi: Emirati, pilot of UA Flight 175.
- Mohand al-Shehri: Saudi, one of the musclemen on UA Flight 175.
- Wail al-Shehri: Saudi, one of the musclemen on AA Flight 11.
- Waleed al-Shehri: Saudi, one of the musclemen on AA Flight 11.
- Satam al-Suqami: Saudi, one of the musclemen on AA Flight 11.

ACRONYMS

AA/AAL	American Airlines/FAA Alaska Region
ACARS	Aircraft Communications and Reporting System (FAA)
ACFD	Arlington County Fire Department
ADIC	ATS Interfacility Data Communications (FAA)
ADW	Andrews AFB, Maryland (FAA designation)
AEA	FAA Eastern Region, Jamaica, New York
AFB	Air Force base
AGL	FAA Great Lakes Region, Des Plaines, Illinois
ANE	FAA New England Region, Burlington, Massachusetts
ANG	Air National Guard
ANGB	Air National Guard Base
ATA	Air Transport Association
ATC	air traffic control
ATCC	Air Threat Conference Call (DOD)
ATCT	Airport Traffic Control Tower (FAA)
ATCSCC	Air Traffic Control System Command Center
ATF	(Bureau of) Alcohol, Tobacco, and Firearms
AWACS	Airborne Warning and Control System
AWP	FAA Western Pacific Region, El Segundo, California
BOS	Boston Logan (FAA)
CAP	combat air patrol
CAPPS	Computer Assisted Passenger Prescreening System
CARF	Central Altitude Reservation Function (FAA)
CAT	Crisis Action Team
CD	command director (NORAD)
CDC	Centers for Disease Control and Prevention
CENTCOM	US Central Command
CFB	Canadian Forces Base
CIA	Central Intelligence Agency
CINC	commander in chief
CINCPAC	Commander in Chief Pacific Command

CJCS	Chairman of the Joint Chief of Staff
CLE	Cleveland
CMOC	Cheyenne Mountain Operations Center (NORAD)
COA	Continental Airlines
COD	chief of department
COG	continuity of government
CONR	Continental US NORAD Region (NORAD), Tyndall AFB, Florida
CONUS	continental United States
CT	counterterrorism
CVR	cockpit voice recorder
CWTC-4D	citywide tour commander 4D
D1	first division chief
DAL	Delta Air Lines
DCA	Reagan Washington National Airport (FAA designation)
DDO	Deputy Director of Operations (Joint Staff, DOD)
DEFCON	Defense (Readiness) Condition
DIA	Defense Intelligence Agency/Denver International Airport
DOD	Department of Defense
DOT	Department of Transportation
EDT	Eastern Daylight Time
ELT	emergency locator transmitter
EMS	Emergency Medical Services
ESCAT	Emergency Security Control of Air Traffic
EWR	Newark International Airport (FAA designation)
FAA	Federal Aviation Administration
FBI	Federal Bureau of Investigation
FDNY	Fire Department of the City of New York
FEMA	Federal Emergency Management Agency
FORSCOM	Army Forces Command
FPCON	Force Protection Condition
IAD	Dulles International Airport (FAA designation)
IAP	international airport
ICP	incident command post
IFF	identification friend or foe
IFR	instrument flight rules
INS	Immigration and Naturalization Service
ISI	Inter-Services Intelligence, Pakistan's military intelligence
ISN	internment serial number
JFCOM	US Joint Forces Command
JOC	Joint Operations Center
JTTF	Joint Terrorism Task Force (FBI)

LAX	Los Angeles airport (FAA designation)
LINDEN	FAA VORTAC, Linden, Virginia
MCC	Mission Crew Commander (NORAD NEADS)
MDW	Military District of Washington
NAOC	National Airborne Operations Center
NATO	North Atlantic Treaty Organization
NCIS	Naval Criminal Investigative Service
NCRS	National Capital Response Squad/Region Support (FBI)
NEADS	Northeast Air Defense Sector (NORAD), Rome, New York
NIST	National Institute of Standards and Technology
NMCC	National Military Command Center
NOIWON	National Operational Intelligence Watch Officer's Network
NORAD	North American Aerospace Defense Command
NOTAM	Notice to Airmen
NSA	National Security Agency
NSC	National Security Council
NTSB	National Transportation Safety Board
NW	northwest
NYPD	New York City Police Department
OP-1	Operations Post 1
ORD	Chicago International Airport (FAA designation)
ORF	Norfolk Airport Traffic Control Tower (FAA)
OSD	Office of the Secretary of Defense
PA	Port Authority
PACOM	US Pacific Command
PAPD	Port Authority Police Department
PATH	Port Authority Trans-Hudson Transportation System
PDB	President's Daily Brief
PEOC	Presidential Emergency Operations Center
PIT	Pittsburgh IAP (FAA)
PWM	Portland (Maine) International Jetport (FAA)
QDR	Quadrennial Defense Review
RADES	Radar Evaluation Squadron (Air Force)
RCO	remote communications outlet
ROC	Regional Operations Center (FAA)
ROE	rules of engagement
SCATANA	Security Control of Air Traffic and Air Navigation Aids
SecDef	Secretary of Defense
SFO	San Francisco airport (FAA designation)
SIEC	Significant Event Conference (DOD)
SIOC	Strategic Information Operations Center (FBI)

SOC	Service Operations/Oversight Center, American Airlines
SPACECOM	US Space Command
STRATCOM	US Strategic Command
TEB	Teterboro, NJ (FAA)
THREATCON	Threat Condition (DOD force protection designation)
TMU	Traffic Management Unit (FAA)
TRACON	Terminal Radar Approach Control[1245]
UA/UAL	United Airlines
USCG	US Coast Guard
USMS	US Marshals Service
VACAPES	Virginia Capes Operating Area (NORAD)
VFR	Visual Flight Rules
WADS	Western Air Defense Sector
WD	weapons director (NORAD)
WFO	Washington Field Office (FBI)
WHMO	White House Military Office
WHSR	White House Situation Room
WMD	weapons of mass destruction
WOC	Washington Operations Center (FAA)
WTC	World Trade Center
WTC 1	World Trade Center, North Tower
WTC 2	World Trade Center, South Tower
WTC 3	World Trade Center Building 3 (Marriott Hotel)
WTC 5	World Trade Center Building 5
WTC 7	World Trade Center Building 7
ZAU	Chicago Air Route Traffic Control Center (FAA)
ZBW	Boston Air Route Traffic Control Center, Nashua, New Hampshire (FAA)
ZDC	Washington Air Route Traffic Control Center (FAA)
ZID	Indianapolis (Indy) Air Route Traffic Control Center (FAA)
ZJX	Jacksonville Air Route Traffic Control Center (FAA)
ZKC	Kansas City Air Route Traffic Control Center (FAA)
ZLA	Los Angeles Air Route Traffic Control Center (FAA)
ZNY	New York Air Route Traffic Control Center (FAA)
ZOA	Oakland Air Route Traffic Control Center (FAA)
ZOB	Cleveland Air Route Traffic Control Center (FAA)
ZP	White House Shelter Tunnel basement level of the White House

---

1245. A terminal ATC facility that uses radar and nonradar capabilities to provide approach control services to aircraft arriving, departing, or transiting airspace controlled by the facility.

ACKNOWLEDGMENTS

Writing a timeline is a ridiculous endeavor, solitary, individualistic, time-consuming, and, in my case, a lifelong addiction. My timeline of 9/11—first of the events leading up to that day, then of what happened afterward, and then of the day itself—grew and then grew into an obsession until, all of a sudden, the 20th anniversary of the attacks loomed, and I wanted to see it published. I organized and reorganized the materials for America's most studied day to condense second by second into minute by minute and thought I might have a book. Only through the assistance of Peter Pringle, a lifelong friend, mentor, and collaborator, did that manuscript gel. And Clive Priddle at PublicAffairs immediately saw the value, and the uniqueness, that even after 20 years no such definitive chronology existed.

Crashing to finish, I'd like to especially thank Jacques and Christine, Debbie Ershler, Kathy Robbins, and Barbara Aplington, who fed and supported me, and my great friends Peter and Eleanor Randolph, Nancy Spillane, Barbara Brooks, Luciana Frigerio, and Cynthia McFadden, who are always there for me. My finest collaborator over the years in understanding 9/11 is Bob Windrem, to whom I owe much thanks. Jason Sommer provided support from the beginning, and Jason Mojica is a great friend. Thanks, too, to Nancy Cooper, Sultana Khan, and Marianne Manilov, and to Tom Powers for his unwavering support over many years. And of course, thank you and all my love to Rikki and Hannah, who are the best.

To my sources and friends in the national security establishment, thank you. Over the years, when I've identified individuals, there have always been negative implications, and so again, because of the world we live in, I won't name names.

Credit: Kathy Robbins

William M. Arkin is an award-winning journalist and best-selling author. He writes for *Newsweek* magazine and has previously served as a columnist, reporter, and consultant to the *Los Angeles Times*, the *Washington Post*, the *New York Times*, and the *Bulletin of the Atomic Scientists*. His almost 30-year association with NBC News included reporting on 9/11 and its aftermath as on-air commentator, reporter, and consultant.

Arkin is the author of over a dozen works of nonfiction, including *The Generals Have No Clothes: The Untold Story of Our Endless Wars*, *Code Names: Deciphering US Military Plans, Programs and Operations in the 9/11 World*, and *American Coup: How a Terrified Government Is Destroying the Constitution*. His novel about 9/11, *History in One Act*, was published in 2021.

Arkin has served as a consultant to diverse organizations, from the US Air Force and the United Nations office of the Secretary-General to Greenpeace, the Federation of American Scientists, Human Rights Watch, and the Natural Resources Defense Council. He was one of the first independent analysts to visit Afghanistan after 9/11 to evaluate the effects of American bombing. He has also traveled and reported from numerous Middle East war zones, particularly Iraq, Lebanon, and Israel. Arkin served as an intelligence analyst in the US Army in West Berlin during the Cold War. He lives in Encinitas, California.

PublicAffairs is a publishing house founded in 1997. It is a tribute to the standards, values, and flair of three persons who have served as mentors to countless reporters, writers, editors, and book people of all kinds, including me.

I. F. STONE, proprietor of *I. F. Stone's Weekly*, combined a commitment to the First Amendment with entrepreneurial zeal and reporting skill and became one of the great independent journalists in American history. At the age of eighty, Izzy published *The Trial of Socrates*, which was a national bestseller. He wrote the book after he taught himself ancient Greek.

BENJAMIN C. BRADLEE was for nearly thirty years the charismatic editorial leader of *The Washington Post*. It was Ben who gave the *Post* the range and courage to pursue such historic issues as Watergate. He supported his reporters with a tenacity that made them fearless and it is no accident that so many became authors of influential, best-selling books.

ROBERT L. BERNSTEIN, the chief executive of Random House for more than a quarter century, guided one of the nation's premier publishing houses. Bob was personally responsible for many books of political dissent and argument that challenged tyranny around the globe. He is also the founder and longtime chair of Human Rights Watch, one of the most respected human rights organizations in the world.

·　　·　　·

For fifty years, the banner of Public Affairs Press was carried by its owner Morris B. Schnapper, who published Gandhi, Nasser, Toynbee, Truman, and about 1,500 other authors. In 1983, Schnapper was described by *The Washington Post* as "a redoubtable gadfly." His legacy will endure in the books to come.

Peter Osnos, *Founder*